IN MEMORY OF

ARTHUR COMPTON-RICKETT

WITH WHOM I WROTE
"RING UP THE CURTAIN"

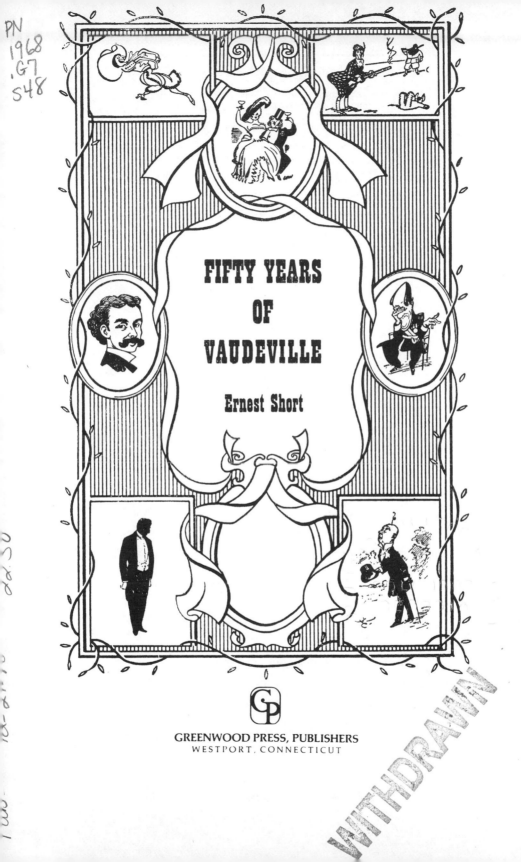

FIFTY YEARS
OF
VAUDEVILLE

Ernest Short

GREENWOOD PRESS, PUBLISHERS
WESTPORT, CONNECTICUT

Library of Congress Cataloging in Publication Data

Short, Ernest Henry, 1875-1959.
  Fifty years of vaudeville.

  Reprint of the 1946 ed. published by Eyre & Spottis-
woode, London.
  Includes index.
    1. Vaudeville--England--London. 2. London--Amuse-
ments. I. Title.
PN1968.G7S48 1978   792.7'09421   78-16385
ISBN 0-313-20576-0

First printed 1946

Reprinted with the permission of Associated Book
Publishers Limited

Reprinted in 1978 by Greenwood Press, Inc.
51 Riverside Avenue, Westport, CT 06880

Printed in the United States of America

10 9 8 7 6 5 4 3 2 1

PREFACE

Of old-time music-hall songs, Rudyard Kipling once wrote: "They supply a gap in the national history, and people haven't yet realised how much they have to do with the national life."

Kipling might well have added musical comedy, revue and concert-party ditties to his tally, for Vaudeville, in its various forms, constitutes a goodly part of social life in the twentieth century.

Numerous books treating the theme have been written by or about well-known actors and actresses, and there have been some interesting reprints of theatrical criticism, in particular those from Mr. James Agate. *Fifty Years of Vaudeville* differs from these inasmuch as it seeks to give a connected story covering the period and relates it, roughly perhaps, to current social happenings.

Mr. John Parker, most generous of critics, and Major John Munro have been good enough to read my proofs, and Mr. Tolmie has compiled my index. Mr. Bateman and Mr. Low, too, have kindly given leave to reproduce their drawings. To them all, my thanks.

E. H. S.

March 1946

CONTENTS

ILLUSTRATIONS

PLATES

PICTURES IN THE TEXT

Chapter I

INTRODUCTION. THEN AND NOW

FIFTY YEARS OF VAUDEVILLE! THOUSANDS OF COMICS AND serio-comics have contributed to the "Rippling, Roaring, Rushing, Rollicking River of Risibility" which constitutes our story, and the best of them move through these pages, for it is a record of the men and women who have shaped comic-opera, burlesque, musical comedy, pantomime, revue, and music-hall variety in the lifetime of present-day theatre-goers. Some are remembered for the quick-fire of their wit or the solid quality of their humour; others for their virtuosity in the management of audiences; or, maybe, because of pleasing features or figures. Who would wish to lose the memory of Marie Studholme, with the gold of her ruddle hair framed by the big white bonnet which she wore when the New Gaiety was opened in 1903 ? Or Gaby Deslys, about the same time one hundred per cent femininity, and with all a woman's love for dress and jewels, coupled with all a player's gift for thrusting her glamour across the footlights?

At the beginning of the present century, when Edward the Seventh was London's social arbiter, Jazz had not issued from its birthplace, the dusky Southern States of America. Nor had the hobble skirt of Parisian invention prepared the way for the transformation of feminine fashion, which led an eminent divine to whisper:

Half an inch, half an inch, half an inch shorter,
The skirts are the same for mother and daughter;
When the wind blows, each of them shows
Half an inch, half an inch more than she oughter.

It was about the time George the Fifth came to the throne that London displayed the first symptoms of the quickened tempo in fashion, dress, and dance which characterises the past twenty-five years, in comparison with the quarter of a century when Edward ruled as Prince and King. The "harem-scarem" skirt was launched upon an astonished world at the Auteuil Races in the spring of 1911, and about the same time the one-step began to find its way into dance programmes, associated with the strains of Irving Berlin's "Alexander's Ragtime Band," which Ethel Levey was popularising in a Hippodrome revue.

What was in progress proved to be a reaction against overfed and under-exercised femininity in favour of what is now called the flapper type, and which has characterised principal girls and ladies of the chorus ever since, as it has characterised the feminine half of vaudeville audiences. Possibly the shortage of butter and sugar between 1914 and 1918 encouraged slimming, and simultaneously ended the vogue of the Victorian and Edwardian petticoat and brought

I

in such fashions as bobbed hair and the Eton crop. I make no apology for recording such facts. They are not mere accessories to vaudeville but of primary importance, as part of the players' stock-in-trade for working upon the senses and sensibilities of audiences. Indeed, dress may be the determining factor in big stretches of behaviour which characterise a theatrical period. In this connection Athene Seyler, in *The Craft of Comedy*, recalled that the very steps taken in walking vary in the different periods. She went on to discuss the consequences upon the art of the actor and actress.

"I should say that a woman ought to *dance* as she moves in a seventeenth-century play, to *sail* in an eighteenth-century one, to *swim* in a nineteenth-century dress (with tiny, even steps under crinoline or bustle) and to stride in the twentieth century."

When Miss Seyler went on the stage in 1909 it was a cardinal rule that a woman should never cross her legs, whereas the twentieth-century young woman adopts this attitude quite normally. The period covered by *Fifty Years of Vaudeville* is largely that in which "slacks" have superseded the outsize corset and bustle and young women feel fully free to cross their legs when and how they please.

Vaudeville takes its name from the French *Vau de Vire*, that is to say, from the town and river valley of Vire, which came into the war news during the invasion of France in 1944. The Valley of the Vire is one through which flowed the stream which drove the fulling mill of Olivier Basselin, composer of the cider drinking songs which eventually gave a name to a much larger class of popular entertainment. Following the miller Basselin, an unsophisticated art of popular balladry established itself in the fifteenth and sixteenth centuries. By the end of the seventeenth century, ballads accompanied by spoken dialogue were given at the larger French fairs, such as St. Germain, and the entertainment was known as "vaudeville." In France, vaudeville gave rise to *opéra comique*, but when American audiences were required to distinguish between the simple sing-songs of the nineteenth century and the fully fledged and double-sexed Variety of the twentieth century, the word "vaudeville" passed into common usage in the Anglo-Saxon world. It may now be regarded as embracing not only music-hall variety, but all forms of extravaganza, burlesque, comic opera, cabaret, and revue.

The pageant of entertainment which *Fifty Years of Vaudeville* promises belongs to the very stuff of social history. Born in the confusion of the industrial revolution, when millions of workers were flocking from villages and country towns into the monster factory centres of modern times, British vaudeville bears the scars and the adornments of its origin. Within our period lies half a century of popular newspapers and periodicals, thirty years of popular cinema and what amounts to as many years of world-wide war. Our story, therefore, promises to display a not unimportant cross-section of the medley of generous impulses and selfish antago-nisms which have occupied the non-working hours of Britain's town-dwellers. Just because so many millions have contributed desires which called for satisfaction, a high intellectuality cannot be expected from vaudeville, but if occasional lapses from good taste reveal themselves, the fault will lie less with the art itself than with the society which vaudeville serves. When work is done and the sleeping hours have not been reached, the surplus energy of a community asserts itself and seeks satisfaction for its cravings for colour, melody, or the byways of sex. We work for eight hours, we sleep for eight hours, and for eight hours we amuse ourselves; some with sport, some with study, and some sampling the musical fare which is the subject of this book.

Now a snatch from a familiar chorus will recall a popular singer; now a comedian's gag will bring to mind a laugh which rocked hall or theatre. Frequently, there will be the human interest of a man or woman making good perhaps after years of endeavour; or perhaps, by what seems just easy-coming luck, as when little Cissie Loftus, in the early 'nineties, revealed her happy talent as a mimic and awoke next morning to find herself a star.

English vaudeville is rich in such episodes and, plainly, its story is not to be recovered in the cold light of scientific research. The raw material belongs to hours when the canons of criticism are relaxed. Nor should it be forgotten that, as often as not, the original experience followed an hour in a gaily lighted grill-room, with fellow theatre-lovers also scampering through a light meal lest they should miss the first glow of the footlights upon a new musical comedy or revue. Less often, and only if funds were available, a remembered music-hall turn may have followed a luxurious lingering over wine and liqueurs, in the comfortable assurance that Harry Fragson or Victoria Monks was not on before nine-thirty and that either would amply suffice to close the day. Writing in 1945, wine and liqueurs savour of super-luxury, but before the first World War a liqueur only added 9*d.* or 1*s.* to a dinner bill, while a Soho restaurant meal cost no more than four shillings.

Even when the prelude to the show was a cold wait outside a pit or gallery, vaudeville-lovers would not have called for artistic standards proper to Bloomsbury, Chelsea, or St. John's Wood. More rough and ready canons of criticism were required. In general, if a song, a dance, a sketch, a revue, a light opera, or a musical comedy once delighted audiences, it will call for appreciation. After all, the Muse who presides over vaudeville is a thought less learned, and not quite so modest, discreet, courteous, and full of virtue as her eight sisters. She can properly demand a canon of criticism, which will cover, let us say, the wisecrackery of Max Miller. As Fred Leslie said of his associates, "We are not educational; we are dinner digestives."

My own research has revealed no principles governing the craft of vaudeville, apart from the value of hard work. If there is one, it lies in the importance of rhythm which pervades all the dramatic arts. The outstanding vaudeville stars have known how to punctuate song and patter so that song and patter meant something fundamentally different to what they did when a man or woman with a lesser sense of rhythm sought to give them life.

Not all the folk who will have a place in our pageant were stars of the first

magnitude. Those who held the stage in between the star turns will not be
forgotten. Even the lesser-known comedians and comediennes of the Victorian
and Edwardian theatre were trained to recognise a laugh round the corner and
moved forward to greet it and let it loose upon a crowded house at the very moment
its welcome was assured. This talent is less common to-day. In variety, spectacular
revue and not a little cabaret work, an under-dressed chorus too often takes the
place of genuine personality, equipped by years of hard work to impress itself
upon an audience. This is not surprising. In mid-Victorian times, a music-hall
singer was a lone man or woman with no more support than a small orchestra
in front and a painted back-cloth behind. To-day, glorious colour devices in
scenery and costume, a body of highly competent singers and dancers and, perhaps,
a loud speaker are there to assist. Is it to be wondered that too many men and
women are content with something less than the arduous training of the old-time
vaudeville star? Similarly, in the realm of music, melodies, hard to come by, have
been largely replaced by rhythms which, to an old-fashioned taste, have little
rhyme and no reason. Just as the minuet passed out when the Industrial Revolution established itself, so the waltz received its death-blow during the first World
War, which sent the entertainment world upon a feverish search for change.
Thenceforward, a hybrid of negroid, Jewish, and Tin Pan Alley growth seemed
to mirror the social mood more accurately than the old-time melodies.

Incidentally, it is to be recalled that the gay self-confidence of the early jazz
music seemed less appropriate when the boom which followed the first World
War collapsed. Accordingly, public taste favoured the maudlin self-pitying mood
of "The Blues," while the words which accompanied "blue" music emphasised
the woes of society's failures. As if the sense of frustration was not sufficiently
emphasised already the singers mooned about among the easy-come and easy-go
rhythms of the ordinary speaking voice, instead of developing the more difficult
technique of the robust singing voice, capable of filling a large hall. It was the
crooners who first demanded aid from the microphone, which makes a whisper
as audible as the full-voice tones of a trained singer had been in the old-time
theatres.

What strikes an elderly playgoer in the super-halls of to-day is the variety of
the lighting effects, as the electrician plays whether upon background or a moving
singer and chorus, just beyond the footlights. In the 'eighties, when Marie Lloyd,
Vesta Tilley, and other stars of the past were learning their craft, the limelight-man
was much less gifted. As Miss Soldene has told us, his stuff would fizz, sparkle,
splutter, and then, with an alarming hiss, disappear altogether. Yet the singer
had to hold on tight to his or her audience, even if the assistant light refused to
co-operate. Equally striking is the rich variety of scenery and costume. Indeed,
the play of light and shade upon colourful costume and highly trained choruses
has so large a part in the entertainments of our time that not a little of the simplicity
of the old-time comic has gone and with it much of the old-time comicality.
Those who remember the past, sigh for five minutes of Tom Costello, with his

game knee, singing "At Trinity Church I met my doom," or another of the songs which were written expressly for a personality and, accordingly, provided players with humour which they could quickly make their very own.

Nevertheless, if *Fifty Years of Vaudeville* is the story of declension in one direction, it is also the story of the passing of the Victorian "flea-pit" and the coming of the spacious super-halls of the pre-war years, not only in the West End of London, but in all the larger provincial towns. With the old-time music-hall has gone the red-nosed comedian and his other number, the flaxen-haired serio-comic, who figured so largely in Victorian programmes. Partly because the music-hall theme has been treated so adequately by Willson Disher in his *Winkles and Champagne*, and partly because the subject occupied considerable space in *Ring Up the Curtain*, which I wrote with Arthur Compton-Rickett, the music-hall will occupy less of this book than musical comedy and revue. Readers of *Ring Up the Curtain* will, however, forgive an occasional quotation from the earlier book when this seems part of the general story of vaudeville.

In general, what has happened in vaudeville has been the introduction of women into what was primarily a masculine institution. Nowadays, if a man goes to a revue, a cabaret entertainment, or musical comedy, it is because he is giving his wife, his daughter, or somebody else's daughter an evening out. Nowadays, women tend to dictate the entertainment when their men-folk are moved to the welcome proposal, "Let's go to a show to-night."

Sing-song to Syndicate Hall

There are Londoners alive, though in a quickly decreasing number, who, in early youth, partook of hot chops and roast potatoes at Evans's Supper Rooms. The modern equivalent is a kipper or eggs and bacon at The Ivy, which Herbert Farjeon impudently described as "a quaint, old eating-house of the 'thirties."

To reach Evans's, our grandfathers turned off the Strand, crossed to the north side of Covent Garden, where they came upon what had once been the town house of Sir Kenelm Digby. Early in the nineteenth century, a well-known comedian, W. C. Evans, converted Digby House into a concert hall, and he carried on until 1844, when the eating-house came into the possession of the even more famous "Paddy" Green.

Picture the scene in mid-Victorian times. A small doorway in the Covent Garden piazza opened upon a flight of stairs, which led to the supper-rooms. Here a cheery old gentleman with snowy-white hair and rosy cheeks would greet favoured patrons by offering a pinch from his snuff-box and possibly a place at his own table. This was Paddy Green, whose mission in life was to keep the fun at Evans's alive. A boys' choir, singing glees and madrigals by Arne, Purcell, Sir Henry Bishop, and other recognised composers, was very popular, but there were less highbrow folk; for example, Harry Sydney, who sang topical songs of his own composition. One of them was entitled "The Signs of the Times in the A.B.C." Each letter of the alphabet represented a topical personality or incident, "V" standing for Victoria and bringing forth the pronouncement: "You cannot find her equal in the wide-wide-world."

Until the 'seventies, lady guests were not encouraged at Evans's, and when they came the vogue of Evans's ended. By the time women began to frequent Evans's, a professional element had been introduced into public-house or supper-room entertainment. Set stages became general, and when the Great Mogul public-house in Drury Lane (The Old Mo) added a music-hall to its attractions, footlights were introduced into the go-as-you-please evenings. The Old Mo is represented by the Winter Garden Theatre to-day. About the same time Charles Morton, on the south side of Westminster Bridge, was adding respectability and feminine patronage to vaudeville at the Canterbury Arms. Born in 1819 and dying in 1904, he converted, built, and managed music-halls for half a century. Very early, Morton visualised a place of entertainment where men and women could foregather. Accordingly, at the back of the Canterbury Arms Tavern, he built a music-hall for 1,500 people. This was in 1852. It had a large platform, but no curtain, and music came from a piano and a harmonium.

To the Canterbury came that Lion-comique, George Leybourne, in 1867. The title "lion-comique" was the invention of the well-known manager, J. J. Poole, who was laughing at one of Leybourne's songs, when he happened to say, "Why, the fellow's a regular lion. A comic lion. I've got it—a lion-comique!" It was Leybourne who established the principle of adequate monetary recognition for "star" turns, by demanding £25 a week for singing the highly popular "Champagne Charlie." By 1944 Tommy Trinder was getting ten or twenty times as much for imitating Leybourne singing the song. In childhood Dame Madge Kendal and Kate Bishop once sang "Champagne Charlie" as a duet in a West Country pantomime, but, properly, the ditty was sung by a gentleman for gentlemen. A lion-comique's idea of a gentleman was a bewhiskered entity wearing a puce jacket, checkered trousers, and a gaily coloured waistcoat. Such a lady-killer was Leybourne himself, singing:

> I've seen a deal of gaiety, throughout my noisy life,
> With all my grand accomplishments, I ne'er could get a wife.
> The thing I most excel in is the P.R.F.G. Game,
> A noise all night, in bed all day, and swimming in champagne.
> *Chorus:* For Champagne Charlie is my name.

The Great Macdermott, famous for his "By Jingo" effort during the Anglo-Russian troubles of 1878, was another singer of dude songs. He is to be pictured in evening dress, with a blue silk tie, white waistcoat, red silk handkerchief, gold fob chain, and patent-leather shoes, hammering out the rhythm of "Jeremiah" with elbows and hands, aided by exceptionally clear enunciation in song and speech.

My name is Jeremiah Jones, and when I was a child,
I used to play a little game which drove my mother wild.
I'd take the bellows on my knee, to blow the fire I'd try,
And when the fire began to blaze, I lustily would cry.

Chorus:
Jeremiah, blow the fire, puff, puff, puff;
First you do it gently, then you come it rather rough.
Jeremiah, blow the fire, puff, puff, puff!

Macdermott's climax came in a later verse:

In time I loved a pretty girl, and strange tho' it may be,
The lady in her younger days was just the same as me.
And when I asked her to be mine, she bowed her lovely head,
And as I pressed my lips to hers, in artful tones she said:
Jeremiah, blow the fire . . .

If the Great Macdermott and his associates were welcome in their dude impersonations, they also created characters of more democratic origin. What we know
as the Coster Song also has a long history in vaudeville. Year in and year out,
successful comedians have made play with the loves and doves of the working
classes as the basis of their appeal to pit and gallery, and that is why so many
successful music-hall singers come from the North Country. Fred Karno, of
"Mumming Birds" fame, once said that, when seeking talent, he went to Manchester, to Birmingham, to Wigan, to Rochdale, and the smaller North Country
towns, and he added, "The old-school-tie style of humour is all very well in
London, but if any of the old-school-tie comedians found themselves in a
Lancashire music-hall, off the beaten track, they'd have to have their jokes
translated."

Only a stage in social custom separates the coster studies of the Great Vance
and his fellows, from those of Albert Chevalier, and this name only serves to
recall Gus Elen, Alec Hurley, and others. An East End study by Vance, which
ended with a cellar-flap dance, ran thus:

I'm a Chickaleary bloke, with my vun-two-three—
Vitechapel was the village I was born in;
    To catch me on the hop
    Or on my tibby drop,
You must vake up very early in the mornin'!

A generation later, Gus Elen created the Covent Garden porter, Jack Jones, who

Came into a little bit of splosh
And dunno where 'e are.

In 1945, comparable impersonations would be in the hands of Gracie Fields, George Formby, Elsie and Doris Waters, Jack Warner, Suzette Tarri, or Lupino Lane, of "Lambeth Walk" fame. In that sense the Cockney is still with us, though the coster type in its old-time purity has vanished and fifty years of board-school education militate strongly against the marked characteristics which used to differentiate such London types as the Billingsgate, the Smithfield, or the Covent Garden porter.

Jack Warner came to vaudeville by way of Wireless fame, in company with Joan Winters ("Programmes! Chocolates! Cigarettes!"), and his asset was his discovery that, in addition to the old-time Cockney, with the broad vowels, another Cockney is acceptable, who flattens his *ahs* into *ees* and his *ees* into *i's*, so that Warner's *eels* become "*ills*" and his *girls*, "*gels*." Such a Cockney represents a rise in the social world, in comparison with Victorian and Edwardian equiva-lents, but a declension from the coster song as part of the folk-music of the proletariat in a developing industrial era. Popular songs dating back to the turn of the century reflected the humorous outlook of the Cockney, the Lancashire lad, the Yorkshire lassies, the Tynesider, and the factory hand from "Glasgie," rather than that of some alien with no firmer hold upon a traditional social atmosphere than an East Side New Yorker in the pay of Tin Pan Alley, as is so often the case to-day.

Transition to Jazz

Turning to music and generalising somewhat roughly, one may say that while English women wore skirts of normal length and permitted their hair to reach their waists, waltz melodies maintained their popularity in ball-room and vaude-ville. In 1911 or 1912, when Irving Berlin launched "Alexander's Ragtime Band" upon London (it was written some years earlier), a couple of young professional dancers, Irene and Vernon Castle, were inventing dancing-steps to match it. Lilting airs from *The Merry Widow, The Count of Luxembourg,* or *The Girl in the Taxi* and other sources of waltz rhythm constituted 75 per cent of the dance programmes. But already there were one-steps enough to suggest that syncopated song and dance might ere long end the long supremacy of the waltz. George Grossmith, dancing with Phyllis Dare in *The Sunshine Girl* at the Gaiety, was one of the first exponents of the tango in London and when *The Sunshine Girl* was transferred to New York, Vernon Castle (George Gros-smith's brother-in-law) danced the tango and eventually married his dancing partner, the American girl who was to become famous as Mrs. Vernon Castle. Fame did not come from their appearances in *The Sunshine Girl*, but flashed upon them in a night, as a result of a chance appearance at the Café de Paris. Mr. and Mrs. Vernon Castle happened to be in the café, when a millionaire acquaintance recognised them and said: "Here, you two, get up and show 'em."

The Vernon Castles did "show 'em" and woke up next morning to find the rewards of full success crowding in upon them. Soon they were the best-known

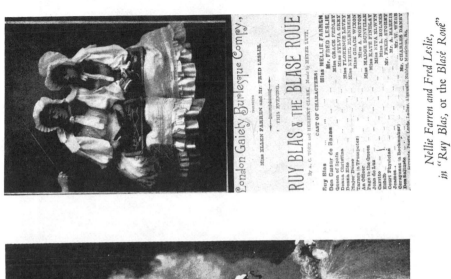

Nellie Farren and Fred Leslie,
in "Ruy Blas, or the Blasé Roué"

Letty Lind, of the Gaiety and Daly's

Night Life in the Twentieth Century

[An Hebblethwaite Cartoon

Night Life in the Nineteenth Century

dancing couple in two continents. Vernon gave up the certainty of a fortune in order to fight in the first World War and towards the end died as the result of an accident, while giving flying lessons to American aviators. Irene Castle went on bravely with the work of creating art out of the chaos of possibilities to which jazz measures were giving rise, and her beauty and grace did much to dignify an art-form which from the first was sadly in need of refinement.

The final embodiment of jazz was "swing," which may be described as jazz civilised, as Louis Armstrong has explained in his *Swing that Music*. His own reputation was made as a jazz trumpeter. It became world-wide owing to gramo-phone records, which sold by tens of thousands. Benny Goodman, Fats Waller, Teddy Wilson, and Bob Crosby were other popularisers of "swing," the "sweet" being simple tunes, played softly, and the "hot," harsh melodies and rhythms, chiefly remarkable for their "kick."

It will not be easy to give form to these freely moving happenings. I ask pardon for inevitable omissions, and also indulgence if the time factor is ignored because a trick of memory suggests an excursus in this direction or that. Half a century of vaudeville is not to be confined within any simple and fixed sequence. I can, however, offer a beginning and an end, with a promise that the intervening episodes shall be of sufficient variety to banish boredom. A certain sense of unity will, I trust, arise from the whole, even if it is not apparent in passing.

And the beginning? Where may that best be made that our story may rest upon sound foundations? The Victorian flea-pit, from which the vaudeville houses of Edwardian times evolved? That is a possibility. Or Gilbert and Sullivan comic opera at the Savoy, which set a standard, not only for librettists and composers, but for producers and players, and one, moreover, which has persisted to this day? Here, at any rate, is an achievement which shows that the best of British vaudeville is not ephemeral, but can delight from generation to generation. My choice, however, is the pioneer work of Madame Vestris and J. R. Planché at the Old Olympic, inasmuch as it covered comic opera, revue, burlesque, and pantomime—and also included innovations in the management of a vaudeville theatre comparable with those of the Bancrofts in the realm of straight comedy.

Ladies and gentlemen, *Olympic Revels*!

Chapter II

OLYMPIC REVELS. BURLESQUE AND THE OLD GAIETY, 1871 TO 1893

John Hollingshead and George Edwardes

APART FROM GILBERT AND SULLIVAN COMIC' OPERA, AND SONG and dance in the London eating-houses, burlesque constituted the staple vaudeville during the greater part of the Victorian era. When musical comedy superseded burlesque, the revolution was completed and Edwardian and Georgian vaudeville, as opposed to the Victorian brand, was in being.

Burlesque, in its English form, originated with J. R. Planché and attained the dignity of a recognised art-form when Madame Vestris produced *Olympic Revels*. During the following sixty years, that is from 1831 to 1891, classical mythology, history, the plays of Shakespeare, opera and current drama were explored continually by men of letters who were masters of the decasyllabic couplet and the popular art of punning. *Olympic Revels* was an epoch-making production, not only from the standpoint of authorship but of production, for Madame Vestris was a theatrical innovator comparable with Marie Wilton and her managerial reforms at the Old Olympic, Wych Street, were as far-reaching as those of the Bancrofts at "The Dust Hole" off Tottenham Court Road a generation later. Like Marie Wilton, the Vestris was bewitching in breeches parts, and the turn of her limbs, the grace of her movements, and the gaiety of her manner made her the idol of the bucks in the boxes and no less beloved by the humbler occupants of pit and gallery. Moreover, in 1831, when she opened the newly decorated Olympic, no woman had ever controlled a London theatre. In the prologue which she spoke on the opening night, Eliza Vestris could rightly claim:

> Noble and gentle Matrons, Patrons, Friends!
> Before you here a venturous woman bends!
> A warrior woman, that in strife embarks,
> The first of all dramatic Joan of Arcs!

Technically, *Olympic Revels* was "burletta," the term signifying that it was produced at a London theatre which was not allowed to play legitimate drama, this being the monopoly of houses specially licensed by the Lord Chamberlain, i.e. the Patent houses, Drury Lane and Covent Garden. Forbidden to offer their customers the heavy fare of a square meal such as the Patent houses provided, the lesser West End theatres produced "burlettas." The word disappeared from the play-bills when the minor theatres were legally emancipated.

In the West End theatres devoted to "burletta," the *élite* sat in boxes, each party

10

separated from another by a low partition, in that part of the auditorium where the dress circle now is. Madame Vestris began her reforms by converting the front part of her pit into rows of stalls. A little later the semi-public boxes were abolished. Instead, private boxes at the sides of the auditorium were introduced,

MADAME VESTRIS,

AS SINGING

MY HEART'S TRUE BLUE,

thus leaving the circle open. The new boxes made it easier for ladies to patronise the light musical plays and constituted a real advance in the direction of an entertainment which women could share with men. Thus Eliza Vestris succeeded in converting the Olympic Theatre into a place where playgoers could enjoy a very agreeable repast, consisting, as a writer in the *New Monthly Magazine* had it, "of jellies, cheese-cakes, custards and trifles light as air, served upon the best Dresden china, in the most elegant style."

"Served in the best Dresden china" meant that Brussels carpet was laid down on the stage, that real curtains hung in place of those the scene-painters simulated, and that period furniture replaced oddments from the property-room. In fact, Madame Vestris introduced stage realism into vaudeville forty years before the Bancrofts initiated the stage reforms in comedy which made their twenty years of management famous.

J. R. Planché

Planché's contribution to the revolution was only less important. Born in 1796, his first burlesque was produced at Drury Lane in 1818. Twelve years later fortune put Planché in the path of Madame Vestris. She was contemplating management at "the most despised nook in the dramatic world," The Old Olympic. From his desk Planché promptly produced a classical libretto, in which Vestris was to play Pandora, "the mettlesome Lady forged by Vulcan." What was novel in the production was that the mythology was accurate, within the limits of extravaganza, and the costumes, as later at the Savoy, were not only in character, but as charming as possible.

Planché, as principal chef, prepared the Vestris refections for several years and, in doing so, offered W. S. Gilbert recipes, which the Savoyard elaborated and possibly improved, but assuredly did not invent. In *Olympic Revels*, following upon a delightful scene of mock love-making with Prometheus, Pandora prepares to open the fateful box. As the rosy rogue sings:

> Can it be lip salve,
> Or sweet lollipops,
> Pretty pearl ear-rings,
> Or Peppermint Drops!

who can but recall Buttercup, the rosiest, the roundest, and the reddest beauty in all Spithead, singing:

> I've treacle and toffee and excellent coffee,
> Soft tommy and succulent chops.
> I've chickens and conies and pretty polonies,
> And excellent Peppermint Drops.

Similarly, when Planché adapted Perrault's *Sleeping Beauty* for production at Covent Garden in 1840, with Madame Vestris as Princess Is-a-Belle, one of the supporting characters was Baron Factotum, "Great Grand Lord Everything," plainly a precursor of Gilbert's Pooh-Bah, for Factotum was Lord Chamberlain, Lord High Steward, and Lord High Constable, as well as Lord High Treasurer (with the devil to pay).

Apropos of the conscious or unconscious influence of Planché upon W. S. Gilbert, it is amusing to note that in Planché's pantomime, *Puss in Boots*, a rabbit was given to King Pumpkin. The monarch duly handed it to the Princess, who passed it on to the First Maid of Honour, who gave it to the Second Maid. It was not until it had come to Maid of Honour Number Three that Kitchenstuff, the Royal Cook, received the dainty. In his *Grand Duke* Gilbert made similar play with a ducal snuff-box and handkerchief, when these were presented through the line of the Seven Chamberlains.

DUKE RUDOLPH: Observe. (*To* CHAMBERLAINS) My handkerchief.
> (*Handkerchief is handed by* JUNIOR CHAMBERLAIN *to the next in order, and so on until it reaches* RUDOLPH, *who is much inconvenienced by the delay.*)
DUKE (*singing*): It's sometimes inconvenient, but it's always very cheap.

A permissible elaboration and, maybe, an improvement upon Planché, but scarcely an invention of Gilbert.

When Planché's long career as writer of extravaganza ended, his well-furnished wit and neat craftsmanship were sadly missed. Lacking Planché's wit, writers of burlesque punned unceasingly and so often without point that players were forced to "gag" instead of keeping to the author's script, as they had done under Planché, and as they certainly did when Gilbert directed his productions at the Savoy. Henry J. Byron, Robert Reece, William and Robert Brough, George Augustus Sala, and Burnand were the best known of the writers of burlesque, and the brew which they were expected to produce is fairly summed up in the opening scene of a Keeley extravaganza, produced at the Lyceum in 1846. The curtain rose upon three authors circumambulating a huge inkstand, akin to the cauldron in *Macbeth* and manifestly intended to hold the ingredients of the new burlesque. The authors sang:

> Railway jests of various uses—
> Workhouse tyrants and abuses—
> Surrey combats, scenes to tally,
> Parodies on opera-ballet.
> London slang and quaint dog-Latin—
> Ah! put that in. Yes, put that in!
> Sly allusion, only spare
> What the Licenser won't bear.
> Bubble, bubble, toil and trouble,
> Brains ferment, and burlesque bubble!

A miniature Robin Hood then arose from the ink-pot and the title of the new extravaganza was revealed.

The great Little Robson sustained extravaganza and burlesque through the opening years of the period of over-punning. Thus he was "the best of mothers, with a brute of a husband" in a skit upon the *Medea* of Euripides, written by Robert Brough in 1856. A high light of the show was Robson's singing of "He's going to marry Creusa."

Medea. I've done for this man.
All that tenderness can,
I have followed him half the world through, Sir,
I've not seen him this year,
And the first thing I hear,
Is, "he's going to marry Creusa,
 going to marry Creusa,
 going to marry Creusa."
Ting a ting ting,
Ting a ting ting,
All I can say, Sir, is *do*, Sir.

With *Perdita*, written by William Brough for the Lyceum in 1856, living playgoers come upon familiar personalities, for Lady Bancroft and J. L. Toole were in the cast. Little Marie Wilton, with her clear merry laugh and saucy features was beloved by our grandfathers, long before she made theatrical history at the Prince of Wales's and the Haymarket, in alliance with Sir Squire Bancroft. Lovers of vaudeville would talk for an hour about Marie Wilton's Gringoire in *Esmeralda*, when she appeared in a jaunty little coat of white sheepskin and silk fleshings, which displayed her trim legs and tiny feet to perfection. Henry J. Byron was the author of the skit upon Victor Hugo's Esmeralda, which is not to be confused with *Miss Esmeralda*, a later burlesque at the Gaiety. Byron was no mean actor and often appeared in his own plays. Of his quick-fire wit, Lady Bancroft tells that he was on the stage at the Strand Theatre in *The Maid and the Magpie* with Patty Oliver, a merry brunette with a laugh as enchanting as Marie Wilton's own. Suddenly, Byron interpolated this couplet:

Jujubes, oranges and cakes I too did give her,
Pâté de foie gras, which means *Patty Oliver*!

"I shall never forget," added Lady Bancroft, "the chorus of 'oh's' that followed."
   Byron died in 1884, jesting to the last. On his death-bed, his groom reported the illness of a horse and asked if he should give the ailing one "a ball." "Ye-es," murmured Byron, "but don't ask too many people."
   Of such kind was the authorship upon which John Hollingshead could draw when he inaugurated his memorable years of management at the Old Gaiety.
   Born and bred in London, Hollingshead was a cloth merchant and a journalist before he entered upon theatrical life as stage director at the Old Alhambra, and was daring enough to take a lease of the Old Gaiety Theatre, at the eastern and unfashionable end of the Strand. As he was responsible for forty musical bur-lesques in a period of eighteen years, and these were only a part of his work as manager at the Gaiety, the theatre was plainly in his blood. In his prime he was proud to describe himself as:

John Hollingshead, licensed dealer in legs, short skirts, French adaptations, Shakespeare, Taste and the Musical Glasses.

The famous island-site in the Strand, within a stone's throw of the present Gaiety Theatre, had been occupied in the 'sixties by the Strand Musick Hall. At the time the *Daily Telegraph* was coining money for the Lawson family, and Lionel Lawson, brother of the first Lord Burnham, came upon the brilliant idea of a new theatre on what promised to be a cheap site. He secured the Musick Hall for the proverbial "song," and made up his mind to spend his money upon a really comfortable theatre and run it in conjunction with a restaurant next door, both catering for the new middle class which the success of the *Daily Telegraph* was revealing.

Learning of Lionel Lawson's scheme, John Hollingshead formed a play production syndicate, with a capital of £5,000. In addition to the £3,500 rental, he had to find £1,000 for "bars," a laughable figure, judged by modern standards, but substantial in the early 'seventies. Altogether, a profit of £6,000 was needed if the venture was to pay. Hollingshead made no mistake. During the eighteen years he took close upon £700,000 from the public, and for the £200 which he personally put into the venture he exchanged £120,000. "Honest John" got into financial difficulties towards the end of his career, but these were not due to theatrical speculations, but to losses in other directions.

Hollingshead was the first manager to recruit burlesque players from the music-halls, as Sir Augustus Harris was the first producer of pantomime to draw largely upon music-hall talent. Both gathered together bodies of players with a technique which differed from that developed in melodrama and romance. Moreover, Hollingshead had the personal gifts needed if the best was to be made of his company. As he said, the problem resolved itself into a conflict between tact and temper, that is to say, "managerial tact, acting on a multitude of men, women and children, each one of whom is fearfully and wonderfully human— filled with ambition, vanity, desire to shine, belief in latent or checked ability, pettishness, insubordination—in fact, *the* profession."

In relation to the general public Hollingshead also showed perspicacity. He was not catering for well-to-do folk, who dined late, but, largely, for middle-class folk wanting a full evening of fun. His doors opened at 6.30; drama began at 7 o'clock, the burlesque being timed for 9.30, and "carriages" for 11.15. Hollings-head further revealed his quality by enlisting the services of W. S. Gilbert and Arthur Sullivan several years before the D'Oyly Carte production of *Trial by Jury* in 1875. It is worth remembering that the first Gilbert and Sullivan association was in *Thespis* or *The Gods Grown Old*, which opened on Boxing Day, 1871. As for the Gaiety company, Hollingshead early enlisted J. L. Toole, Edward Terry, E. W. Royce, Nellie Farren, and Kate Vaughan, and before Gaiety burlesque ended, Fred Leslie, Arthur Roberts, David James, Letty Lind, Florence St. John, E. J. Lonnen, Sylvia Grey, Marian Hood, Phyllis Broughton, and Willie Warde had been added, though at the end George Edwardes had a voice in the selection. These names suffice to prove that the Old Gaiety was a first-rate training-ground, not only for vaudeville but for the legitimate drama. Kate Vaughan, a dancer of genius, later showed herself a delightful player in eighteenth-century comedy, and Constance Collier, who began her career as "Connie" Collier in the Gaiety chorus, was later to charm two continents in comedy, as in tragedy. Ethel Irving was "Birdie" Irving, in the days when she was playing with Nellie Farren and Fred Leslie in *Monte Cristo, Junior*.

Edward Terry was the Alfred Lester of the Gaiety company, for Terry was by no means a light-hearted comedian. A characteristic effort was his Ali Baba in *The Forty Thieves*, in which he completely lost his voice outside the Cave with crying "Open Sausages" instead of "Open Sesame." The weaker the voice became the more melancholy was Terry. At times his despair could reach tragic heights, as when Petipois played too freely with the hair-dye of "Bluebeard." "It won't come out!" cried the unhappy Edward. Another typical Terryism depended upon the fact that, at the Aquarium in the 'eighties, a damsel, Zazel by name, was fired out of a cannon nightly. Accordingly, in *Little Doctor Faustus*, Edward Terry, as Mephistopheles, pushed Nellie Farren into a big wooden cannon and asked, in turn, "Are you in? Are you far in?", concluding with, "Are you Nellie Far-in?"

Of course the Gaiety gallery boys chuckled over the elaborate pun, and even more over their own chorus of "Oh's."

I was born too late to develop a taste for Gaiety burlesque, so my personal experience is confined to George Grossmith's *The Linkman* in 1902, and occasional revivals of individual turns, for example, in the "Teddy" Payne benefit matinée, a lengthy but happy memory. Later, in 1921, George Grossmith staged *Faust on Toast*, with a cast including Jack Buchanan, Phyllis Monkman, Nancie Lovat, Robert Hale, and Morris Harvey. Somehow, the puns failed to carry and the gallery boys plainly disliked the ladies of the chorus as they appeared in tights. In the 'twenties Victorian burlesque might have furnished material for a half-hour's skit in revue, but it failed to fill the bill for an evening, even at the Gaiety, the home of burlesque.

Taking the many years of her service into account, Nellie Farren was Hollings-head's brightest star. At an early age she appeared at the Old Vic, in the Waterloo Road, and was then fortunate enough to come under the tutelage of Horace Wigan, at the Olympic, playing in melodrama, as well as burlesque. An outstanding memory is her "Street Arab" song in *Aladdin*, a number written by Robert Reece, with music by Meyer Lutz.

The modern equivalent of Nellie Farren's "Street Arab" would be:

> Shoe-Shine Boy.
> You work hard all day, Shoe-Shine Boy!
> Got no time to play.
> Every nickel helps a lot.
> So, shine, shine, Shoe-Shine Boy . . .

Those who saw her say that sex appeal played no part at all in Nellie Farren's popularity. Women loved her just as much as men. When she donned the rags of the Street Arab, she might as easily been taken for a boy as a girl. What never left her during the years she was principal "boy" at the Gaiety was the energy of spirit and joy of life which belong to all youth, masculine and feminine.

Out at dawn, nothing got to do.
Nothing but skulking round and prowling,
Getting kicked and howling,
Bobbies grimly scowling,
Wretched little Arab forced to stir!
"Please, Sir, hold your nag, Sir!
"Take your little bag, Sir!
"Wer-ry hard to live,
"Just what you'll give!
     Thank you, Sir!"

What Victorian players and playgoers thought of Nellie Farren was shown when a matinée was arranged in her honour, when her health broke down and she could delight London no longer. Over £7,000 was taken. The Rothschilds banked the money, gave Nellie 10 per cent each year and, at her death, handed the whole amount over to her heirs and assigns. Only Dame Ellen Terry's matinée will bear comparison with that which honoured Nellie Farren.

A male star of Gaiety burlesque who persisted into the musical comedy period was E. J. Lonnen. He sprang into fame when he sang "Killaloe" in the role of Claude Frollo, the monk, in *Miss Esmeralda*, cementing his reputation with "The Bogie Man," in *Carmen Up to Data*. Lonnen not only sang the song but introduced it to George Edwardes, after hearing something of the sort at a nigger minstrel show. Meyer Lutz, the composer of *Carmen up to Data*, objected to a strange song being added to his score, so a new one was written based upon Lonnen's general idea. Lutz's version proved infinitely the better, and the song not only saved the

---

NOTE. The delightful Charles Harrison drawing on p. 19 is a souvenir of the most amazing Harlequinade ever staged on a London or any other stage. Drawing Harlequinade graced Nellie Farren's Benefit at Drury Lane in 1898.

The School=Room Scene from the Drury Lane Pantomime,

THE BABES IN THE WOOD,

By ARTHUR STURGESS and ARTHUR COLLINS.
Music by J. M. GLOVER.

Prince Paragon	... Miss ADA BLANCHE
Marian	Miss VIOLET ROBINSON
Miss Gertie Girton	...Miss ALICE BARNETT
The Baron Banbury	Mr. JOHN A. WARDEN
Reggie } The Babes	{ Mr. DAN LENO
Chrissie}	{ Mr. HERBERT CAMPBELL

Lord Chamberlain, Miss NELLIE HUXLEY; Field Marshal, Miss HOOTEN; Master of the Horse, Miss WALTERS; Master of the Buckhounds, Miss LILLIE HENSHAW; Captain of Hussars, Miss LILIAN LEE; Captain of the Guard, Miss E. RUSSELL: Aide-de-Camp, Miss RITA HARRISON; Music Master, Mr. E. MORGAN; Porter, Mr. W. MORGAN; and the Members of the Drury Lane Company.

TO BE FOLLOWED BY A

HARLEQUINADE

Concocted by W. PALINGS and HORACE LENNARD.

Music arranged by J. M. GLOVER.   Stage Manager: J. A. E. MALONE.

Scene—A LONDON STREET (Bruce Smith).

Fairy Queen	Miss ELLALINE TERRISS
Columbine	Miss LETTY LIND
Harlequin	Mr. WILLIE WARDE
Pantaloon	Mr. FRED STOREY
Clown	Mr. EDMUND PAYNE
Police Sergeant XX	Mr. ARTHUR ROBERTS
Cheesemonger	Mr. ARTHUR WILLIAMS
Fishmonger	Mr. HARRY MONKHOUSE
Rummun, the Restaurateur	Mr. HARRY NICHOLLS
Waiter at Rummun's	...Mr. FRED KAYE
Pawnbroker	Mr. WILLIE EDOUIN
Street Orator	Mr. SEYMOUR HICKS
Newspaper Boy	Mr. TOM THORNE
Soldier	Mr. WILL BISHOP
Singing Swell	Mr. HUNTLEY WRIGHT
Butcher Boy	... Mr. A. BOUCICAULT
Deaf and Dumb Man	Mr. HARRY PAULTON
Sandwich Man	Mr. ARTHUR BOURCHIER
Sandwich Girl	... Miss DECIMA MOORE
Simple Simon	Mr. EDWARD RIGHTON
Susannah (*Maid of all work*)	Miss LOUIE FREEAR
Registry Office Keeper	Miss CONNIE EDISS
Tinker	Mr. JOHN LE HAY
Pieman	...Mr. HARRY RANDALL
Two Babes	Miss EVA MOORE and Mr. H. V. ESMOND
Their Nurse	...Miss SUSIE VAUGHAN
Walking Gent	... Mr. ROBB HARWOOD
Cheeky Boy...	Master BOTTOMLEY
The Boy's Mother	Miss M. A. VICTOR
Two Little Vagabonds	Miss KATE TYNDALL and Miss SIDNEY FAIRBROTHER
Organ Grinder	Mr. H. DE LANGE

Constables—Mr. W. L. ABINGDON, Mr. PAUL ARTHUR, Mr. SYDNEY BROUGH, Mr. H. O. CLAREY, Mr. LESLIE HOLLAND, Mr. G. HUMPHERY, Mr. LUIGI LABLACHE, Mr. F. H. MACKLIN, Mr. R. NAINBY, Mr. EDWARD SASS, Mr. GEORGE SHELTON, Mr. FRED TERRY, Mr. F. WRIGHT, Jr.

Street Dancing Girls—Miss PHYLLIS BROUGHTON, Miss MADGE GREET, Miss KATE JAMES, Miss ALICE LETHBRIDGE, Miss KITTY LOFTUS, Miss MARIE LLOYD, Miss KATIE SEYMOUR, Miss TOPSEY SINDEN.

Street Singers—Mr. C. HAYDEN COFFIN, Mr. LAWRENCE KELLIE, Mr. BARTON McGUCKIN, Mr. NORMAN SALMOND.

play but went round the world. One of the criticisms next morning was headed, "Saved by a Song." There was nothing comic about Lonnen's rendering. It was sung with dead seriousness and the "muted" chorus and the twilight enshrouding Lonnen added to the mysterious effect.

As for the dancers of burlesque, Kate Vaughan's contribution has already been mentioned and that of Letty Lind is reserved for later debate. Mention, however, must be made of the willowy Alice Lethbridge, the pretty and athletic Mabel Love, and the ingenious and hard-working Topsy Sinden. An Alice Lethbridge

Willie Warde

Edmund Payne

Ellaline Terriss

Fred Storey

Arthur Roberts

Harry Monkhouse

Arthur Williams

Harry Nicholls

Fred Kaye

Willie Edouin

Will Bishop

A. Boucicault

A. Bourchier

Seymour Hicks   Harry Randall   Louie Freear

memory is the close of her Marionette scene, with E. J. Lonnen, in *Little Christopher Columbus*. Holding on to a stick, Miss Lethbridge was flung over Lonnen's head and, to the amazement of onlookers, alighted safely on the farther side of the stage. Edward, Prince of Wales, was fond of burlesque and Alice Lethbridge was among the Royal favourites. Sylvia Grey also belonged to the period of Gaiety burlesque, as she married in 1893. A stepdancer of charm, her first speaking part was a flowergirl in *Miss Esmeralda*, with this typical snatch of punning dialogue:

> *Customer:* How much are your hyacinths?
> *Sylvia:* Two shillings a bunch, Sir.
> *Customer:* Why, yesterday they were a shilling.
> *Sylvai:* Yes, but they're *higher since*.

In 1887, when *Miss Esmeralda* was being played, the days of burlesque were numbered. The well of possible puns was running dry, and the store of potential themes capable of furnishing burlesque material was diminishing. Romance, History, Shakespeare, Victor Hugo, and other possible sources had been searched and researched. A new invention was urgently called for if musical shows were not only to survive, but attract the women who were becoming an increasingly important element in vaudeville audiences. The invention proved to be Edwardean musical comedy, Edwardean in a double sense, as it associated itself at once with the social leadership of Edward VII as Prince and King and with George Edwardes as producer and financier. Whether it be Edward's or Edwardes's, the new type of vaudeville had to express what Herbert Farjeon once summed up as "spanking days," when:

> Hats were hats of startling size,
> And waists were waists and thighs were thighs!

Enter George Edwardes

The mention of George Edwardes shows that not all Gaiety burlesque was associated with John Hollingshead. His last burlesque, *Jack Sheppard*, was produced in 1885. Already financial trouble was threatening and, in 1886, George Edwardes took over the Gaiety. His productions were *Monte Cristo*, *Miss Esmeralda*, a new skit upon Victor Hugo's "Notre Dame," and *Ruy Blas*. They differed from earlier burlesque mainly because vaudeville writers had practically exhausted the possible themes, and the Gaiety management was forced to rely upon the inventive powers of Fred Leslie, Arthur Roberts, and Nellie Farren. As someone wrote at the time, "The backbone of narrative which once ran through burlesque has become gelatinous." The comedians, accordingly, had not only to act but to create laughtercausing incident. Indeed, Leslie was partauthor of the last burlesque in which he appeared, *Ruy Blas*, or *The Blasé Roué*.

Thenceforward, actors in increasing numbers wrote the books for musical plays, as the titles to the credit of Seymour Hicks, George Grossmith, junior, and Harry

Grattan prove. Literary quality, as Planché and W. S. Gilbert understood the phrase, and as Herbert Farjeon understood it in our day, was no longer welcomed. Opportunities for topical invention were judged of more importance than plot or carefully devised verbal wit. Leslie was seldom at a loss for a stage impromptu. On one occasion he tripped over a lady's dress. "Be careful with that special train," he said. Turning, Leslie collided with yet another character, and exclaimed, "Cannon Street." He died young or his fame as a burlesque actor would have equalled that of the great Little Robson, of the previous generation.

There was a considerable element of revue in Gaiety burlesque. In *Ruy Blas*, Nellie Farren not only played the name part, the lovelorn lacquey of Don Caesar, but disguised herself so that she might imitate Ellen Terry as Portia, appeared as a toreador, and wore a white frock and pinafore in order to burlesque Minnie Palmer in *My Sweetheart*, and yet put on the rags of a Victorian crossing-sweeper, in order to sing her "Street Arab" song. Similarly, Fred Leslie, in the role of Don Caesar, was a strolling player and a Scotsman and an Irishman rolled into one, and yet found opportunities to put on a skirt as Madame Katti Lanner, the ballet trainer, and finally disguised himself as Henry Irving, in order to take part in the *pas de quatre*, which he had already given in *Faust Up to Date*.

The mention of Fred Leslie calls to mind the high level of craft skill called for from those who reach the heights in vaudeville. Leave out of account the sharpness of intelligence which detects the characteristics worthy of reproduction; remember only the tricks of voice, which are the equivalent of the draughtsmanship of a caricaturist. Dr. Lennox Browne was the throat specialist to the theatrical profession for many years, and among his clients was Fred Leslie, an imitator of admitted genius. Dr. Lennox Browne tells that Leslie's natural voice was a light baritone, with a compass of two octaves, G to G, but his imitations were generally produced on the middle A and most of them depended upon minute alterations in the resonators and subtle changes in the lip muscles. Thus, in order to imitate the *brek-ek-ek-kez-coax-coax* of a frog, Leslie agitated his vocal chords by an inward current of air from the mouth, while the imitation of a turkey cock was produced by a very rapid trill between the tip of the tongue and the upper lip. On the contrary, the report of a popgun was produced by a falsetto note, with the lips closed, so that the sound escaped through the nose, this being followed by a loud explosion caused by suction with the tongue. In a single song, "Love in the Orchestra," Leslie imitated a clarinet, a 'cello, cymbals, a violin, and a banjo. Plainly, hours of work, extending over months, were necessary to perfect the muscular movements which produced such results, and imitations were only an item in Fred Leslie's equipment as an artist in vaudeville.

Similarly, Louis Calvert said (and there is no more sure authority) that a big factor in Harry Lauder's success was the consummate skill with which he used his voice. He gave the impression of perfect spontaneity, and, though he always appeared to be "just talking," he, in fact, used an astonishing range of voice. Calvert continued, "The delectable, winning inflections, which somehow cajole and stroke an audience into just the warm mood he wishes, are not, I venture to say, so unstudied as they seem. Night after night he deftly touches the identical notes so expertly and easily that it all seems the naïve and almost accidental charm of a delightful personality."

Lauder himself has told us that it took him a year to make perfect the laugh which accompanied the patter of his song "Tobermory." For months he practised that laugh until it was natural and effervescent enough. But when "Tobermory" was right, Lauder sang it ten thousand times in all parts of the globe. Lauder happened to hear a boatload of holiday-makers from Glasgow embarking and two of them shouted to their friends ashore what they would do in Tobermory. An idea for a song, thought Lauder; the hard work followed.

Dan Leno said of his own art, "It may seem easy now, but I've had to dig for everything I've got."

The Edwardes productions were to dominate the light musical stage in London, the provinces, and the Overseas Dominions for a full quarter of a century, but before they come up for review the contribution of W. S. Gilbert and Arthur Sullivan to English vaudeville must be assessed and its worth acclaimed. Regarded as an expression of current social life, Savoy Opera was less significant than the productions at Daly's and the Gaiety, but, artistically, comic opera, as it was produced and played in the palmy days of the Savoy, was unsurpassed. Which is why it promises to be a vital element in the theatre of Britain fifty years hence.

Chapter III

GILBERT AND SULLIVAN COMIC OPERA, 1871 TO 1896

IT ALL BEGAN IN THE PAGES OF "FUN" A WEEKLY PERIODICAL akin to *Punch*, which flourished in the 'sixties under the editorship of H. J. Byron, the writer of extravanganza, and Tom Hood, the punster poet. Tom Robertson, George R. Sims, Clement Scott, Boyd Houghton, and Fred Barnard were others who contributed comic sketches and pictures. In the pages of *Fun*, Gilbert

When a felon's not engaged in his employment,
Or maturing his felonious little plans,
His capacity for innocent enjoyment
Is just as great as any honest man's.

developed his topsy-turvy sense of humour, literary as well as pictorial, for Gilbert, like Thackeray, was in his early days fully as promising a comic artist as he was a writer.

Thanks to *Fun*, Gilbert brought a fully fledged fancy to the creation of a new form of vaudeville when chance thrust him into an alliance with Arthur Sullivan. I am assured that Gilbert imagined, devised, and inspired the Savoy operas; he was the driving force. Hesketh Pearson was dead right when he wrote that it was part of Sullivan's greatness that he allowed Gilbert to call the tune. When the experiment began, Gilbert was immensely more experienced in theatrical affairs and his financial position was assured. In the year he wrote *Thespis* for the Gaiety Theatre (his first piece with Sullivan's music) Gilbert also wrote *Pygmalion and Galatea*, a play which was to bring him in £40,000 in royalties. Moreover,

3   23

the *Bab Ballads* had not only been written, but the best of them were in book form. Thus Gilbert was a mature writer, aged forty, when *Trial by Jury*, the first Gilbert and Sullivan success, had its run at the Royalty in 1875.

It is true that a section of the playgoing public was slow to recognise the rare contribution which Gilbert made to the alliance. When Queen Victoria ordered a command performance of *The Gondoliers* at Windsor Castle in 1891, the opera was described as "by Sir Arthur Sullivan"; to the chagrin of the librettist, his name was omitted from the Court Circular, an omission Gilbert did not forget. The error is the more curious as Queen Victoria had a personal acquaintance with the operas. When an old lady, she sang a duet from *Patience* with Mr. Alick Yorke. Obeying the royal command, Mr. Yorke began, "Prithee, pretty maiden, will you marry me?" When Victoria's turn came, a very clear, soft voice sang, "Gentle sir, although to marry I'm inclined . . ." In the middle of the song the little Queen stopped to say, "You know, Mr. Yorke, I was taught singing by Mendelssohn."

It would seem that mid-Victorian taste underrated the potentialities of a comic-opera librettist, in spite of the manifest services which Planché had rendered to extravaganza. For many years before the production of *Trial by Jury* the operas of Offenbach and Lecocq, which were the staple vaudeville of the period, had been so maltreated in translation that all the wit and most of the intelligibility vanished before they reached production. We know now that a witty and well-planned book of the words is far rarer than the tuneful music which has brought fame and fortune to the authors of many light operas. Arthur Sullivan is much more than a writer of tuneful music and a full share in the popularity of the Savoy operas is his due. Nevertheless, Gilbert was the energising force and it was his experience and drive which assured the venture triumphant success.

Gilbert was born within a stone's throw of the Opera Comique, whence H.M.S. *Pinafore* set sail on May 25th, 1878. The theatre stood on the island site in the Strand, between what is now Bush House and Australia House. Nearby was Southampton Street, and at Number 17, William Schwenck Gilbert was born on November 18th, 1836. Princess Victoria was not yet a queen and, in 1855, when William Schwenck was nineteen, he wanted to be a soldier and serve in the Crimea. The war ended too quickly, so Gilbert commenced his life's work with four years in the Education Department of the Privy Council. Then came a bit of luck. Young Gilbert inherited £400. He spent £200 in fees to the Inner Temple which ensured a Call; another £100 gave the budding barrister-at-law access to a conveyancer's chambers, and the rest of the money was spent upon furnishing suitable chambers in Clement's Inn. In other words, Gilbert "went to the Bar as a very young man," and contemplated a career ending as England's Lord High Chancellor.

Happily, briefs were hard to come by, and like many another budding lawyer Gilbert was tempted to test his talents in other directions. After H. J. Byron brought *Fun* into existence in 1861, Gilbert sent in an article, illustrated by a half-page drawing on wood, the 'sixties being the days of wood-blocks. Byron asked for more; indeed, for a column every week, plus a half-page drawing. Whereas two years' work as a barrister brought in no more than £75, comic articles and sketches promised a livelihood.

Even better prospects opened up when the young barrister sold his first stage piece, the reward being £30 for a fortnight's work. This success justified another burlesque, this time founded upon Donizetti's *Daughter of the Regiment*, with Toole and Lionel Brough in the cast. It ran for 120 nights and brought forth a commission from John Hollingshead to write a piece for the opening performance of the Gaiety. This time the burlesque was founded upon the opera, *Robert the Devil*, and the extravaganza was supported by the whole comic, vocal, and pantomimic strength of the Gaiety Company. Nellie Farren played Robert.

Burlesque was the mood of the decade in vaudeville, and punning the trump card of the librettist. In a burlesque upon *Ruy Blas*, published in 1866, Gilbert showed that he could pun with the best of his rivals. Here are a few lines from the complaint of the Queen, who finds herself wooed by Ruy Blas, in the disguise of Don Caesar de Bazan:

> Unhappy Queen, unhappy maiden I!
> In vain to get a wink of sleep I try,
> But wander, dressing gowny and night-cappy,
> I seldom get a nap—I'm so unnappy!

In Savoy opera, however, Gilbert was chary with his puns.

Enter Arthur Sullivan

Four years later Gilbert was introduced to Sullivan, then twenty-eight years old and Gilbert's junior by seven years. The immediate consequence was another commission from John Hollingshead and the production of *Thespis*, or *The Gods Grown Old*, at the Gaiety. It was put together in three weeks and produced after a week's rehearsal, so poetic justice ordained that it should only run for a month. Probably Sullivan's music was still somewhat "churchy." Nevertheless, Gilbert's share of the work was full of promise, as indeed was the basal idea, by which the Thespians, armed with Olympian powers, promised to put the poor old world to rights and failed so lamentably that the Old Gods resumed their duties to the satisfaction of everyone.

Perhaps the jolliest memorial of *Thespis* is an illustration reproduced in Hollingshead's *Gaiety Chronicles*, picturing a bewhiskered Gilbert, in a top hat, rehearsing the extravaganza. Nellie Farren and another lady of the company, both in bustles, are staging a mock combat with a dragon, the episode burlesquing Perseus rescuing Andromeda.

Arthur Sullivan was of Irish descent, with an added touch of the Jew to give artistry. Born on May 13th, 1842, he was a Londoner, and his early days were associated with Kneller Hall, where his father was a military bandmaster. When he was eight Sullivan attended his father's rehearsals regularly. By the time he was fourteen he could play every instrument with ease, and so, in later life, could show any player how to handle a passage. For the rest his schoolboy days were associated with the Chapel Royal, where he wore the scarlet and gold uniform of a chorister and revealed manifest promise. At fourteen he won the Mendelssohn travelling scholarship at the Academy of Music and went to Leipzig to study. At twenty, his *Tempest* music was given at the Crystal Palace and promise became proved achievement. An outstanding asset which Sullivan enjoyed and exploited to the full arose from the fact that he was a trained musician. He was not forced to ask another mind to orchestrate numbers. It is often forgotten that music which occupies a couple of minutes of stage-time may give the composer three days of heavy manual work, working up and writing down the orchestrations. Most musical comedy and revue composers shirk this hard work and not a few lack the needful musical training.

Sullivan, as a trained musician, knew just what he wanted from a theatre orchestra of thirty, consisting of a couple of flutes, an oboe, two clarinets, one or two bassoons, two horns, a couple of cornets, two trombones, to which were added percussion and strings. Given Gilbert's words, Sullivan was able to compose in terms of a theatre orchestra and hundreds of happy inventions reveal the value of his musicianly gifts; for example, the cymbals in "the screw may twist and the rack may turn" in Dame Carruthers's song in *The Yeomen*. In general, Sullivan sketched out the rhythms for a lyric and later evolved the melodies which identify themselves so closely with Gilbert's words, that, to-day, words and music seem a single invention. As a preliminary to setting Phoebe's song in *The Yeomen*, "Were I thy bride," Sullivan made eight essays in rhythm, each represented by a series of dots and dashes. Most of them seemed commonplace, but the selected one precisely suited the sentiment of the lyric and was, therefore, fittest for translation into melody.

Though his first interest was sacred music, and ecclesiastical harmonies and cadences can be readily found in the Savoy operas, Sullivan always drew upon a rich fund of humour. When organist of St. Peter's, Cranley Gardens, a certain Bishop was late and Sullivan patiently improvised. His first effort was based upon "I waited for the Lord." There followed some passages recalling his own "Will He Come?" When his Lordship at length appeared fully robed from the vestry, the organist was playing "We that endure to the end."

A hundred passages in the Savoy operas witness to Sullivan's sense of musical humour; among them Lady Jane's recitative in *Patience*, caricaturing the mock heroics of Italian "recitativo parlant," and the reminiscence of a passage from Wagner's *Tristan*, as Iolanthe rises clad in water-weeds, singing "With humbled breast and every hope laid low." Again, there is the Bach-like introduction to the Lord Chancellor's Nightmare Song, "When you're lying awake with a dismal headache."

Here Sullivan's ingenuity rivals the verbal skill of Gilbert, though, very properly, the music is subordinated to the all-important patter of the low comedian. Oddly enough, one of the rare occasions when Gilbert's sense of humour deserted him was when he complained that the splendid setting to the Ghost Song in *Ruddigore* was "out of place in a comic opera" and asked for something more humorous! "I fancy," added Gilbert, "that Sullivan thought his professional position demanded something grander and more impressive than the words suggested." In fact, Gilbert underrated his own powers of suggestion. The underlying skit upon operatic melodrama called for just the setting demanded by:

> When the night wind howls in the chimney cowls, and the bat in the moonlight flies,
> And inky clouds, like funeral shrouds, sail over the midnight skies,
> When the footpads quail at the night-birds wail, and black dogs bay the moon,
> This is the spectre's holiday—then is the ghosts' high noon!

Admit that the music of the Savoy operas owed something to Mozart and Mendelssohn, and it is still plain that the borrowings passed through the alembic of a comparable talent and what remained in the crucible was genuine Sullivan. How could a musician of Sullivan's capacity escape the influence of Mozart or write the fairy passages in *Iolanthe* without occasionally remembering that Mendelssohn had given the world a musical recension of *A Midsummer Night's Dream*? For the rest, Arthur Sullivan composed with amazing facility. The overtures to *Iolanthe* and *The Yeomen of the Guard* were written, the one in a night, and the other in twelve hours.

Such efforts are the more remarkable as Sullivan, after 1872, suffered from stone in the kidney, and much of his work was done while under great pain. He only finished the music for *Princess Ida* four days before the opening performance in January 1884. On New Year's Day, he rehearsed the Savoy Orchestra all the morning, spent several hours at the dress rehearsal, and then walked home through a snowstorm to Queen's Mansions and worked until the small hours of the morning upon the Princess's Song, "I Built Upon a Rock," and Gama's "Nothing to Grumble at." On the eve of the first night of *Princess Ida*, morphia was injected to allay the pain from which Sullivan was suffering, and in the morning he lay in bed, inert and helpless. When he tried to get up, he fell to the floor in agony. Yet he was resolved to be in the conductor's seat that night. At 7 p.m. another hypodermic injection was given and with it a strong cup of coffee to keep Sullivan awake. Thus he managed to drive to the Savoy. He wrote in his diary, "Tremendous house—usual reception. Very fine performance—not a hitch. Brilliant success. After the performance I turned very faint and could not stand."

"And be it remembered, a composer cannot dictate to a secretary or get his rough draft typed. Every note must be written by your own hand," said Sullivan of his compositions. "There is no other way of getting it done. Every opera means four or five hundred folio sheets of music, every crochet and quaver of which has to be written out by the composer, often with his ideas pages and pages ahead of his fingers."

In general, Gilbert's rhythmic versalility and his ingenuity as a rhymester kept Sullivan's inventive capacity fully alive, while the melodies of Sullivan softened the acerbities of Gilbert's humour. It was also a virtue in Sullivan that he was always prepared to set the words of his lyricist to music and not demand that words should be fitted to his melodies, as is the modern method, particularly in the innumerable musical shows derived from the Continent. Basil Hood was in the habit of reading his lyrics to Sullivan, who allowed his imagination to roam until the required rhythm suggested itself, when Sullivan added the melody suited to the verses.

Gilbert's Contribution

William Archer said no more than the bare truth when he stated that Gilbert, with his librettos, restored literary self-respect to the English stage. Victorian books of the words, so far as they could be distinguished from the gagging of low comedians, were little more than vulgar doggerel. Gilbert gave the librettos of his day an Aristophanic flavour, the adjective suggesting not only full artistry but satirical contacts with many aspects of social and political life. In particular, Gilbert's dramatic use of the chorus was an outstanding contribution to English comic opera, and the biggest factor in ensuring artistic unification. The "sisters, cousins, and aunts" of *H.M.S. Pinafore*, the fairies and the Peers of *Iolanthe*, and the love-sick maidens of *Patience* were devised in the mood of *The Frogs* or *The Birds* of Aristophanes. Akin was the unification of character in the Imported Flowers of Progress in *Utopia Limited*, and the theatrical company in Greek attire, which introduced the second act of *The Grand Duke*, as brilliant a bit of work as ever the Savoyards accomplished. Recall the opening chorus, "Eloia! Eloia!", Rutland Barrington's patter song, "At the outset I may mention it's my sovereign intention, to revive the classic memories of Athens at its best," and Ilka von Palmay's contribution to the memorable Mad Duet:

> I have a rival! Frenzy thrilled
> I find you both together!
> My heart stands still—with horror chilled—
> Hard as the millstone nether!
> Then softly, slyly, snaily, snaky,
> Crawly, creepy, quaily, quaky,
> I track her on her homeward way.

There follows the chorus, "Your Highness, there's a party at the door," Julia's "Broken every promise plighted," and the duet:

> If the light of love's lingering ember
> Has faded in gloom,
> You cannot neglect, O remember,
> A voice from the tomb.

If *The Grand Duke* is the weakest of the Savoy operas, how high must be the standard of all the rest.

From the first, Gilbert and Sullivan determined that no derogatory element should associate itself with their stage work. Unlike current burlesque or *opéra bouffe*, the chorus was never permitted to don tights, nor were men allowed to play women's parts, or vice versa. Careful as they were, Gilbert and Sullivan did not placate every purist. Lewis Carroll, apparently troubled by the Great Big "D" in *Pinafore*, wrote, "How Mr. Gilbert could have stooped to write or Sir Arthur Sullivan could have prostituted his noble art to set to music such vile trash, it passes my skill to understand." This from the author of *Alice in Wonderland* is, surely, proof positive that Gilbert and Sullivan accomplished a difficult task when they persuaded Victorian England to take the new comic-opera form to its heart. After all, the outstanding thing about the partnership was that it attracted a vast new class of theatre-goers to vaudeville.

However, such strictures were few and far between and, after three-quarters of a century, only serve to emphasise the achievement of the great Savoyards. To their other gifts must be added the high standard of craftsmanship which librettist and composer continually impressed upon their players. In this respect, Gilbert was once more the prime mover. He was the stage-manager and, it may be added, one of the most talented who ever directed rehearsals, his ideals being firm-based upon those of his friend, Tom Robertson, of *Caste* fame. Gilbert selected his own scenery and many of the costumes in the operas were made from his drawings. When a spinning-wheel was needed for Phoebe's opening song in *The Yeomen of the Guard*, Gilbert found just what was wanted in an antique shop. Lastly, his was the primary voice in the selection of the actors and actresses, few of whom were men and women of established reputation. Always, Gilbert was convinced that the author was all-important in comic opera and that gagging and the "business" of low comedians were cardinal crimes at the Opera Comique or the Savoy. "And why not?" said Gilbert, "I planned out the whole stage-management beforehand on my model stage, with blocks three inches high to represent men and two and a half inches high to represent women. . . . I had it all clear in my head before going down to the theatre."

During rehearsals at the Savoy a scaffold was raised in the stalls, so that Gilbert might have the correct "audience view" of the stage. And woe to the player who interfered with the all-important continuity, whether the actor was up to tricks with Gilbert's words or Sullivan's music. Once a bold fellow attempted to retort, "Look here, Mr. Gilbert, I know my words backwards." "I know you do," said Gilbert, "but I don't want them said that way."

Gilbert's readiness of wit has seldom been surpassed. Oscar Wilde was ready, but not more ready than Gilbert. During a rehearsal Durward Lely, the Lieutenant the Duke of Dunstable in *Patience*, was told to sit down "in a pensive fashion." In doing so, Lely upset an elaborate bit of scenery. "No, no!" said Gilbert. "I said pensively, not ex-pensively."

Another story relates to the lovely Miss Fortescue, who was a member of the Savoy Company for a time, and a lifelong friend of the Gilberts. At a dinner-party Miss Fortescue chanced to mention that the Greeks had the custom of carving inscriptions upon their seats.

"I've forgotten what they called them," she added, with a glance towards Gilbert.

"*Arrière-pensées*, I expect," was the reply.

Nor would one like to forget the crisp, though somewhat unkindly, reply to the secretary of an amateur choral society, after a struggle with one of the operas:

"What do you think of the Club?"

"Well, it's not so much a club as a bundle of sticks."

Nevertheless, old George Grossmith testified to Gilbert's infinite patience, when he had talent to his liking, and Jessie Bond, a Savoyard of twenty years' experience, was pronouncedly pro-Gilbert, when any discussion regarding the relative merits of the three Savoyards was under way.

The Savoy Company came into being at the Opera Comique, when *The Sorcerer* was produced by the D'Oyly Carte Comedy Opera Company. *Trial by Jury* had been only a one-act affair and the text came from a Gilbertian effort in *Fun*, written seven years earlier, to which Sullivan added the music in a couple of weeks. But the success of the collaboration was so plain that D'Oyly Carte, manager of the Royalty Theatre, where *Trial by Jury* was first played, suggested a full-length comic opera and formed a syndicate to produce it at the Opera Comique in the Strand. Looking out for interpreters of what he hoped would prove a new brand of vaudeville, Gilbert bethought him of George Grossmith, whom he knew as a police-court reporter in the daytime and a musical entertainer at night. Grossmith was told about the magician, who was to bring about such strange happenings in the village of Ploverleigh.

"But, Mr. Gilbert, you require a fine man with a large voice."

"No, that is exactly what we don't want," said the dramatist.

I did not see George Grossmith until the production of *His Excellency*, and in that pleasant opera he certainly was not a fine man with a large voice. His virtue from Gilbert's standpoint was that he avoided exaggerated gestures and did not lack the emotional appeal which all comedians of the first rank have at their command. Moreover, he was intelligent enough never to miss a humorous point, whether in dialogue or music. Lastly, he was a first-rate dancer, as those who saw his bat-like movements in the third verse of the "If You Go In" trio, with Tolloler and Mountarrat in *Iolanthe*, testify.

Unlike Hollingshead, George Edwardes, and Augustus Harris, Gilbert did not draw his stars from the music-hall or the burlesque houses. Rutland Barrington was a young baritone when he was engaged to play Dr. Daly in *The Sorcerer*. Gilbert nursed Barrington into a perfect instrument for unfolding his topsy-turvydoms. Jessie Bond was the daughter of a Camden Town piano-maker who migrated to Liverpool, where Miss Bond made an early appearance as a child

Jessie Bond as Margaret, in "Ruddigore" (top left)
'Three Little Maids' (Leonora Braham, Sybil Grey and Jessie Bond)
'Dear Little Buttercup' (Bertha Lewis) (lower)

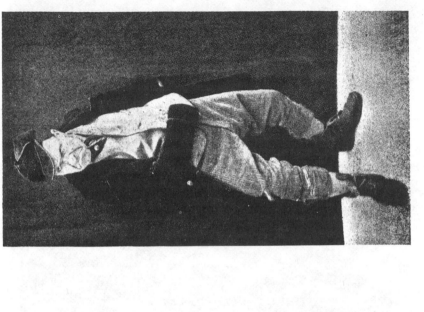

Albert Chevalier
in "The Lag's Lament"

Arthur Roberts in "Gentleman Joe"
(The Hansom Cabbie)

pianist. At seventeen she was a popular singer in Lancashire, and her very first appearance on the stage was as Hebe in *Pinafore*. Mrs. Howard Paul, the Lady Sangazure of *The Sorcerer*, had walked out of the Opera Comique when she saw the role with which Gilbert had fitted her. In a quandary, D'Oyly Carte bethought him of little Jessie Bond. She could sing, but could she act? In doubt, Gilbert cut the part of Hebe drastically, and that is why *Pinafore* is the shortest of the Savoy operas and often played with *Cox and Box* or *Trial by Jury*.

And what was the result? Gilbert became a staunch friend and admirer of Jessie Bond and taught her the craft of vaudeville acting, until she was one of the best players who ever graced the Savoy stage. She had a part in every opera from *Pinafore* in 1878 to *The Gondoliers* in 1889, beginning at £3 a week and ending at £40. She was never better than as the distraught Mad Margaret in *Ruddigore*, though she was her charming self as Phoebe, in *The Yeomen of the Guard*.

"Here you are, Jessie," said Gilbert, as he handed her the part. "You needn't act this. It's you."

Pinafore established the fame of Gilbert, Sullivan, and D'Oyly Carte the world over. There was a time when it was played at eight theatres in New York alone. But its success was not instantaneous. The Opera Comique was an uncomfortable little theatre, on the edge of a rookery which extended from the Strand to Holborn. One approached its pit through a subterranean tunnel. It was only when Sullivan played a selection from the opera at the Promenade Concerts, where he was conductor, and was encored four times, that London awoke to the tunefulness of *Pinafore*.

The Pirates of Penzance and *Patience* followed. By this time the success of Gilbert and Sullivan vaudeville was so well-assured that D'Oyly Carte decided to build a new theatre on the cleaner side of the Strand. So great had been the success of *Pinafore* in America, that *The Pirates of Penzance* had its first production there, with an English company including Jessie Bond and Rosina Brandram. Three companies were touring in the States before the first night in London on April 3rd, 1880.

Patience was produced on April 23rd, 1881, at the Opera Comique, and transferred on October 10th to the new Savoy. Within a year there had been 365 performances in London, 323 in the provinces, 180 in New York, and 111 in other American towns: a total of 977, representing 870,000 playgoers and box-office takings totalling £138,000. In London, the amenities of the new theatre enhanced the popular appeal of the operas. Here, electric light was installed for the first time in theatrical history: an innovation which was to invade the stage in *Iolanthe*, when the chorus of fairies tripped on, each with a star-like electric light in her hair. The apparatus was concealed in the small of each lady's back. Another Savoy innovation was the stage lake, from which Iolanthe emerged. A zealous property man, anxious to enhance the realism of the scene, once added some real frogs, until Jessie Bond, the Iolanthe, objected. The frogs were fished out of the water trough, with the aid of an inverted umbrella, and only then did

Jessie Bond answer the Invocation of her estranged mother, clad in the water-weeds of her long exile.

1891, when *The Gondoliers* ended its run, was the time of the unhappy quarrel. The actual break seems to have been over a carpet which D'Oyly Carte judged necessary for the foyer and for which Gilbert resented paying one-third of the cost. We can now see that the break would have come in any case. Sullivan had been

The Savoy

restless for a long time. He considered himself worthy of better things than putting music to Gilbert's special brand of topsy-turvy nonsense. Events were to prove Sullivan wrong. *The Maid of Antioch, Ivanhoe,* and even *The Golden Legend* are forgotten things, in comparison with the comic operas. These are destined to carry the fame of Arthur Sullivan down the centuries, if not in company with Mozart, Bizet, and Rossini, then with Delibes, Offenbach, and Strauss. Charming as was some of the music in *Haddon Hall* and *The Rose of Persia*, it never touched the heights reached continually when Gilbert's words were the inspiration.

The three Savoyards joined forces once again in 1893 for *Utopia Limited*, and *The Grand Duke*, the last of the operas, followed in 1896. Only Rutland Barrington and Rosina Brandram now remained, but an accomplished band of new-comers, most of them trained by Gilbert, were there, among them Walter Passmore, John le

Hay, Scott Russell, Charles Kenningham, Scott Fishe, Nancy McIntosh, Florence Perry, and Emmie Owen. They were to render great service to the Savoy for five years or more.

Some of the virtues of *The Grand Duke* have been recorded. *Utopia Limited* furnishes such a memory as Lady Sophy's

> Bold-faced ranger,
> (Perfect stranger)
> Meets two well-behaved young ladies.

The King's song:

> First you're born, and I'll be bound you
> Find a dozen strangers round you;

the patter song: "A complicated gentleman allow me to present," and the two songs by the Stockbroker: "Some seven men form an Association" and "The delightful English Girl," are other memorable things.

Almost to the end influences derived from the *Fun* days persisted. Again and again Gilbert drew upon humorous ideas adumbrated in the 'sixties, but the pliancy of his wit was such that very little seemed dated. In *Pinafore*, Captain Corcoran is, plainly, a variant upon Captain Reece, commanding of the *Mantel-piece*; an able seaman, Joe Golightly, who receives a dozen lashes daily for making love to the daughter of the First Lord of the Admiralty, also reappears with differences. The *Bab Ballads* also include a Bumboat Woman, the Buttercup of *Pinafore*.

The origins of *Iolanthe* are particularly well documented. Gilbert invented a fairy curate who got into trouble with his bishop for embracing an airily attired young lady, who turned out to be his fairy mother, an imbroglio which first found expression in a *Bab Ballad*. Mr. Malcolm Salaman has told us how the plot was evolved, his guide being the fat note-books in which Gilbert jotted down the several chops and changes. The first notion was that the fairy had been guilty of the imprudence of marrying a solicitor, aged forty-five, while engaged upon a fairy mission on earth. After a trial in Fairyland, the erring damsel was banished, as was Iolanthe, while her son, a barrister, achieved fame owing to his uncanny influence with juries, a result of his fairy origin. Salaman tells that Gilbert turned the plot about twenty or thirty times before the existing story came to him. Each time there was an alteration in the scheme, the whole growing in scope, and gathering, at each fresh writing incidents, suggestions for stage dialogue, lyrics, or business, while the characters developed precision, aided by the vivacious pen-and-ink sketches with which Gilbert enlivened his fat note-books.

At first thought, this habit of utilising any material which lay to hand might be regarded as suggesting that Gilbert did not take his talent very seriously, but the underlying truth is that originality in plot is no great virtue in the theatre world. Shakespeare did without it. So did the Greek tragedians. What mattered to Gilbert was that he should be unsparing in his efforts after perfection. He wanted present success, not fame. On one occasion he said, "I fancy posterity will know as little of me as I shall know of posterity."

Seventy-five years of theatre-going and more than one generation of theatre lovers testify that Gilbert underrated the staying-powers of the operas. Perhaps he was deceived by their relative unpopularity in London early in the century, when the value of the copyrights was at their lowest. The temporary eclipse is one of the mysteries of Gilbertiana, as was the sudden revival of popularity after the first World War, when a memorable season at the Prince's Theatre showed that a new generation had arisen to welcome the Savoy confections, while the delight of the elderly remained unabated. Perhaps the growing popularity of the Savoy operas with the amateur dramatic societies furnishes a clue to the mystery. In a Prince's Theatre audience one could detect two strata: one Victorian and the other Georgian; a full decade of theatre lovers seemed to be missing.

Happily, in the post-war era, a company of players existed capable of carrying on the Savoy tradition with full assurance. Though the interest of provincial audiences had waned between 1910 and 1920, it had not failed. The elements of a first-rate London company were there when the best of the provincial players made their appearance at the Prince's. Walter Passmore, in the George Grossmith parts, had been a tower of strength in the revivals of the 'nineties, being a good singer of the patter songs, a brilliant dancer, and a resourceful comedian. Never have Ko-Ko's dances been better done, the climax of "Here's a How-de-do" being specially memorable. Passmore had left to establish himself in a tobacconist's business in Golders Green, an end which, to Savoyards, must have seemed akin to the tragedy which assailed Prince Florizel of Bohemia, in Stevenson's *New Arabian Nights*.

I have been tempted to visit Golders Green for a smoke and a chat, but always courage has failed. Heigh-ho! With what an Olympian outlook Passmore could have debated the moot problem of Jack Point's end. Did the jester just faint, or did he die, dropping dead at Elsie's feet, after kissing the hem of the girl's dress, while she bent compassionately over him? George Thorne, the comedian of the principal touring company, had introduced the change, and with such success that Gilbert had not the heart to intervene. But he was adamant when Passmore proposed the same business in London.

"Elsie does not care a hoot about Jack Point," was Gilbert's objection; but, after a rehearsal, Gilbert consented and, since then, Jack Points have been free to live or die, as they pleased.

Passmore's successor in the low comedy roles was C. H. Workman, excellent alike as singer and actor. The long and worthy service of Sir Henry Lytton followed and persisted well into the experience of latter-day lovers of Gilbert and Sullivan. Lytton played thirty roles in Savoy operas during his career and was associated with the Company for the greater part of fifty years. A very worthy record which was symbolised when the follysticks, which he used in the *Yeomen of the Guard*, were laid upon his coffin when he was cremated at Golders Green.

It was as though they were the baton of some field-marshal. And so they were in the sense that they represented Henry Lytton's contribution to the world's work through a long life. He made them himself fifty years earlier. As for Sullivan's music, Lady Lytton felt that nothing could be more fitting for her husband's passing than the airs he loved so well. So "I hear the soft note," from *Patience*, and "Hail Poetry," from *The Pirates*, were played instead of hymns.

Lytton was as good as any Savoyard as the Lord Chancellor in *Iolanthe*, his staccato delivery and clear-cut articulation suiting the part admirably. He was equally effective as the Judge in *Trial by Jury*. Robert Evett as Earl Tolloller, R. Crompton's singing of the Sentry Song, Isabel Jay's Patience, George Thorne's pathetic Jack Point, Leo Sheffield's Don Alhambra, Marjorie Eyre's Mad Margaret, and the brilliant work of Bertha Lewis after Rosina Brandram's retirement, also call for record. Miss Lewis's Lady Blanche in *Princess Ida*, her Buttercup, her Katisha, her Lady Jane in *Patience*, and her Lady Sangazure in *The Sorcerer* were all perfect. Bertha Lewis joined the Savoy Company when she was nineteen years old and was the outstanding success of the repertory season at the Prince's Theatre in 1919-20. She was only forty-four when she was killed in a motoring accident in company with Sir Henry Lytton, who narrowly escaped with his life.

The careful presentation of Sullivan's music in these later revivals, when Malcolm Sargent and Geoffrey Toye trained the chorus and conducted the orchestra, was an important factor in making for their success. Beautiful as were the dresses and scenery which Charles Ricketts designed for the Savoy revival of *The Mikado* in 1929, I am not sure that they helped the opera. The great hats and trains were highly picturesque, but, perhaps, were a thought too beautiful and of the period to carry the needful humour. The new Mikado's costume was based upon that of a Shogun, a relatively unimportant ruler, the idea being to spare the feelings of the real Emperor of Japan. Somehow the personal reactions of a foreign potentate seemed far removed from the stage requirements of a Gilbert and Sullivan opera. Ricketts' designs were eventually purchased by the National Arts Collection Fund and are now a national possession. One would not have missed Bertha Lewis's wonder-gown as Katisha at the end of the first act of *The Mikado*, but Nanki-Poo, as minstrel, was better served by the dress which Gilbert had approved. The Three Little Maids, too, were more amusing when they had no hats; the change converted them into "young ladies."

Nor did I particularly welcome the new scenery of *The Yeomen*, though Peter Goffin devised a novel and pleasant colour-scheme from the scarlet of the uniforms and the greys of the Tower Green. However, these personal predilections did not disturb the welcome accorded to the operas. Derek Oldham, in the tenor roles, Darrell Fancourt, a Mikado as telling as Scott Fishe had been, Nellie Briercliffe, a latter-day Yum-Yum, Sydney Granville, Martyn Green, Winifred Lawson, Elsie Griffin, and Leo Sheffield—all were now accepted exponents of their several roles and, thanks to the abiding influence of Gilbert's stage management, this generation continued to receive its Savoy opera from an uncontaminated well.

In February 1945, while a World War was in progress, there were eighty amateur dramatic societies producing musical shows in Great Britain, and no fewer than twenty-eight were rehearsing Gilbert and Sullivan operas. Five of them were at work upon *Pinafore* and five upon *The Gondoliers*. Can there be any doubt that the genre still has power to please a third and a fourth generation of vaudeville lovers?

One thing more: a tribute to Mrs. D'Oyly Carte, from the early days, when she was Miss Lenoir and D'Oyly Carte's secretary. By common consent Mrs. D'Oyly Carte was one of the outstanding women of her time. Sir James Barrie, in conversation with Lord Esher, once suggested that the two of them should write down the name of "the most remarkable woman they had known." Both wrote "Mrs. D'Oyly Carte." Gilbert and Sullivan were devoted to her. After taking a degree at London University, "Helen Lenoir," as she was called, joined D'Oyly Carte as a clerk, when her chief was a dramatic and musical agent, and contemplating the production of *The Sorcerer*. She laboured by day and by night, settling tours, engaging artists, and generally ensuring the success of the venture. When D'Oyly Carte's health broke down she took over complete control of his complicated affairs, including the arrangement of lecture tours by such a man as H. M. Stanley and the management of the Savoy Hotel. For years the profits of the Savoy Theatre were in the neighbourhood of £60,000 a year. They were divided equally between Sullivan, Gilbert, and D'Oyly Carte. In a juster world the division would have been into four and the last part would have gone to Helen Lenoir. She was the simplest, the kindest, and yet the most competent of women. The highest tribute to her gifts came from Gilbert. It ran:

> *My dear Miss Lenoir,*
>   *I have the honour to be,*
>   *Madam,*
>   *Your very obliged and*
>   *truly humble servant,*
>   *W. S. GILBERT*
> *and will therefore sign any blessed thing you tell me to.*

Chapter IV

THE SAVOY. POST-GILBERT ERA. EDWARD GERMAN'S OPERAS

BETWEEN 1875 WHEN "TRIAL BY JURY" WAS PRODUCED AND 1896 when *The Grand Duke* enjoyed its only run, Gilbert established a standard for English libretto-writing which holds to-day, though the moods and methods of authors, composers, producers, and public alike have changed so greatly. The best wits in Britain have found it impossible to reach the achievements of the famous Savoyard. Following *The Grand Duke*, Burnand and R. C. Lehmann, editors of *Punch* both of them, wrote *His Majesty* for the Savoy company, when a new Gilbert and Sullivan opera was not available. The music was by Sir Alexander Mackenzie; George Grossmith, senior, and the talented Ilka von Palmay were in the cast, but the play would not run.

Somewhat earlier, in 1891, while *The Gondoliers* was still delighting audiences at the Savoy, Edward Solomon's *The Nautch Girl* was brought to D'Oyly Carte, with a book by George Dance. The libretto was no worse than that of the average successful comic opera, and Solomon's music was distinctly better, but neither were good enough for Savoy audiences. Yet another score from Edward Solomon was set to a libretto by Sydney Grundy. Grundy lacked the deft touch of George Dance, but he was a competent dramatist and knew how to fit an old-world tale for the stage. With the *The Vicar of Bray* as his title, a lively chapter of English social life seemed to offer itself. Moreover, *The Vicar of Bray* was a revival and Grundy had ample opportunities for revising his lyrics during the ten years between 1882 and 1892. The Solomon-Grundy comic opera was not a failure. It ran for half a year, but it never established itself, in spite of some tuneful music. The same must be said for Sydney Grundy's *Haddon Hall*, which he wrote for Sullivan and the Savoy company in 1892. A straightforward plot and passable lyrics were not enough to inspire the musician to his best.

Sir Arthur Pinero, at the height of his fame, collaborated with J. Comyns Carr in *The Beauty Stone*, and Sullivan provided the music, but, again, the libretto was not what the genius of Sullivan required or the Savoy public wanted to see. There was far too much plot. Moreover, Satan is not a happy principal character for Anglo-Saxon vaudeville and Walter Passmore, literally, "played the devil" in and with the piece. Rosina Brandram as the Weaver's wife, and Ruth Vincent singing the Cripple Girl's Prayer to the Virgin, are the outstanding memories.

Again, in an effort to find another Gilbert, D'Oyly Carte commissioned Charles Hallam Edward Brookfield, a merry wit, to explore French *opéra bouffe*, and see if the popularity which had attached to Offenbach and Lecocq a generation earlier could be reclaimed. But still, no real success.

Better fortune attended the Savoy management when Sullivan was associated with Basil Hood, a connection of Tom Hood, and like his more famous relative a punster of uncanny ingenuity. Basil Hood, moreover, had written *Gentleman Joe* for Arthur Roberts and was not likely to fall into the trap awaiting straight dramatists, such as Sydney Grundy and Sir Arthur Pinero. In fact, Basil Hood's libretti were the best in the post-Gilbert era, and those for *The Emerald Isle* and *Merrie England* had real merit. Too much of Basil Hood's work was of the musical-comedy order and he was unlucky in having to transform so many continental books of the words into an English form, thus writing lyrics to music which was already composed, instead of providing words which the musician could fit to music, as Sullivan had done.

The Emerald Isle, Basil Hood's masterpiece, reached a climax of inventiveness in Professor Bunn's patter-song, "Imitations," also sung by Walter Passmore.

> Oh, the age in which we're living strikes a man of any sense
> As an age of make-believe, of imitation, and pretence. . . .
> While silly servant maidies
>   Dress in imitation silk,
> And think *they* look like ladies
>   When they're taking in the milk—
> But though they take the milk in,
>   That's the only thing they do,
> For the milk takes *them* in sometimes,
>   Being imitation too!

In *The Emerald Isle*, too, it was a real pleasure to listen to neatly turned lines, not only in the patter-songs and character lyrics, but in the choruses. Following the opening dance, the Irish girls broke into this protest:

> Now be aisy with taisin'
> And squazin' and saizin'
> My waist wid your arm like a bundle o' hay!
> It's meself that is dressed
> In my best and distressed
> To be tumbled and pressed in that impudent way.

The "Song of the Devonshire Men," with a bimble and a bumble and the best of 'em, is a Basil Hood number in *The Emerald Isle*, and Reginald Crompton singing the lyric to the music of Edward German is remembered. So is Isabel Jay as the heroine, Rosie, singing "Oh, setting sun!" Had Basil Hood been able to maintain the standard achieved in *The Emerald Isle* and *Merrie England*, his name would have loomed more largely in the story of English vaudeville.

About the time *The Emerald Isle* was produced, Sir Charles Stanford composed his *Shamus O'Brien*, with a book by Alfred Graves, father of the latter-day poet. Three reputations established themselves during the run of *Shamus O'Brien* at the Opera Comique, those of Joseph O'Mara, the tenor, Kirkby Lunn, the contralto heroine of the opera, and Henry J. Wood, its young conductor. Kirkby Lunn had studied under Stanford at the Royal College of Music, and many of the chorus were drawn from students at the Guildhall and other London Colleges of Music. From *Shamus* Kirkby Lunn passed to the Carl Rosa Company and, eventually, to the great Wagner contralto roles at Covent Garden. Joseph O'Mara was a Limerick lad and had made his first appearance in Sullivan's *Ivanhoe*. When D'Oyly Carte's venture at the Royal English Opera House failed, O'Mara joined Sir Augustus Harris at Covent Garden. As Mike Murphy in *Shamus O'Brien*, O'Mara touched heights, though the fruits of his success were garnered by the public in the United States, and not in London. Like many another lover of English vaudeville, I saw *Shamus O'Brien* again and again from the shilling gallery of the Opera Comique and the pleasure never exhausted itself.

Stanford had the talent for light opera, and the sense of humour, but his musical interests were too widely distributed. In the event, Edward German proved the only possible successor to Arthur Sullivan. And how English he was. Born at Whitchurch in Shropshire in 1862, his talent was mature when an obvious career as a light-opera composer opened up, owing to the passing of Sullivan. German's father had been an organist and the family was musical, so it was not surprising that at fifteen years of age young German could conduct a small orchestra and was already bent upon a career as a composer. After training in Germany, he made his first contacts with the theatrical world as a conductor. His incidental music for Richard Mansfield's production of *Richard the Third* in 1889, when German was twenty-six, was not only promising, it represented proved achievement. The battle scenes were specially well handled; so were those covering the murder of the little Princes in the Tower.

Three years later Irving commissioned the incidental music for his *Henry the Eighth* revival at the Lyceum, and the familiar Three Dances established German's reputation. Five other similar commissions followed between 1895 and 1900, the last being the music for *English Nell* at the Prince of Wales's, 1900. The songs, as sung by Marie Tempest, showed that German had the makings of a highly successful comic-opera composer and his opportunity came when he was required to finish the score of Sullivan's *The Emerald Isle* for the Savoy Company. Only two of Sullivan's numbers had been completed, though the melodies for fifteen others were in manuscript. Edward German worked through the winter of 1900-01, finishing Sullivan's work and everyone admitted that a difficult task could not have been better done.

Merrie England followed in 1902, after the lease of the Savoy had passed from Mrs. D'Oyly Carte to William Greet. Basil Hood's plot was concerned with the love-affairs of Sir Walter Raleigh and Queen Elizabeth and the Earl of Essex were among the characters. More inspiring for Edward German were the rustic scenes in Windsor Park and the May Day revels which figure so prominently in the book. The quintet, "Love is made to make us glad,' was comparable with anything of the kind in Gilbert and Sullivan opera. As Isabel Jay left the Savoy

Company to marry Frank Curzon, Agnes Fraser was called upon to play Raleigh's lover, Bessie Throckmorton, and Henry Lytton, Robert Evett, Walter Passmore, and Reginald Crompton (the Big Ben) were also in the cast. Since then *Merrie England* has been popular with amateur operatic companies, and was revived at Prince's Theatre in the 'thirties, with W. S. Percy as Walter Wilkins, and Miss Cruickshank in Rosina Brandram's part of Elizabeth. Nancy Fraser played Bessie Throckmorton, the part her mother, Agnes Fraser, played in 1902. Pretty Louie Pounds, a sister of Courtice Pounds, played Jill All Alone in 1902, this being Rosalinde Fuller's part in 1934; 1945 witnessed yet another revival.

A third Edward German and Basil Hood opera, *A Princess of Kensington*, was produced at the Savoy in 1903 and again Passmore, Robert Evett, Louie Pounds, Rosina Brandram, and Agnes Fraser played and sang. The plot, however, proved too complex and the outstanding memory is the rollicking "Four Jolly Sailormen," a number in Edward German's best manner. The failure of the play heralded the end of the splendid adventure, which sought successors to Gilbert and Sullivan and so nearly found them in Edward German and Basil Hood. Denied an outlet at the Savoy, Edward German turned to Robert Courtneidge, who had established himself as a producer of musical shows with *The Arcadians*. A splendid product of the new alliance was *Tom Jones*, a musical version of Fielding's novel, with a book by A. M. Thompson and Robert Courtneidge. Robert Courtneidge produced it at the Apollo in 1907, and this time Edward German had a first-rate opportunity. The plot was concerned with Tom's love for Sophia; the heroine's flight from home; Tom's lapse with Lady Bellaston; and the reconciliation of the lovers in Ranelagh Gardens. As a Salopian, who was born a "Jones"—for Edward German had dropped his original surname in favour of his second Christian name—Fielding's novel promised a background pleasantly attuned to the composer's genius. Always there was the sunny freshness of the West Country in German's music and "Don't you find the weather charming?" is only an example of it. The septet, "The Barley Mow," and Squire Western's song, "The Maid and the Cuckoo," sung by Ambrose Manning, are other examples.

> On a Januairy morning in Zummerzetsheer
> Two pretty maidens were walking alone
> When suddenly there came from a coppice, zo clear,
> The call of a cuckoo in zong.
> It astonished those pretty maids the cuckoo for to hear,
> On Januairy morning in Zummerzetsheer.

German's songs and choruses being worthy of good singing, Robert Court-neidge was careful to provide players with the necessary experience. Hayden Coffin played Tom Jones, and the role offered acting opportunities which came to Hayden Coffin very seldom; Dan Rolyat was the Benjamin Partridge, and Ruth Vincent, Sophia Western. German's Waltz Song could not have been rendered more delightfully than it was by Ruth Vincent, fresh from her successes in Gilbert and Sullivan roles and with a career in grand opera in prospect.

Carrie Moore, as Sophia's maid, Honour, sang:

> All for a green ribbon he bought at the Fair,
> All for a ribbon to tie in her hair.

Among the lighter memories of *Tom Jones* is Dan Rolyat in search of Lizzie, the Leech, and the neat quartet:

> Here's a paradox for lovers,
> Love is weakest when he's strong,
> When he thinks he most discovers
> Blindest all the gods among,
>   Fa la la la.

In 1909, German collaborated with W. S. Gilbert in another Savoy opera, this being the unlucky *Fallen Fairies*. The first night reception seemed to give promise of another *Iolanthe*, but Gilbert hampered the Savoy management by cutting out a male chorus. Indeed, he only used three male characters to tell his story. *Fallen Fairies* was a version of his own play, *The Wicked World*, which had been acted at the Haymarket more than thirty years earlier. It told how three men were introduced into Fairyland, much as three men were introduced into the mock kingdom of Princess Ida. The result of the masculine invasion was that Queen Selene fell in love with a mortal and, forthwith, every sort of human passion invaded the land of the fairies. By this time C. H. Workman controlled the Savoy and he played the leading comedy part, supported by Nancy McIntosh (Selene), Miriam Lycett, and pretty Maidie Hope. Possibly *Fallen Fairies* was somewhat too ambitious; at any rate, it did not establish itself. Queen Selene's song came near to being a grand opera number:

> Oh, wondrous Love, pure as the silver sky!
> Even when Death has set the loved one free,
> This Love supernal doth not,—cannot—die;
> It lives upon the loved one's memory.

The German operas were a brave effort to endow musical comedy with fuller plots and with more varied opportunities for well-trained players and composers of real talent. Edward German would have been more fortunate if a series of his operas had been maintained in production. *Tom Jones, A Princess of Kensington*, even *Fallen Fairies*, all reached a high level, but there was no management to do them full justice. The composer's fame would stand still higher if the D'Oyly Carte companies of to-day included German, as well as Sullivan, operas in their repertory. Perhaps this reform may come.

Chapter V

THE GIRLS OF THE GAIETY, 1893 TO 1914
COMING OF MUSICAL COMEDY

ENOUGH HAS BEEN SAID TO INDICATE THE CONTRIBUTION OF George Edwardes to the declining years of burlesque at the Gaiety. This was not, however, the type of vaudeville which theatrical history will associate with his name. He is better remembered as the creator of musical comedy, though there must be added "Owen Hall," writer of *A Gaiety Girl*, and Arthur Roberts, principal comedian in the first of all musical comedies, *In Town*.

Musical comedy, as George Edwardes saw it, was characterised by a certain contemporary realism which had been lacking in extravaganza, burlesque, and comic opera. Tights were banned and Bruton Street frocks and Savile Row coats and trousers were substituted for the costumes which the wardrobe mistresses or Covent Garden costumiers had run up for earlier vaudeville players. When Arthur Roberts appeared in the role of Captain Coddington in *In Town* at the Prince of Wales's in 1892, the necessity for contemporary realism took him right away from his methods as a burlesque actor or pantomime comic. He was nearly akin to his merry self, in the setting of modernity which the title, *In Town*, was intended to suggest. As Coddington, Arthur Roberts proved not only a source of laughter but a leader of fashion. The masculine youth of London copied Arthur's coats, cravats, monocles, spats, and buttonholes, just as the hansom‑cabbies of London, a few years later, sought to emulate Arthur's "turn‑out," when he appeared in *Gentleman Joe*. This was an early musical comedy from the lively pen of Basil Hood. Elderly playgoers will not have forgotten "A Trilby Hat," embodied in *Gentleman Joe*, with Roberts as Tree‑Svengali. They will also recall the buxom Sadie Jerome from the States, singing "Lalage Potts, that's me!"

In Town did not establish the vogue of musical comedy. From the Prince of Wales's, Roberts returned to the Gaiety to play in another burlesque, *Don Juan*, and it required the amazing success of *A Gaiety Girl* to persuade George Edwardes that he had hit upon a gold‑mine in musical comedy. But, as the first Captain Coddington, Roberts had a decisive influence upon the form, as indeed, he had upon other types of musical entertainment in his era.

For a glimpse of Arthur's talent in burlesque, recall his appearance as Stanley the explorer, singing "I went to find Emin," with music by Osmond Carr and a lyric by Adrian Ross and J. L. Shine. A *tour de force*, this song, with puns in six languages—the Coster tongue, French, German, Italian, and Niggery from Margate. Here is an English verse:

Dudley Hardy's poster for "A Gaiety Girl"

Some Gaiety Girls

Jean Aylwin (top left)
Camille Clifford, the "Gibson Girl" (with Leslie Stiles)
Gertie Millar (Gertrude, Countess of Dudley) and (right)
Phyllis Dare

Oh, I went to find Emin Pasha, and started away for fun,
With a box of weeds and a bag of beads, some tracts, and a Maxim gun . . .
I went to find Emin, I did, I looked for him far and wide;
I found him right, I found him tight, and a lot of folks beside,
Away through Darkest Africa, though it cost me lots of tin,
For without a doubt I'd find him out, when I went to find Emin!

As Roberts vitalised burlesque and pantomime, so he brought fortune to West
End music-halls, while no convivial gathering was complete without him, and
no "benefit" or "charity" performance could afford to ignore him. In a single
turn at the Empire, then a music-hall, Arthur Roberts judged the taste of fre-
quenters of the Promenade to a nicety, and his dry staccato manner relieved the
most suggestive lines of offence, for Arthur never underlined a doubtful jest.
Arthur Compton-Rickett used to recall how on one occasion a little lady on the
stage was recounting her adventures. "One night——" she began. "*His* name!"
snapped Roberts laconically, without a twinkle.

No comedian of his period, or indeed any other period, had greater powers of
pantomimic suggestion, and to this was added a genius for improvising. Aware
of his inventive faculty, his managers used to give him a free hand.

"I had a blank sheet—and a bottle of champagne," declared Arthur. "This
constituted *my* part in a new show."

Dear old Arthur Roberts. Nothing could restrain his exuberant humour. At
the end of his long life, the Eccentric Club organised a matinée in his honour and
he was called upon for the final speech of thanks, the immediate occasion being
the presentation of a big bunch of flowers. Arthur was properly sentimental and
there were moist eyes and dry throats in the crowded Alhambra. Arthur Roberts
ended:

"I look on these flowers, roses, lilies, violets, and all bring back fond memories,
but (and a sob came into the old man's voice) my favourite flower is missing
—Hops!"

The First of the Girls

A Gaiety Girl came to London in 1893 and was a George Edwardes production
at the Prince of Wales's, with a book by Owen Hall, lyrics by Harry Greenbank
and music by Sidney Jones. A star cast included handsome Hayden Coffin,
the burly Harry Monkhouse, the resilient Louis Bradfield, the dapper Eric Lewis,
the demure Decima Moore, the natty Kate Cutler, the stately Maud Hobson, the
shapely Louie Pounds, the dainty Juliette Nesville, the lovely Marie Studholme,
and blithesome Lottie Venne, a galaxy of beauty, energy, and efficiency which
has never been excelled in musical comedy, and possibly not in all vaudeville.

"Owen Hall" was a *nom de theatre*, which both hid and revealed the personality
of Mr. Jimmy Davis, a member of a clever Jewish family. One of his sisters was
"Frank Danby," the mother of Gilbert Frankau, the novelist, and grandmother of
Pamela Frankau. Nominally, Jimmy Davis was a solicitor, but in his spare time

a talent for dramatic and other criticism was displayed in Jimmy's somewhat scurrilous publications, *The Bat, The Cuckoo,* and *The Phoenix.* For the rest, he was a man-about-town, and, as his *nom de théâtre* suggests, money, with Jimmy Davis, was easy come and easy go. On one occasion Mrs. Dennis Eadie asked Davis to write something in her autograph book. Now, Mrs. Eadie's father was Savile Parker, the money-lender. What "Owen Hall" wrote was "I wish your father was as anxious for my signature as you are." Arthur Roberts devised an *alias* akin to "Owen Hall" when he wrote under the name, "Payne Nunn."

As regards *A Gaiety Girl,* what happened was this. With no more practical acquaintance with the drama than occasional criticism, Jimmy Davis chanced to meet George Edwardes in a railway carriage and bluntly told him that if he, Jimmy Davis, couldn't write a better musical comedy than that running at the Gaiety, he would be damned. Edwardes promptly told "Jimmy" to "get on with the job," and, in due time, the script of *A Gaiety Girl* materialised. *An Artist's Model, A Greek Slave,* and *The Geisha* followed.

The contribution of Owen Hall to the new type of musical play was considerable, but an even more important element was the music of Sidney Jones. Born in 1869, Sidney Jones's father had conducted an orchestra for Wilson Barrett, and his son wrote the incidental music for *The Sign of the Cross,* including the "Shepherd of Souls" anthem, sung by the Early Christians. Returning from an Australian tour, young Sidney Jones wrote "Linger longer, Lucy, linger longer, Loo" as a test piece for George Edwardes, who liked the song so much that he added it to *Don Juan* with such success that Edwardes commissioned Sidney Jones to compose the music for Owen Hall's promised play.

By the way, a brilliant touring company introduced *A Gaiety Girl* to Australia. Louis Bradfield, Leedham Bantock, Decima Moore, Florence Lloyd, Maud Hobson, Madge Russell, and Grace Palotta were among the principals. Musical comedy in the 'nineties had become not only a "dinner digestive" for Londoners, but a square meal for audiences all over the Empire.

Following upon *A Gaiety Girl* came *The Shop Girl,* with music by Ivan Caryll, which ran at the Gaiety for two years after its production in 1894. The shares of the Gaiety Company which had been standing at 3s. quickly advanced to over £1. Plainly, there was big money in musical comedy, and not only in London but throughout the Anglo-Saxon world. The new type of vaudeville also promised opportunities for a new type of actor and actress which was entering the profession and replacing the players who had their training in the provincial stock companies and the even rougher school of the "sing-songs," attached to public-houses. Ellaline Terriss and Seymour Hicks and George Grossmith, junior, were typical of the new order of players.

As for the play itself, there were enough memorable songs and danceable tunes in *The Shop Girl* to establish the fortunes of half a dozen modern musical plays. Though the music was by Ivan Caryll, the best-remembered number, "Her golden hair was hanging down her back," chanced to be an importation from

America. "A pink song for pale people" was Seymour Hick's description of the ditty. It was also sung by Alice Leamar, one of two daughters of a New Cut coal vendor, who introduced themselves to their audience in this fashion:

> Two girls of good society. We dance, we sing
> We're models of propriety—too wise to wear the ring!

It is on record that Seymour Hicks sang "Her Golden Hair" for six hundred nights without a holiday. On one occasion it fell to the young comedian to sing the song before Alexandra, Princess of Wales. It was during a dance at Cadogan House, and as the song was regarded as daring at the Gaiety, Hicks was in doubt whether it would be approved by Royalty in the home of a real Earl. He therefore suggested that the Princess should hear a verse spoken before the song was sung. Standing before a row of peers, peeresses, and other terrifying critics, Hicks solemnly recited:

> Oh, Flo, what a change you know,
> When she left the village she was shy.
> But alas and alack,
> She came back
> With a naughty little twinkle in her eye.

Princess Alexandra was somewhat deaf and her verdict was that the words were "charming," certainly the first and only time this adjective suggested itself. Thus fortified, Seymour sang his song. A quarter of a century later, in 1920, Seymour Hicks revived *The Shop Girl*, with some additions by Arthur Wimperis and Herman Darewski. The outstanding change was Evelyn Laye's singing "The Guards Brigade," for which Hicks engaged a band of sixty, who marched on to the stage in uniform from the great staircase which was so prominent in the scenery of the second act.

In the early years of musical comedy at the Gaiety, Ivan Caryll, a bearded Belgian, whose real name was John Tilkin, was doing the heavy musical work. He was responsible, perhaps, for two-thirds of any score, including the difficult finales and the outstanding dance tunes, the better-known songs being usually from the pens of Lionel Monckton or Paul Rubens. Caryll studied at the Paris Conservatoire as a singer and came to England in 1882. His first opera, *The Lily of Leoville*, was produced at the Comedy, and persuaded George Edwardes to commission some songs for *Monte Cristo, Junior*, in 1886. When *The Shop Girl* was produced Ivan Caryll came to the Gaiety as conductor. His music for May Yohe in *Little Christopher Columbus* won a big success elsewhere and had shown that a master of light melody was to be installed as musical director at the Gaiety. His Gaiety achievements enabled Ivan Caryll to prove himself a master showman, as well as a competent musician. He drove up to the Gaiety for each performance in a pair-horse Victoria, with a couple of men on the box. Among Caryll's non-Gaiety successes was the delightful vocal gavotte, which the chorus sang in *The Earl and the Girl*, together with the "Pink Lady Waltz" and "Goo-Goo."

My Girl, by J. T. Tanner, Adrian Ross, and Osmond Carr, followed the two years' run of *The Shop Girl*, and then came *The Circus Girl*, which ran through 1897 and until May 1898, when *A Runaway Girl* was substituted. This was written by Seymour Hicks and Harry Nicholls, the Adelphi comedian, to the music of the veteran Ivan Caryll, though, by this time Seymour himself had left the Gaiety company and been replaced by the volatile Louis Bradfield. To Ivan Caryll's score in *The Runaway Girl* Lionel Monckton added the "Soldiers in the Park," first sung by Grace Palotta, and that unhappy reminiscence of young Jack, who was welcomed by his master, with his hand behind his back, saying: "Guess what I've got for you," this being an Ellaline Terriss effort:

> The boy guessed right the very first time,
> Very first time, very first time!
> He guessed right away it was not a cricket bat,—
> I wonder how he came to think of that?

However, Sir Seymour and Lady Hicks were to prove very much more than pleasant interludes in two or three Gaiety shows, and a fuller account of their contributions to vaudeville is reserved for a later chapter.

> The cuckoo is calling aloud to his mate,
> The turtle dove coos in its nest;
> And, oh, I am longing to meet with my fate,
> Who's photo lies hid in my breast.
> Ah, will he be tender and loving and sweet
> To one so unworthy as me,
> And fondle me much as I sit at his feet,
> Or, sometimes, perhaps on his knee?

Yes, it is Caroline singing in *The Orchid*, and a few moments later on, Meakin, a gardener, was answering with another riddle:

> Life is an omelet, Love is an egg.
> Oh, what a true practical view,
> Listen to me I beg.
> Excellent cooking will not avail,
> All will depend upon this in the end,
> Is the egg fresh or stale?

And the singers? Connie Ediss and Teddy Payne, of course. When *The Orchid* was blooming in the eastern end of the Strand in 1903, Connie Ediss was an established favourite at the Gaiety. She came into the company in 1896, when Lillie Belmore relinquished the low-comedy part of Ada Smith in *The Shop Girl*. As George Edwardes put it, Connie was a "comfortable-looking comedienne." Her early appearances were as a music-hall singer at her birthplace, Brighton, under the name Connie Coates. Coming to the Trocadero, a music-hall on the

Teddy Payne in "The Orchid"

site of the present restaurant in Shaftesbury Avenue, Albert Chevalier exploited the talents of the shapely and winsome maiden from Brighton, introducing her to the public as the "New Nelly Power." Later, Connie Ediss was just her plump and pleasing self, and no musical comedy of the decade seemed quite complete without a Connie Ediss role, even if Miss Ediss did not fill it. Its latter-day equivalent is a Vera Pearce part. The Mayoress in *My Girl*, with her "Lady Tom" song, Mrs. Hoppings in *The Toreador*, Caroline Vokins in *The Orchid*, Mrs. Drivelli in *The Circus Girl*, and Carmenita in *The Runaway Girl* were other Connie Ediss roles. As Carmenita, she sang:

> Though my family's pedigree
> Isn't all that it ought to be,
> I've a face that is not so bad
> And a figure that drives 'em mad,
> All my manners are so refined,
> Dukes and Duchesses fill my mind,
> With the swells I would dine and dance
> If they'd give me a chance!
> Oh!
> I!

Chorus: Love Society!
                High Society!
Carmenita: I should be called an attractive girl
                If my papa was a noble hearl.

The equally memorable "Class" was a non-Gaiety effort. Connie Ediss migrated for a while to Shaftesbury Avenue, where she appeared in Leslie Stuart's extravaganza, *The Silver Slipper*.

What can be said of Teddy Payne, save to recall the inimitable lisp, the grotesqueries of costume, and the unfailing powers of comic invention? Edmund (Teddy) Payne was not so much a low comedian as a natural droll. He was one of Nature's comics, and his physical appearance accentuated by make-up, together with a dozen quaint little mannerisms, made the most ordinary dialogue seem funny. Gee-Gee Grossmith tells that Payne once asked him to come to the Athenaeum, after a matinée.

"Do you mean the Club?" asked Gee-Gee doubtfully.

"Certainly," lisped Teddy. "They have the beth glath of port in London."

"Gee-Gee" was still doubtful, but Teddy took him along to Waterloo Place, and then down some steps, into the Club basement.

"The head waiter is a friend of mine," explained Teddy.

This simple creature had an admirable foil in Katie Seymour, whose graces displayed the funniments of her partner, as the charms of Kate Vaughan enhanced the humours of Edward Royce in Gaiety burlesque.

Born in 1869, Katie Seymour appeared in pantomime at the age of seven and drifted into music-hall entertainment. In the early 'nineties she came to the Gaiety, waving a tiny lace handkerchief in token that she proposed to take up the dainty mantle which Kate Vaughan had let fall. Recall the Goblins' duet in *The Runaway Girl*, and the Pierrot and Pierrette dance in *The Circus Girl*. Payne played Biggs, the American bar-tender, who, in an effort to win Miss Seymour, dared to measure his strength against Toothpick Pasha, the Terrible Turk. Teddy Payne was never more amusing than when he was expressing dismay. Here is a snatch from a typical Teddie Payne ditty:

> It was an evil hour when I met my Mary Ann,
> Oh woe! woe the day!

She was living with her mother on the vegetable plan,
Yea, verily yea!
She said if I would try it,
The cold potato diet,
'Twould regulate my liver, I'd become another man.
Though seriously doubting,
I took to Brussels sprouting,
And now you see what's left of me, a Vegetarian.

During the Kaffir boom on the Stock Exchange in the middle 'nineties, London enjoyed a theatrical boom. Money poured into the coffers of the Gaiety, as an accepted purveyor of light entertainment. Men who were making fortunes on 'Change and in big business felt honoured if they were permitted to entertain the ladies of the Gaiety Company.

Constance Collier tells a pleasant story in this connection. She was sixteen at the time, and a member of the chorus, when an invitation came for a party at the Savoy. Alas, her part was a small one from every standpoint. She entered carrying a very small box and her only line ran:

This box contains my costume for the fancy dress ball.

Plainly, the role afforded small promise of any other frock, not to mention the equally important petticoats of the period and other incidentals to a party at the Savoy. "Connie" deferred her reply to the invitation to the last moment, but knew that it must be an insistent "No." Then she found laid out in her dressing-room an evening dress, a cloak to match, the petticoats of the period, stockings, gloves, and a fan. They had been subscribed for and selected by her comrades in the Gaiety Chorus. Years later, "Connie" said: "It was the loveliest present I have ever had." And another welcome surprise was to be added. Under her plate at dessert-time, Miss Collier discovered £50 worth of South African mining shares, and each of the Gaiety girls at the Savoy had a similar gift. It was a welcome tribute to the far-reaching influence of Gaiety Girls, in the days when Marie Studholme, in *The Messenger Boy*, was singing "When the Boys Come Marching Home."

About this time Ellaline Terriss left the Gaiety Company and the reign of Queen Gertrude began. She began in *The Toreador* in 1901 and stayed for seven years. Constance Collier has described Gertie Millar's reed-like figure and tiny, breathless voice, "the words half-spoken and half-sung," so that one had to listen hard to catch their full significance. Miss Millar was a Bradford girl, and her early public appearances were as an infant phenomenon at the Bradford Mechanics' Institute, in pantomime, at the Princes' Theatre, and with Brogden's Swiss Choir, of which she was a member for several years.

In *The Orchid*, Gertie Millar, along with Fred Wright, played her happy Bradford self, in clogs and shawl. She had married Lionel Monckton, the composer, and, one day, had been washing her hair, when her husband caught her with a couple of long plaits hanging one over each shoulder.

An "Orchid" Memory

Lady Vi. (*Gertie Millar*). I'm flaid.

Zaccary (*Fred Wright*). What art *flaid* about?

Lady Vi. I'm flaid you might kiss me!

Zaccary. How can I kiss thee wi' a can in other hand?

Lady Vi. I might 'old cans!

"Well! You *do* look a Yorkshire lass," said Monckton.

"Yes, I feel a bit of a Liza Ann," replied Gertie.

Monckton went off to his study and wrote an air for the Liza Ann theme, while his wife, in the process of completing the hair-dressing, helped with the words.

> Liza Ann is a neat young lass
> And she's working up at Briggs's mill.
> Every morning at six o'clock,
> You can see her walking up the hill.
> There she goes with her turned-up nose
> And her dinner in a nice tin can,
> Oh, you'll all of you be mad, when you see another lad,
> Is a-taking out Liza Ann!

After Lionel Monckton's death Miss Millar married the Earl of Dudley and to this day there is no more welcome personality at a London first-night than the Liza Ann from Yorkshire. She owed a good deal to "Lally" Monckton's insistence upon her talent in the early days. The son of a popular Town Clerk of the City of London whose mother, Lady Monckton, was an actress of acknow-ledged ability, Lionel was curiously reserved when he came to man's estate. Only a piano and Gertie Millar made him really unbend, but he developed a talent for writing tuneful songs, so precisely suited to Edwardean musical comedy, that it approached genius. Melody, rhythm, gossamer lightness of treatment, and endless variety within the genre—all the qualities needed were there. His parents wanted "Lally" to go to the Bar, and he was called in 1885, but the lure of the theatre prevailed. Already, at Oxford, Lionel Monckton had been a leading light among the Philo-Thespians and when George Edwardes commissioned his first song, "What will you have to drink?" (in *Cinder Ellen*, 1891), the talent for song-writing was sufficiently plain. When the time came to produce *The Runaway Girl*, seven years later, Monckton could share the music with Ivan Caryll and, in fact, contributed "The Boy guessed right" for Ellaline Terriss, "I don't think that's the sort of girl I care about" for Louis Bradfield, "Follow the Man from Cook's" (an octet), "The Soldiers in the Park" for Grace Palotta, and "Society" for Connie Ediss, sufficient in quality and variety to establish the fortunes of any musical show.

"Lal" Monckton, apart from his curiously deliberate speech and marked reserve, displayed some strange habits. During the run of *The Arcadians* he used to stand near the pit or gallery door, with a little checking machine in his pocket. A touch, and another pittite or galleryite was registered! No one ever heard that any use was made of the record. Again, after a very late supper at the Greenroom Club, he would walk to his home in Russell Square, wake up his dogs, and walk them round for hours, perhaps, on a fine night, until daylight. In fact, Monckton was never truly alive unless he was putting to paper the almost infinite variety of airs which bubbled up in his musical imagination. And the wonder was that there was no marked similarity between the several numbers which went round the world, and, for that matter are still going round the world, for there is no more popular vendor of wireless melody. The patter song, "The Valley of Bhong," bears no resemblance to the breezy, "Yo, ho, little girls, yo, ho," or "Follow the man from Cook's" and "The Pipes of Pan" (which Monckton wrote for Florence Smithson) is utterly unlike the songs he provided for Gertie Millar, among them the amusing "Chalk Farm to Camberwell Green," a number from the Palace revue, *Bric-a-brac*, in 1916.

> Chalk Farm to Camberwell Green,
>   All on a summer's day,
> We went on top of a motor 'bus
>   And started right away.
> When we came to the end of the ride,
>   He wanted to go for a walk,
> But I wasn't Camberwell green
>   By a long chalk.

The earlier "Little Mary" owed its being to Sir James Barrie's "uncomfortable" play of the same name:

> Now Mamma is very delicate, as anyone can see,
> Because of Mary, Little Mary!
> And it's not her fault she's given up
> Her coffee and her tea!
> It's Little Mary, Little Mary!
>
> Mary, Mary, dainty little Mary!
> She's a fickle but a fascinating fairy.
> When you're crossing o'er the channel,
> You must wrap her up in flannel,
> Oh, take care of "little Mary!"

"Little Mary" comes from *The Orchid*, while "Keep off the Grass" is from *The Toreador*, in which Miss Millar was Captivating Cora, the bridesmaid who "makes the bride look small." And what a cast, for Gertie Millar was only a "starlet" in *The Toreador*. Marie Studholme, Connie Ediss, Ethel Sydney (in boy's attire, proposing to smoke three cigars at once), Queenie Leighton, and Violet Lloyd were among the ladies, and Fred Wright, Lionel Mackinder, and Herbert Clayton among the supporting males.

Lionel Mackinder was a victim of the first World War. Over forty years of age, he went to Clarkson's, bought a toupee, and went to the front as a trooper, riddled with rheumatism though he was. He got a bullet in his throat in January 1915, while telling a funny story to the members of his company. He was the husband of Gracie Leigh.

Our Miss Gibbs, a second romance of a shop girl, dates from 1909, when

Gertie Millar returned to the Gaiety, after an American tour. She betrayed her Bradford origin in Act I, singing her husband's "Yorkshire," where—

> A chap takes a ticket, excursion, third-class,
> And he won't call a porter, he's not such an ass.
> He tips himself sixpence and pockets the brass!
> Sixpence is sixpence in Yorkshire!

At the White City, in the last act, however, Miss Millar was fantasy incarnate, wearing a dark blue satin pierrot costume, with white pom-pom and a huge white satin bow under her chin. Eight attendant pierrots, in pale blue costumes, a-tumble on the stage, made up the background, though a flutter of ill-fitting gloves should be recalled if the stage picture is to be complete. Then a bewitching

*Miss
Gertie
Millar*

little voice made its caressing chant felt through the half-light, and a lithe form moved about the stage like a capful of invigorating wind off a summer sea.

> I'm such a silly when the moon comes out,
> I hardly seem to know what I'm about,
> Skipping, hopping,
> Never, never stopping.
>
> I'm all a-quiver when the moonbeams glance,
> That is the moment when I long to dance
> When the moon comes creeping up the sky.

James Tanner was the carpenter of *Our Miss Gibbs*, the material being provided by "Cryptos," a *nom de théâtre* which included Adrian Ross and Percy Greenbank, the lyric writers, and Ivan Caryll and Lally Monckton, the composers. The final scene was attuned to "Moonstruck," being a symphony in blue. Not only were lovely Denise Orme. the distinguished Jean Aylwin, and the stately Gladys

Homfrey in varying shades of blue, but the chorus of dudes wore blue dress-coats, blue knee-breeches, and blue silk stockings. This was possibly an effort of the Gaiety Company to revolutionise male evening attire, on the lines of an earlier effort by Seymour Hicks, when he put his chorus into silk stockings and knee-breeches in the *Catch of the Season* and persuaded a party of young aristocrats to introduce similar evening attire at West End gatherings. Both efforts failed.

Some years before "Moonstruck" and *Our Miss Gibbs*, the theatre of Lionel Lawson and John Hollingshead had disappeared and a new Gaiety had arisen at the eastern corner of Aldwych. A main street connecting the Strand and Holborn had been under discussion for half a century. When the 100-feet-wide Kingsway and Aldwych finally came into being, one of the ugliest of the London slums was cleared away and with them Holywell Street (the Booksellers Row of London), Wych Street (with the old Globe Theatre and the Olympic), and the old Gaiety, with the restaurant attached to it.

King Edward and Queen Alexandra were in the Royal Box when the New Gaiety opened on October 26th, 1903, with *The Orchid*, by Tanner, Adrian Ross, Monckton, and Caryll, with extraneous aid. A souvenir of *The Orchid* lies before me, but it preserves the secret of the carpentry shop to the full, authors, composers, and stage producers being represented by black silhouettes which are nameless. What is certain is that Teddy Payne was the gardener Meakin, who posed as Rupert Vandeleur, a lady-killer, and called forth the song already quoted from the amorous Connie Ediss:

> The cuckoo is calling aloud to his mate.

The Orchid blossomed for 559 performances, and there followed soon after *The New Aladdin*, a relative failure, as the magic lamp lost its potency after 203 appearances. *The New Aladdin* was burlesque, with a difference. Gertie Millar certainly appeared in the clothes of a principal boy, one memorable opportunity being as a coster in pearlies, in company with Teddy Payne, singing "Down where the vegetables grow." Who will have forgotten?

> Oh, I tell you straight and plain
> There's a lot of human brain
> Down where the vegetables grow!

Again, in white knickers this time, Gertie Millar sang the Lionel Monckton number, "Bedtime at the Zoo":

> Every beast is thinking of his bed!
> Good night, Mister Elephant,
> Tiger cease your play,
> Lie down and you're sure to dream
> That you're ro ring in the jungle far away,
> Sleep well, Miss Ourang Outang, Good night, Kangaroo,
> When another day is breaking
> You'll all of you be waking
> In the Zoo. In the Zoo.

The New Aladdin also included a Spirit of the Ring, but it proved to be the well-beloved Connie Ediss, singing "In the Strand." Even George Grossmith as the Genie of the Lamp, who created an Ideal London for the second act, smacked of musical comedy rather than of old-time burlesque. In retrospect, *The New Aladdin* is chiefly remarkable for the coming of Jean Aylwin from Hawick, over the Border, who arrived in London armed with a letter of introduction to Dion Boucicault the Younger, from Lady Forbes-Robertson (Gertrude Elliott). A pronounced Glasgow accent proved a handicap and the best Jean could discover was a series of melodramatic roles in a minor touring company, which perhaps was the luckiest thing that could have happened to her career. Then came a tour as a shop assistant in *The Girl from Kay's*, which led to a chorus engagement for the run of *The New Aladdin*.

Now Gaby Deslys had been engaged to play the part of a French maid, but was eventually introduced into the Gaiety show as her pretty self—a beauty with an international reputation. To Jean Aylwin fell the role of the French maid, Fossette. When *The New Aladdin* reached its second edition, Jean's Scottish origin had asserted itself, and she was "Jennie," with a pronounced Scottish accent and making great play with her braw Highlander, Dougail. The critics accepted Jean as *the* discovery of the evening and she joined the growing list of starlets, who associated themselves with the Gaiety of late Victorian and Edwardian times, and bring up such memories as Grace Palotta singing "The Soldiers in the Park," Rosie Boote (later Marchioness of Headfort), with her dark eyes and wistful manners and reed-like movements, singing "Maisie was a daisy," or, as I said before, the golden hair and golden smile of Marie Studholme, in the dove-grey gown and great white bonnet which she wore as Josephine Zaccary in *The Orchid*. Ay, and Julia James, with a male chorus, singing "Widows are Wonderful" in *Yes, Uncle*, if only because it recalls the quip of Douglas Jerrold, that the whole tragedy of the years between 1914 and 1919 was summed up in the conjunction of two songs, "We don't want to lose you" and "Widows are Wonderful."

These secondary memories of the Gaiety, Old and New, are as vivid as those attaching to stars who sparkled more continuously. Gaby Deslys was one of these secondary memories, though she certainly drew the salary of a constellation when she obliged George Edwardes by embodying the charm of Paris as she sailed across the stage on a boat-truck in *The New Aladdin*, for Gaby had a vast company of admirers in her day. She was a pocket Venus and her big, wondering eyes, pearl-pink complexion, and glossy hair offered a curious contrast to her energetic acrobatics in company with her dancing partner, Harry Pilcer, when they played in *A Day in the Life of a Parisienne*, which filled the Palace Theatre for many weeks. In one scene, Gaby took up a cane and flogged a wealthy and elderly admirer off the stage, an episode which might have been edifying in Gaby's career as a beauty, but seemed somewhat shocking to Edwardian Londoners. She had a genius for money-making on and off the stage. Her weekly wage in New York

5

at the height of her career was £1,000, and she could earn £500 a week in London. A good deal of the money was spent upon the great gilded bed and the life-sized Madonna, hung about with real pearls, which adorned her luxury bedroom in Kensington Gore. Priceless chinchilla rugs covered the floor. A strange episode in a strange career was James Barrie falling a victim to her exotic graces. He wrote the revue *Rosy Rapture* for her. Gaby was only thirty-six when she died from cancer in the throat.

The Girls of Gottenburg (1907) is remembered for its associations with the famous Koepenick spoof which made Germany the laughing-stock of the civilised world. The idea came to young George Grossmith to give the episode a musical-comedy setting by turning Edmund Payne into a variant upon the cobbler, Koepenick, and putting the rest of the Gaiety Company into German attire, in itself something of a novelty. Earlier German musical shows tended to associate themselves with Austria, rather than with the Prussians, who were the victims of Koepenick's ruse. In *The Girls of Gottenburg* George Grossmith cast himself for the part of Prince Otto, commanding a detachment of the Blue Hussars, which was in friendly rivalry with the Red Dragoons, commanded by Robert Hale. Max Moddelkopf, the resourceful valet of Prince Otto, was moved to put himself into one of Otto's uniforms and pose as Special Envoy of the Emperor, Wilhelm II. Played by Edmund Payne, the Special Envoy proved a "scream." He dominated his little world until the Blue Hussars were comfortably ensconced in the neighbourhood of the Ladies' University at Gottenburg, in place of the less resourceful Red Dragoons. Ivan Caryll and Lionel Monckton provided the music, one comedy number being "Prince Otto of Roses," which "Gee-Gee" wrote for himself, with music by Ivan Caryll. Here is the gist of the lyric:

> My dear mother said to me
> At the early age of three,
> "Darling Otto, for the army you're intended."
> I said, "All right, mother dear,
> I will model my career
> So that bravery and caution may be blended."
>
> *Chorus:*
> Oh, girls all call me Otto, what oh!
> They know that my heart never closes,
> If you don't like what you've got oh,
> Pick another from the grotto,
> Is the motto of Otto of Roses!

Using a refrain of the Wagnerian Rhine maidens, Lionel Monckton wrote a Rheingold number for Gertie Millar, which she sang with a chorus of the town girls of Gottenburg. More in the Gaiety spirit was a Basil Hood lyric, which Monckton put to music and Gertie Millar sang in company with Edmund Payne:

Berlin is on the Spree,
And that's the place we want to see,
So we've packed our little slippers
And we're trotting off as trippers—
Just as happy as can be . . .
And we'll never go to bed
Till we've painted Berlin red.
Oh, they'll talk about our walking tour to Berlin!

The triumphs of Gertie Millar at the Gaiety were followed by those of Phyllis Dare. She was the younger daughter of Arthur Dones, a good-looking judge's clerk, who was also the father of Zena Dare, and the two girls made their first appearance in public as the Babes in the Wood, in the Coronet Pantomime of 1899, Zena being the boy Babe and Phyllis the girl. Two years later Seymour Hicks persuaded Mr. and Mrs. Dones to allow their lovely younger daughter to appear in *Bluebell in Fairyland*, and from the Vaudeville Phyllis passed to the Gaiety. The play was *The Sunshine Girl*, with words by Cecil Raleigh, music by Paul Rubens, and lyrics by Arthur Wimperis, and the plot was laid in Port Sunshine, where the hero fell in love with the lovely Delia Dale, played by Phyllis in a blue frock. The quartet, "The Butler kissed the Housemaid, the Footman kissed the Cook," which included Tom Walls, may be recalled, while the prize for the best couplet must be awarded to Connie Ediss, when she announced with proper vim:

Oh, I went to the Durbar! Didn't we have a spree?
They say I tickled the Rajahs, but they *all* tickled me.

Rajahs had a symbolic significance in Gaiety and Daly circles in the years preceding the first World War. George Edwardes was once discussing salaries with an established musical-comedy star, prior to a world tour. He offered £100 a week, including a trip to Australia, but mademoiselle asked £200. When he entered management, Edwardes had been able to pick up "stars" for £15 a week and mould them to his heart's desires. He learnt generosity in the years, but on this occasion he hesitated, and pointed out that the proposed tour included India. "Rajahs, Jams, and Nabobs," he recalled, "are in the habit of presenting stage favourites with ropes of pearls and rubies." The young lady promised to consider the proposal and, next morning, George Edwardes received a note: "Dear Mr. Edwardes—If you accept my terms, you can have the Rajah's presents."

Phyllis Dare's career in musical comedy was as closely associated with that of Paul Rubens, as that of Gertie Millar was with "Lally" Monckton. Rubens was a Winchester boy, and, like Monckton, studied law until the musical numbers he wrote for *Florodora* justified a bigger commission in connection with *A Country Girl* (1902) and *The Cingalee* (1904). Rubens was fifteen years older than Miss Dare and a sick man, but he worshipped her. Towards the end, Phyllis Dare was appearing at the Brighton Hippodrome, when a tall, pale man came to the manager's room, with a roll of music. He whispered: "A new song for Phyl. Would you let us try it out at second house? I'm so anxious." "Does Phyl know?" "Oh, yes. I have orchestrated it myself. Here are the band parts."

During the second house Phyllis sang three songs, and then as an encore:

> I love the moon, I love the sun,
> I love the forest, the flowers and fun.
> I love the wild birds, the dawn and the dew,
> But best of all I love you, I love you.

It was Paul Rubens's swan song and he wept as Phyl sang it for the first time. Rubens died in 1917 and left a small fortune to Miss Dare.

In *Sunshine Girl*, Phyllis Dare sang the musical comedy songs of Paul Rubens, but in *Peggy*, a jolly Gaiety show of 1911, the music was by Leslie Stuart, the melodist who gave us "Louisiana Lou," "Soldiers of the Queen," and the "Lily of Laguna." In his early 'teens, Leslie Stuart was organist and choirmaster at the Roman Catholic Cathedral at Salford, so Church music from Palestrina onwards to Gounod was in his blood. Perhaps because Catholic Church music is essentially dramatic, Leslie Stuart passed to music-hall and musical-comedy songs with no great difficulty. *Peggy* followed such an outstanding success as *Florodora* and is memorable for Olive May's singing of "The Lass with the Lasso" and Robert Hale's chorus-song, "Whistle and the girls come round," the climax of which was reached when ten ladies of the Beauty Chorus were on the singer's knee at the same time. The feat sounds difficult, but Hale achieved it by a process of deputising.

In *Peggy* Phyllis Dare, as a manicurist, made Gaiety history by being engaged for a time to Teddy Payne; the comedian usually having to be content with something less than the caresses of a leading lady. In the course of a go-as-you-please plot, Phyllis played Juliet (with a head cold) to the Romeo of Teddy Payne. Albert Umbles, the barber, with his guitar, looking up to pretty Peggy on an improvised balcony, is to be remembered though thirty years have passed.

Umbles: Hark! Hark! Love, a cadenza. Your troubadour comes to sing to you.
Peggy: Go, go, or influenza
       The biting wind will soon bring to you.
       Highly critical,
       Soon will become your condition.
Umbles: Laryngitical,
       Is the trouble I see in store!
Peggy: Oh, Robeo!
Umbles: Oh, Juliet, Juliet!
Both: Night winds blow
       Uncommonly coolly yet

       Under $\genfrac{}{}{0pt}{}{my}{your}$ window $\genfrac{}{}{0pt}{}{you}{I}$ sing like a star,
       Although I am suffering
       From slight catarrh.

Blue-eyed George

What had been accomplished during the twenty years since George Edwardes first experimented with musical comedy? In the first place, runs had been vastly extended. A successful production at the Gaiety in the 'seventies and 'eighties

did not run for a couple of years, so comedians, dancers, and singers, as well as authors and managers, were continually required to rehearse new productions. There was no easy resting upon established reputations. As for the brand of vaudeville which Edwardes made his own, it is impossible to define the dividing line between Gaiety and non-Gaiety musical comedy. A Gaiety mood was recognisable; that is all that can be said, and this mood differed in some subtle way from the mood which could be aroused in a playgoer at Daly's, the Adelphi, the Prince of Wales's, the Lyric, or the Shaftesbury. Authors, producers, and players were dimly aware that a reasoned and reasonable plot had little value in creating the Gaiety atmosphere, so librettists and composers tended to reserve their more ambitious efforts for some other stage, where principals and chorus were attuned to a higher level of singing and acting of a less go-as-you-please order.

In general, George Edwardes spared nothing to make his companies of players worthy of the theatres they represented. He provided singing, dancing, and fencing masters and sent the ladies of the chorus to experts who taught them how to wear expensive clothes on the stage, and this without competing unduly with the leading ladies. Moreover, blue-eyed George had a faculty for using subordinates and his productions owed more than can be told to such men as Edward Royce, a son of Teddy Royce, and J. A. E. Malone, who later managed and produced important ventures on his own account. George Edwardes also probably owed very much to the judgment of Walter Pallant, a stockbroker and a fellow director of the Gaiety Company Limited. Of Willie Warde, with his genius for inventing dances and amusing business, Edwardes said, "He's my mascot." Warde seldom had more than a line of dialogue, but he made the very most of a tiny opportunity; for example, as a speechless Chinaman carrying an umbrella of State over the Marquess in *The Geisha*, and hard put to it to follow his master round the stage.

It is easy to throw critical stones at the producers of musical shows, and *Vanity Fair* perpetrated the following at the expense of Blue-eyed George, based, of course, upon the familiar lines of J. K. Stephens:

> Will there never come a season
> Free from incoherent rot,
> Free from rhymes that know no reason
> And a "book" that has no plot;
> When a girl in man's apparel
> Shall not make the pittite roar;
> When the Ivans cease to Caryll
> And the Rubens Paul no more?

Probably Edwardes was wiser than his critics. From time to time authors of musical comedy essayed a full-scale plot, but it never seemed to increase box-office takings materially. At any rate, we know now that what musical comedy developed into was plotless revue and not the play with a story set to music, which would seem to be the foundation of comedy, musical or otherwise. In fact, the change began in the early days, when George Edwardes engaged the versatile talents of Fred Leslie and put them to work at the Gaiety. Thenceforward, the author in vaudeville was almost a nonentity, apart from Gilbert and, upon occasion, Basil Hood, until Noel Coward and Herbert Farjeon restored the balance.

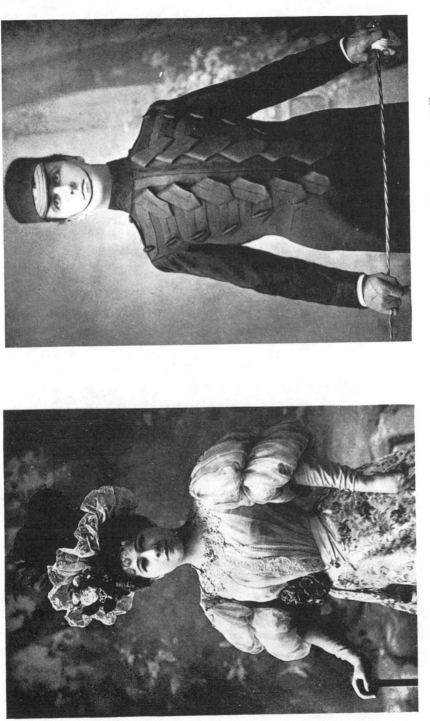

Hayden Coffin, in " A Gaiety Girl"

Marie Tempest

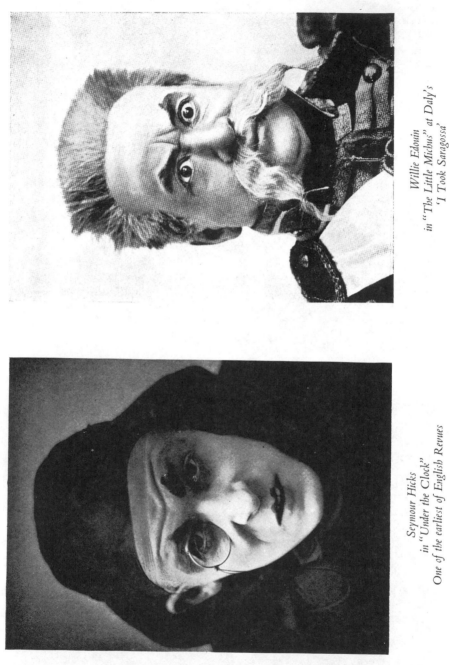

Willie Edouin
in "The Little Michus" at Daly's
'I Took Saragossa'

Seymour Hicks
in "Under the Clock"
One of the earliest of English Revues

Born in 1852, George Edwardes was educated for the Army. While he was at his crammers, Michael Gunn, a Dublin manager who had business connections with D'Oyly Carte, asked George to superintend a company touring in *The Lady of Lyons*. Afterwards, Gunn arranged that Edwardes should join D'Oyly Carte at the Savoy. Thus a curious blend of the simple and the sophisticated drifted into London vaudeville. In person, Edwardes was a tall, big-built, good-looking Irishman, with a pair of markedly straight eyebrows over two very blue eyes. The lighter stage, horse-racing, chess, and poker filled Edwardes's life and from time to time a coup on the turf saved a tottering theatrical investment or unexpected good fortune with a play made gambling losses payable. It was no unusual thing for Edwardes to win or lose £500 at poker in a night. After his death his estate realised about £250,000, but, mainly, because Daly's Theatre was carefully nursed by Robert Evett, on behalf of the executors, until another gambler, James White, came along to relieve the Edwardes family of the liability. Continually, big sums of money changed hands in connection with the Edwardes enterprises. It has been said that in Britain, America, and Australia £2,000,000 was paid into the box-offices in connection with *The Geisha*, and *San Toy* and *The Merry Widow* were no less successful. Yet George Edwardes did not know the difference between Tolstoi and Tosti, or rather, he had heard of Tosti, the ballad-writer, but had never happened to come across the author of *War and Peace*. What George Edwardes did know was that his public "never makes a mistake." Fortified by this conviction, he dominated English vaudeville for thirty years.

Anything less like the autocratic rule of W. S. Gilbert cannot be imagined. It is on record that on one famous occasion George cabled to America for a leading lady and then forgot all about her until she presented her card at Daly's Theatre and intimated that she was ready to perform. The amiable George was in no way abashed. "It will be all right on the night, my dear." And it was. George requested his tame authors and musicians to provide what was necessary and Marie Tempest, the wanderer in question, duly made her entrance in *An Artist's Model* as Adele, singing "*On y revient toujours*," with the aid of a chorus of students. The song was a pleasant reminder that the heroine of *Dorothy* had been absent from the London stage too long, and thus George redeemed a situation which under the Gilbertian régime would have been impossible. Redeemed is too strong a word. In fact, *An Artist's Model* was a semi-failure on the opening night. When the curtain fell, George Edwardes went "in front" and asked Daly's audience what it thought of the play.

"Half and half," was the answering call from the gallery boys.

"Come again in three weeks and I'll have bettered the other half," replied George confidently.

And come the gallery boys did, confident in the ingenuity of Daly's manager and his company of go-as-you-please authors and composers. And yet the method succeeded in the sense that *An Artist's Model* had a run of 393 performances and elderly playgoers still prick up their ears and move their feet when a band breaks into "Gay Bohemi-ah," murmuring:

> Of course it's only fair to add
> If we're not so good, we're not so bad,
> In gay Bohemi-ah!

The ways of Gaiety composers were as casual as those of the authors. During rehearsals at the Gaiety or Daly's it was the custom of "Lal" Monckton to sit at a cottage piano, tapping out new airs or orchestral effects, regardless of the irritating effects upon players on the stage who were trying to concentrate upon their lines. However, the habit had its value in the easy-going world in which musical comedies came to life. During rehearsals of *A Greek Slave* at Daly's, Edwardes suddenly demanded a new song for Letty Lind.

"Have you anything up your sleeve, Moncky?" he asked. At once "Lal" got to work upon the cottage piano, humming the words and strumming the tune of "I am a naughty girl."

As for George's general knowledge, it was abysmal. When it was suggested that the hoax of the cobbler Koepenick, in Germany, was promising material for a comic-opera plot, Edwardes dissented. "I think this fellow, Kubelik, has had advertisement enough." The difference between the cobbler and the violinist meant no more to the amiable director of the Gaiety than the distinction between Tosti, Tostig, and Tolstoi. Moreover, he had little ear for music, and the smallest insight into the problems of libretto-writing. His contribution to the vaudeville of his time can best be estimated when his productions are compared with the numerous revivals which have been attempted since. Rarely have the modern variants borne comparison with their predecessors. The talents of the players apart, the revivals suffered from a marked absence of what can only be described as style. When George Edwardes and his body of factors had done with a production, they had impressed a certain character upon all departments of the show—principals, chorus, scenery, dresses, lyrics, and music, and, as the book of the words was negligible in the Edwardean tradition, the whole thing, at least, had a character of its own, which can best be defined as "style."

No small part of successful production at the Gaiety depended upon the stately Big Eight of the chorus, a little bored by the smaller fry singing, cracking jests, and pirouetting around and about them, but fully assured of their own splendour of feature, figure, and limb, as these were displayed in Edwardian hats, frocks, and petticoats. Maud Hobson, Hetty Hamer, "Connie" Collier, Maud Hill, and Birdie Sutherland, to take a few names at random, served to display the Cockney-isms of Connie Ediss and Teddy Payne, as they displayed the lissom graces of Topsy Sinden, Katie Seymour, and "Gabs" Ray. The stately Big Eight of a Gaiety chorus were an essential element in "style" as it was displayed under George Edwardes. All of which means that musical comedy, thirty or forty years ago, was not quite what modern producers seem to suppose. Indeed, I doubt if the petticoatless, small-breasted, slight-hipped ladies of a latter-day chorus can recover the all-important stateliness and without this element of assured success the various Gaiety Girls would have been quite different from what, in fact, they were. Before he died, George Edwardes produced well over sixty original pieces, and, if a manager of similar authority was available, it is unlikely that so popular a theatre as the Gaiety would be tenantless, merely because no one has the courage to put up £20,000 for alterations required by the London County Council before the lease can be renewed.

All of which suggests that it will never be known precisely how much musical comedy owed to "Blue-eyed George." His chief business asset was a *flair* for what theatre-goers wanted. As he said: "Our public to-day will tolerate a young girl playing a young girl character whether she is a good artist or not. What our public will not tolerate is an old woman trying to look young." Given oppor-tunities for love-making with an embroidery of humour, George Edwardes felt safe. Lively lieutenants and loose purse-strings would bring forth the necessary players, and, as has been said, George was not ungenerous when big monies were being made.

Contrary to general belief, profits were by no means always made out of the London runs, long as most of them were. The salary roll, the rents, and the running expenses at the Gaiety and Daly's were high. Frequently, the Edwardes syndicates had to look to American and Australian rights, or the profits on provincial tours, for the money to carry on. *An Artist's Model* was often running at a loss at Daly's, as £1,400 a week had to be taken at the box-office before any week showed a profit. *A Country Girl*, too, enjoyed a long London run, but failed to show a balance on the right side. *The Lady Dandies* cost George Edwardes £10,000 before the curtain rose on the first night, and this was not recouped in London. *The Girl from Kays* ended its run of 432 performances at the Apollo in 1902 with a debit of £20,000, which was made good in the provinces or the United States. And here, too, there were occasional miscalculations. £10,000 was lost in America over *The Duchess of Dantzic* and £20,000 over *Veronique*.

In view of the gambling element in his vaudeville ventures, it is not surprising that the worth of George Edwardes's personal estate was problematical when he died in the first year of the first World War. He was at Carlsbad in August 1914, and many months passed before he was exchanged. He was not ill-treated by the Germans, but came back a dying man, his eyes dulled, his hair white, and his body shrunken. When he died in 1915, the best asset in his estate was his interest in Daly's Theatre and the good-will attaching to his twenty years' associa-tion with Daly musical comedy. As we shall see, George Edwardes's wife, Julia Gwynne the actress, and her daughter were fortunate in their association with Robert Evett. His production of the all-British *Maid of the Mountains* closed the Edwardes's régime at Daly's with a triumph. The Edwardes family were able to sell their rights in Daly's Theatre to James White for £200,000.

Chapter VI

MUSICAL COMEDY AT DALY'S
1895 TO 1905

DALY'S THEATRE WAS NOT BUILT BY THE MANAGER WHO GAVE his name to it, but by the ubiquitous George Edwardes. Not content with the Gaiety, the Empire, and other West End houses which from time to time tended to come under his control, George Edwardes found the capital to build a theatre in the nineties of the last century at which the American star, Agnes Huntington, might appear, under the aegis of Augustin Daly. Miss Huntington, a burlesque actress of parts and a beauty of statuesque proportions, appeared at the Prince of Wales's Theatre in *Paul Jones*, a comic opera from the French, with music by Planquette. Miss Huntingdon, however, fell out with George Edwardes before Daly's Theatre was completed, and Daly decided to make the new theatre in Leicester Square a place where his comedy company could play when they were in London. A large stage was called for, and as money was plentiful £60,000 was spent upon the building, which incidentally was one of the first theatres in London built upon the cantilever principle. This means that the circle tiers were supported upon girders radiating from the surrounding walls and kept in position by their own weight, thus doing away with interior pillars which tended to obstruct the view of theatre-goers.

The theatre opened in the summer of 1893, with Ada Rehan in a revival of *The Taming of the Shrew*, but the high gods decided against its owner's plan. In fact, Daly's Theatre was destined to be the home of a new brand of vaudeville, owing something to Owen Hall's *A Gaiety Girl* and something to an unfortunate misjudgment of George Edwardes in connection with the comic opera *Dorothy*, a misjudgment which cost the amiable George a small fortune and which he never forgot.

Precisely how or why a George Edwardes production in Leicester Square differed from one at the Gaiety in the Strand cannot be stated. In general, the music at Daly's called for more skilled singers and the plots of the operas were somewhat better defined and more dramatic in treatment. There is also a certain significance in the fact that the manager distinguished sharply between his Gaiety and his Daly companies. Members of the latter were expected always to be on their best behaviour. The "Guv'ner" once said to José Collins:

"If you go out to supper, my dear, I shall have to send you on to the Gaiety."

No doubt the same line of thought was uppermost when Edwardes once asked a potential chorus-girl, "Do you run straight?" "Oh, yes, Mr. Edwardes," was the reply, "but not very far and not very fast."

When George Edwardes took over a comedian like Rutland Barrington or such leading ladies as Ruth Vincent and Isabel Jay from the Savoy, with its tradition of musical training and Gilbertian discipline, it was to Daly's that Edwardes sent them, not to the go-as-you-please Gaiety. At any rate, when a typical Daly's show, *Havana*, was produced at the Gaiety owing to the obstinacy of *The Merry Widow* in prolonging a run which was to have been for six weeks but continued for more than two years, *Havana* was not what Edwardes would have called a "hitter." Somehow, it seemed out of place. In fact, it was a romantic comic opera and not a Gaiety musical comedy, and the lovely and talented Evie Greene failed to charm her Strand audience, as she charmed stalls, circles, and gallery at Daly's. The why and the wherefore cannot be put into words, but theatre-goers sensed a differing psychological atmosphere.

Incidentally, the psychology of playhouses has never received elucidation. An established tradition has something to do with the fact that a certain class of entertainment associates itself with a certain theatre and not with one across the road. I do not mean so obvious a factor as seating capacity, for this reduces the problem to mere finance. What I have in mind is the affection keen theatre-goers display towards a certain type of entertainment as played at a certain theatre. How long does such a tradition need before it has an established box-office value? How much does such a tradition owe to a continuity in the band of players, such a continuity, for example, as the Gaiety had in Hollingshead times and in that of George Edwardes, or the Savoy, when the Savoy really was the Savoy? The Adelphi developed such a tradition over a period of years when Bill Berry was the chief laughter-monger in a special brand of musical comedy. When Cochran was most successful he created a similar atmosphere at the Ambassadors. Perhaps the pleasure theatre-goers take in following the development of a talent in players or producers, has something to do with the problem. Nowadays, a certain theatre does not associate itself naturally with a familiar entertainment form and with a company trusted because it has been sampled in the past and not found wanting, and I believe the theatre suffers. The public memory needs all the aid it can get from such a continuity of interest.

To return to *Dorothy*, which was a George Edwardes and Gaiety production in 1886 and yet made a fortune for H. J. Leslie at the Prince of Wales's and the Lyric, which was actually built at a cost of £77,000 from Leslie's profits from *Dorothy*. The reason will never be plain, but, certainly, the fortunes of *Dorothy* changed directly H. J. Leslie moved it from the Gaiety, added Ben Davies to the cast as Wilder, and replaced Marion Hood by Marie Tempest. Miss Tempest played the title part as a fresh schoolgirl, rejecting the chillsome and stately *prima-donna* role which Marion Hood had chosen.

Another factor in the romantic success of *Dorothy* was young Hayden Coffin's singing of "Queen of my Heart," though this had nothing to do with Leslie. Curiously enough, Alfred Cellier, the composer, always resented the presence of the song in a pastoral musical play of the *Dorothy* type. It was introduced during rehearsals, because George Edwardes thought Hayden Coffin, in the role of

Dorothy's lover, needed a sentimental song. At the time Cellier was in Australia, but his publishers, Chappell and Company, unearthed an earlier effort, with a taking melody. B. C. Stephenson, who was responsible for the book, put the printed copy on the top of the piano and, in red ink, re-wrote the ballad there and then. For "It was a year ago, Love, in the balmy Summer-time," were substituted the more definite sentiments of "You're Queen of My Heart, To-night." It proved to be the song-hit of the piece and established the fame of Hayden Coffin.

Born in Manchester in 1862, Hayden Coffin was the son of a dentist, and was intended for his father's profession, until the call of the Stage proved too strong. Within three years he was established as the leading *jeune premier* of his day and entered upon an alliance with George Edwardes's ventures which extended through the greater part of Coffin's career. He knew to a nicety how much of swagger and assurance a potential hero could display if he was to hold his public, masculine as well as feminine, and he knew, moreover, just how to put a senti-mental or patriotic song over the footlights. Add to these gifts no mean powers as a straight actor and it will be seen that George Edwardes was lucky when he established relations with Hayden Coffin.

Following his Harry Sherwood in *Dorothy*, Hayden Coffin played in *La Cigale*, some of the time in the United States. He was recalled to London to play the hero in *A Gaiety Girl*, with yet another song-hit, this time "Tommy, Tommy Atkins," a song which had not exhausted its welcome when the South African War put a premium upon the robust patriotism which Coffin thrust upon audiences so effectively.

The Daly Stars

Thus one of the *Dorothy* principals was working under George Edwardes when a successor to *A Gaiety Girl* was called for. Bent upon making his first musical show at Daly's fully worthy, Edwardes bethought him of *Dorothy's* heroine, Marie Tempest, who was also in America and had been for a considerable time. I have told how Marie came and found the management had provided for every contingency except her part in the proposed play. When this was remedied Miss Tempest and Hayden Coffin were supported by a wonderful cast. It will be found on the opposite page.

Letty Lind sang her ever-popular "Gay Tom-tit":

> A Tom-tit lived on a tip-top tree,
> And a mad little, bad little bird was he;
> He'd bachelor tastes, but then—oh dear!—
> He'd a gay little way with the girls, I fear.
> Now a Jenny Wren lived on a branch below,
> And it's plain she was vain as ladies go.
> For she pinched her waist and she rouged a bit—
> With a sigh for the eye of the gay Tom-tit.

This song and dance, and half a dozen comparable efforts at Daly's, was of
a pattern which Letty Lind and Charles Danby had popularised in *Ruy Blas*:

> A little peach in an Orchard grew,
> Listen to my tale of woe.
> A little peach of em'rald hue,
> Warmed by the sun and wet by the dew.
> It grew, it grew . . .
> Listen to my tale of woe . . .
>
> Now John took a bite, and so did Sue,
> Listen to my tale of woe.
> And then the trouble began to brew.
> A trouble that the doctor couldn't subdue,
> Poor John, poor Sue!

Born in 1862, Letty Lind came of theatrical stock, her sisters being Millie
Hylton, Lydia Flopp, Fanny Dango, and Adelaide Astor, who married George
Grossmith, junior. She made her earliest appearance on the stage at the Theatre
Royal, Birmingham, as Eva in *Uncle Tom's Cabin*, aged five. Though she had
no more than a thread of a voice, her pretty stage manners ensured a welcome
as singer, reciter, and, at last, as a dancer at the Gaiety, in company and in competi-
tion with the stars who twinkled in the Strand when Nellie Farren and Fred Leslie
topped the bills. "Click, click! I'm a monkey on a stick," in *The Geisha*, was a
Letty Lind invention. So was the memorable "A frog he lived in a pond⸝O," the
Aristophanic lyric, which Adrian Ross wrote for her in *A Greek Slave*:

> *Iris:*   A frog he lived in a pond⸝O.
> *Chorus:*   A pond⸝O! A pond⸝O!
> *Iris:*   He warbled a plaintive rondo—
>   Of brek⸝ek⸝ek⸝ex⸝koax!
> *Chorus:*   Koax!

In the climax, and Letty Lind had to reach it more than once in a typical evening at Daly's, "an owl flew out from a hole, O":

> Now an owl likes eggs, and an owl likes mice,
> But he thinks frogs' legs are extremely nice.
> He made a swoop with an open throat
> And nobody heard the frog's top note!

Adrian Ross, author of this pleasant lyric, was the best-equipped versifier associated with musical comedy in his generation. He had not a Sullivan to work upon his lyrics, but he proved a tower of strength at the Gaiety, Daly's, and elsewhere. Born in 1859, Arthur Reed Ropes, as "Adrian Ross" was christened, had a brilliant career at Cambridge, being a "wrangler," as well as winner of the Chancellor's Medal for English verse. It seemed that another Planché had come to the aid of vaudeville when Adrian Ross collaborated in the production of *In Town* in 1892, *Morocco Bound* in 1893, and *My Girl* in 1896, and then showed his talent at its bright best in *A Greek Slave* at Daly's. For the *Transit of Venus*, a James Tanner and Lambelet opera, for which Adrian Ross provided the lyrics, no fewer than nine sets of words were needed for the close of the highly ingenious first act, including those for eight principals and a chorus of gendarmes. Yet all the rhymes were adequate, and the proper rhythm was preserved throughout. Indeed, the whole of Ross's contribution to *The Transit of Venus* is worthy of study. Oddly enough, Adrian Ross never became fully acclimatised to the theatre. On one occasion, Letty Lind, in a burst of wondering enthusiasm, kissed him on the stage at rehearsal time. The lyricist fled the theatre.

The Geisha, which followed *An Artist's Model* in 1896, was not another *Mikado*, though comparison with Gilbert's masterpiece was inevitable and not unjust. Owen Hall saw an opportunity for an ambitious effort. The book he provided, however, was somewhat banal, though Harry Greenbank's lyrics and Sidney Jones's score were pleasantly tuneful and Lionel Monckton added two welcome numbers, so that all the members of a first-rate company were supplied with worthy material, judged by any standard less testing than that of Gilbert and Sullivan.

As for Owen Hall's plot, Molly Seamore is visiting Japan and, foolishly, puts on the dress of a *geisha*, and thus finds herself put up for public auction, and in the possession of a Japanese marquis, who proposes to make the English girl his wife. Fortunately, Reginald Fairfax (Hayden Coffin) of H.M.S. *Turtle* is at hand and with the aid of Mimosa San (Marie Tempest), a real *geisha*, rescues the imprudent Molly. Plainly, an adequate plot for a musical comedy, but scarcely inspired. However, few of Daly's patrons were critical when Huntley Wright as Wun-hi was there to sing "Chin-chin, Chinaman," and Louis Bradfield to lead a small company of naval officers in the gay, "We're going to call on the Marquis." And this leaves out of the reckoning Marie Tempest singing "The

Amorous Goldfish," the wiles of Juliette Nesville, bent upon marrying herself to the Marquis, and two lovely sets by W. Telbin, The Tea House of Ten Thousand Joys and a Chrysanthemum Fête in the Palace Gardens.

Huntley Wright was a Daly star during the first decade of George Edwardes's tenancy. He made his first stage appearance as a baby in arms in his father's company, so he had "theatre" pulsing in every artery when he came to Daly's. Haidée Wright was a sister and Fred Wright, of the Gaiety, a brother, while the Betty Huntley-Wright of to-day is a daughter. A trouper, this, if ever there was one, so that songs, dances, and snatches of humorous dialogue associate themselves with half a dozen roles, which are memorable, not because they are of great dramatic importance, but because they precisely met the needs of a given theatrical situation. Huntley Wright's "Chinee Soje-man" in *San Toy* was a fresh creation; not a duplicate of Wun-hi. Excellent, too, were dapper little Barry in *A Country Girl*, singing "Yo, ho, little girls, yo, ho" and the nicely turned Bagnolet in attendance upon the peppery General des Ifs in *The Little Michus*, and singing "The Regiment of Frocks and Frills."

A Greek Slave deserved better than it got. Owen Hall, Harry Greenbank, and Sidney Jones were all spurred by the success of *The Geisha* to a master-effort, and George Edwardes allowed them to get to work upon what was hoped would be a definite and dramatic story. The Daly's cast was strengthened by Rutland Barring-ton and Scott Russell from the Savoy, and the Roman scenery and costumes were as novel in musical comedy as they were lovely in presentation. But the run only extended to 349 performances. Was it to be wondered that the Far East, having proved so much more lucrative than Ancient Rome, to the Far East Edwardes went once more for his next background; instead of Japan, China, the result being *San Toy*. A minor memory is Akerman May's astonishing make-up as Sing-hi, President of the Board of Ceremonies. The aged Chinaman was there to the finger-nails and the strange collection of curios which the actor made to complete his portrait, included the thumb-ring of white jade, the tortoise-shell spectacles, complete with case, and the Cantonese fan and tassel. Three "foundations" were required to assure the proper complexion, the first two being pale pink and the third a dark yellow. A touch of white added prominence to the frontal bone while the cheeks were sunk with the aid of a dark shading. After forty years one can remember Sing-hi, and this without the least recollection of any song, dance, or jest, if the part of Sing-hi was thus dowered.

Owen Hall and Sidney Jones were seeking pastures new by this time, and the book of *San Toy* was written by Edward Morton to the music of Sidney Jones, the scenery of Joseph Harker and Hawes Craven, and the costumes of Percy Anderson. Rutland Barrington, who was not very well suited in *A Greek Slave*, created a second professional reputation as a singer of topical patter-songs, these being the Daly's variant upon Gilbert's famous patter-songs. He was at his best in *San Toy*, playing the mandarin Yen How, with his six little wives. Harry

BILL of the PLAY

TO-NIGHT FRIDAY, MAY 29th and Every Evening at 8-15.

MR. GEORGE EDWARDES

will produce a Japanese Musical Play in Two Acts, entitled

THE GEISHA

A STORY OF A TEA HOUSE.

The Book by OWEN HALL   Lyrics by HARRY GREENBANK   Music by SIDNEY JONES.

O Mimosa San	Chief Geisha		Miss MARIE TEMPEST
Juliette Diamant	(A French girl, attached to Tea House as interpreter)		Miss JULIETTE NESVILLE
Nami (Wave of the Sea)	(an attendant)		Miss KRISTINE YUDALL
O Kiku San (Chrysanthemum)			Miss EMILIE HERVE
O Hana San (Blossom)		Geisha	Miss MARY FAWCETT
O Kinkoto San (Golden Harp)			Miss ELISE COOKE
Komurasaki San (Little Violet)			Miss MARY COLLETTE
Lady Constance Wynne	(an English visitor in Japan, travelling in her Yacht)		Miss MAUD HOBSON
Miss Marie Worthington			Miss BLANCHE MASSEY
Miss Ethel Hurst		English Ladies,	Miss HETTY HAMER
Miss Mabel Grant		guests of	Miss ALICE DAVIS
Miss Louie Plumpton		Lady Constance	Miss MARGARET FRASER
Miss Molly Seamore			Miss LETTY LIND
Reginald Fairfax			Mr C. HAYDEN-COFFIN
Dick Cunningham		Officers	Mr LOUIS BRADFIELD
Arthur Cuddy		of	Mr LEEDHAM BANTOCK
George Grimston		H.M.S. "The Turtle."	Mr SYDNEY ELLISON
Tommy Stanley (Midshipman)			Miss LYDIA FLOPP
Captain Katana	(Captain of the Governor's Guard)		Mr WILLIAM PHILP
Takamine	(Governor's Agent)		Mr FREDK. ROSSE
Wun-hi	(A Chinaman ; Proprietor of Tea House)		Mr HUNTLEY WRIGHT
The Marquis Imari	(Chief of Police and Governor of the Province)		Mr HARRY MONKHOUSE
	Coolies, Attendants, Mousmés, Guards, &c.		
Conductor	Mr ERNEST FORD		

DALY'S THEATRE

Greenbank died before he could finish the lyrics, and Adrian Ross completed them.

Here is Greenbank's swan song:

Yen How: Oh, my name is Yen How, I'm a mandarin great,
And this is my famous umbrella of state.
And these are the robes that my office contrives,
And these, if you please, are my six little wives.

Wives: Yes, we are his six little wives.

All: Kow-tow, kow-tow
To the great Yen How,
And wish him the longest of lives.
With his one little, two little, three little, four little,
five little, six little wives!

Only less effective was Adrian Ross's effort on Rutland Barrington's behalf: "I mean to introduce it into China." Popular as this proved, it was eclipsed by Rutland Barrington's tit-bit in *A Country Girl*:

Peace! Peace! Oh, for some peace!
I think all this bustle is wrong.
And I'd like to repose in the sight of the snows,
Of the beautiful Valley of Bhong.

It seemed as if encores of the Rajah's song would never cease. Much of their appeal was due to the extra topical verses, introduced to fit a bit of news, fresh

from the evening papers. And there really were evening papers in London about the turn of the century, when Barrington was playing the Rajah of Bhong. *Evening News, Evening Standard, Globe, Westminster Gazette, Echo,* and *Star*—any of which might include a tit-bit which would inspire the Daly lyricists to a new verse. Similarly, Hayden Coffin sang "Hands off, Germany" with the manuscript music in his hands. The title was suggested by the leading article in an evening paper. A reference to the Kaiser, "Let pinchbeck Caesar strut and crow," troubled the Foreign Office, but reached the footlights.

For the rest, *A Country Girl* included pretty Evie Greene as Nan, singing "Molly the Marchioness" and "Try Again, Johnnie"; Huntley Wright, as "a bold A.B.," in company with Ethel Irving in song and dance, and the haunting "Under the Deodar." The Devonshire setting, the humours of Huntley Wright, and the acting and singing of Evie Greene, combined to justify a run which was only eclipsed, so far as Daly's is concerned, by the 768 performances of *San Toy*. Gertie Millar played Nan in a revival of *A Country Girl* at Daly's in 1914.

Changes, indeed, were in the air at Daly's in 1899. After a few weeks Marie Tempest left the cast of *San Toy*, being replaced by the sweet-voiced Florence Collingbourne. The "Guv'ner" wanted Miss Tempest to wear a pair of Chinese trousers, whereas the wilful *prima donna* chose to see herself in boylike "shorts," and literally "shorts," as Marie had just cut away the lower parts of the offending garment. The trouble culminated in an ultimatum. Trousers or go! Marie went and *San Toy* continued its triumphant run. By this time, Sidney Jones had also left Daly's, so the music for *A Country Girl* came from Lionel Monckton, with help from Paul Rubens. Sidney Jones went on to write *My Lady Molly*, which was given at Terry's Theatre in 1903, and included some of the composer's most tuneful numbers, and, moreover, had the advantage of a production by Sidney Ellison, who had done so much for *Florodora*. Sidney Jones also wrote the music for *See See*, a Chinese play translated from the French by Charles Brookfield, which seemed fully as good as *San Toy*. Huntley Wright, "Gabs" Ray, Adrienne Augarde, Maurice Farkoa, and W. H. Berry were in the cast, together with the popular Fred Emney of "A Sister to Assist 'Er" fame, and father of the Fred Emney of our own times. Yet, at the Prince of Wales's in 1906, *See See* failed to attract as George Edwardes's production at Daly's had done.

Gabrielle Ray was an attraction in various George Edwardes productions. She was discovered by Bannister Howard, who produced many musical-comedy successes in the provinces, and put "Gabs" Ray into one of his *Belle of New York* companies. At the time, she was one of the Sisters Ray and Howard was impressed by what he described as her "left foot kick." His admiration for the dancer chanced to coincide with the fact that Miss Ray's sister was about to be married, so the three years' contract to play in *The Belle* seemed a gift from the gods. George Edwardes borrowed "Gabs" from Bannister Howard and the young beauty reached a postcard fame which rivalled that of Marie Studholme, Phyllis Dare, or Mabel Love about 1909, when she was principal dancer at Daly's and in partnership with such comedians as Willie Warde and W. H. Berry. "Gabs" Ray, being lightly built, was specially good in acrobatic dances. Berry has admitted that, after a bout following "For I am such a simpleton," he was impelled to make inquiries regarding the damage done:

"How's your where I dropped you last night?" he asked diplomatically.

Chapter VII

DALY'S, THE SECOND PHASE, 1905 TO 1920

AFTER A DECADE THE PERIOD OF HIGH PROSPERITY DUE TO THE tuneful music of Sidney Jones and the novel form of musical comedy which George Edwardes had established at Daly's, threatened to end. Lionel Monckton and Paul Rubens had been good, as their Gaiety record assured, but in the end they had nothing new to give Daly's public. Requiring rather more serious music than Monckton or Rubens could offer, Edwardes looked abroad. French and Austrian musicians and stories from overseas of the Ruritanian type characterised Vaudeville at Daly's during the second ten years of George Edwardes's tenure, André Messager, Edmond Audran, and Franz Lehar being his instruments.

Nor is the reason far to seek. Frenchmen and Austrians have artistry in their blood, and this because Frenchmen and Austrians take their pleasures seriously and respect all forms of artistry as the average Englishman does not. We have agreed that the essential in comic opera is the presence of a recognisable and consistent plot, as opposed to the "get-along-as-best-you-can-to-the-next-tuneful-number" which so many British librettists regard as the basis of their art efforts. Given this outlook, plots permitting of lyrics which interested composers as Gilbert's humours and rhythms inspired Arthur Sullivan, were rare. The inherent weakness in English vaudeville was revealed years ago by that theatrical light o' heart, Seymour Hicks. It was the morning after the first night, when judges of stage effect are in the closest touch with the box-office. Quoth Hicks:

"Now we've got good notices from the critics, let's call a rehearsal and cut out the plot."

The story, even if it is apocryphal, reveals why artistic Frenchmen rather than inartistic Britons developed comic opera in its dual form, opéra comique, in which there was no element of burlesque, and opéra bouffe, in which not even the love-making was to be taken seriously. *Veronique* and *La Poupée* are examples of successful opéra comique, while the works of Offenbach and Hervé are styled opéra bouffe.

The tendency to establish French comic opera, with a recognisable plot and musicianly composition, was not a new one. *La Cigale* with Audran's music was an experiment of the 'nineties, and it was followed by the same composer's *Miss Decima*, a dainty morsel, served daintily at the Criterion. When *Veronique*, with music by André Messager, reached London in 1904 it proved a great draw. The composer being a director of the Opéra-Comique in Paris, was a real musician and, being an artist, he demanded a lively and clearly defined story. Beginning with a production at the Coronet in French, the English version came to the Apollo, with the advantage of a production by Sydney Ellison, of *Florodora*

73

fame. This included costumes from the brush of Percy Anderson and a charming apple-green opening scene in Coquenard's flower-shop, with the shop girls in costumes which chimed in with the scenic background. The blossoming chestnuts in the second scene and the mauve and silver hall in the Tuileries were scarcely less charming.

As for the plot of *Veronique*, it revealed that Count Florestan was under the obligation of marrying a certain Mlle Helene, whom he had never seen and, being a confirmed bachelor, selected the alternative—a term in a debtor's prison. Needless to say, he met Helene in Coquenard's shop, fell in love with her at once in approved comic-opera fashion, whereupon, to punish him, Helene posed as Veronique, a flower-shop girl and, in this guise, was invited to the chestnut-haunted tea-garden of the second act and the royal reception at the Tuileries, which gave material for Messager's closing scene. Here, at last, Helene, *alias* Veronique, gave the Count his long-denied kiss. Apart from the lovely Ruth Vincent, riding the donkey, which was fed upon carrots to ensure perfect stage manners, there were George Graves, the Coquenard, dark-eyed Maudi Darrell, and Rosina Brandram, the latter as the Countess singing "The Garden of Love":

> Like the bee to the garden of roses
> Comes man to the garden of love,
> To flit round its daintiest posies
> And hover their petals above. . . .

Another comic opera from the French which was universally acclaimed was *La Poupée*, given at the Prince of Wales's in 1897. Thanks to the music by Edmond Audran, the opera had a successful run in Paris and Arthur Roberts, who was in partnership with Henry Lowenfeld in connection with *Gentleman Joe*, secured an interest in it, despite the fact that George Edwardes, Horace Ledger, and other London managers had turned down the play, chiefly because they feared the jovial monk of the story might offend patrons, in itself a curious commentary upon late Victorian ethics. Before the first night Arthur Roberts, too, had joined the doubters and finally refused a half-share in a production which would have earned him £100,000. Lowenfeld was thus left to bear the burden alone. The dress rehearsal gave every indication of a pronounced flop, but the first night proved a triumph for everyone concerned. Even when Mlle Favier, the delightful little Frenchwoman who played the doll, became home-sick and left London, *La Poupée* continued to delight audiences not only in London, but the Provinces. Willie Edouin headed the cast in the part of Hilarius, which Arthur Roberts was to have played. After forty years one can see him touch his nose wisely, give a sweep to his coat-tails, and look proudly upon his handicraft:

"All my own work. My wife had nothing to do with that!"

The witticisms had the more point as Hilarius's own stage daughter was posing as the doll, which had been broken. Courtice Pounds as the novice and Norman

Willie Edouin in "La Poupée"

Salmond, singing "A Jovial Monk am I," shared the triumphs with Willie Edouin.

Remembering *Veronique*, it is not strange that George Edwardes turned to a French composer when he wanted a successor to Sidney Jones at Daly's. What he got was *The Little Michus*, with music by André Messager. It came to Daly's in 1905, a year after Messager's success with *Veronique*. The book had a Gilbertian flavour, as Blanche Marie and Marie Blanche had been mixed up in the bath when they were a month old. "Why don't people mark things when they send them to the wash?" In the event, no one could tell which was the daughter of General des Ifs and which was her foster-sister. The girls were happy enough until marriage-time came and the dashing young officer Gaston (Robert Evett) was foolish enough to engage in a game of blind-man's buff. In his blindness he kissed Blanche, only to find that the turn of the plot seemed to make it certain that Marie was the General's daughter. Mabel Green played Marie, while Blanche was pretty Adrienne Augarde, niece of Amy Augarde, who was playing her foster-mother. For the rest there was Willie Edouin as the General, with his wonderful wide-open eyes, his vast moustache, and even vaster military boots, and Huntley Wright singing:

> Oh, the Regiment of Frocks
>   And the Regiment of Frills,
> Though they use the smokeless powder
>   It's the glance that really kills.
> There is little noise or bustle
>   On the battlefield, it's true,
> Only petticoats that rustle, rustle,
>   With a frou, frou, frou, frou, frou!

Willie Edouin was the first General des Ifs, but George Graves was later to impress his guileful personality upon the role, thanks to his nimble gagging. There was, for example, the General sampling a draught of home-brewed wine, which had such a "bite" that it dislocated the General's false teeth! The gestures, grimaces, and gyrations which followed upon the "bite" threatened Daly's audiences with a similar physical collapse. In the shop scene, one of the ladies behind the counter assured the General, "we have had testimonials for this wine," to which Graves retorted, with a shudder, "Yes, and memorial cards." Lastly, there was the patter which accompanied the invention of the Gazeka, a beast of prehistoric ancestry, which will go down to posterity with Hetty the Hen, a product of *Merry Widow* days.

From boyhood days, Graves's imagination had been obsessed with nightmare beasts and the trick of mind suggested the Gazeka, when the part of the General seemed to need strengthening during rehearsals of *The Little Michus*. As George Graves pictured the Gazeka it was a toad-like creature, characterised by a pro-nounced wink. Four fingers and four toes, instead of the customary five and a patch of fur upon his chest, were other characteristics. Among the peculiarities of Hetty the Hen was the power to lay "a bent egg." Another evening, Graves calmly assured Daly audiences that a door-knob had been found in Hetty's nest and the strange bird was judged to be responsible. A foolish neighbour had been feeding the bird with brass filings. The nightly bulletins upon Hetty's health were eagerly awaited, finally taking the form of the injunction, "Eat more Bent Eggs." This amazing capacity for inventing picturesque happenings accounted

George Graves, by H. M. Bateman, in "Princess Caprice"

for much of the comic appeal of George Graves and made him the accepted successor of Dan Leno in Drury Lane pantomime.

He began his business career at sixteen, addressing envelopes in a Chancery Lane business-house at 7s. 6d. a thousand. Prospects were so uninviting that Graves and three other youngsters determined to start a concert-party in the Isle of Wight. When this failed George Graves toured in *The Shop Girl*, at £2 a week, and five years later he was still only worth £6 a week, in the judgment of theatrical managers. All this was changed in 1905, when Graves took over the part of General des Ifs from Willie Edouin. He ended by getting close upon £400 a week from Arthur Collins during the pantomime season at Drury Lane.

It was in 1909 that George Graves was persuaded to forsake musical comedy at Christmas-time, in order to play the villain Abanazar in *Aladdin* at the Lane. In a polar setting, Mr. Graves attempted to teach a penguin to lay an egg. The penguin refused. Mr. Graves tried persuasion. He pleaded for that egg. He cajoled, he wheedled, he coaxed. The penguin would not oblige. In 1913/14, when *The Sleeping Beauty* had her turn at the Lane, George Graves and Will Evans developed a photograph. The house rocked from stalls to gallery when Will told George "to take a bath," George regarding the instruction as an aspersion upon his personal habits. However, a hip-bath was procured and an ounce of this and a penny-weight of that were duly put in. Later, Mr. Graves danced a tango, which he described as "not a dance, but an 'assault,'" and made the stalls chuckle by a reference to "the girl with the R.S.V.P. eyes," a phrase which may well pass into the language. Some of Graves's quips were really funny. Of *The Times*, he said, with a tearful shudder of disappointment at noticing that it no longer cost 3*d.*:

"But this isn't *The Times*, Pompey. This isn't the good old threepenn'orth I used to sleep behind at the club."

Perhaps Graves's most telling quip was to the effect that "the meanest man he ever knew was the man who would not even spend Christmas." In Drury Lane pantomime Graves, on one occasion, took a "call" with half a dozen prompters who had helped with his gags and topical verses. The prompters popped up from behind furniture on the stage and all parts of the wings. There was a yell from the delighted house.

Les Merveilleuses, which London's cab-drivers called "The Marvellous 'Ouses," and a few uninstructed professionals *The Lady Dandies*, came to Daly's in 1906. The story was devised by Victorien Sardou, after George Edwardes had expressed a desire for a comic opera with a definite plot. Sardou selected the period of the Directoire in Paris, between 1795 and 1799. Illyria (lovely Denise Orme) had been divorced from her husband that she might marry Saint Amour, Chief of the Secret Police of the Director Barras. The Tricolour Fête at the Palace of the Luxembourg furnished the background of Sardou's third act, in which Evie Greene led a lovely company of ladies in a memorable dance with the Dandies, headed by Louis Bradfield. Throughout, the music of Dr. Hugo Felix was masterly, in particular the brilliant finale to the second act. Evie Greene's Merveilleuse Song and her "Ring-a-Ring-a-Roses" at the end of the first scene in the Palais Royal are also memorable, as are Denise Orme's "Cuckoo," Robert Evett's dramatic "How I took the Redoubt," and his duet with Denise Orme, "It might have been." W. H. Berry ("Always Berry and Bright") began his ten years' connection with Daly's in *Les Merveilleuses*. He was originally engaged to play a detective, but George Graves had to leave the cast and Berry was called upon to play Saint Amour at two days' notice. He took with him his detective song, "It comes from an authoritative source."

Akin to *Les Merveilleuses* was *The Duchess of Dantzic*, a musical version of the story of Madame Sans Gêne, with Evie Greene in the title part and music by Ivan Caryll. The play cost £15,000 before the curtain went up at the Lyric on the first night, and this was a lot of money even for George Edwardes. With a chorus of sixty, an orchestra of forty, and an excellent supporting cast, the opening performances were full of promise. The opera, however, called for continued good acting and singing, and when the first-night enthusiasm waned, the players, principals as well as chorus, slackened their efforts. In an ordinary musical comedy, this might not have mattered. A song could have been introduced or a passage of low comedian's patter might have brightened a dull patch, but *The Duchess of Dantzic* did not permit of such interpolations. Courtneidge, who produced for George Edwardes, called some rehearsals with a view to tuning-up the production, but failed to do any permanent good and a very promising opera came to a premature end.

When French comic opera, like English musical comedy, failed to meet the needs of Daly's Theatre, George Edwardes turned to Austria, and found his culminating triumph in *The Merry Widow*. The music was by Franz Lehar, an ex-bandmaster in the Austrian army, and it pleased all ears, as the beauty of Lily Elsie delighted all eyes, and the charm of Joseph Coyne won all hearts. There had not been a comparable triumph in light "theatre" since *The Gondoliers*. *Die Lustige Witwe* was first produced in 1906 at the An der Wien Theatre, Vienna, and was played at some 450 European theatres before London discovered its virtues. Twelve thousand performances were given in Germany alone in the early years after its production, and Bernardt Herzmansky, the Viennese music publisher, made £70,000 from sales of the score, his success being duplicated by that of Messrs. Chappell, with the English edition. Two hundred thousand copies of the famous waltz were sold before the London run ended. Finally, Franz Lehar, then in the thirties, profited to the extent of £60,000, in spite of poor original contracts, while the lucky librettists made £40,000.

The chief reason for this sensational success was that *The Merry Widow* combined the virtues of romantic light opera with those of musical comedy. The latter were dominant in the first act and the romantic opera elements in the second, when Robert Evett and Elizabeth Firth sang their duet, and Coyne and Miss Elsie the "Vilia" song. The third act, at Maxim's, brought musical comedy to the fore once more.

In view of its Continental record, it might have been expected that George Edwardes anticipated big profits from *The Merry Widow*. On the contrary, it had been running for three years before he could be persuaded to venture a miserable £1,000 upon it. Only the insistence of Pat Malone, who saw the play in Vienna, persuaded him. When George did agree, it was with the idea that a six-weeks' run would suffice, pending the production of *The Dollar Princess*. Similarly, Edwardes did not approve of Coyne's Danilo; nor, by the way, did Joe himself, being of opinion that he was a comedian and not a romantic lover in a musical play. A good deal of persuasion was also necessary before George Edwardes agreed to entrust the name-part to Lily Elsie. Which shows that the showman who said "No" to *Dorothy*, *La Poupée*, and *The Belle of New York* was fallible. In fact, £250,000 was taken at Daly's in two years and Lily Elsie and

Joseph Coyne won all hearts, while Lehar's music, including the famous waltz, entranced all ears, and has been going round the globe ever since. As for the comedians, there were George Graves as Baron Popoff, "barging down to the footlights and barking the funny ones into the abyss" (Graves's own description of his nightly task) and the popular Bill Berry. Nor must the male sextet escape mention. Freddy Kaye, portly Lennox Pawle, Coyne, Graves, Valentine O'Connor, and Berry sang the number and in every verse each one had a single line.

> Women! Women! Women! Women! Women!
> You may study their ways if you can,
> But a woman's too much for a man.
> It is deeper than diving for pearls,
> Courting, girls, girls, girls, girls, girls.
> With her fair flaxen hair, eyes of blue,
> She's a long way too knowing for you.
> She is dark, she is fair, you may smile, you may frown,
> Never mind, you will get done brown.

I include Coyne among the singers. More strictly, as he confessed, "he spoke through the music."

Like most of the outstanding vaudeville stars, Lily Elsie was caught young. She was a member of the Cotton family, and as "Little Elsie" began as a mimic and clog-dancer. Soon she was playing leading roles in pantomime. Her first London success was in *A Chinese Honeymoon*, in which the wondering eyes seemed the more mysterious when veiled by the great basket hat of her role, with its multitudinous tassels. The combination of youth and beauty persuaded Edwardes to give her the title role in *The Merry Widow*, when it was declined by Marie Tempest. Miss Elsie played the part more than seven hundred times and was fully as popular with the women as she was with the men. What happened was that *The Merry Widow* set the seal of public approval upon romance-cum-music, this being the mood specially suited for girls who were bringing their young men in thousands to musical plays in the years immediately before the first World War. The popularity of dancing which revealed itself in "Merry Widow Lancers," a "Merry Widow Waltz," and "Merry Widow Quadrilles" helped greatly. The younger patrons of pit and gallery were less interested in the burlesque element of vaudeville than in the fallings-out and comings together of women as pretty as Lily Elsie and men as charming as Joseph Coyne. Almost against his better judgment George Edwardes and his lieutenants had tumbled to the change in public taste and given patrons at Daly's the very thing they had been wanting.

Lily Elsie was not the only Sonia. The part was so replete with elements that delight theatre-goers, that failure was almost impossible, and Constance Drever, Gertrude Lester, Clara Evelyn, Emmy Wehlen, and Gertrude Glyn all have admirers who associate them with the Vilia Song or some other highlight in *The Widow*. The latest revival, in the middle of the second World War, gave

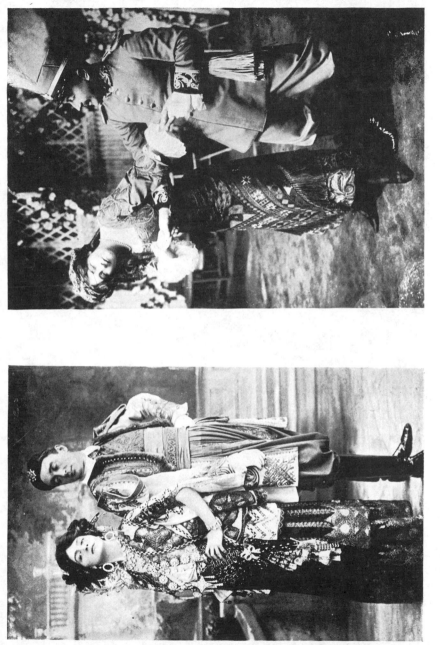

"The Chocolate Soldier"
Constance Drever, as Nadine ;
C. H. Workman, as Bumerli

"The Merry Widow" (1907)
Lily Elsie, as Sonia
Joseph Coyne as Prince Danilo

Gabrielle Raye,
of Daly's and the Gaiety

Rosie Boote, of the Gaiety
(Marchioness of Headfort)

Florence Smithson
in "The Arcadians"

us the Widow of Madge Elliott, playing with her husband, Cyril Ritchard, the Prince Danilo.

One other memory of *The Merry Widow*, Mabel Russell, with the uptilted nose and the pretty rotundities, who played Fi Fi and danced with such splendid spirit upon one of the tables in the cabaret scene in the third act. Miss Russell was climbing to stardom when *The Merry Widow* came to Daly's and theatre-lovers have had a grudge against politics, combined with the institution of marriage, ever since these persuaded Miss Russell to change her name to Philipson and become a Parliamentarian. Membership of the House of Commons was the climax of a career which began in the box-office of the Shakespeare Theatre, Clapham. During the pantomime season someone remembered the bright-eyed girl in the box-office, when one of the principals fell ill and someone was wanted in a hurry to fill the gap in the cast. Mabel Russell took up the part and was an immediate success. Leading roles in musical comedies on tour followed, among them Nan in *A Country Girl*, and then Daly's.

The Dollar Princess succeeded *The Merry Widow*, and again Lily Elsie was the heroine. The story had a German origin and was a variant upon Shakespeare's *Taming of the Shrew*. Robert Michaelis proved a very gentlemanly Petruchio and Lily Elsie the most amiable of Katharinas, so "rings and things and fine array" for the bride, ay, "and kisses," were not unduly delayed. More memorable than the love encounters with Michaelis were the comedy episodes between Lily Elsie and her stage brother, Joseph Coyne, among them the Hansel and Gretel duet, in which the singers wore dunce's caps and swished light canes, while they recalled the delinquencies and other memories of their childhood days, to a pretty setting by Leo Fall.

> *Lily:* I'll dance a ring of roses,
> Taking hands with you,
> You're Hansel and I'm Gretel,
> That's the way they do.

The second act of *The Dollar Princess* also gave us "Bill" Berry's play with an astonishing tennis racket, which had a pliable india-rubber handle. Just as George Graves specialised in strange beasts, so Berry specialised in curious properties. In *A Waltz Dream* he sang the "Piccolo Duet," telling of the wedding of a violin and a piccolo. The singers occupied two roomy high-backed cane chairs.

> *Berry:* A violin who'd lost her beau,
> She met a toney piccolo.
> *Elsie:* His tone was so extremely high.
> She gave a *pizzicato* sigh.
> *Berry:* Said he, "Oh, come, my lady fair,
> Be with me when I take the air."
> *Elsie:* Said she, "It wouldn't seem quite right
> Accompanying you to-night."

When the duet ended, Berry was surrounded by a whole family of curious instruments, the progeny of the marriage which followed upon the happy flirtation. Edward Royce, who produced *A Waltz Dream* at Daly's, put a couple of baskets behind the high-backed cane chairs and as Lily Elsie and "Bill" Berry moved round in their dance, they took the baby instruments from the baskets, each smaller than the other. When the singers were seated once more they displayed the smallest of the piccolos and violins. The music was by Oscar Straus, the lyrics by Adrian Ross. *A Waltz Dream* was originally given at the Hicks Theatre in 1908, with Gertie Millar as Franzi, leader of the women's orchestra in a Viennese beer-garden, which Lily Elsie played later at Daly's. When *A Waltz Dream* was revived at the Winter Garden in 1934, Berry again played Count Lothar and once more helped to bring the brood of piccolos and violins to birth.

The Count of Luxembourg was a Daly's production in 1911, with music by Franz Lehar, who had given *The Merry Widow* to vaudeville. The composition occupied no more than two months. The original Viennese book was in three acts; Basil Hood reduced them to two. As the Viennese libretto lacked humour in character and situations, the English adaptor also devised the part of Brissard for W. H. Berry. Only thirty lines of the original dialogue remained when Basil Hood had finished his adaptation and, admittedly, he improved it. As for the plot, a comic grand duke, played by Huntley Wright, wanted to marry a vaudeville artist (Lily Elsie). As a title was deemed an essential preliminary to marriage with a grand duke, a mock wedding was arranged with the spendthrift Count René (Bertram Wallis), the condition being that the Count should never see his bride and divorce her at the end of three months. A cheque for £20,000 sealed the bargain between Count and Grand Duke and Countess Angela awaited her real marriage. The action of the second scene took place in the reception hall of the Grand Duke's palace, with its great golden stairway, embowered with roses and the abiding memory will be the Staircase Waltz which Edward Royce devised for Lily Elsie and Bertram Wallis. King George and Queen Mary were present at the first night, and Lily Elsie, who was recovering from an operation for appendicitis, only managed to finish her performance with the aid of repeated injections of morphia. But those who watched the Golden Stairs Waltz saw only effortless beauty and grace as Lily Elsie and her partner moved up the stairway, in and out of the pillars supporting the crossing, and down the stairs on the other side. Momentarily, they were in the Fairyland of the song, "where all may wander hand in hand."

Bertram Wallis was a gold medallist at the Royal Academy of Music in his student days and after years of solid work as a straight actor, began to tour in Daly musicals in the year 1902. His first appearance as a star was in *The King of Cadonia*, supporting Isabel Jay, in 1908. King George V saw Wallis at the Prince of Wales's and chanced to remark: "This man ought to be at Daly's." This came to George Edwardes and the transfer took place in 1911. In the next ten or fifteen years there was no more acceptable hero in comic opera. A manly presence, a pleasing voice, and a welcome personality helped to fill the stage in a long series of successes.

How the Edwardes tradition was maintained at the Gaiety by the Grossmith-Laurillard management will be told in another chapter, but, at Daly's, a brave bit of team-work not only made theatrical history, but carried on the Edwardes tradition for five critical years.

When Edwardes died, Robert Evett, the tenor, was in control of affairs at Daly's, and he made up his mind that the memorable thirty years deserved a worthier memorial than a bankrupt estate. Looking around, he came upon *The Maid of the Mountains*, assembled the essential players and, finally, produced the play with such success that not only were all debts paid, but the Edwardes family left the London theatre world with a substantial fortune. A triumph, indeed, for professional fealty.

Strictly, *The Maid of the Mountains* was opéra comique, rather than musical comedy. Its romantic book was the invention of Freddy Lonsdale, the lyrics being by Harry Graham, writer of the familiar *Nonsense Verses*, and the music by Harold Fraser-Simson. As is so frequently the case, many managers turned down Lonsdale's idea before its money-making capacity was realised. The original script went back to 1908 and Harold Fraser-Simson wrote the music for a totally different plot. To Oscar Asche, the producer, belongs the principal responsibility for the changes which proved so successful. In particular, he designed a highly romantic mountain lair instead of the beach scene originally proposed. His lighting of the scene was masterly. Lastly, after a successful try-out at the Prince's Theatre, Manchester, James W. Tate added some interpolated numbers. He was José Collins's stepfather and she had been singing his songs at music-halls, among them, "I've built a bamboo bungalow for you." For *The Maid* he wrote "A Bachelor Gay" and "A Paradise for Two."

When the curtain rose, Teresa, the lovely Maid of the Mountains, had been captured by the police, about the time the brigand band had captured the Governor of Santo. Aided by credentials taken from the Governor, the brigands came to Santo and released Teresa. Complications, however, arose, from jealousies incidental to life "somewhere in the south of Europe." Lauri de Frece, as the merry-man of the robber band, and Mabel Sealby provided the humour, as José Collins and Thorpe Bates provided the romantic melody. Lauri de Frece (with the lobster), pleading that his wife should "be kind to little Leonard," lingers in the memory.

Born in 1893, José Collins's first stage appearance was made when she was ten, and she was only thirteen when she was with Harry Lauder in his "Scotch Bluebell." She danced in a tartan frock and glengarry, while Lauder sang "I love a lassie." Four years later, after a stern struggle, she reached the London Pavilion. At twenty-four Robert Evett persuaded Miss Collins to return from America, to play a leading part in *The Happy Day*. The three years' run of *The Maid of the Mountains* followed, 1,352 performances, a record apart from *Chu-Chin-Chow*.

The daughter of Lottie Collins had just the combination of singing and acting ability needed to bring comic opera back into favour. Though her American experiences had raised her to stardom, José was content with £50 a week when the run of *The Maid of the Mountains* began. She did not draw more until the £80,000 debt owing by the Edwardes estate was paid off. Then she received £300 a week. Robert Evett also had a part in this self-denial, for his own salary was limited to £30 a week. He was bent upon showing that George Edwardes had died solvent. *The Maid* was produced in February 1917, and by Christmas it was plain that Daly's had found a gold-mine in José and the music she had to sing. At one time there were fourteen touring companies.

The Maid was not Evett's first war-time production. It was preceded by *Betty*, with music by the Viennese Ernst Steffen. Throughout the war, the unlucky musician could not draw a penny of his royalties and at the end of 1918 he was glad to accept a job as pianist in a Viennese restaurant. To Steffen it seemed nothing less than a miracle when the management at Daly's sent a cheque for £13,000, being deferred payment for the royalties.

José Collins followed her Teresa with her Dolores in *A Southern Maid* and her Sybil in a musical comedy with a Russian background. Better remembered is her Countess Vera Lisaveta in *The Last Waltz* at the Gaiety in 1923, to the music of Oscar Straus.

> If this should be the last waltz,
> If dawn must break too soon,
> Just hold me to your heart, dear,
> And love shall call the tune.
> Our dreams of joy are ended,
> And tears are all in vain.
> Then let us dance together
> That last sweet waltz again.

By this time, José Collins was earning £800 a week, including the income from gramophone records of the Gaiety songs.

Harold Fraser-Simson, who contributed so much to the record-breaking run of *The Maid of the Mountains*, was a shipowner before he turned comic-opera composer, and revealed the talent for singable melody which José Collins displayed to such advantage. *A Southern Maid* did not achieve the success of *The Maid of the Mountains*, but such songs as "Love will find a way" and Beppo's "Live for To-day" ensure that Harold Fraser-Simson will not be forgotten by lovers of English vaudeville.

Nor must mention be omitted of Harry Graham, who wrote the words for familiar songs in *The Maid of the Mountains*, the *White Horse Inn*, *Toni*, and other musical plays, and was part author in some of them. Graham was an Etonian, who passed on to the Coldstreams, an odd beginning for one who devoted so much of his time to musical comedy. He was also private secretary to the late

Lord Rosebery for a time. A theatrical manager who had dealings with Harry Graham was driven to this comment:

"Captain Graham, what I likes about yer is that you're my idea of a fine old English gentleman."

From which it may be surmised that Captain Graham was not a master in contract-making.

James White, who bought Daly's Theatre from the Edwardes estate for £200,000, had neither the temper, the knowledge, nor the common honesty to make a success as a theatrical manager. After a hectic few months he double-crossed his general manager, Robert Evett, and, with Evett's departure from Daly's, the end was not long delayed. White committed suicide and Daly's degenerated into a home for more or less unsuccessful revivals. The sad tale is told in Forbes-Winslow's *Biography of a Theatre*. When the film magnates took over the site, a glory departed from Leicester Square.

Chapter VIII

THE MANTLE OF EDWARDES, 1900 TO 1925

THE PHRASE, "THE MANTLE OF" SHOULD BE RESERVED FOR personalities of the highest distinction. It can justly be associated with a Garrick or an Irving; yes, and with a Gilbert or a Sullivan. For the succession to George Edwardes a more prosaic image is required. Should it be the white tie, starched shirt, and black "tails" of evening wear which Blue-eyed George filled with such distinction on a first night at the Gaiety or Daly's? Whatever be the image selected, the musical-comedy managements deriving from the Edwardes tradition constitute an important chapter in the story of Anglo-Saxon vaudeville in the first quarter of the present century. Indeed, the tradition passed from the Gaiety and Daly's well before the first World War and in not a few cases with Edwardes himself as part-owner of the show and one of his lieutenants as producer. For example, the Adelphi Theatre was captured for musical comedy in November 1910, when the Gaiety released Gertie Millar from *Our Miss Gibbs*, in order that she might appear in a play in which all the music was by her husband, Lionel Monckton. It was *The Quaker Girl*, and Miss Millar, as Prudence, opened the story by being caught drinking champagne, a variant upon Joseph Coyne's predicament in the first act of *The Merry Widow*. Primarily, because of a delightful waltz number, "Come to the Ball," and Monckton's tuneful songs, *The Quaker Girl* seemed good and enjoyed 536 performances. Joseph Coyne was the Quaker girl's lover, James Blakeley, the low comedian, and Gracie Leigh and Elsie Spain, the dancers. In 1944 *The Quaker Girl* enjoyed a new lease of life at the Coliseum, with Celia Lipton as Prudence.

More interesting than the shows patterned upon Gaiety and Daly successes were the musical comedies which revealed a spice of originality, either because of a fresh managerial approach or the coming of a star with a personality. About the time George Edwardes was experimenting with *In Town* and *The Shop Girl*, the personality of May Yohe called for exploitation and her success was largely due to the skill with which Ivan Caryll fitted her very limited vocal powers with suitable songs, as in *Little Christopher Columbus*. May Yohe's deep contralto voice had a range of five or six notes, but Ivan Caryll's "Oh, honey, ma honey," the earliest of the imitation coon songs, was written with the fact in mind. For the rest, May Yohe's plantation costume, with its big straw hat, white blouse, and striped knickers (one "leg" neatly turned just above the knee) suited the singer's trim figure to a nicety. The daughter of a Pennsylvanian iron-moulder, May Yohe was born in 1869 and made her stage debut in Chicago when she was eighteen. Lord Francis Clinton-Hope, a brother of the Duke of Newcastle, introduced Miss Yohe to London managers six years later, and the Sims-Caryll opera, *Christopher Columbus,* established the actress's vogue. *Dandy Dick Whittington* and *The Lady Slavey* were followed by May Yohe's marriage to Lord Francis, and her association with 'the misfortunes attaching to the famous blue Hope Diamond.

Apart from George Edwardes, there was no producer of musical comedy more ingenious, knowledgeable, and successful than Sir George Dance. His big discovery was Louie Freear. Dance devoted more attention to provincial productions than did his great rival, and there were times in the first decade of the

century when Dance had sixteen musical-comedy companies on the road in Great Britain.

In addition to his business gifts, George Dance was a master-hand as a writer of low-comedy lyrics. An early effort was "His lordship Winked at the Counsel," sung by the Great Macdermott; somewhat later came "Come where the booze is cheaper." The air was played by a Guards band one Sunday afternoon on the Terrace at Windsor Castle and attracted the attention of Queen Victoria. Her Majesty sent Lady Antrim to find out what the tune might be. The bandmaster thought twice before he permitted Lady Antrim to inform the old Queen that she had been listening to a "common music-hall song" about strong drink and that the words ran:

> Come where the booze is cheaper,
> Come where the pots hold more,
> Come where the boss is the deuce of a joss,
> Come to the pub next door.

George Dance not only invented successful songs and produced musical shows, but wrote the books of a number of well-known pieces. Indeed, it has been claimed that Dance's *A Modern Don Quixote,* produced in 1893, has a joint claim with *In Town* to be regarded as the first musical comedy. *Lord Tom Noddy,* exploiting the quaint personality of Little Tich, followed, and then a triumph, *A Chinese Honeymoon,* exploiting the equally quaint personality of Louis Freear.

Among vaudeville shows, only *Chu-Chin-Chow* and *The Maid of the Mountains*
have excelled the 1,075 performances of *A Chinese Honeymoon*. Both the others
had the advantage of production during the years of the first World War, when
no fewer than four London plays enjoyed runs of more than one thousand
performances.

Sir George himself wrote *A Chinese Honeymoon* to music of Howard Talbot
and produced it at the old Strand Theatre, on the site of the existing Tube railway
station. It attracted a new type of audience to musical comedy. Visiting pit or
gallery, it was plain that a goodly proportion of the patrons of the cheaper seats
turned eastwards, when making for home and bed, rather than north, south, or
west, as the majority of London theatre-goers did at the turn of the century.
Before he died, his sense of what his public wanted made Dance one of the
wealthiest men in the theatrical profession. In a time of crisis he gave £30,000 to
save the Old Vic and, very properly, received a knighthood.

It is, perhaps, to be deplored that much of Sir George's good fortune was due
to the frailties of man, rather than man's nobler qualities. He was the owner of
the bars at a number of West End houses, a form of theatrical investment which
is much more assured of dividends than authorship or production. Indeed, it
has been said, the worse the play, the greater the profits of the bar. Poor vaudeville
has sent many a playgoer out for a whisky and soda. The big profits in *A Chinese
Honeymoon* were shared with Frank Curzon, manager of the Strand in those days,
who saw the play in the provinces and brought it to London. When the
Shuberts presented the play at the Casino, New York, it ran for 500 performances,
a record at the time for a musical play. In Melbourne, it ran at the Princess's
Theatre for 165 performances, another record.

Like most vaudeville stars, Louie Freear was caught early. A Cockney, of
Irish extraction, her first stage appearances were made as "Baby Freear," while in
early youth she gained invaluable experience, playing such a role as Puck in one
of Ben Greet's repertory companies. Her first big London success was as the
Slavey in *The Gay Parisienne*, which was played at the Duke of York's in 1896.
Miss Freear contributed that immortal ditty, "Sister Mary Jane's Top Note":

> Sit tight! Hold fast!
>   Mary's going to sing!
> She's going to try her best to crack her throat.
> She starts the bird's a-singing
> And she sets the bells a-ringing—
> Sister Mary Jane's top note.

In *A Chinese Honeymoon* she sang another musical ditty, "Martha spanks the
Grand Pianner."

The Belle of New York

As May Yohe's pretty voice and figure carried *Little Christopher Columbus* to
success and Louie Freear's quaint personality accounted for the runs of *The Gay*

Parisienne and *A Chinese Honeymoon,* so *The Belle of New York* was in debt to Edna May, though Gustav Kerker's music was the outstanding factor. Indeed, Kerker's music has some claim to be regarded as the most tuneful score ever put to a musical-comedy plot. Fifi's "Teach me how to kiss, dear," Ichabod's "Far from Cohoes," "Ze American girl, she walks like zis," "Follow on," Blinky Bill's "She is the Belle of New York"—and all of it in the first act! "When we are married," "The Purity Brigade," "Plump girls and slender girls, solid girls and tender girls," followed and every one was an air to whistle or dance to. The odd characters and a novel background added to the attraction of *The Belle.*

Charles McLellan, who wrote the book, was a brother of George McLellan, director of the New York Casino in 1897, and, with no great faith in the production, George put it on the stage with the aid of George Lederer. Edna May, at the time was only a chorus girl, but during rehearsals the Casino management had the happy idea that she was fitted to the part of the Salvation lassie. However, the first production had no success, almost the only hopeful sign being that Charles Frohman liked it. George Musgrove chanced to be passing through New York, and he also saw *The Belle.* It struck him that it might be worth transplanting to the unlucky Shaftesbury Theatre in London, with which he had family associations, through a marriage into

J. HASSALL

the family of Henrietta Hodson (Mrs. Labouchere). To the amazement of everyone, *The Belle of New York* had a rapturous reception, though the dresses, scenery, and properties were all old. Musgrove, in fact, promised the Shaftesbury company new costumes, if the show was a success.

The Belle earned a profit of £100,000 in its first run and the Musgrove estate later took £87,000 profit from the provincial rights, which McLellan and Lederer had sold for a beggarly £2,000. Needless to say, the company had their new costumes long before the first season ended and Edna May's salary had risen well

above the £8 a week, with which she started at the Shaftesbury. She had a
pretty little voice, but so small experience as an actress that chalk marks on the
stage were needed to show her where to take her stance.

In fact, all the original salaries were small—"summer salaries." J. E. Sullivan,
the polite lunatic, received £13 a week, though he was taking £80 a week when
The Belle was in the full flood of success. Harry Davenport, the Harry Bronson,
Phyllis Rankin, the Fifi, Dan Daly as Ichabod, and Frank Lawton, as Blinky
Bill, all made their names. Blinky Bill's best scene was in the candy store in the
second act. He came in, bought some chocolate, ordered a soft drink, flirted
with the shop-girls, and at last bade them good-bye, and all without uttering a
word, only whistling. Lawton died of consumption in 1914 and left a ten-year-old
boy, the Frank Lawton of to-day, and the husband of Evelyn Laye, who was
the Salvation Army lassie in a revival at the Coliseum in 1942.

Edna May's bewitching face and girlish figure did much for *The Belle*, but
the American chorus did more. George Edwardes sent his Gaiety and Daly's
chorus girls to the Shaftesbury, six at a time, that they might acquire the American
"pep," and English musical comedy has never lost the bias it received from *The
Belle of New York*. The play was revived at the Adelphi in 1901 and at the Lyceum
in 1914, and these only drove home the impression that its power to charm was
imperishable. In addition, it toured the English provinces continuously for thirty
years and, at their height, these provincial rights brought in their lucky owners
£1,000 a week. Bannister Howard and Ben Greet owned them for many years.

Apart from the "great little girl in her queer little gown, the pride of the
Salvation Army," what Edwardian could resist Fifi's:

> O teach me how to kiss, dear,
> Teach me how to squeeze.
> Teach me how to sit upon your sympathetic knees.
> Teach me how to coo, dear,
> Like a turtle dove,
> Teach me how to fondle you,
> Oh, teach me how to love.

They were unsophisticated, the maidens of the days when *The Belle* conquered
London. The American lyric was accepted as very daring.

Edna May was never so well suited to a role again. Perhaps her second best
part was in *Kitty Grey*, at the Apollo in 1901. It had a French original, which
accounted for the fact that there was more plot than patrons of musical comedy
had been led to expect. Edna May played an aggrieved wife, who came to Ada
Reeve, an actress, for advice as to how Maurice Farkoa (Edna May's stage husband) might be redeemed from promiscuous flirtation.

> *Ada Reeve:* Why do men make love to me? Because they never know how they'll find
>   me. You good wives are like safe Consols. A husband is sure of his 2¾ per cent,
>   but he knows he'll never get any more. That's why he speculates.
> *Edna May:* Teach me to speculate.

The part of the actress was played on the first night by the unlucky Evie Greene. When she resigned, the Apollo management was fortunate in finding a brilliant substitute. Miss Reeve began as a child in East End melodrama, and has confessed that her stage manners in the *Kitty Grey* days were less than circumspect. Johnnies, with gold-knobbed ebony sticks, frequented the stalls of musical-comedy houses, and Ada Reeve was not without unknown admirers, who sent flowers, letters, and invitations to supper. In the dressing-room scene Kitty Grey had to open similar letters from imaginary admirers and, reading them, she said to her dresser:

No, Auntie, I'm too tired to see anybody or go out to supper either. Tell them, No!

Upon occasion, Ada Reeve, in the role of Kitty, would produce a letter from a living admirer and read it aloud from the stage, smiling the while upon an offending Johnnie with the eyeglass and white camellia, whose only known address was "The Stalls, Apollo Theatre, Shaftesbury Avenue." Ada Reeve also learnt her job in life in a hard school. When she was fourteen she was singing "I'm a little too young to know, you know," and so well understood by the gallery boys that, at the old Cambridge, they always demanded a concluding Catherine Wheel, which Ada had learnt from her brothers. For several years Ada "obliged" when the boys and girls shouted, "Over, Ada!" But, at last, Ada rebelled. "No, no, I'm grown up now!" As late as 1935, Ada Reeve appeared in cabaret at the Trocadero, where, as a music-hall star, she had earned her first £5. As I write, she is playing still.

Ellaline Terriss and Seymour Hicks

Neither George Dance nor George Musgrove, the discoverer of *The Belle of New York*, belonged to the Edwardes group, but there was a definite secession from the Gaiety when Ellaline Terriss and Seymour Hicks decided to produce musical shows on their own account and went into management at the Vaudeville, with Charles Frohman as capitalist-in-chief. A very few years as leading man at the Gaiety had rendered Seymour far too fiery a brand for the amiable George to handle with comfort. Not only was he an actor, but he was writing musical comedies, melodramas, and other plays, literally by the score. Here are some of the pieces which owe a goodly proportion of their vim to the volatile Seymour, and the list could be easily supplemented—the *Talk of the Town*, the *Earl and the Girl*, *Blue Bell in Fairyland*, *The Cherry Girl*, *My Darling*, *The Gay Gordons*, *A Runaway Girl*, *The Beauty of Bath*, *The Catch of the Season*, constituting no small contribution to the literature of Vaudeville about the turn of the century.

The contribution of Sir Seymour to theatrical history extends beyond musical plays but, from the time George Edwardes baited his book with the magical words, "Leading parts at the Gaiety," it was manifest that musical comedy was destined to develop on lines very different from the old-time burlesque, when Edward Terry, Nellie Farren, Arthur Roberts, and Fred Leslie held the stage.

The personalities of Ellaline Terriss and Seymour Hicks had not a little to do with the change.

It is on record that Ellaline Terriss was nicknamed "The Little Oil-can" in the theatres where she worked. Hers was the faculty of soothing troubled spirits. Caustic wit, physical vim, and other qualities associated with leading ladies in quick-fire musicals did not belong to Ellaline Terriss. The only daughter of William Terriss, beyond a doubt the most popular actor of his time, she escaped the early struggle for recognition which is the lot of most players. At twelve, she danced a hornpipe in a Liverpool pantomime, in which Vesta Tilley was the principal boy, but the solitary appearance was in the nature of a jest, such as friends and relations naturally staged for "Bill" Terriss's pretty little daughter.

Ellaline Terriss's second dramatic effort was no less spontaneous and natural. She wanted to give her father a surprise, and Alfred Calmour, the author, offered to write a playlet. He called it *Cupid's Messenger*, and it was staged in the Theatre Royal drawing-room, with Ellaline in the leading role and Mrs. Terriss and Alfred Calmour supporting. The father of the leading lady was the only member of an enthusiastic audience.

Now it chanced that Beerbohm Tree, at the Haymarket, wanted a one-act play and someone mentioned *Cupid's Messenger*. Momentarily, a lady to play the lead was wanting. Why not Ellaline? The idea no sooner formed itself than a telegram was dispatched, and a career began which was to influence vaudeville history during a couple of decades. The musical comedy achievements of Sir Seymour Hicks were closely associated with those of his future bride.

Miss Terriss, aged seventeen, did not suffer from stage fright. On the contrary, she enjoyed every minute of her week's engagement. At the end she was richer by five pounds, which she spent upon a ruby ring, christened "Herbert." "Herbert" is in her jewel casket to this day. Indeed, the debut of "Bill" Terriss's pretty daughter was so successful that Charles Wyndham offered a three-years' engagement, the salary being £1 a week for the first year, £8 a week for the second year, and £12 a week for the third year.

No better coach for a young actress could have been found. While understudying Mary Moore, Ellaline learnt to be a trouper, ready to give as well as to take. She has told us that it has been her custom throughout life to go to bed every afternoon, before acting in the evening. Marie Tempest cultivated the same habit.

Edward Seymour Hicks was about three months Ellaline's senior. Before they exchanged a word Hicks had written the words for two little songs, composed by his future wife, and they had been published by Chappell. They met at the Court Theatre, where both of them were members of a company, for which Hicks had written a playlet, *The New Sub*. It was part of a famous triple bill, in which *A Pantomime Rehearsal* was the principal item. Terriss was touring in America and there was no one to stop the young people falling in love.

Moreover, as they were earning something like £22 a week, there seemed no reason for postponing marriage until Papa Terriss could be consulted. Ellaline and Seymour, therefore, indulged in the nearest thing to a runaway marriage which such a bride could contemplate. They were married at a London registry office and the wedding breakfast, a dish of Irish stew, at the Café Monico, was followed by a matinée appearance.

The following Christmas witnessed Ellaline in Oscar Barrett's pantomime at the Lyceum, as the perfect Cinderella. The eve of the performance was devoted to taking the frills and furbelows off Cinderella's dress in order that she might be the real household drudge of the fairy-tale, before she suffered the sea change into the Prince's bride. The last-minute change assured a triumph.

Meanwhile, what of Sir Seymour as actor? He was a Jersey boy and the son of a Major in the 42nd Highlanders, but he did not reach the stage by way of the public school and the University, as some young actors were doing at the time. His beginning was an engagement at the Grand, Islington, as a super at a shilling an hour. For this modest stipend he appeared as a Guardsman, a convict, and gamekeeper in the melodrama, *In the Ranks*, in which Charles Warner was the suffering hero. To his exploits as actor, Sir Seymour added some skill in maintaining pressure upon the india-rubber bags which fed the limelight in those days. Later, Seymour learnt more of the actor's craft from Mrs. Kendal, as Ellaline learnt her job in life from Charles Wyndham. Thus, at the age of twenty-two, Seymour was able to make a small hit in Barrie's *Walker, London*. The engagement at the Court followed.

Now, in 1894, George Edwardes not only wanted a leading lady for the Gaiety, but a light comedian, likely to develop into a successor of Arthur Roberts. Ellaline Terriss selected herself, after her triumph as Cinderella, and Seymour was manifestly a vital spark. So Edwardes decided to engage both of them. Ellaline rehearsed for *The Shop Girl*, but fell ill and Ada Reeve played Bessie Brent in her stead on the first night. Later, Ellaline joined the company and sang Leslie Stuart's "Louisiana Lou" and the haunting American melody, "I want yer, ma honey." Her success was immediate and she stayed at the Gaiety for five years, playing leading lady in *My Girl*, *The Circus Girl*, and *The Runaway Girl*. She was playing in *The Circus Girl* on December 16th, 1897, when Terriss was murdered outside the Adelphi by a lunatic actor. The time was just before curtain-rise and an understudy was hurriedly sent on to the Gaiety stage, in place of Seymour Hicks. The understudy played through his opening scene without guessing the reason for the manifest excitement among the audience.

Miss Terriss's fresh charm and arch humour made her an ideal heroine in musical comedy. Her sense of humour, indeed, followed her in semi-private life. Years after their Gaiety appearances, Hicks was holding an audition at a West End theatre, when a heavily veiled lady appeared. At once, the quick-eyed Seymour said quietly: "Give that old lady a chair."

Two or three actresses displayed their youthful paces, and then the call: "Next, please," brought the new-comer to the piano. She sang "The boy guessed right." At the end of the first verse, Seymour said: "Please go on."

The elderly lady was assured that she had scored. "Really, Mr. Hicks?" she piped.

"Yes, my wife used to do that song, but you sing it a thousand times better than she ever did!" was the retort.

If George Edwardes had had his will, Ellaline would have stayed in musical comedy indefinitely. Ellen Terry was responsible for ending the engagement. She said:

"Ella, my child, this form of entertainment, when you have achieved all you can (as you have), only means standing on the top of a ladder, with a hundred young women pulling at your pretty petticoats. Make an end of it!"

Seymour Hicks being like-minded, the young couple from the Gaiety joined forces with Charles Frohman, at a joint salary of £75 a week, plus one-third of any profits. As they ran no financial risks, it was an ideal contract. There were a couple of failures at the Criterion and then a long series of successes at the Vaudeville, including Barrie's *Quality Street*. Among the musical shows at the Vaudeville were *Bluebell in Fairyland*, with a book by Seymour Hicks and music by Walter Slaughter, which had 294 performances, and *The Catch of the Season*, with a book by Hicks and Cosmo Hamilton, and music by Herbert Haines and Evelyn Baker, which achieved 621 performances. Zena Dare was "the Catch of the Season," this being her first grown-up part, and Ethel Matthews, Olive Morell, Rosina Fillippi, Laurence Caird, Alexandra Carlisle, Eva Carrington, Sylvia Storey, Camille Clifford, and Barbara Deane were other members of one of the strongest companies which has ever appeared in musical comedy. Barbara Deane, with her fine voice, was destined for big successes, but she left the stage to be married. Camille Clifford was the Gibson Girl, with the uptilted nose, the Empire gown, which displayed shoulders and hips so happily, and the not-to-be-forgotten glide which made her voiceless appearance in the *Prince of Pilsen* so memorable in 1903. Later Miss Clifford sang "A Gibson Girl" song in musical comedy, but it was the first non-speaking role at the Shaftesbury which constitutes the real memory.

As the hero in *The Catch of the Season*, Seymour made an attempt to convert the young males of the metropolis to wear knee-breeches and silk stockings, in place of the customary black trousers of evening wear. The effort failed.

In *Bluebell in Fairyland*, Ellaline sang "Only a Penny, Sir," a variant upon Nellie Farren's famous number. For the rest, the author emphasised the London note. *Bluebell* opens in the Strand, and then passes to Bluebell's garret in Drury Lane, the time being midnight. Thence, the transition to Fairyland and the garden of the Castle was easy. The chorus included flower-girls, shoeblacks, fairies, birds, trumpeters, and pages at the Court of the Sleepy King, a very seasonable mixture. It is not surprising that Barrie wrote the part of Wendy in *Peter Pan* for Ellaline, after seeing her in *Bluebell*. Seymour Hicks was to have been the original Captain Hook, but other engagements necessitated changes in Barrie's plan, so Gerald du Maurier replaced Hicks and Hilda Trevelyan was the Wendy.

When Frohman's agreement with the Gatti Brothers expired, Seymour Hicks had accumulated such evidence of success that a bigger theatre than the Vaudeville seemed essential. The time was before 1914 and money was to be had on easy terms. Seymour was a product of what he called "The Vintage Years," and there was no reason to think they might not be prolonged indefinitely. They were years when an income-tax of 1s. in the £ was regarded as somewhat scandalous and oysters cost no more than 3s. 6d. a dozen, "gaspers" a farthing apiece, and whisky a mere 3s. 6d. a bottle. Accordingly, Hicks built a theatre of his own, the Aldwych, and acquired substantial interests in others, including one named after himself, but later known as the Globe. At the Hicks in 1907, Seymour produced *My Darling*, with a Palais Royal plot, though Marie Stud-holme was cast for the part of Joy Blossom, in order to fit the Parisian café scenes for London consumption. For himself and Ellaline, Seymour wrote and produced *The Beauty of Bath*, with music by Herbert Haines, who had written the score for *My Darling*. Before the first night of *The Beauty of Bath*, Hicks trained a black cat to walk across the stage in front of the footlights before the curtain rose. The cat made history, for *The Beauty of Bath* ran a year, mainly owing to Ellaline Terriss, whose charm had a delightful setting, thanks to the talent of her husband as a producer of musical shows. The curtain rose upon the foyer of the Mascot Theatre at Bath, where Sir Timothy Bun was to be seen with his adopted daughters, the Twelve Bath Buns. To them was added Ellaline Terriss, duly fitted with an ingénue lyric of the period, "The Things you never learnt at school":

> When I left school I had been taught
> So many things that, oh!
> I thought I knew just everything
> A little girl could know.
> I studied all the simple rules of plain arithmetic,
> But when I went out in the world
> I found out very quick . . . there are . . .
>
> Lots of things you never learn at school,
> And I found them most upsetting as a rule.
> I found out, for example, that the simplest rule of three,
> Was bringing two together, and a third for gooseberry.
> Now they never, never, never taught me that at school.
> No, they never taught me that at school.

In the second act Ellaline Terriss made a spectacular entry in a flower-covered litter, borne by flunkies in uniforms and accompanied by a chorus of girls gowned in blues, pinks, and whites. They were associated with an early Herman Darewski

8

song, "Au revoir, my little Hyacinth," and led to the "David Garrick" episode, in which the hero pretended to be tipsy and only succeeded in making Ellaline still more sure that this was the man of her heart. In token thereof the two of them, white hair and bespectacled, sang the Bridge Duet, with kisses as the only stakes.

> What do you say?
> Partner, I leave it to you.

For the rest, Seymour added a fellow Jersey woman to his company, in the person of Ivy St. Helier, and she stayed three years, this being her first London engagement. An amusing quarrel scene was played by Maudi Darrell and Sydney Fairbrother, the first being dressed as Edna May, while Miss Fairbrother wore the black velvet of Camille Clifford's Gibson Girl. Maudi Darrell was a daughter of Didcott, the music-hall agent, and had talent which would have carried her far, if she had not died in early womanhood. She was the first wife of Ian Bullough, whom Lily Elsie married afterwards.

From Bath, the versatile Seymour moved to the Scottish Highlands, and the *The Gay Gordons* was the result. It was produced at the Aldwych in 1907, with music by Guy Jones, a brother of Sidney, the composer of *A Gaiety Girl*, though Herman Darewski composed the popular Ellaline Terriss number, "Humpty, Dumpty," with its pantomime play with a knotted handkerchief. Peggy, the heiress, wanted to be loved for herself alone and changed places with the daughter of a touring Punch-and-Judy man. As the daughter, Zena Dare sang "Flies around the honey-pot." Of course, Ellaline won her Earl before curtain-fall and Zena did not leave the footlights heart-broken. Seymour Hicks, as maker of the libretto, saw to that.

It was all too good to last. Sad to relate, Seymour was running into trouble and the first hint came when *The Dashing Little Duke* was staged at the Hicks, with Ellaline playing the young Duc de Richelieu. A French version with music by Lecocq had been very popular in the 'seventies and Frank Tours provided some pretty music for the book by Seymour Hicks, but, in spite of the charm of Ellaline, in a Louis Quatorze breeches part, *The Dashing Little Duke* failed commercially. The venture lost £13,000. By the middle of 1914, Sir Seymour found himself facing a loss of £47,000 and liabilities totalling £14,000 more. "Don't go bankrupt!" was Ellaline's advice and her husband accepted it fully. While his wife earned a big salary playing sketches in the music-halls, Seymour went on tour, earning £400 and £500 a week, figures which could not be approached in London, apart from theatrical gambles. In six years the popular couple had put the financial situation to rights and the incubus of debt was removed. A courageous effort, and fully rewarded.

Frank Curzon in Management

Frank Curzon was the son of a successful business man in Chester, proprietor of the Dee Oil Company, and became interested in theatrical affairs as a member of an amateur theatrical club in Manchester. After some small experience as an actor, Frank Curzon went into partnership with Charles Hawtrey and shared in the fortune made by the 544 performance-run of *A Message from Mars*, at the Avenue in 1899. Then he bought the Strand and soon was controlling seven or eight London theatres. The amazing success of *A Chinese Honeymoon*, done at the Old Strand in 1901 (1,075 performances), persuaded Curzon to turn his attention to musical comedy and alone, or in partnership with George Edwardes, he presented at the Prince of Wales's *Three Little Maids*, *The School Girl*, *Lady Madcap*, *The Little Cherub*, *Miss Hook of Holland*, *My Mimosa Maid*, the *King of Cadonia*, and *The Balkan Princess*. The later theatrical career of Frank Curzon, in association with Gerald du Maurier, Dennis Eadie, and Gladys Cooper, was concerned with straight drama.

Frank Curzon's second wife was pretty Isabel Jay, of the Savoy Company, who had appeared as Elsie Maynard at the Savoy, when she was only eighteen and fresh from the Royal Academy of Music. It was an appropriate training-ground, as she was a descendant of Dr. Jay, a well-known composer and violinist in the eighteenth century, who also had associations with the Academy. Isabel Jay had won the first medal for operatic singing at the Academy, so she was just the material which Gilbert wanted. She stayed at the Savoy until 1901, playing soprano leads in the famous revivals of the period. Her appearances under Frank Curzon's management included Winnie Willoughby in *The Girl Behind the Counter*, Olivia in *The Vicar of Wakefield*, Sally in *Miss Hook of Holland*, Paulette in *My Mimosa Maid*, Princess Marie in *King of Cadonia*, Christine in *Dear Little Denmark*, and Princess Stephanie in *The Balkan Princess*.

The Balkan Princess was a typical Curzon production. It had a Ruritanian background and was from the pen of Freddy Lonsdale, assisted by Frank Curzon. Bertram Wallis, the Grand Duke Sergius, had been banished from the Court of Balaria, and was revenging himself upon the late King by writing treasonable articles against the reigning Princess in the Radical newspapers. Isabel Jay (Princess Stephanie) determined to tame the rebel duke, and, duly disguised, came upon him at a Bohemian restaurant, where the Duke was drinking to the "downfall of Stephanie of Balaria." The lady promptly lost her temper and her sense of humour, so the Archduke was arrested. Manifestly, there could be only one way out of such a situation. It was found when Princess and Sergius agreed to "rule together." Lauri de Frece as Blatz and James Blakeley, with the famous smirk, as Henri the waiter, provided the necessary humour, and with them was Mabel Sealby as Magda.

> I char at two and three and four,
> I char at five, and then,
> To-morrow at five,
> If I'm alive,
> I char all over again.

Lady Madcap was another typical Frank Curzon production. It was given at the Prince of Wales's in 1904, the book being by Colonel Newnham-Davis, with aid from Paul Rubens, who also wrote some very tuneful music. The first leading lady was Adrienne Augarde, but early in the run she handed over the part of Betty to dainty Madge Crichton. The plot was concerned with the daughter of an Earl, who, in her father's absence, converted Egbert Castle into a Liberty Hall for the officers of the East Anglian Hussars. Thus Egbert Castle became the background for a troop of plump little page-boys, pretty housemaids, and aristocratic footmen, who assisted Lady Betty in her love-affair with a certain Trooper Smith, whom the exigencies of the plot compelled "to buttle," though, in fact, he was a millionaire.

G. P. Huntley was the millionaire trooper who "liked to buttle fearfully," at any rate when pretty Lady Betty was in cap and apron. Though his eyeglass, his "super-fatted" voice, his rambling patter, and his "half-past eight feet" tended to deceive, G. P. was an accomplished actor. Like Seymour Hicks, he learnt his trade under Mrs. Kendal, and, at his best, could improvise for minutes upon end, possibly upon a theme as abstruse as "the sex-appeal of the olive," or as simple as the homely telephone, which, somehow, reminded G. P. of a skinny widow, with her mouth wide open. The reason for the malice displayed towards this bit of official furniture was that Huntley rang up his sweetheart and the call took so long to come through that the girl was married and, moreover, had six children! "Filleted Flappers" were a curiosity of the animal kingdom which also interested Huntley. During the long run of *The Kiss Call* at the Gaiety, with Binnie Hale, Stanley Lupino, and Gwendoline Brogden, G. P. was particularly agile in his patter, Evelyn Laye being one of the "filleted flappers" who stirred him to reminiscence.

West End audiences tended to identify G. P. Huntley with dude roles, but he was equally good as an elderly comic; for example, in *Miss Hook of Holland*, a Frank Curzon production at the Prince of Wales's in 1907, for which Paul Rubens was primarily responsible. The first act was laid in the Cheese Market at Arndyk and later scenes in Hook's liqueur distillery at Amsterdam, offering opportunities for quaint characterisation and novel incident. Thus, Isabel Jay, with a chorus in Dutch attire, sang:

> Little Miss Wooden Shoes,
> Goes where she choose.
> All the neighbourhood were knowing
> Which direction she was going,
> By the clatter, clatter, clatter,
> Of her little wooden shoes.

As for the second leading lady, Gracie Leigh, maidservant to the Hooks, she dilated upon the number and variety of feminine petticoats in Holland:

I've a little pink petty from Peter,
And a little blue petty from John,
And I've one, green and yellow,
From some other fellow—
And one that I haven't got on.

Like Lionel Monckton, Paul Rubens was of the public-school type, and his first song, "Trixie, from the Town of Upper Tooting," was commissioned by George Edwardes while Rubens was still at the 'Varsity. He composed it on a small-scale yacht piano in George Grossmith's dressing-room at the Gaiety, where Jerome Kern was later to write "They didn't believe me" and other popular "Gee-Gee" numbers. From this beginning, Paul Rubens went on to write the numbers which Ellaline Terriss sang in the second edition of *The Shop Girl*, "The Little Chinchilla" and "The China Egg." Quickly he developed astonishing facility in turning out librettos, lyrics, and music. Seated at a piano, he could write a successful song in a few minutes. He had great charm and wit, but was hampered by ill-health. Typical of his humour was the song which Leedham Bantock sang as the Colonel in *Lady Madcap*:

Oh, the boot loved the beetle,
The beetle barred the boot.
The beetle never thought the boot
Could be so big a brute.
But a foot was in the boot
And the beetle didn't scoot;
So the boot got the beetle
And the beetle got the boot!

Other memories of *Lady Madcap* are Madge Crichton singing "Love a maid, love her little dog," and Maurice Farkoa making love to pretty Delia Mason to the lilt of another effort by Paul Rubens:

I like you in velvet,
I love you in plush
In satin you're like your own lovely blush.
You're charming in silk or a plain woollen shawl,
But you're simply delightful in—(then came a prolonged
pause and Farkoa's climax)—in *anything* at all!

Early in the century Maurice Farkoa, with his tuft of white hair and his charming impudences, enjoyed immense popularity. Born in Smyrna, he was half French and half English, but on the stage the French side was dominant. His early stage appearances were as a duettist, with his cousin, Fysher—the Fysher-Farkoa duettist. Maurice Farkoa finally drifted to America, where he died.

For his own *Three Little Maids*, at the Apollo in 1902, Rubens wrote the tuneful "Miller's Daughter." Hilda Moody sang the song:

> She was a miller's daughter,
> And lived beside the mill;
> Yes, there were flies on the water,
> But she was flier still!

Robert Courtneidge comes from Manchester

Robert Courtneidge was another purveyor of vaudeville in the years between 1900 and 1914. To his credit stand two outstanding achievements, *The Arcadians* and Edward German's *Tom Jones*.

Robert Courtneidge came of sturdy but poor Scottish stock. After he ran away from home to join a theatrical company, he had more than his share of the kicks which were incidental to provincial touring in the 'seventies and 'eighties. In youth, Courtneidge played small parts in the companies of such tragedians as Barry Sullivan and Charles Dillon, earning 12s. a week. A spell of exceptional good fortune might mean 25s. a week. Late in the 'eighties Courtneidge had achieved a certain position and George Musgrove gave him £25 a week, to join a Gaiety company touring in Australia, in *Esmeralda* and *Faust Up to Date*. He stayed on to play Gama in *Princess Ida*. Thus, his daughter Cicely was born in Sydney, before her father returned to England to begin a seven years' management of the Prince's Theatre, Manchester, where Cicely made her first stage appearance as Peaseblossom in *A Midsummer Night's Dream*.

A remarkable production of *Cinderella* in Manchester, which was later brought to the Adelphi, London, revealed Courtneidge's capacity as a producer of musical shows and George Edwardes called him in to direct the production of *The Duchess of Dantzic*, as has been told. When this very promising play came to a premature end, Courtneidge determined to test his fortunes alone and produced *The Blue Moon*, by Harold Ellis and Percy Greenbank, with music by Howard Talbot and Paul Rubens, at the Lyric. The venture was successful, thanks to a brilliant cast, including Willie Edouin, Walter Passmore, Carrie Moore, Billie Burke, and Florence Smithson (her first London appearance). *The Dairymaids*, by A. M. Thompson and Paul Rubens, followed in 1906, and ran a year at the Apollo, with Dan Rolyat making his first London appearance and Phyllis Dare as the heroine. A feature was the novel scene in which the chorus swung Indian clubs.

By this time Courtneidge had proved his worth as a musical-comedy manager and was ready for even bigger things. He bought a long lease of the Shaftesbury Theatre, and also spent £12,000 upon improvements in the auditorium. For the all-important play, Mark Ambient came along with the first rough idea, based upon a mortal accidentally falling into Arcadia from an aeroplane, and then coming to earth at the head of a mission, charged with the task of converting London to Arcadian manners and morals. Mark Ambient could not carry his

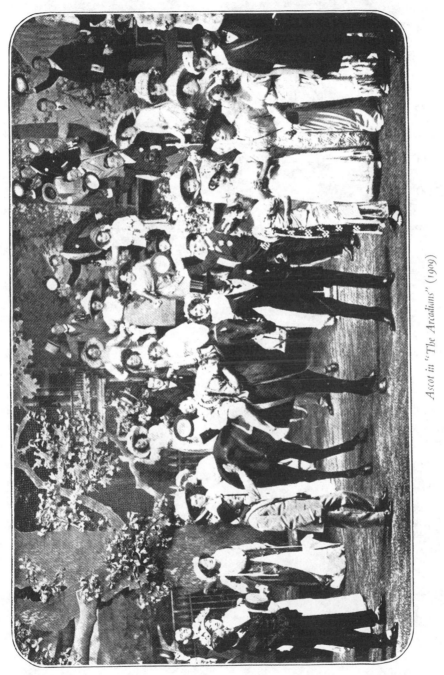

Ascot in "The Arcadians" (1909)

Nelson Keys   *The Deuce and*   *Harry Welchman and*   *Phyllis Dare and*
'Bobbie'   *Dan Rolyat*   *Florence Smithson*   *Ada Blanche*

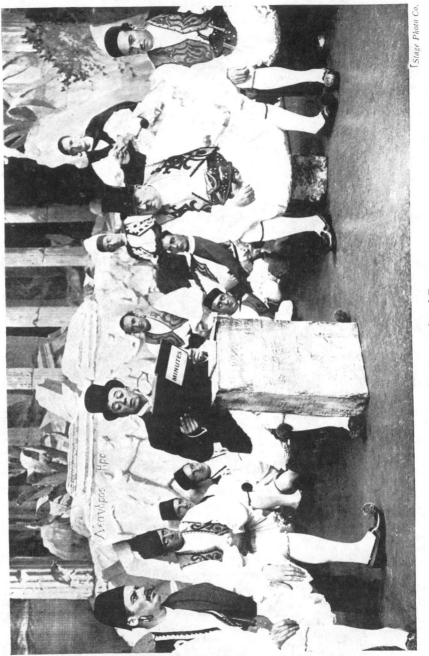

Leslie Henson and Fred Emney
in "Going Greek," at the Gaiety, 1937

promising scheme through and A. M. Thompson was called in to finish the book. He did so with some aid from Courtneidge, who suggested the matter for the third and concluding act. Doody the Jockey was Thompson's contribution to Mark Ambient's story, and he also suggested the "motter" which Arthur Wimperis used so effectively, in the unhappy Doody's famous song, "Always merry and bright.."

Apparently, Courtneidge was the only principal who really believed in the future of *The Arcadians*, yet it proved as popular as the best of its rivals. The music by Lionel Monckton and Howard Talbot delights to this day and, after a first run of two and a half years, the play toured the provinces for another ten years. And this without any excessive expenditure upon production and a cast which did not include any very highly paid principals. Dan Rolyat took £50 a week as chief comedian, Lester £35, Phyllis Dare £45, and Florence Smithson £30. Nelson Keys, making his first London appearance, was content with £5 a week, and the chorus of Arcadians included Marie Blanche and Cicely Debenham at £2 a week apiece. Nevertheless, from the moment Mr. James Smith descended in his aeroplane upon the glade in Arcadia and was dispossessed of his mutton-chop whiskers in the magical Well of Truth, the success of Courtneidge's venture was assured. Something new was promised and something new was accomplished. The Arcadian Sombra was played by Florence Smithson, "the Nightingale of Wales," whose most characteristic effort was "Glad is my Heart," in which she reached a long *F* in alt. and even the high *A*.

Nothing in *The Arcadians* remains more vividly in memory than the unhappy jockey, Peter Doody. In 1905, Alfred Lester was playing in a sketch, in which he enacted a disgruntled scene-shifter, whose ambition was to play Hamlet. Sir Alfred Butt heard of the turn and gave Lester a chance at the Palace. The scene-shifter was followed by Lester's "Waiter," in which the forlorn Lester was asked: "Where's the proprietor?" His answer was: "Gone out to his dinner." Unhappy Lester, he had been "waiting" for sixteen years, and his tips over the period totalled 3*s*.! No customer ever came to that restaurant twice! In the role, Lester's invention was tireless. A piece of linoleum was discovered in a customer's soup! "It may not have been strained," explained the funereal one. There were fears that the champagne might be flat! The waiter inflated a sugar-bag and burst it, to ensure the requisite "pop." But at all times and in all parts the same lugubrious tones, the same comic despair, and, always, chuckles from fully satisfied audiences.

Alfred Lester came of theatrical stock and had toured the provinces for twenty years before he came to the Palace. Later, at the Gaiety, Lester played in *The New Aladdin* and *Havana*, and then the Shaftesbury, and the part of Peter Doody, in which he plumbed the depths of self-imposed melancholy when pretty Phyllis Dare offered him a flower "for luck." The Jockey was about to mount an ill-favoured brute in the race for the Ascot Gold Cup.

"What might you call this flower, Miss?" asked Lester.

"Love lies bleeding."

"That's what I expect to be doing in a minute," moaned the unhappy Alfred.

Oddly enough, Courtneidge was slow to appreciate how much *The Arcadians* owed to Lester. When the actor dressed for Peter Doody on the first night there was a letter on his table giving him a fortnight's notice, though he only stood at £10 a week on the pay-roll of the Shaftesbury. By chance, Lester did not open the envelope until after the famous first night. Next morning he was in a position to sign a fresh agreement with Courtneidge, but at £30 a week, instead of the original £10.

Courtneidge's production of the racing scene was superb; in particular, the ingenious device by which the stage players followed the horses with their racing glasses, as the race proceeded, in imagination, somewhere about the line of the dress-circle. In the same scene an effort was made to reproduce fully up-to-date feminine fashion, the "horrible hobble" skirt being one example and its successor, "the divided skirt," another. The very long run made numerous redressings of *The Arcadians* necessary, and more than one eccentricity of fashion exhausted its vogue before the play exhausted its popular appeal.

Florence Smithson was the daughter of a Welsh theatrical manager, and was only three years old when she made her first stage appearance in pantomime. Her first London hit was in *The Blue Moon* in 1905, when the Nightingale of Wales imitated the song of birds with astonishing ease and finish. Plainly, comic opera had a recruit with the talents of a real opera singer and Robert Courtneidge, who had discovered the girl, intended to exploit them. Her first husband was Dan Rolyat, the Simplicitas in *The Arcadians*, who rode the Deuce in that memorable race for the Ascot Gold Cup. During a later tour Rolyat was kicked by the racehorse and never fully recovered. He returned to the stage for a while, but died in 1927, aged forty-five.

The Mousmé followed *The Arcadians*. It was a Japanese play with an astonishing earthquake scene, part of a remarkable effort by Conrad Tritschler, who spent two years devising the scenic effects. Lionel Monckton, Howard Talbot, and Wimperis, fresh from their *Arcadians* triumph, all worked hard, and Alexander Thompson's story of the geisha who sold her voice, but not her love, to the proprietor of a tea-shop, seemed promising. The lovely cherry-blossom scene in Act One and the Tea-shop gardens, with the hanging wistarias, are still remembered, so is Florence Smithson singing "The Temple Bell" song, yet *The Mousmé* involved Courtneidge in a loss of £20,000 and destroyed his confidence in large-scale musical productions. He restored his theatrical fortunes by less spectacular ventures. *Princess Caprice*, starring George Graves; *Oh, Oh, Delphine*, a musical comedy from the French with music by Ivan Caryll followed; then *The Pearl Girl*, by Basil Hood, with music by Hugo Felix and Howard Talbot; and *The Cinema Star*, chiefly remarkable because it was adapted from the German by Jack Hulbert, Courtneidge's son-in-law, for he had married the highly popular Cicely.

By this time the first World War was imminent and in the war period Court' neidge's chief production in the realm of musical comedy was *My Lady Frayle*. Arthur Wimperis and Max Pemberton told how Lady Frayle, in Faust'like fashion, was rejuvenated by the Devil, played as a modern character by Cecil Humphreys. Cicely Debenham, promoted from the chorus, was the Lady Frayle. He also produced *Young England* at Daly's, that is, the light opera of the name by Basil Hood, with some charming music by the Australian, G. H. Clutsam, and Hubert Bath. Some years earlier Sir Thomas Beecham produced Clutsam's *A Summer Night*, with a setting in Tuscany and a plot taken from Margaret of Navarre's *Heptameron*. The fanciful and humorous score of *Young England* was promising, but Basil Hood's book failed to give the musicians a full opportunity.

Berriment at the Adelphi

Mention has been made of a periodic longing among players, composers, and even producers for well'knit plots and not a few concerted efforts were made to satisfy it. One of the most successful was at the Adelphi during the first World War, where two of Pinero's farces were put to music and had highly successful runs under the titles of *The Boy*, a version of *The Magistrate*, and *Who's Hooper*, a version of *In Chancery*.

The Magistrate was produced at the Court in 1885, and the plot required that a highly respectable official should permit a stepson to take him to a night club, at a time when it was to be raided by the police. Edward Terry and Arthur Cecil had identified themselves with the part of Mr. Posket, so W. H. Berry had no easy task when he proposed to play the principal part in *The Boy*. In fact, the police'court scene was played without any music and Berry aimed at a charac' terisation as true to type as that of Arthur Cecil, when he created Mr. Posket at the Court Theatre.

Some of the success of *The Boy* was due to Bill Berry's topical song, "I want to go to Bye'bye," in the last act, and his amusing business with the pumping quill'pens, the climax of which was Berry's insane query as he pointed to the ink'pot, "Who's been filling this with india'rubber ink?" Neither the song nor the business with the quill'pens were attuned to the mood of Pinero's farce, but the dramatist's excellent story went far to explain and justify the run of just over 800 performances. In his day Berry was almost alone among English comedians in his capacity for inducing the full'throated laughter, which makes theatrical audiences rock in their seats, from stalls to gallery. The jests which produce these "belly'laughs" are never subtle. For example, Connie Ediss was once asked:

"Where did you meet all those women?"

"Cowes," replied Connie.

"Yes, I know," retorted Berry, "but where did you meet them?"

The audience roared, without troubling to remember that, in any case, the witticism was only a variation upon a familiar W. S. Gilbert jest. Gilbert looked in at the Savoy box'office and asked for Miss Bond.

"She's round behind," was the reply.

"Yes, I know," said Gilbert, "but where is she?"

A typical "berriment" occurs in a couple of lines in Jerome Kern's romance, *Blue Eyes*, the play in which Evelyn Laye had to make love to Bertram Wallis, as the Duke of Cumberland, the "butcher" of Culloden. Berry was Pilbeam, one of His Majesty's Company of Players.

> *Moll:* I always put violet in my bath.
> *Pilbeam:* So would I, but I don't know Violet.

Bill Berry had to work hard before his laughter-creating capacity came to him. As a young man he was a clerk in the employ of Keith Prowse, the theatre-ticket agents. In this capacity, he saw all the stars of the day—Irving, Nellie Farren, Arthur Roberts, and the rest—from the inside of the theatre and bethought himself of the possibility of adding a pound or two a week to his slender earnings by singing at cricket or football clubs in the Tottenham district. He might make 7s. 6d. a night plus "beer," if he was lucky, though 4s. was a more usual fee. Then Berry discovered that his happy capacity for radiating good-humour seemed to be creating a Bill Berry public at Yarmouth, where he went for a couple of weeks' holiday in 1895. He stayed for six long summers, working on the old Wellington Pier. Soon the 4s. a night had increased to 50s. a week; an improvement, but not enough. Accordingly, Berry wrote the sketch, *Music Mad*, and played it with his pretty red-headed wife, Kitty Hanson. He was now working with the Bohemians, a pierrot troupe, with its headquarters at Bournemouth.

By this time Berry had a considerable gramophone public, as a singer of comic songs. On the strength of this he and his wife were called to the London Pavilion for a few weeks. Berry was a husband troubled by a singing wife who trilled at breakfast and rouladed at lunch, Berry replying with prosaic refrains from current comic songs. A few weeks later the struggle towards the West End of London ended. "Gee-Gee" Grossmith and his wife, together with H. B. Irving and Dorothea Baird, chanced to see Bill Berry and Kitty Hanson in one of their musical sketches at Bournemouth, and Grossmith, in search of talent for George Edwardes's many enterprises, asked Berry to come to London for an audition. Berry came, saw George Edwardes, and conquered.

His comic features went some way, but, primarily, Berry's success was due to the ten years of hard work at Yarmouth and Broadstairs, before all sorts of holiday folk, in fair and foul weather. It was with Berry as with Leslie Henson, Renee and Billie Houston, Stanley Holloway, Elsie and Doris Waters, Dave Burnaby and the Western Brothers, all of whom learnt to hold audiences through long experience with pierrot troupes. Appearances at a seaside pavilion were not quite so testing as those at a provincial music-hall where an earlier generation of entertainers learnt their business, but they were enough.

Fortified by such experience, Berry entered upon his ten years at Daly's and the Gaiety before he passed to the Adelphi, after the death of George Edwardes.

The first World War was in progress and soldiers on leave found the full-fruited comedian greatly to their liking. He timed his retorts so neatly and could put over a comic song so surely.

In *Tina*, Berry's first show at the Adelphi, there was a jolly duet with Phyllis Dare, "Let me introduce you to my father." *High Jinks* was another successful production, which exuded "berriment," thanks to Dr. Wilkie Thorne, with the big bath sponge which bounced, in as unexpected a fashion as the quill-pens in *The Boy*. Maisie Gay, Marie Blanche, Peter Gawthorne, Tom Walls, the statuesque Violet Blythe and her diminutive husband, "Nipper" Lupino Lane, were other members of a strong cast. In 1921 was produced *The Golden Moth*, a story written round Robert Macaire and Jacques Strop, his manservant, Robert Michaelis being in his best form as Robert. Bill Berry, as the Duchess, in a dress of green sequins, supplemented with nodding ostrich plumes, made the third act of *The Golden Moth* memorable. P. G. Wodehouse and Fred Thompson wrote the book and Ivor Novello provided the music.

Various managements were responsible for Adelphi productions during that memorable decade, William Boosey, Grossmith and Laurillard and William Gaunt, the Bradford millionaire, among them, but always Bill Berry was the principal attraction. After he had made 2,000 appearances, the Adelphi management produced a new contract.

"I think I go with the gas brackets," sighed W. H. B., with a lift of the expressive eyebrows, as he added his signature to the contract.

In this record of Anglo-Saxon vaudeville, little need be said of the line of operettas based upon the lives and music of Schubert (*Lilac Time*) and Tschaikowsky (*Catherine*). Similarly, the airs of Chopin were exploited by Mr. Clutsam, in *The Damask Rose*, which Robert Courtneidge produced, seeking a success comparable with *Lilac Time*. But Chopin's love romances proved less suitable for a comic opera than the happy-go-lucky existence of Schubert and his student friends in *Lilac Time*. However, the Ballade in A Flat and the A Major Polonaise gave Mr. Clutsam far more engaging melodies than the popular jazz rhythms of the hour and wedded to a chorus in spreading skirts of the 1830's resulted in an entertainment pleasant enough to deserve more success than, in fact, it achieved.

The delightful *Chocolate Soldier*, with its Anglo-Irish flavour and charming music by Oscar Straus, calls for more than bare mention, the more because it was freely adapted from Bernard Shaw's *Arms and the Man*, and, therefore, operetta, as opposed to go-as-you-please musical comedy or old-time burlesque.

In fact, only the first act of the musical play bore any resemblance to Mr. Shaw's original, so it is not surprising that the programme on the opening night offered "apologies to Mr. Shaw for an unauthorised parody on one of his comedies." In fact, Oscar Straus composed the music before libretto and music were sent to Mr. Shaw for inspection and approval, with a cheque for several thousand pounds. To the astonishment of the promoting syndicate, the cheque was returned. Shaw refused his sanction. An appeal to Shaw's good-nature, as opposed to

Shaw's banking account, was more successful. He granted permission to the adaptors to use his plot, but refused to accept payment in any form. He saw very clearly that the only part of the book which showed any real invention was his own contribution, in which the Chocolate Soldier entered Nadina's bedroom and was hidden for the night. With Act II the opera reverted to type, and type plays are not plays with which Mr. Shaw desires intimate associations. The original cast was delightful. C. H. Workman, the Bumerli; Constance Drever, as Nadina, the Raina of Shaw's play; the handsome Tasmanian, Roland Cunningham, as Alexis Spiridoff. Never did baritone twirl a moustache with better effect. "I am never wrong." Or again:

> *Nadina:* My hero! I ought to be very proud of you.
> *Alexis:* Indeed, you ought.

The point of the jest lay in the fact that both were posing and Nadina, in particular, knew that her heart had already been transferred to the matter-of-fact but dependable Bumerli. Apart from the very welcome comedy element in the basic plot, *The Chocolate Soldier* owed its vogue to Oscar Straus's music. In the opening act, audiences sensed that this was not just pleasant melody furbished up with alien orchestrations, but musicianly light opera, rendered by real singers and supported by an orchestra which knew its business. The duet, "Oh, you little chocolate soldier man," and Nadina's letter song were delightful numbers, while Lempriere Pringle, as Massakroff, showed the value operatic training could lend to the lighter musical forms. The words fitted to the famous waltz ran:

> Come! Come! I love you only,
>   My heart is true.
> Come! Come! my life is lonely
>   I long for you. . . .

Another interesting migrant from Vienna in the pre-war period was *Night Birds*, a version of *Die Fledermaus*, with the music of Johann Strauss, which was produced at the Lyric by Michael Faraday, following the highly successful run of *The Chocolate Soldier*. Constance Drever played the Countess Rosalinda, the part which Ruth Naylor played in the still more effective revival in 1945. *Gay Rosalinda* at the Palace Theatre, with Richard Tauber in the conductor's chair, was the version produced for Max Reinhardt and had the sparkle of its Continental origin. Crowded houses, paying 16s. for a stall, welcomed the new *Die Fledermaus*, with a story which was worth telling, incidents which were worth acting, and music which was worth singing. Irene Ambrus was a gay Adele, singing the delightful "Letter Song" and "Laughing Song." A few words, too, are the due of Johann Strauss's *A Night in Venice*, a very pleasant amalgam of melodies in song and dance.

Reverting to Faraday's *Night Birds*, one recalls the magic gown which Miss Drever wore in the Prison Scene, with the silver fern-leaves set in zigzag fashion, uniting the black and white of the dress, the magpie effect being repeated in Miss Drever's black velvet hat, with its great white and black ostrich feathers. Michael Faraday was an amateur who intruded into vaudeville more than once in the early years of the century. A successful estate agent by profession, he wrote the music for the Egyptian comic opera, *Amasis*, and entered upon a career of management when he helped to produce *The Chocolate Soldier*. *The Girl in the Taxi* was a Faraday production.

One category remains for mention and classification, the romantic musical play. Here there is a serious love interest, instead of the element of burlesque love which is found in opéra bouffe or the inconsequential love-making which fills out the comedy scenes in the typical musical comedy. *The Vagabond King* is a typical romantic musical play, with its background of underworld Paris in the days of Villon and its chorus of thieves. So is *The Student Prince*, though in a very different mood. The plot was derived from *Old Heidelberg*, which made it possible for George Alexander and Eva Moore to delight audiences at the St. James's with a feast of sentiment, extending over months. The story of Prince Karl and his love for the innkeeper's niece Kathie invited music and when Sigmund Romberg provided this the public reception was no less generous. Apart from the production at His Majesty's in 1926, *The Student Prince* has been revived more than once, largely because of the male-voice choruses of the Heidelberg students, among them the familiar "Gaudeamus Igitur."

The Rebel Maid was a costume play written during the first World War by a couple of lieutenants in the Royal Naval Volunteer Reserve, Montague Phillips doing the music, and Gerald Dodson, later a Recorder of London, the libretto, with aid from Alexander Thompson. It was produced by Robert Courtneidge at the Empire in 1921, and included the highly popular song for baritones, "The Fishermen of England." The rebel maid was a certain Lady Mary Trefusis, who was supposed to have played a not unimportant part in the landing of William of Orange in Devon in 1688. *The Three Musketeers*, as given at Drury Lane, with music by Rudolf Friml, was yet another romantic musical play, Dennis King, who played D'Artagnan, showing himself to be a music-loving Lewis Waller. Lilian Davies was an attractive Queen of France and proved her versatility by taking up the role after a successful appearance as principal boy in a Drury Lane pantomime. Leo Fall's *The Pompadour*, at Daly's in 1924, with Evelyn Laye as the frail favourite of Louis XV, must also be classed as a romantic musical, though this is uncertain in view of the fact that the lady was discovered in her bedroom with a lover who certainly had no claim to the Crown of France. Even more surprising, the injured monarch was moved to this curious snatch of recitative:

> Take that fellow to prison,
> To-morrow we'll discuss what's arisen.

One of the latest examples of the genre was *The Lisbon Story*, which had a run at the Hippodrome in 1944 and was unique among musical plays, inasmuch as Patricia Burke, the heroine, was shot by the German Gestapo and her dead body was carried back-stage through a frightened chorus as the final curtain fell. The Portuguese folk-songs gave some character to *The Lisbon Story*, which also revealed its modernity by the number of the scenes and characters required to tell its story. The pretty duet, "You must never say Good-bye," was composed by Harry Parr Davies and was sung by Patricia Burke and Joseph Dollinger, Patricia singing from a balcony and Dollinger from his fruit stall on the stage below.

Around and About the Lyric, Hammersmith

Some memorable musical productions were associated with Sir Nigel Playfair's years of management at the Lyric, Hammersmith. Perhaps A. P. Herbert was Sir Nigel's outstanding discovery, inasmuch as talent in libretto and lyric writing is rarer than a gift for melody in music and, on analysis, fully as important. That more of promise than of achievement resulted was not Playfair's fault. At the time, Herbert was forty years of age, and had Irish blood, a Winchester education, a First Class in Law, and service as an A.B. in the Royal Naval Volunteers as assets, not to mention a seat at the weekly luncheon-table of Mr. Punch. The combination suggested a potential Planché or Gilbert, and as concrete evidence of potentialities, Herbert wrote *The Policeman's Serenade*, with George Baker as the Policeman, for the revue *Riverside Nights*. He followed up his success with an Offenbach book, suitable for the Offenbach airs, embodied in *La Vie Parisienne*. With welcome *naiveté*, a programme note admitted that A. P. Herbert had never read the original book of *La Vie Parisienne*, and was only told as much of the story as the producer considered would be useful.

A wholly original work, *Tantivy Towers*, with music by Thomas Dunhill, followed, and at last *Derby Day*, Mr. Herbert's Cockney comic opera, with Mabel Constanduros, of Wireless fame, in a leading part. It was transferred from Hammersmith to the Lyric, Shaftesbury Avenue, but did not prove a financial success. Indeed, A. P. Herbert summed up his comic-opera experiences under Sir Nigel Playfair as most enjoyable, "but no money in it." It may be that author and management were just unlucky. *Riverside Nights* coincided with the year of the Great Strike and *Tantivy Towers* and *Derby Day* with the world economic crisis of 1931-2. It may, however, be that A. P. Herbert's work as humorist, politician, sailor, and the rest left all too little leisure for full success in the difficult task of comic-opera and revue authorship. He is hampered by the fact that, to the present, he has not picked up the knack of writing lyrics which are not only witty but easily singable and therefore easily heard in a theatre, where colourful movement and other distractions make it specially necessary to be plain and even blunt. It is not easy for composers or singers to put over such lines as:

> Chelsea! Chelsea! Home of Culture!
> Wretches who do not live here
> Suffer premature sepulture,

if only because vaudeville audiences are not accustomed to wed culture with sepulture. The Earl's insistence upon the use of Monogamee would seem to be another example, though the chorus is amusing:

> As my poor father used to say in 1863,
> Once people start on all this art,
> Good-bye Monogamee!
> And what my father used to say
> Is good enough for me.

However, the compensations were the "pretty, frilly, fluffy, filly, dilettante Jenny Jay," Viscount Harkaway, with his "huntin' and fishin' and shootin'," and Lady Ann Gallop, with a characteristically funny but not markedly singable self-introduction:

> And is my lovely liberty to cease,
> Must I go back to my appointed lord,
> Master of Foxhounds, Justice of the Peace,
> To be beloved, to be embraced—and bored?

Probably *Tantivy Towers* would have been more amenable to stage treatment if Herbert had not chosen to rely entirely upon rhymed verse. Lest criticism should seem ungenerous, be it added that *Tantivy Towers* displayed satirical fun enough to stock half a dozen average musical shows, while the solid quality of Thomas Dunhill's musical gifts is sufficiently indicated by recalling the Trefor Jones song, with male chorus, at the end of the second act. Vaudeville can do with more brave experiments of this kind. Too few creators of the art-form can cry with Hugh Heather:

> We are the makers of tunes,
> We are the singers of songs,
> We are the dreamers of dreams,

any more than they can say with assurance, "We are the minters of mirth," a claim which is plainly within the dower of A. P. Herbert.

Derby Day's music was by Alfred Reynolds, the conductor at the Lyric, who had already collaborated with Herbert in *The Policeman's Serenade*. A. P. began with a characteristic Preface, which sufficiently indicated his purpose. It ran:

> Bold is the poet and his face unsure
> Who makes an opera about the poor . . .
> The Derby! Muse, I am afraid of you.
> We have bit off more than we can chew . . .
> You want a moral? Well, then, is the pub
> The root of evil, or the Jockey Club?

The quality of the humour can be judged from Eddy's song, "Derby Day." Eddy being a demi-aristocrat, as the son of Sir Horace Waters, J.P., and therefore an essential contrast to Bert Bones, the tipster; Rose, the barmaid of the Old Black Horse, and John Bitter, its landlord.

> The boy with virtuous parents is a most unlucky lad,
> For by the law of averages he almost must be bad.
> The miser's child invariably lives beyond his means,
> While Pentonville is crowded with the younger sons of Deans.
> Had I been mothered by a crook or born of burglar stock
> I must have been a decent chap from sheer disgust and shock,
> But since my dear progenitors are righteous all the time
> My natural reaction is to wickedness and crime . . .
> So grave upon my tomb, I beg, this melancholy verse,
> *He might have been much better if his parents had been worse.*

In general, the Lyric, Hammersmith, fully lived up to the expectations aroused by its name, after Nigel Playfair, Arnold Bennett, and Amner Hall took over what had been called "the blood and flea pit." The theatre cost them no more than £2,050, while the capital of the syndicate was "not enough to run a musical comedy for a week," as Playfair used to say. Yet the venture included the famous three-and-a-half-years' run of *The Beggar's Opera*, and had as a consequence the interesting revival of *Polly*, which was not even produced in Gay's lifetime. Apropos of *The Beggar's Opera*, it is almost unbelievable, yet a fact, that as Gay wrote the play it had no music. The Duchess of Queensberry of the time suggested the addition of an orchestra during rehearsals, causing Gay to search out the tunes which Pepusch orchestrated. At the Lyric, the airs which Gay had chosen were orchestrated by Frederic Austin with a skill which amounted to fresh composition. *Polly* was a Kingsway Theatre production in 1923, and Frederic Austin worked upon lyrics fitted for a revision of Gay's book, due to Clifford Bax. The production was remarkable for the acting and singing of Lilian Davies, who made, literally, her first stage appearance in *Polly*. She had been a singer of songs, picking up occasional guineas by entertaining at City dinners. However, Nigel Playfair was at his wits' end for an actress who would not look ridiculous in knee-breeches. Someone suggested "Lilian Davies." "Never heard of her," retorted Playfair. "Then do," was the reply, and Playfair did. The first song settled that particular problem and Lilian Davies was engaged. She triumphed alike as wearer of the knee-breeches, actress, dancer, and singer. Unhappily, she died in tragic circumstances less than ten years later, aged thirty-seven.

The loss to British vaudeville was comparable with that suffered when Sari Petrass, beloved of Daly's audiences, was drowned through her motor-car plunging into a river, and when Anny Ahlers, the leading lady at His Majesty's, died during the run of *The Dubarry*, not to be confused with *Dubarry was a Lady*, quite a different show. Theatre-goers have not yet forgotten Anny Ahlers singing "I give my heart," to the haunting music of Millöcker.

It is to be hoped that A. P. Herbert's "Most enjoyable, but no money in it" is not the last word regarding such a venture as that which radiated from the Lyric, Hammersmith, in the 'twenties and 'thirties, even on its vaudeville side.

Chapter IX

THE PALACES OF VARIETY. UP THE CHORUS
1910 TO 1925

THE PALACES OF VARIETY ARE THINGS OF THE PAST, THOUGH they flourished well into the time of the present generation in the shape of the Alhambra, the Empire, and the Palace. The twists and turns of latter-day entertainment have either brought them to the housebreakers, or so changed their character that the description "Palace of Variety" no longer applies. Nevertheless, for a generation the phrase represented an important stage in the passage from the Victorian "flea-pit" to the super-halls of to-day. The characteristic in the entertainment at the Palaces was usually a colourful ballet or similar attraction, added to the song and dance of the ordinary music-hall, the difference being due to the size of the auditorium and the need for pleasing outsize audiences.

The story of the Alhambra is typical, and the theatre itself had an interesting beginning. Leicester Square, in Stuart times, was known as Leicester Fields, and Leicester House, built by Robert Sidney, Earl of Leicester, about 1635, stood in the north-east corner of the Square, until it was pulled down in 1806. In 1851, some of the land was in the possession of Mr. Wyld, a geographer, who set up a monster globe, in a circular building—"Wyld's Great Globe." This attracted public attention for a while, but when it was removed in 1862, the nakedness of the district stood revealed. Mr. Albert Grant, M.P. (Baron Grant) did good service to Leicester Square when he planted the central gardens, and thus regu-larised the position of a curious Moorish building, "The Royal Panopticon of Science and Art," to the east. It had been built in 1854, "for the diffusion of useful knowledge, the improvement of the arts, and the elevation of the social, moral, and intellectual condition of the masses." London's millions, however, declined to be improved, so, in 1858, the Panopticon became the Alhambra Palace. An American circus troupe was an early attraction. Later came trapeze artistes such as the Flying Leotard, and Lulu the Circassian catapultist. Lulu originally appeared as one of a troupe of acrobats at the Cremorne Gardens. She was believed to be a girl, and was shot thirty feet into the air by a powerful spring. Really, Lulu was a boy.

An Alhambra programme was generous. It was timed to begin at 7.45 and lasted until 11.30. The principal attraction came when M. Jules Riviere was appointed chief of a big orchestra in the early 'seventies and inaugurated a memor-able series of ballets. Odell the "Savage," Harry Paulton, of *Niobe*, *All-Smiles*, Emily Soldene, and Fred Leslie were players who amused the shilling pit and sixpenny gallery of the Alhambra in the 'seventies, supplementing Riviere's orchestra and the ballets.

In December 1882, the Moorish palace was burnt, andt after rebuilding, ballets furnished the staple fare. For example, Sullivan's *Merrie England* delighted audiences for many weeks in the early part of the century and, as late as 1919, the Alhambra offered a London home to Serge Diaghileff's ballet. We have not forgotten "La Boutique Fantastique," danced to melodies by Rossini, with Lopo- kova as the doll. Eyelids, lips, finger-tips, as well as arms and legs, danced when Lopokova held the stage. There may have been lovelier dancers, but never a wittier—the pretty wit of pre-revolutionary Petrograd. The can-can danced by the Doll gave rise to a universal chuckle. Alhambra audiences called for the dance again and again. Later, lovers of the ballet identified the dance with Massine and Danilova, but Lopokova was the Alhambra idol.

The Zancigs, that is, Julius Zancig, his very remarkable wife, and "a Shadowy Third," provided another Alhambra sensation. Their's was a thought-reading turn and, to this day, there are music-hall *devots* who are assured that there was something of the miraculous in the Zancigs' powers of "thought transference." In fact, the explanation was a capacity for hard work. Julius Zancig and his hunchback wife practised for a year, ten to fourteen hours daily, before they appeared in public. With his wife on the stage, Julius went among the audience, "talking" in lightning-like gestures, some representing numbers, others days of the week, others again months, years, colours. By touching his tie or his left ear, Julius would give his quick-witted wife a wealth of information. For example, he carried a book similar to that Mrs. Zancig had on the stage and she would start reading at any line or word. A cough might start Mrs. Z. counting, another sound stopped her at the proper number, but, always, The Shadowy Third, in the auditorium with Julius Zancig, was a primary factor. Alhambra audiences would soon have spotted direct signals, but, at one remove, they were effectually hidden. Conan Doyle could never be persuaded their act was a fake and done entirely by signals.

"You are psychic. You may not know it, but you are psychic," he said.

The Zancigs were not strictly a vaudeville turn and, indeed, the story of the Alhambra is not rich in purely vaudeville memories. Among them, however, are the three "Bing Boys" of the first World War. *The Bing Boys are Here* dates from April 1916, and was followed by *The Bing Girls*, with Wilkie Bard, Joe Coyne, and Lorna and Toots Pounds the third being *The Bing Boys on Broadway*, produced in February 1918, which brought George Robey back once more to the Alhambra. The title had its origin in Regent Street, where George Gros- smith chanced to read something about *The Bung Boys*. He and Fred Thompson wrote the first of the plays in three weeks, Clifford Grey contributing the lyrics and Nat Ayer the very tuneful music. "If you were the only girl in the world," "The first love is the last love and the best love of all," and "Another little drink won't do us any harm" are still in currency, though the adventures of the characters are less easy to remember. One of them recurs. Robey unexpectedly came into a small but very desirable fortune. Advancing to the footlights, George faced the Alhambra audience with the familiar, "Do you believe in fairies?", a query which was answered as whole-heartedly as it had been by the children watching Barrie's *Peter Pan*.

The apostle of sound, rude, common sense was just the comedian for the roomy Alhambra. His method and sense of humour really could fill the house. He had the advantage of being Cockney-born, though the greater part of his boyhood was spent at Birmingham. His father was a civil engineer, and for a time Robey was at Jesus College, Cambridge, but some skill as a mandoline player led to concert engagements in early youth and, by 1891, there were stage appearances at the London Aquarium, as assistant to a spoof mesmerist. Young Robey's job was to accept hypnotisation and not raise any objection if pins and needles were driven into his manly bosom with zest. Having been mesmerised, George sang a Gaiety song, "A little peach in an orchard grew," and thus learnt to face an audience. The manager of the Oxford Music-hall, in Tottenham Court Road, heard young Robey and offered him the opportunity of an extra turn at a matinée. Wise in his generation, Robey appealed to the baser instincts of the Oxford audience, dressed himself as a curate, and sang: "You can tell her by the pimple, simple pimple on her nose."

A twelve months' engagement followed. In a few months he was billed as "The coming comedian." Within ten or twelve years he had a brougham of his own, with a coachman and a dresser on the box, and was doing four houses a night. The first turn might be at the Metropolitan, Edgware Road, then Collins's at Islington, and by 10.30 the Oxford, ending with an appearance at the Pavilion as the clock struck 11 p.m. The years had brought full assurance. A lift of the hand, the single word, "Desist!", and Robey could silence even the men and women in the huge promenade which surrounded the whole ground-floor at the Old Oxford and go on to make his song and patter plain to the last boy or girl at the back of the gallery. Robey's idea of a good music-hall song has always been one with an idea which would induce patter, and he taught his public to expect character-creation and vivacious comment upon what they believed to be "life." Always, the patter has come with the precision of a tommy-gun, though no battle-field equivalent suggests itself for the familiar lift of the Robey eyebrows, with its expression of pained surprise, "I mean-ter-say!"

Occasionally, George Robey is indebted to John P. Long for an idea, as in his nudist colony song. With aid from J. P. Long, Robey's "Nudism only started with Adam and Eve," was lengthened into "Yes, and she was a wise woman. She always had a bunch of holly, for when the party got rough." Our George can be troubling at times, but, if cross-examined, he would assuredly quote a line which Arthur Wimperis gave to Beatrice Lillie, in *Elopement*:

"Wot I sez is, take wot's good for yer inside, even if it's bad for yer morals."

Our George believes in the medicinal value of laughter.

Robey's transition from full-blooded Variety to spectacular Revue was a war-time measure, but persisted because he proved to be one of the few comedians

George Robey

Will. A. Bradley

Sing us one of the old songs, George,
One of the songs we know!
Try, old man; do what you can
And we'll let the chorus go.

able to hold the bits and pieces of revue together in an outsize house. When, in April 1916, Sir Oswald Stoll suddenly decided to mount a revue at the Alhambra, he offered Robey a record salary if he would play Lucifer Bing, in "a picture of London Life in a Prologue and six Panels." The show was destined to assist in naming a British Army, "The Byng Boys," and shared with *The Maid of the Mountains* and *Chu-Chin-Chow* the glory of being the outstanding theatrical success of the war. As support, Robey had Alfred Lester, the more diffident of the Bing boys, and mercurial Vi Loraine, while the Gresham Singers contributed an important turn disguised as itinerant musicians.

Violet Loraine had just made a big success with her first character study, that of an elderly Cockney, in charge of a winkle stall, the background being Piccadilly Circus, during a thick fog. A couple of dudes tested the old lady's "oysters," whereupon Vi entertained them with "Dear Old Saturday Night," to the music of Herman Darewski. On the evening the sketch was produced at the Hippo-drome the audience wept tears of delighted surprise as it penetrated Miss Loraine's disguise. Stoll made an excellent bargain when he offered four times what she was getting at the Hippodrome and persuaded her to become leading lady in the Bing Boys series. She displayed an astonishing versatility alike as singer, dancer, and actress. The duet, "If you were the only girl in the World and I were the only boy" was rendered as a straight love-song, to the delight of audiences which did not expect this sort of thing from Robey. He is listening to Vi:

> If I were the only girl in the world
> And you were the only boy,
> Nothing else would matter in the world to-day,
> We could go on loving in the same old way.
> A Garden of Eden just made for two,
> With nothing to mar our joy;
> I would say such wonderful things to you,
> There would be such wonderful things to do,
> If I were the only girl in the world
> And you were the only boy.

Following the success of *The Bing Boys*, and while *The Bing Girls* was being played at the Alhambra, Robey went to *Zig Zag*, a De Courville revue at the Hippodrome. In *Zig Zag* Robey's song about Prehistoric Man was converted into a scenic sketch, with Daphne Pollard as She of the Tireless Tongue and George Clarke as He of the Knotted Knees, that is to say, as a prehistoric dude, in competition with the muscular Robey for the attention of Miss Daphne. No sooner was the run of *Zig Zag* over than Sir Oswald Stoll recalled Robey to the Alhambra, for an addition to the adventures of *The Bing Boys*, this time having an American background. The United States were now in the war, so Lucifer Bing was associated with his American cousin Potifer, a character played by Peter Wiser. Again Violet was Emma, and George Grossmith assisted Fred

"The Bing Boys are Here"
Alfred Lester and George Robey

Maud Allan
in "The Vision of Salome"
at the Palace Theatre in 1908

[*Photo Foulsham and Banfield*

4946 L ROTARY PHOTO. E C MISS MAUD ALLAN, AS SALOME

1.	Selection ... "Reminiscence
2.	**TALBOT AN** In a Japanese Musical Sc
3.	**BI-BO-BI.** In
4.	**MISS OUIDA M** In a Song Scena entitle
5.	**THE PALAC**
6.	**HALL AND EARLE** The
7.	**JACK LORIMER**
8.	**BROTHERS MILLE**
9.	**MISS CLAR** At the Piano in Selections from her Répertoire.

10.	**ALFRED LESTER** in "A Restaurant Episode" Assisted by Miss MABEL ORMONDE.	9.30

11. **Intermezzo—** 9.45
Selection "Vive la Danse" ... *Arranged by Herman Finck.*
A Pot-pourri of popular dance melodies of the past and present time, introducing Characteristic Dance Tunes of many countries, intermingled with those made popular in Ballroom and Theatre.

MATINÉE OF THE FULL EVENING PROGRAMME EVERY SATURDAY AT 2.
Reduced Prices to all Parts. *Seats can now be Booked.*

12.	**MAS-ANDRES** Eccentric French Duettists in a Burlesque of a Revue.	10.0
13.	First Appearance in England. **MISS MAUD ALLAN** In Selections from her famous Classical Dances.	10.15

(a) CHOPIN ... Valse, A minor. | (b) MENDELSSOHN ... "Spring Song."
(c) "The Vision of Salome."
During Miss ALLAN's Engagement she will present further Selections from her Répertoire of Classical Dances.

14.	**JOSEPH DUMOND TRIO** Parisian Street Singers and Instrumentalists.	10.40
15	**Mlle. ROBERTY,** et ses Danseurs. In her Whirlwind Dances.	10.50
16.	**THE BIOSCOPE** Showing the World's Events from Day to Day.	11.0

Thompson and Harry Vernon with the script, while Nat. D. Ayer and Clifford Grey contributed the music and lyrics.

As *The Bing Girls* in 1917 lacked the Robey touch, so did the successor to the *Bing Boys on Broadway*, as the genial George returned to the Hippodrome to play the lead in *Joy Bells*. It had a year's run and then Robey returned once more to the Alhambra, this time in *Johnny Jones*, the book being by Harry Vernon, and some very tuneful music by Charles Cuvillier. The programme described the piece as "A Robey Salad, with musical dressing, or The Adventures of a Naughty Boy." Aided by Ivy St. Helier as his sister, Sue, Robey passed from Paris to Venice and Bagdad, gathering adventures not only in space but in time. In one scene Johnny Jones was knocked out by a boxer and, in trance, found himself to be Louis Quinze, in search of a pretty girl whom he had foolishly omitted to kiss. Still more surprisingly, when the background changed and Versailles disappeared, Johnny Jones was back in the boxing-ring singing his topical song, "It wouldn't surprise me a bit." The Robey Salad had variety in plenty. We saw its hero as a Dervish, wearing a twenty-year-old beard, and as a Persian ploughman, lecturing Alhambra audiences upon worms—"helmin-thology," as Robey termed it, in his anxiety to display the classical lore he picked up at Cambridge. Yet another bright spot was disclosed when Robey began to pluck cherries from Ivy's hat, throwing the stones dexterously among the orchestra. As each stone alighted, there was a big bang on the big drum. Altogether, a very merry evening.

A year later, in March 1921, Robey was *en casserole* at the Alhambra, and the highlight of another kaleidoscopic entertainment. His appearance at the head of a ballet, in which the ladies of the chorus wore policeman's uniform from the waist upwards and were fairies in saucer skirts in the lower regions, will not be forgotten by those who supported spectacular revue in the early 'twenties. Robey also appeared as Millais's Bubbles, replete with a big clay pipe.

By this time Robey revue was an established variety of vaudeville, characterised by tuneful music, frequent changes of scenic background, and little more con-tinuity than arose from the Robey features, with the familiar domed forehead and lifted eyebrows and a fund of relatively unfamiliar back-chat.

Round in Fifty at the Hippodrome promised to have a golfing background, but, in fact, was a recension of Jules Verne's *Round the World in Eighty Days*, with music by James Tate and Herman Finck. We were told how Philias Fogg, a spendthrift son of Verne's Phineas, won a wager similar to that propounded by Jules Verne, and visited in turn Boulogne, Brindisi, Hong Kong, San Fran-cisco, New York, Portsmouth, and London. In one scene Philias (George Robey) was a convict under sentence of death in Sing Sing Prison and, simultaneously, the victim of an amateur musical entertainment. He came to the conclusion that electrocution was preferable. As Jill Carey, a lady journalist, Helen Gilliland supported Robey in this musical adventure in many climes. An orange-grove, seen first in daytime and later at night, was one memorable stage picture. Julian

Wylie, the producer, also staged a very effective race between an Atlantic liner and a motor-launch, Philias's wager being dependent upon victory between one craft or the other.

Nor were the Robey spectacular revues confined to their original homes, the Alhambra and the Hippodrome. Sir Oswald Stoll persuaded Robey to appear at Covent Garden in a top-speed American revue, entitled *You'd be Surprised.* Lydia Lopokova, Leonide Massine, and Ninette de Valois, supported by fifty English dancers, helped to fill the great opera-house stage, as did the Savoy Havana Band. Finally George Robey organised a touring spectacular revue, *Bits and Pieces,* which began by making the round of the Moss Empires and ran for four years, between 1926 and 1930. A company numbering twenty-five included Marie Blanche and toured 15,000 miles. *Bits and Pieces* included so many tit-bits from the Robey salad or casserole that it never exhausted its popu-larity. It just ended. The ballad of "The Pigs" was one item, so was the familiar "I stopped—I looked—I listened." Perhaps the most memorable line was given to a bride, in the traditional silk gown and orange-blossom wreath, whose opening exclamation was:

"The strife is o'er, the battle won."

As a Palace of Variety the Alhambra ended a long and varied career in 1937, being converted into a cinema-house by Oscar Deutsch, of the Odeon circuit. Oddly enough, the Alhambra had seen the birth of the modern "movie" forty years earlier. The first topical film was shown there in 1896—the screening of the Derby, which had been run at Epsom a day earlier. Mr. Deutsch contemplated something very different from the "flicker" of the early "movies." He had opened 125 cinema-houses and, in six or seven years, had seventy-five other picture-houses under construction, his business policy being to add one new cinema-house each week to Britain's amusement world. Even the Alhambra succumbed to such dynamic force.

The Empire

The Empire Theatre of Varieties on the northern side of Leicester Square, was not built until 1884, though a music-hall, the El Dorado, occupied the site earlier. The El Dorado was burnt to the ground in 1865, the catastrophe passing into social history as the occasion of King Edward's term of service as a fire-brigade officer. The heir to the throne jumped upon a fire-engine when he heard that the El Dorado was ablaze and did his best to save the building. When the Empire was built it was fortunate in having a roomy site, which afforded space for a spacious promenade at the back of the dress-circle. Here men-about-town fore-gathered in the 'eighties and 'nineties, to the distress of Mrs. Ormiston Chant and other "Prudes on the Prowl," to recall a somewhat ungenerous phrase coined by Mr. Clement Scott, of the *Daily Telegraph.* On one occasion the Empire manage-ment made a vigorous effort to remove any cause for offence in the dress-circle foyer, but the "bloods" of the Town would have none of it. Led by Mr. Winston

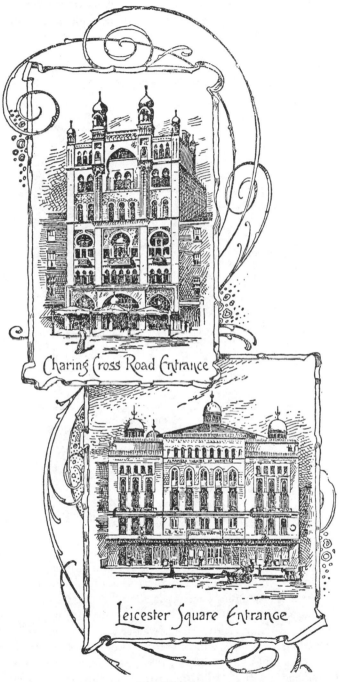

Charing Cross Road Entrance

Leicester Square Entrance

The Alhambra

Churchill, they tore down the screens of Moorish woodwork placed round the promenade and carried the wreckage in procession through Piccadilly. The Promenade survived until 1916. When it disappeared the "Empire," as Victorian and Edwardians knew it, went too.

The glorious years of the Empire were associated with the management of "Druriolanus" Harris and George Edwardes. In 1884 Mr. Edwardes was

proprietor of the Edwardes Menu Company. Indeed, his theatrical interest at that time was primarily due to his ownership of refreshment bars and the right to sell programmes. As manager of the Menu Company, Mr. Edwardes sometimes had to seek out promising stage productions, because an idle theatre meant no bar and no programme receipts. About the same time, in partnership with John Hollingshead at the Gaiety, Mr. Edwardes became interested in the production of *Little Jack Sheppard*, so he was in a position to assist Sir Augustus in staging spectacular ballet at the Empire, interspersed with variety turns. When Sir Augustus and Edwardes failed to agree upon Empire policy and parted company, Edwardes produced a modern-dress ballet, *Round the Town*, which won success for much the same reasons that made *In Town* and "Girl" musical comedies attractive novelties at the Prince of Wales's, Daly's, and the Gaiety.

Adeline Genée, for ten years after 1897, and Lydia Kyasht (after 1908) were the attractions in Empire ballet for years. In her day and generation Adeline Genée was a London institution. A Dane by birth, Queen Alexandra gave her fellow-countrywoman a wedding present, when she was married, and a Duke gave the bride away. She had come to the Empire in 1897, to fulfil an eight-weeks' engagement. The contract was renewed until it reached the amazing total of 572 weeks. She made her debut when she was seventeen and practically all her stage career belonged to the Empire.

Among the variety singers Arthur Roberts was a typical Empire star, and displayed qualities akin to genius in playing-up to the Promenade. The Empire Theatre of Varieties was also the scene of the early London appearances of Yvette Guilbert, and the house of the 'nineties will have a place in vaudeville history on that account alone. The tall woman with corn-coloured hair, her low-cut frock, the black band at the waist. Yes, "a poster-impression, primeval in its simplicity," but Mlle Guilbert was determined to cultivate the extremes of individuality and,

STEINLEN

above all, to avoid the berouged and bespangled vulgarities associated with many Variety singers of the period. The famous black gloves, in contrast to the white dress, were due to considerations of economy, though there would appear to be a special virtue attaching to black gloves in association with vaudeville. Some years earlier Kate Vaughan had appeared in a Gaiety burlesque wearing black gloves! On the following evening a troop of admirers in the stalls, Guardsmen or officers in crack cavalry regiments for the most part, all donned black gloves and clapped their favourite until she blushed with satisfaction.

Yvette Guilbert's life-story affords proof of the necessity for hard work when public entertainers are in the making. A needlewoman, tramping for hours in snow and rain, in search of a shop which would buy the morning's work of herself and her mother—that was the beginning. Then a casino paid Yvette Guilbert £48 a month to sing. The result, "Cat-calls." "She's left her figure in her trunk." "Good!" murmured the brave Yvette. "You've been paying me £48 a month. I'll come back, and you shall pay me £48 a night." Yvette began by reading Maupassant, Zola, and the other realists. "I want to do for song what they did for fiction." The purchase of a tiny book of songs on a bookstall for sixpence, *Les Chansons Sans Gene*, furnished the required material. A Brussels engagement at £40 a day followed, and Paris demanded her return. Yet another struggle, and Yvette won through. It took London some time to appreciate Mlle Guilbert, but even the Empire Promenade surrendered to her talents in the end. Odette Dulac, another diseuse of the Boulevards, conquered Empire audiences with the "Honeysuckle and the Bee." When Yvette Guilbert deigned to sing in English, her choice was "I want yer, ma honey."

In later years Yvette Guilbert's art associated itself with folk-songs, usually with a background of mysticism, whereas, in earlier times, there was always a flavour of naughtiness in her character-sketches. Yvette had learnt much of the seaminess of life when she tramped the muddy pavements of Paris in broken boots, selling her home-made millinery and she did not propose that her ever-growing public should escape a similar knowledge. She intended to shock, and was very well aware that the absence of make-up, the simple white frock and the economy black gloves added point to her sophisticated irony. Yvette Guilbert's range was remarkable. By voice and gesture, she could bring a street-walker to life for vaudeville audiences, but also suggest the awe of the Woman of Samaria when she met Jesus at the Well.

Apart from Variety, as Victorian and Edwardian audiences understood it at the Empire, the house was primarily a home of ballet, or revue with an element of ballet in it. Two memorable musical shows, however, call for record. They are *The Lilac Domino* and *Irene*. The first brought fame to Clara Butterworth and the second brought Edith Day from the States to London. In *The Lilac Domino*, the music of Charles Cuvillier, with extras by Howard Carr, was well above the average and has more than justified revival, including that by Jack Hylton in 1944, with Pat Taylor in Miss Butterworth's part and Elizabeth French in the role of Leonie. The duet, "I have loved in days gone by," the quartet, "Every day is Lady's Day," Andre's drinking song, and "We'll let the music play away, play, play, play away," linger pleasantly in the memory and are the more attractive because they fit neatly on the colourful backgrounds of Palm Beach, Florida, and the Carnival in the Court of Palms which the plot permitted. As Irene O'Dare, Miss Day had her big moment when she sang that fascinating, though naïve, lyric:

> In my sweet little Alice-blue gown,
> When I first wandered down into Town
> I was both proud and shy, as I felt every eye,
> But in every shop window I'd primp, passing by.
> Then in manner of fashion I'd frown
> And the world seem'd to smile all around
> Till it wilted I wore it,
> I'll always adore it,
> My sweet little Alice-blue gown.

Robert Michaelis, Daisy Hancox, singing "Castle of Dreams," and Robert Hale were also associated with *Irene*, which was to win another lease of life, when Anna

The Dear Old "Empire" 1842.

"Damme, Bessie, I shouldn't be surprised if some cads came one day and turned the old place into a cinema or something."

Neagle took over Edith Day's part in a film version. Pat Taylor and Arthur Riscoe are playing in *Irene* at His Majesty's as I write. Tuneful songs have a long life.

But the real romance of *The Lilac Domino* and *Irene* was not in composers or players, but in Joe Sacks, the producer. A Russian by birth, he began his theatrical career as page-boy in a South African circus, whence he was promoted to clowning, with the added duty of cleaning the horse-boxes. At the time of the first World War Joe Sacks was in funds and he partnered Andre Charlot in the Harry Lauder revue *Three Cheers*, chiefly remarkable because Lauder received £800 a week, surely a record salary for a London vaudeville appearance. In 1918 Joe struck lucky when he made £150,000 out of *The Lilac Domino*. Thenceforward the colour lilac was Joe Sacks's mascot. He rode in a lilac motor-car, wore lilac suitings, and had his office letters typed on lilac note-paper. The success of *Irene* followed and came to a man who confessed he could neither read nor write the King's English. It is not to be wondered that this admixture of the shrewd with the futile ended in the bankruptcy court, but not before Joe Sacks had impressed his personality upon the vaudeville of his time through ten or a dozen productions at West End theatres.

The great days of the Empire were between 1885 and 1915. After fifty years of activity, the house was sold to an American syndicate for £750,000, and a big cinema-house replaced the old-time Theatre of Varieties.

Moss's Hippodrome

The Hippodrome, as the name suggests, began in 1900 as a circus ring, and included a water-pool, in which De Rougemont rode his turtle nightly and Annette Kellerman dived and swam. Miss Kellerman reached stardom in a curious fashion. With some Australian reputation as a swimmer, she came to America and was billed to swim from Boston Bridge to Charlestown. She failed, but her charms of face and figure, coupled with a momentary publicity value, seemed to justify a two-weeks' stage engagement at the Hut House. The management realised that Annette's toe-dancing and diving act was not strong enough, and this characteristic solo conversation took place at the end of Annette's first performance:

> *Albee, the Manager:* What are we selling? We're selling back-sides, aren't we? All right. If one back-side is good a hundred back-sides are many times better. Go down to the cellar and bring up those mirrors.

And so it was. Albee's intuition brought Annette Kellerman's act to life. In particular, leading American doctors pronounced her "a perfectly proportioned woman." Attired in a blue jersey, knickers, stockings, and a coquettish scarlet cap, her manager arranged a series of matinées, at which Annette explained how she kept in perfect physical condition. She also gave swimming lessons and, indeed, was a dominant influence in persuading women to discard the mid-Victorian bathing-costume and adopt the close-fitting stockingette costume of later fashion. When she first came to London, her agent had thousands of tape measures specially printed with Annette's physical measurements—neck, ankles, bust, waist, calves, thighs, and arms. Women wrote in for the tape measures from all parts of Britain. For months, her swimming and diving act was a Hippodrome sensation.

Necessarily, there were few individuals, either singers or speciality artists, who could fill the Hippodrome stage, so gymnasts, acrobatic cycling acts, jugglers, wood-cutters, and sawmen and living statuary had a big share of a typical bill. *The Typhoon*, a Dramatic Spectacle, by Alicia Ramsay and Rudolph de Cordova, with music by Carl Kiefert, was the outstanding item in a programme which lies before me. The final scene included a wreck, the explosion of the ship's boilers, the storm, and, at long last, a rescue by the lifeboat.

Another typical Hippodrome scena was devised by Sydney Blow, and showed Hyde Park, near the Achilles Statue. Twelve horses and their riders, four motor-cars and two broughams appeared, together with 150 actors and actresses. Unfortunately, the scena played for forty minutes, and thus transgressed the licensing laws of the period. The Bow Street magistrate accordingly fined the Hippodrome management for exceeding the time-limit. About 1909, owners of West End theatres were in the habit of employing "informers," who attended the vaudeville houses with watches, to ascertain if the variety managers were producing sketches which ran for more than thirty minutes.

The Hippodrome touched high prosperity after 1912, when Sir Edward Moss died, and Albert de Courville staged "display revues," that is to say, a combination of pantomime spectacle and topical-variety. It gathered what logic it was destined to possess from an ingenious blending of spectacle and the personality of the all-important leading lady. Shirley Kellogg, Ethel Levey, and Violet Loraine were brightly shining planets in de Courville revues at the Hippodrome. Miss Kellogg's outstanding asset was robust loveliness; Miss Loraine, vigorous and resourceful personality; and Miss Levey a voice which ranged from *basso profundo* upwards, coupled with irrepressible vim.

Ethel Levey, by H. M. Bateman

Thus, in the summer of 1913 *Hullo, Ragtime* met with sensational success at the Hippodrome, largely because of the energies of Miss Ethel Levey in a principal part. Shirley Kellogg and Maud Tiffany, whose career was strangely short, supported Ethel Levey. Maud Tiffany was an American, whose good looks and vivacity gave her full control over audiences. Following an engagement at the Victoria Palace, de Courville offered her £100 a week to sing "Everybody's Doing It" and "Alexander's Ragtime Band" in *Hullo, Ragtime*. Her success was immediate and gave promise of a long and successful career. When the war of 1914 opened, Maud Tiffany was appearing at the Holborn Empire, but she disappeared without any warning, leaving her theatrical "props" in her dressing-room, and was not seen again.

Apart from Ethel Levey and her associates on the stage, *Hullo, Ragtime* owed most to Albert de Courville, who produced the show and brought dancing, singing, costumes, stage-grouping, and scenic effects to a high degree of perfection. Albert de Courville, like George Black after him, was concerned with the amusement of big popular audiences, rather than the small sophisticated gatherings to whom Intimate Revue appeals. Both producers disdained plot, holding that incessant change was the primary essential. "Run things in quickly and trust to luck," was the rule, though they were very well aware that scenes had to be blended in such a way that the audience sensed a logical continuity, even if they could not explain how it had arisen. Always, the basis was the players available and the outstanding difficulty the fewness of the available stars. Beauty and charm in a woman or vigour and strength in a man, allied with personality sufficient to fill a large stage during the greater part of an evening, represented a rare combina-tion. Often, a well-trained chorus was necessary to make up for the shortage of stars with the necessary qualifications.

By 1913, the public was a little tired of the pretty sentiment of Gaiety and Daly's musical comedy and ready for an entertainment with more of vim and ginger. The changing public mood showed itself in directions other than theatrical. When *Hullo, Ragtime* had been seen by 400,000 Londoners, a "Do, Do Dance" was given at the Hotel Cecil. Relatively impecunious officers of the Guards, and relatively wealthy members of the Metal, the Wool, the Wheat, or the Stock Exchanges made merry with the beauties of musical comedy, the stars of Revue and mannequins from Regent Street, and ten thousand gaily tinted celluloid balls were distributed, which served for friendly bombardments. Great reels of coloured paper were also distributed, which the skilful could throw from one end of a dancing-room to the other, while the Chicken Scramble, the Bunny Hug, and similar importations from the States were being danced. Mass-production methods were being applied to London entertainment, and, quickly, it was evident that they could add punch to various forms of vaudeville. An early consequence was a Hippodrome revue, in which a Joy Plank was projected into the auditorium, and thus seemed to offer exceptional value for the half-guinea charged for a stall.

Sumptuous as were some of the London reproductions of American shows which followed in the wake of *Hullo, Ragtime*, the lavish displays possible in New York were never possible in London. A London theatre would have had to take an equivalent of £7,000 a week if such a show as the Ziegfeld Follies was to pay its way. Even Drury Lane could not contemplate such costly productions.

For a time, Harry Tate, like George Robey, was in demand as a comedian capable of filling the ample stage of one of the larger spectacular revue houses. An early appearance of the kind was in *Hullo, Tango!* at the Hippodrome in 1913, and he was at the Hippodrome again in 1918 in *Box o' Tricks*, a title which aptly summed up Harry Tate's whole career as a comedian, whether in revue or straight

Harry Tate, by H. M. Bateman

Variety. It might be a motor-car it might be an aeroplane it might be just the furniture of any go-as-you-please business office in Greater London. Out of the Tate box o' tricks came an unfailing supply of homely japes, with the assistance, maybe, of a small boy in a top hat and Eton jacket. Then the memorable drawl, and the equally memorable twitch of the outsize moustache.

"'I don't think! Why do you say, 'I don't think', at the end of a sentence? You should say 'I don't think' at the beginning of a sentence. What would your head-master say if I took you up to the College and said, 'Here's my son, I don't think!' It's absurd."

As a result of the furore aroused by *Hullo, Ragtime, Hullo, Tango* and their like, seventy-five different revues were soon running in the English provinces. Scenery and a suggestion of plot enabled a music-hall to approximate closely to a go-as-you-please musical comedy theatre, while contact with old-time Variety was maintained by devoting the first half of the entertainment to ordinary music-hall turns, the revue-proper coming in the second half. *Chase Me! Splash Me! Go Ahead! Fancy Meeting You! Keep Smiling, Not Likely,* and *Very Nice, Too!* were typical titles. These revues also hit the touring musical shows badly. In the years before the war of 1914 George Edwardes usually had eight or ten musical comedy companies touring the provinces and Sir George Dance at least as many. Indeed, Dance often had sixteen companies "on the road."

Vaudeville as an Industry

Fifty years of ever-growing feminine patronage, by doubling or quadrupling the size of potential audiences, forced vaudeville to organise itself. It is now a major British industry, giving employment to hundreds of thousands of people and allowing the investment of many millions of capital in buildings and the goodwill of successful ventures. Stoll Theatres Corporation, which controls the London Coliseum, has a capital of just over £2,000,000, and its rival, Moss Empires, has a capital of £1,350,000. Yet Moss Empires had the humblest of beginnings. Edward Moss chanced to read an advertisement in an Edinburgh newspaper, to the effect that a certain person, living several miles from the city, would *give* a piano to the first person who called for it. The offer had all the appearances of a "leg pull," but the young Jew decided to take a chance. He hired a barrow and found that the owner had been so tormented by players upon the instrument that he was only too glad to get rid of the thing at the price of a small newspaper advertisement. Accordingly, young Moss put the piano upon the barrow, pushed it back to Edinburgh, and hired a small hall. Here he played the piano and a couple of singers contributed songs, this being Edinburgh's first music-hall, as opposed to the "free and easies," associated with bar parlours. The venture proved so profitable that Moss and his partner created a circuit of music halls, where, before Edward Moss died, 85,000 were being entertained nightly. In 1942, 12½ per cent was being paid upon the ordinary shares of Moss Empires and the company could boast that since the inception of the entertainment tax no less than £4,300,000 had been paid to the Government, apart from ordinary taxation upon profits.

As for the relative earnings of the multitudinous hangers-on to the whirling skirts of vivacious Mademoiselle Vaudeville, evidence of their prosperity as compared with mid-Victorian times will arise again and again from the present study. The change was largely due to the activities of Hugh Didcott, the agent, who had the cream of the profession on his books in the 1890's.

A curious character, Didcott. He entered vaudeville as a ballad singer, his real name being Josephs. He took the name Didcott from the station Didcot. Macdermott, Jennie Hill, Bessie Bellwood, and Albert Chevalier were included among his clients and soon Didcott was drawing £200 a week in commissions upon their ever-growing salaries. Unfortunately, the agent had a lurid past and the details were revealed during a law-suit which he brought against Frank Boyd, of "The Pelican." The action ruined Didcott. Nevertheless, in his day and generation he served the leading Variety artists well, so well that the managers staged a revolt. Adney Payne of the Tivoli, the Canterbury, and the Paragon; Edwin Villiers of the Pavilion and Jennings of the Oxford, formed a Managers' Association and fixed a series of maximum salaries. Edwin Villiers, however, "ratted" and, with Didcott's aid, cornered the leading stars for the Pavilion. Thus, the salaries of stars once more were allowed to find their own level.

In the generation after Didcott, Sam Braff, an agent with a large Continental connection, managed for many vaudeville stars. Braff it was who discovered Maud Allan in Berlin and introduced her to Sir Alfred Butt, with such astonishing consequences. Gertie Millar, Ethel Levey, Delysia, Leon Morton, Ruth St. Denis, the "Indian" dancer, and Lee White were other clients of Sam Braff. Lastly, the firm of Richard Warner and Co. included Sir Walter de Frece, husband of Vesta Tilley, and had a big influence upon the economics of the London theatre world in our period. Little Tich, Louis Freear, Harry Randall, Seymour Hicks, and R. G. Knowles were among the clients of Richard Warner and Co. Nor was the profession itself powerless to protect its interests. The Music Hall Artistes' Association came into being in 1885, and its value was revealed when, some years later, the managers attempted to force music-hall players to give their services at matinées without due payment, that is to say, payment for one matinée was regarded as covering five matinées, *if the managers chose.* Established stars, of course, ignored the added clause, but the little men in vaudeville were frightened into accepting the injustice, until a strike was organised, with the support of Marie Lloyd and other music-hall favourites. For some weeks in 1907 the London Pavilion, the Oxford, the Holborn Empire, and other halls were picketed by popular stars who begged the public not to patronise the offending halls. The managements capitulated.

Up the Chorus. The Coliseum, the Palace, and the Syndicate Halls

The ever-growing salaries of stars was only one item in theatrical expenditure which was increasing. The chorus was also larger and cleverer and better dressed, and consequently more and more expensive. Mention has been made of the Big Eight in musical-comedy choruses and their value in adding substance and style to the humours and sentimentalities of the principals, whether as singers or dancers. What was happening was that all members of a chorus in a large West End theatre were expected to reach the standard set by the Big Eight.

H. B. Farnie, the adapter of Offenbach and Lecocq, has been claimed as the earliest producer to distinguish between front-row chorus girls and the rest and in Farnie's time the phrase "The Big Eight" was already current. The stately Alma Stanley was one of Farnie's display items. Between 1910 and 1920, years largely given over to war and preparations for war, and therefore years when theatrical audiences were suffering major changes, vaudeville choruses altered their character considerably. Experience had shown the value of a fully trained and expensively dressed or under-dressed chorus in the large theatres of the twentieth century, in which audiences were markedly masculine *and* feminine and two sexes and not one had to be entertained.

In Victorian times any hardworking girl was deemed fitting for chorus work, if she could sing and dance in a perfunctory manner, but under twentieth-century conditions managers found it far from easy to recruit women with the requisite physical gifts. Chorus girls in spectacular revues were paid from £2 10s. to £5 a week before the first World War, and even allowing for the low scale of pay for women's work, the remuneration did not seem generous, though the glamour of the footlights promised other advantages. At the Empire, in 1913, where Seymour Hicks chanced to control *All the Winners*, 700 more or less promising women once attended an audition. Of the 700, only 20 proved acceptable. Some had pretty faces, but poor figures; others had good figures, but could not display expensive dresses with due effect. As the then manager of the Empire explained, every girl means the expenditure of 50 to 100 guineas in gowns. "Most girls do not look a whit more impressive in an expensive frock than they do in one costing £5."

Similarly, the London Opera House management in 1913 spent £18,000 in producing *Come Over Here*, the main attraction being a bevy of English and American beauties. They wore 650 frocks in the course of the evening and the central episode was a bathing scena, in which the chorus girls disported themselves in suitable attire. The publicity department of the London Opera House made great play with the rivalry which was supposed to exist between the two beauty troupes. We were told:

"The American girl relies upon her vivacity, her boldness, her swinging gait, and her suggestion of independence in winning the man she loves. The English girl, on the other hand, is softer, more delicately seductive, more daintily alluring. In the heart depth, one is as firm and strong as the other, but the English girl gives the Englishman the impression that she is more intensely feminine than her American cousin."

It would seem that managers were fortunate in getting 20 out of 700 winners, when such allurements were looked for.

Historically, it must be admitted that an American, Florenz Ziegfeld, is to be credited with the discovery of the full value of a vaudeville chorus as a box-office attraction and as a publicity stunt. Born in Chicago, Ziegfeld began his career in Buffalo Bill's Wild West show, which had international renown in the 'eighties. By 1872 he was in charge of a vaudeville show at the World's Fair, Chicago, and he established himself by starring Eugene Sandow, the strong man, and Anna Held, a French lady who made vaudeville history by a daily bath in milk, a publicity stunt which had amazing success and was probably the most active factor in establishing the Ziegfeld Follies.

Flo Ziegfeld has left a record of the physical attractions required by the young ladies of his chorus. Beauty of features was secondary to graceful movement and well-turned limbs. When a potential Folly paraded before Florenz, she was required to stand erect, so that the feet touched at the inner sides and the legs tapered evenly down to the ankles. "I never diverge from these two rules," said Florenz. He went on: "The shoulder-blades, the gluteus muscles of the back, and the muscles of the lower leg must be in direct line with each other." Apparently the Anna Helds of vaudeville have always been distinguished for their sym-metrical backs. With a spine even slightly out of alignment, the shoulder-blades of a Florenz Folly would not move evenly. Only when these physical require-ments had been satisfied, did Florenz set about his real mission—the discovery of personality, whether of the athletic, the statuesque, the Mona Lisa, or what Florenz called "the flower" type.

The English contribution to the chorus in spectacular vaudeville associates itself with John Tiller of Manchester. For a generation the Tiller training school for stage-dancing has provided the greater part of the musical comedy, revue, and pantomime houses with their choruses and dancing troupes. John Tiller was employed on the Manchester Cotton Exchange as a young man, but he had a hobby—conducting an amateur concert party. In this connection, he conceived the idea of training a team of girls to dance in unison and the first four had some professional success as the Four Little Sunbeams, team-dancing being a novelty at the time. Soon Tiller troupes were in general demand, not only in Britain, but on the Continent. The girls came from working-class homes all over the North of England, and John Tiller made all arrangements for their feeding, clothing, and education. Smoking was strictly prohibited, and when a troupe of girls went abroad, a matron was always sent in charge, the secret of John Tiller's success being strict discipline. Respectable parents knew they could trust a pretty daughter at a Tiller dancing school and felt that a decent living was assured if the girl submitted to the discipline. Chorus dancing and singing was to be a real career.

Symptomatic of the ever-increasing importance of the chorus were the publicity stunts which ingenious managers devised, following the Ziegfeld example. Mr. Cochran's campaign on behalf of plumper chorus girls comes to mind. By 1929 the skinny shoulders and bony legs of up-to-date womanhood were pronounced a national, if not an international, danger, so Mr. Cochran called in Sir William Arbuthnot Lane, the dietetic specialist. "What is to be done about it?" "More chocolates," replied Sir William, contemplating the damsels of the Pavilion chorus, whose average weight was precisely 8 stone 4 pounds. Meals including cream, peas, fresh milk, butter, and wholemeal bread were arranged. Quickly a full-figured chorus girl was produced, not only able to sing and mime with vigour, but fitted by her example to save the women of Britain from the dangers which an excessive desire for a slim figure had encouraged. Again, when Mr. Cochran was devising his twenty-second revue, he determined to have done with the somewhat scanty costumes which had characterised earlier shows and, as Mr. Cochran feared, had caused critics moments of anxiety.

"I am not allowing the girls to show an inch of flesh, other than hands and faces. They will be dressed from their chins down. Their legs will be encased in oceans of frills, furbelows, and frou-frous," said Mr. Cochran.

And Mr. Cochran said this with decision. I am well aware that the underlying humour of the declaration was well within Mr. Cochran's ken, but, doubtless, it witnesses to the importance of his Young Ladies in the shows of the 'thirties.

In London, the record-breaking success of Oscar Asche's pantomime *Chu-Chin-Chow* perhaps furnished the most obvious proof that theatrical audiences welcomed the ever-increasing insistence upon exotic spectacle, sensuous colour, and speedy movement, of which a large, well-dressed, and well-trained chorus was the primary exemplification. That amiable robber began his career in August 1916, and held West End London to ransom for five long years. During this time 2,800,000 people visited His Majesty's Theatre. The original production cost Oscar Asche £5,300. By the spring of 1921, the public had paid him £700,000, and Asche's share of the loot was in the region of £200,000. At the time thousands of young men were on leave from the Front or, being demobilised, were in a mood to spend their war gratuities generously. After the stresses of Flanders, Salonica, and Iraq, they felt they could justify blazing away savings, and thus they justified such theatres as Drury Lane, the Hippodrome, the Coliseum, His Majesty's, the new Dominion Theatre in Tottenham Court Road in staging shows with spectacular choruses and elaborate settings. Indeed, this seemed the obvious method of attracting audiences of the requisite size.

Apart from *Chu-Chin-Chow*, Asche's contribution to vaudeville included the stage presentation of *The Maid of the Mountains*, with its charming lighting effects. In general, however, Asche was primarily responsible for revealing the box-office value of under-dressed houris and their attendant males, this being the tendency towards abdominal display which Chance Newton (or was it Lady Tree) summed up so neatly in the phrase, "more navel than millinery." After they had seen *Chu-Chin-Chow* and *Cairo*, managers of the outsize London theatres felt they were on sure ground in following Asche's lead. For example, in 1922 the Drury Lane management spent £40,000 upon *Decameron Nights*. It included eleven scenes, among them full-stage sets representing the Hanging Gardens of Damascus, the Palace of the Soldan, and the Piazza di San Marco at Venice. One scene was manifestly stolen from Shakespeare's *Cymbeline*. It displayed a gallant who had been conveyed into his lady-love's bedroom in a trunk, bent upon winning a wager from the lady's husband by collecting evidence of the wife's unfaithfulness. The proof seemed so complete that the injured husband called upon the Doge to punish his wife, by exposing her naked in the Piazza di San Marco (full-stage set aforesaid). An unexpected eclipse of the sun came at an opportune hour, so the blushes of the citizens of Venice, of Margaret Bannerman (who played the injured wife) and of Drury Lane stall-holders, alike were veiled.

Stoll's Coliseum

As the Hippodrome was the crowning achievement of the Moss Circuit, so the building of the Coliseum formed the apex of the career of Sir Oswald Stoll.

The house arose in a slum area (Bedfordbury), to the east of St. Martin's Lane, which was a cluster of alleys, courts, shops, and old-fashioned dwelling-houses at the end of the nineteenth century. Like Morton and Sir Edward Moss, Stoll, from early manhood, had been staging variety entertainments, fitted for women as well as men, and he built the Coliseum in 1904 as "a family hall." It was brilliantly designed by Frank Matcham, perhaps too brilliantly. Thus, a special tramline was laid from the street right into the Royal box, and on it ran a crystal tram made entirely of glass. About six weeks after the opening King Edward VII and Queen Alexandra paid a visit. They entered the tram, which unfortunately refused to start, and the King himself suggested that it would be better if they walked. The tram was never used again. The lines were taken up and filled in, but the place where they lay can be traced in the tessellated floor.

The happy financial result was primarily due to the fact that Sir Oswald Stoll had been in Variety from boyhood. He knew his job. Born in Melbourne in 1866, he lost his father within a few weeks of his birth. Mrs. Stoll, a remarkable Irish woman, left Melbourne with her son for Liverpool when the infant was three months old, and here she married John Stoll, proprietor of the Parthenon Music Hall. When John Stoll died in 1880, Mrs. Stoll and her fourteen-year-old boy continued to conduct the Parthenon, until they migrated to Cardiff, where they had purchased a music-hall. The Cardiff venture succeeded after a desperate struggle, and Mrs. Stoll celebrated the turn of fortune by spending £1 10s. upon a blue suit for her son. After Sir Oswald Stoll became a wealthy knight, Mrs. Stoll continued as the mascot of her son's box-office, driving up to the theatre in a carriage drawn by dappled greys. She died in 1924.

The declining popularity of Variety in the post-war years, coupled with the size of his theatre, persuaded Sir Oswald Stoll to stage a remarkable musical play at the Coliseum in 1931. This was *White Horse Inn*. On the day the first-night notices appeared the libraries booked £60,000 worth of seats. Sir Oswald Stoll's venture was based upon a German production, which had been playing to crowded houses in Berlin. In it Erik Charell and Ernst Stern applied the production methods which Reinhardt devised for romance and tragedy of *The Miracle* to a comedy theme. The Coliseum inside and outside was transformed into the semblance of a Tyrolean village, with the White Horse Inn as the dominant feature. Aided by 150 players, 3 orchestras, and bands of Tyrolese singers and dancers, patrons of the Coliseum were permitted to take part in the fêtes of a Tyrol village. Charabancs with tourists drove on to the stage; a lake steamer, belching smoke, steamed alongside an improvised landing-stage. Real horses, real dogs, and real goats, as well as real actors and actresses, moved against the background of Professor Stern's mountain scenery, which, in itself, was so realistic that a rain-storm, which included descent of real water, was accepted as a perfectly natural happening. Sir Oswald Stoll spent £50,000 upon *White Horse Inn*, but the money came back. Moreover, for the first time Sir Oswald was able to make full use of the Coliseum's famous revolving stage. A climax in large-scale spectacle was reached when the Coliseum stage was converted into an ice-rink for the presentation of *San Moritz*, the skating revue.

Spectacular vaudeville had saved the Coliseum at a time when Variety had plainly exhausted its popular appeal. Accepting the hint, Sir Oswald produced *Waltzes from Vienna*, at the Alhambra, the music being that of Johann Strauss, father and son. During one scene in *Waltzes from Vienna*, the entire orchestra was raised to the level of the footlights and was moved on rollers across the stage. Another highlight in the piece was Danilova, in the fireworks ballet.

The whole question of German influence upon spectacular revue as it developed in London under Charles Cochran is interesting. Max Reinhardt was the philosopher of the movement which was primarily designed to bring the spectator into the very action of the drama, as the Athenian spectator had been when a play by Aeschylus, Sophocles, or Euripides was played in the theatre of Dionysos in the fifth century. By 1931, when Hitler came into power in Germany, Reinhardt had produced no fewer than 432 plays; they are pictured in a remarkable volume edited by Hans Rothe and call for careful study by those who would understand the development of twentieth-century vaudeville. What Cochran did was to apply the grand-scale experiments of Max Reinhardt to English spectacular revue and as Germany contributed little directly to this art-form, much of Cochran's work was of the pioneer type.

Long before the production of *Follow the Sun* Ernst Stern had won a European reputation as Reinhardt's art director, in charge of scenery, costumes, and properties and, in particular, of the novel colour and lighting effects which made up so much of a typical Reinhardt production. Ernst Stern regarded colour and lighting as dynamic forces, using cadmium yellow, for example, to suggest energy, and blue-greens, tranquillity. Stern's method was not to secure these colour effects directly, but by throwing rays of light upon neutral surfaces, thus achieving much more variety than would have been possible by costume and scenery alone. All this means that, in the Reinhardt system, Stern was responsible for "the stage picture," an entity very different from the conjunction of scenery and costumes, which constituted "the stage picture" in English vaudeville, before Max Reinhardt and Ernst Stern showed Charles Cochran a better way. Apart from these indirect influences, some of the most memorable stage effects on the London stage in the 'twenties and 'thirties were directly due to Ernst Stern, among them the Vienna café scene in *Bitter Sweet*, and the Tyrolean background to *White Horse Inn*. The scenery and dresses in the wordless play *Sumurun*, at the Coliseum in 1911, gave London its first impression of Ernst Stern's quality. In transplanting the scenic designs from Berlin to London, some calamitous colour clashes were disclosed. There were only a few hours to put the matter right, but Ernst Stern got to work with some outsize brushes and pails of whitewash and black paint. A black-and-white production, which proved one of the attractions of *Sumurun* was the result.

A year or so later, in 1912, another Reinhardt production was staged at the

Palace, this being the comedy-drama *A Venetian Night*. The story was devised by Karl Vollmoeller, who wrote *The Miracle*, and Frederick Bermann added the music. It only ran for three weeks and the failure was almost entirely due to the fact that Ernst Stern's lighting effects went wrong and Palace audiences failed to establish the emotional intimacy with the stage pictures which was all-important if Vollmoeller's fantasy was to be acceptable.

Imagine Venice in the year 1860. A young stranger is approaching his hotel in a gondola, at a moment when a party of Venetians are trooping in to a wedding feast. The Bride has no joy in the match. So much is plain. Plainly, too, the imagination of the Stranger has been stirred by the knowledge.

The story of *A Venetian Night* then passes into Dreamland, where the young stranger finds himself in the bedroom of the Bride. The groom has been drinking and when he reaches the bedroom he finds his lady-love and an unknown youth embracing. At this moment a thief enters the bedroom, kills the Bridegroom, and the Young Stranger, in his dream, finds himself cast with the difficult duty of disposing of the body. In fact, the episode, which alternated between comedy and tragedy, was only the fantasy of a dream. All that really happened was that the Young Stranger was introduced to the Bridegroom during the wedding feast and dropped a rose, the symbol of his admiration for the loveliness of the Bride.

There were thirteen scenes in the Palace production and they alternated between the waking and the dream state of the Young Stranger. They were made possible by a revolving stage, which was set with all the thirteen scenes before the curtain rose. A quarter turn of the revolving stage was all that was necessary to carry the Palace audience from the gay scene on the Grand Canal, with its gondolas, to the hotel interior where the wedding guests were gathering. Another quarter turn and the Young Stranger, in his fantastic dreamland, was in the Bride's bedroom. For the concluding scenes, the revolving stage came once more to the hotel adjoining the Grand Canal and waking reality.

The Palace

Like the Alhambra and the Empire, the Palace, in Cambridge Circus, did not begin as a music-hall. It was built out of profits earned from Gilbert and Sullivan opera. In 1891 D'Oyly Carte produced Sullivan's *Ivanhoe* as the opening venture, hoping to establish an all-English opera-house. Unhappily, *Ivanhoe* proved to be the only English opera forthcoming, and D'Oyly Carte sold the theatre to Sir Augustus Harris. "Druriolanus" was responsible for putting the male attendants at the Palace into knee-breeches, and for powdering their hair.

"This is going to be a gentleman's theatre," he said, and Sir Augustus was not thinking of "gentlemen" of the Champagne Charlie type.

Eventually, the control of the Palace Theatre passed to the Father of the Halls, Charles Morton. He made it pay.

One reminiscence of the public-house "sing-song," from which the modern music-hall shows evolved, was maintained while Morton ruled at the Palace.

He had his own seat at a little table behind the stalls, and sat there, drinking tea and keeping time to the melodies with his spoon upon the saucer. Occasionally, a favoured patron of the house was invited to join Mr. Morton and occupy the extra seat. Mr. Morton's successor was Sir Alfred Butt, who began as an accountant at Harrod's, became Morton's secretary in 1898, and succeeded to the managership when Morton died in 1904. Thenceforward, the Palace made £20,000 a year with admirable regularity.

Maud Allan, with her Salome dance; the triumphs of Pavlova and Mordkin, particularly in Glazounoff's "Bacchanale"; and the classic dances of Lady Constance Stewart-Richardson, are Palace memories. So are Anna Held singing "Won't you come and play with me?"; Fred Russell, the ventriloquist; and Kilanyi's "Living Pictures." Mr. Chance Newton described the last turn as "nude departures," and Charles Morton booked them in fear and trembling. As a fact, Kilanyi's Graces were attired in substantial fleshings which were laced at the back.

Variety has long tended to arouse a desire for the feminine nude, apparently obeying much the same rule as that which persuades certain newspaper proprietors to enliven their back pages with a succession of bathing beauties in the Silly Season. To-day, such turns are known as "Strip-Tease," but in mid-Victorian times there were tableaux vivants at such places as the Cider Cellars in Maiden Lane or the "Coal Hole" in the Strand. In the provinces, too, where the basis of the vaudeville was a judicious mixture of the comic and the sentimental song, the entertainment was frequently varied with tableaux. I have seen a programme from the Parthenon Rooms, Liverpool, dated 1850, in which John Reed, "the old favourite comic vocalist," and Miss M. Baxter, "the celebrated sentimental singer from London and Glasgow concerts," provided the staple fare, but between songs there were tableaux representation such as "Jephthah's Rash Vow" (Sacred History), alternating with "The Sultan's Favourite Returning from the Bath" and "Diana Preparing for the Chase."

In 1908, music-hall patrons flocked to the Pavilion to see La Milo in a living representation of the Velasquez "Venus," which had recently been presented to the National Gallery. In La Milo's case the costume consisted of a thick plaster preparation, which covered the figure from top to toe, but Johnnydom was deceived. La Milo in real life was a Melbourne girl, Pansy Montague, and her turn was invented by her partner, Alec James.

Lady Constance Stewart-Richardson's classical dances, like the Salome dance of Maud Allan, also aroused protests from the unco guid, but only because the player was the granddaughter of a duchess, the daughter of an earl, the cousin of a countess, and the wife of a baronet. There was not a shadow of indelicacy, and the lady also had the justification of charity. Lady Stewart-Richardson had original ideas regarding the education of children, and wished to establish a model school, based upon the upbringing given to her own son, Ian. A swimmer, a diver, a rider, and a huntswoman, Lady Stewart-Richardson wanted dancing, outdoor sports, and gardening to have a large part in the training of small boys.

When Sir Alfred Butt offered 350 golden sovereigns weekly for twenty golden minutes of dancing in diaphanous draperies, valuable financial support for the educational scheme was forthcoming. About the time of the Palace appearances, a West End hostess approached a witty but old-fashioned leader of Society with the news:

"Lady Constance has promised to do her barefoot Persian dance."

"Dear me," replied the Duchess. "I knew something dreadful would happen when I overturned the salt at dinner."

Different in its appeal, but also semi-sensational, was the Apache dance of La Polaire, which was performed to the strains of the "Merry Widow Waltz." In 1909 La Polaire was billed as "the ugliest woman in the world," but she had a fifteen-inch waist and the lithe grace of a python. In the dance she was caught up by her partner and then flung off, only to end by twisting herself with snake-like grace about the body of the man, until, in a paroxysm of passion, he threw his woman to the ground and she crawled back to his feet. It was an early example of the "Treat me rough, kid, treat me rough" love-making, which appealed to disenchanted youth about the time of the World War.

Among Morton's triumphs was the booking of Harry Bootles, better known as Datas, the boy with the phenomenal memory. He was working at the Anerley gasworks when someone noticed his exceptional powers of memory. A music-hall agent took Bootles to Morton and the old man renamed the boy Datas, and gave him a week's engagement as a memory displayer. Datas stayed at the Palace for eighteen months.

In spite of occasional exotic attractions, the Palace was essentially a house to which a man could take his wife. At the Empire and the Alhambra there were ballets, but the Palace, maybe, staged a dramatic interlude. George Alexander and Beerbohm Tree both made their first appearance in Variety at the Palace, tempted by Sir Alfred Butt's offer of £750 a week. Here, too, Granville Barker, fresh from his triumphs with Bernard Shaw plays at the Court, staged some one-act playlets by the Austrian Arthur Schnitzler. A new "Anatol" episode was given each week for six weeks and Palace audiences approved. Glover, the musician, tells a capital story of Sir Herbert's first Palace appearance. He was nervous regarding the manners of music-hall performers, so nervous that he persuaded Lady Tree to accompany him and help to bear the brunt of any shock. His worst fears materialised during rehearsal. A half-dressed, perspiring acrobat approached, and struck Sir Herbert on the back.

" 'Ullo, 'Erbert, 'ow are you? Glad to see you on the 'alls."

Tree, however, proved equal to the situation. "Very well, thank you," he replied. "You know my wife? Maud! Maud—The Two Whacks! The Two Whacks . . . Maud!"

Lady Tree's personal triumph at the Palace was her recitation of Kipling's *Absent-minded Beggar* during the first World War. The *Daily Mail* gave her an advance proof of the poem in order that she might include it in a charity concert at the St. James's Hall. At once Lady Tree saw her opportunity. She approached the Palace management and asked them to give £100 to war charities, if she recited the Kipling poem during a week. In fact, the Palace was crowded nightly for ten weeks and Lady Tree's recitals of the poem did not end until she had earned £20,000 for war charities.

Another Palace memory is Margaret Cooper, in the dress of golden silk, sitting at her piano, but facing the audience all the time, so that every word of "Agatha Green" could be heard to the backmost seat in the gallery. Alfred Butt heard Margaret Cooper singing at a charity concert in aid of Charing Cross Hospital, and determined to give her a chance. Just a pianist at her piano, whose voice, at the beginning, "would not fill an egg-cup." Nevertheless, Miss Cooper won through. She had at least a couple of hundred songs in her repertoire, many of them with lyrics by her husband and tunes by herself. "Waltz me round again, Willie" was a welcome number in at least a thousand programmes, "Dingle, Dongle, Dell," "My Bungalow in Bond Street," and "Beautiful Country of Dreams" being other Margaret Cooper favourites. She was nicknamed "The Lady Corney Grain."

No record of the Palace would be complete without mention of Herman Finck, who became leader of the orchestra in 1896 and was musical director from 1909 to 1921, when he relinquished the post in order to take over the musical direction at Drury Lane. Herman was the son of a Dutch musician, Old Finck, who ran a small orchestra—a couple of fiddles, a harp, a viola, and a piano—which provided light music for dances and parlour entertainment in late Victorian times. Old Finck taught his son the violin, and he was playing in theatrical orchestras at the age of fourteen. Later young Finck blossomed into a tuneful and ingenious composer and not a few song-hits of the first quarter of a century came from his facile pen, among them Arthur Wimperis's recruiting song in *The Passing Show* (1914) and several numbers in *Bric-a-brac*, the Palace revue of 1915, in which Finck was associated with Lionel Monckton. Teddie Gerard's signature song, "Naughty, Naughty, One Gerrard," was an Arthur Wimperis and Herman Finck number. Gerrard was, of course, an exchange which was very familiar to users of the London telephone system. Miss Gerard described herself thus:

> Everybody calls me Teddy,
> T E double D Y.
> Yankee, swanky, full of hanky-panky
> With the R.S.V.P. eye.

The triumphs of Anna Pavlova and Mordkin at the Palace about 1908 belong rather to the history of ballet than vaudeville, but Maud Allan has a definite place in the story of English Vaudeville.

It was at the Palace Theatre that she took pre-war London by storm. Pavlova and the Russian Ballet were still things of the future, and nothing like Maud Allan's classical dancing had ever been seen on the English stage. Dancing hitherto had meant ballet-work, varied with the accordion-skirted type of dancing associated with such a name as Letty Lind. For any dancer to appear stockingless on the stage was unknown—almost inconceivable.

Maud Allan showed how lovely the human body can be in a yard or two of *crêpe de Chine*, with bare legs and arms. She showed also how much more attractive the face could be when practically free from make-up. Above all, she discarded the stereotyped dancer's smile. Her sensational turn, "the Dance of Salome," was the only one in which make-up played a considerable part, and its popularity was due to its daring. Artistically, it was the least excellent of her dances.

Few things more beautiful have been seen on the stage than her interpretation in rhythmic movement of a Chopin valse or Rubinstein's "Valse Caprice." There was charm in her young girl scene, based upon the "Spring Song" from Mendelssohn's "Songs Without Words," which Pelissier guyed with horrid success by capering round the stage wearing a green scarf and carrying a single daffodil. Perhaps for that reason the Chopin valse and the rococo elfishness of the "Valse Caprice" are richer memories. After thirty and more years one can recall the thrill of the moment when, through the simple massive curtains that flanked the stage, there stole a shy, serious-looking young girl, who expressed with rhythmic curves of the body the strange mingling of exotic beauty and wistful grace in Chopin's music. In her art she tried to interpret every mood in terms of rhythm. Surprise, joy, roguishness, the madness of a Pan-intoxicated dryad, she could impersonate them all. Perhaps her art was at its happiest with the music of Grieg.

In her early days, Maud Allan owed a good deal to the generous appreciation of Yvette Guilbert. With view to a Parisian engagement, Mlle Guilbert arranged that Miss Allan should dance at an entertainment given by the Earl and Countess of Dudley, at which King Edward and Queen Alexandra were to be present. One end of the great ball-room was reserved for the young dancer, and she moved against a background of masses of smilax and La France roses—a veritable Fairyland, as Maud Allan judged things. With such Society support, Sir Alfred Butt was on sure ground when he arranged the Palace engagement which established the Maud Allan vogue.

The Syndicate Halls

In many ways the outsize Palaces were less characteristic of London music-halls about the turn of the century than the somewhat smaller houses known as the Syndicate Halls and comprising the Tivoli, the Pavilion, and the Oxford.

The Oxford, Tottenham Court Road, is a Lyons Corner House to-day, with dining space for five thousand people, but elderly Londoners associate the site with Marie Lloyd, Eugene Stratton, Cissie Loftus, and George Robey. Charles Morton's quick eye noted the value of the old posting inn, the Boar and Castle, as an entertainment centre, and when he took control of the house, its reputation was quickly established. Maintaining connection with the hostelry, Morton provided a substantial "Ordinary," price half a crown, which included admission to the vaudeville show. There have been five Oxfords, beginning with Morton's in 1861. The Syndicate Hall arose in 1893, and then the theatre which Charles Cochran built at the end of the first World War at the cost of £80,000. Cochran made a fortune at the Oxford with the war-time comedy, *Old Bill*, and lost it over costly revues. Here is a typical programme dating from the music-hall days:

An Oxford Music-hall Programme

Week commencing Sept. 18th, 1893.

1	**Overture**		*By the Band*
	"Electric," J. WORSWICK.		
2	**Miss Winifred Johnson**		
			Banjoist & Dancer
3	**Mr. Tom Leamore** ...		*Comedian*
4	**Mr. Will Evans and Miss Ada**		
	Luxmore *Eccentric Instrumentalists*		
5	**Miss Ada Lundberg**		*Comedienne*
6	**Miss Flo Hastings**		*Serio Comic*
7	**Mr. Sam Redfern**		*Negro Comedian*
8	**Miss Kate James** ...		*Comedienne*
9	**Miss Lucy Clarke**		*Ballad Vocalist*
10	**The Bros. Horn** *In their Boxing Sketch*		
11	**Miss Florrie Gallimore** *Serio Comic*		
12	**Mr. Harry Atkinson**		
			The Australian Orpheus
13	**Mr. R. G. Knowles** ...		*Comedian*
14	**Miss Minnie Cunningham**		
			Serio Comic &-Dancer
15	**Mr. Leo Stormont**		*Baritone Vocalist*
16	**Miss Nellie Navette**		
			Serio Comic & Dancer
17	**Mr. Charles Godfrey**		*Comedian*
18	**Miss Fannie Leslie** *Burlesque Artist*		
19	**Mr. Dan Leno** ..		*Comedian*
20	**Miss Marie Lloyd**		*Comedienne*
21	**Miss Jenny Valmore**		*Serio Comic*
22	**Mr. Arthur Rigby** ...		*Comedian*

The Pavilion, which is a cinema to-day, had a somewhat similar origin. Its history, more or less connected, dated back to 1859, when a "sing-song" hall was attached to the Black Horse public-house in Piccadilly Circus. The pit and stall space was occupied by marble-topped tables, and a chairman, at a central table, presided over the musical arrangements. Early in the 'eighties, an excellent seat, complete with marble-topped table, cost sixpence. In 1885 and 1886 Piccadilly Circus was enlarged to provide an approach to the newly cut Shaftesbury Avenue, and several buildings in the north-east corner were pulled down, among them the Pavilion, but the music-hall was rebuilt on a new site, at the junction of Coventry Street and Shaftesbury Avenue. The new company also abolished the Chairman and put tip-up seats in place of the tables. Still later, in 1900, the ground floor of the Pavilion was raked and the bars were moved to an underground saloon, under the stalls. Leybourne, Vance, Arthur Roberts, Jennie Hill, and Harriett Vernon were attractions at the old "Pav," as were Cinquevalli, the billiard-ball balancer, and Jolly John Nash. The latter had been a successful Worcester ironmaster in earlier years, but failed in business, and made good once more by utilising a talent for entertainment which he first tested at masonic meetings. In old age he wore a curly black wig, dyed his moustache and whiskers generously, and appeared in evening dress, gloves, and an opera hat. This imitation of the real "gent" apparently made a special appeal to clubmen and on one occasion Nash was included in a party of Variety artists who entertained the guests of a certain nobleman after supper. Edward the Seventh was present and was installed as Chairman. He joined lustily in Nash's nonsensical chorus:

> Hey, hi. Stop, waiter! Waiter! Fizz! Pop!
> I'm Racketty Jack, no money I lack,
> And I'm the boy for a spree!

The Tivoli of to-day, a super-cinema, has only its name in common with the German beer-garden of the 'sixties, which first associated the Strand site with entertainment. The old music-hall, with its memories of "Ta-ra-ra-boom-de-ay" followed in 1890. Miss Lottie Collins is one among a hundred memories. Harry Fragson, the Anglo-Frenchman with his piano, is another. And Ernest Shand, in the role of the polite curate: "It really was a most delightful evening."

Of course it was—with Dutch Daly, wearing a belt and white trousers, in an effort to emphasise his slimness, and coaxing his concertina into an imitation of church bells. "You will observe," said Daly, "that, as the church draws nearer, the sound becomes louder."

Or Number 20 on the Tivoli programme which lies on my desk. Eugene Stratton, the whistling Coon, doubtless singing the ever-popular "Lily of Laguna" or "Little Dolly Daydream," with which Leslie Stuart fitted him so perfectly. Not only as a singer, but as a dancer, he was an artist in a hundred and he was destined to be the forerunner of a long line of dandy coloured coons, of whom G. H. Elliott is still with us, singing "Sue, Sue, Sue, I am very much in love with you." Listen to the first and the best of the coloured comedians:

She's ma lady love, she is ma dove, ma baby love,
She's no gal for sittin' down to dream,
She's de only queen Laguna knows.
I know she likes me, I know she likes me, bekase she says so;
She is de Lily of Laguna, she is my Lily and my Rose.

A TIVOLI PROGRAMME

For Week ending October 7th, 1893.

1	**Overture.**
2	**Arthur Rigby.** *Comedian.*
3	**George Robey.** *Comedian.*
4	**Harry Freeman.** *Comedian.*
5	**Edwin Boyde.** *Comedian.*
6	**Ida Heath.** *Transformation Dancer.*
7	**Fred Mason.** *Comedian.*
8	**Herbert Campbell.** *Comedian.*
9	**Harry Pleon.** *Comedian.*
10.	**Rose Dearing.** *Serio-Comic.*
11	**Sam Redfern.** *The Black Philosopher.*
12	**Dan Leno.** *Comedian.*
13	**Kate James.** *Comedienne.*
14	**Albert Chevalier.** *Comedian.*
15	**Flo. Hastings.** *Serio-Comic.*
16	**Charles Godfrey.** *Comedian.*
17	**F. H. Celli.** *Baritone.*
18	**Harry Atkinson.** *The Australian Orpheus.*
19	**M. Cunningham.** *Serio-Comic.*
20	**Eugene Stratton.**
21	**Bros. Griffiths.**
22	**R. G. Knowles.** *The Very Peculiar.*
23	**Billie Barlow.** *Comedienne.*
24	**Little Tich.** *Comedian.*
25	**Nellie Navette.** *Serio-Comic and Dancer*
26	**Harry Randall.** *Comedian.*
27	**Tom Bass.** *Comedian.*

The above Programme is subject to alteration.

MATINEE EVERY SATURDAY AT 2.30.

What a bill o' fare. Arthur Rigby, the "beginner" with George Robey to
follow. And then Herbert Campbell, Albert Chevalier, Charles Godfrey,
Eugene Stratton, R. G. Knowles, Little Tich, Harry Randall, and, of course,
Dan Leno, best of all Tivoli memories. And the prices—Upper Circle, 1s.;
Pit and Promenade, 1s. 6d.; and Orchestra Stalls, 3s. and 5s. Yes, London knew
how to get cheap entertainment in the days when the Syndicate Halls displayed
the leading lights in Variety.

Since all these talents cannot be characterised, let the memory of Dan Leno,
Number 12 on that memorable evening in the Strand, speak for the twenty-seven.
As Fred Leslie was supreme in the extravaganza of his day, so Dan, with his
twinkling feet and his gentle confidences, was supreme in Variety and Pantomime.

Born in 1860, Dan Leno was the son of Mr. and Mrs. Johnny Wilde, who
played at cheap music-halls in the 'sixties, such as the Rotunda in the Blackfriars
Road. When Wilde died, his widow married one, William Grant, whose stage
name was Leno. Accordingly, Dan began his theatrical career as Dan Patrick
Leno, singing Irish songs, often in company with Johnny Danvers, his uncle,
though, in fact, Danvers was somewhat younger than his nephew.

Travelling in Lancashire when he was seventeen, Dan heard that a free-and-easy
was to be held in a local inn. He was allowed to contribute to the amateur talent
in consideration of taking a hat round after the song and dance with which Dan
obliged. The result was close upon £2, most of it in coppers. Plainly there was
money in song and clog-dancing, especially in the clog-dancing, when, after a
six-days' open contest Dan was proclaimed Champion Clog-dancer of the World.
In Lancashire in the 'eighties clog-dancing was not a mut's game. Clappers in
the shoes were taboo and audiences knew the finer points of the art almost as
well as the judges. At St. Helens, during a contest at the George, a slate slat was
let into the stage floor and the judges were put into the cellar underneath to hear
if the dancer missed a tap in time with the piano, cornet, and drums, which
constituted the orchestra. Dan could dance for twenty minutes without an error
and yet include original steps in his display.

Dan's first London appearance was at the Middlesex on October 5th, 1885, as
"the celebrated Irish comic vocalist and clog-dancer, Dan Leno." A little later
George Conquest engaged Dan for the Surrey pantomime.

Dan's verbal invention eventually proved fully as agile as his india-rubber legs.
Indeed, the essence of the Lenoesque humour was the speed with which absurdity
was piled upon absurdity, leaving time for nothing save laughter, not too far
removed from tears. When Dan was on the stage the laughter was not noisy.
I have referred to the "gentle confidences" which characterised so many of his
impersonations. As an ill-conditioned widow, maybe:

"He's so kind—so different from my fust husband. Oh, I've been married
before, girls. Yes, I'm a twicer. My first husband was a Spaniard. When he was
cross, oh! the way he used to look at me, with his black eyes and dark olive skin.
Oh, girls, beware of olive-skinners."

11

Mrs. Kelly

Or Dan Leno commenting upon Mrs. Kelly: "You see, we had a row once, and it was all through Mrs. Kelly. You know Mrs. Kelly, of course—Mrs. Kelly —Mrs. Kelly? You know Mrs. Kelly? You must know Mrs. Kelly. Good life-a-mighty! don't look so simple. She's a cousin of Mrs. Nipletts, and her husband keeps the what-not shop at the—— Oh, you must know Mrs. Kelly. Everybody knows Mrs. Kelly."

In a very few weeks every patron of the Tivoli *did* know Mrs. Kelly. She popped up in all sorts of queer corners for Dan had given her life, as he gave life to his Beefeater, or the Waiter, wearing those roomy trousers which seemed to sweep the stage. Like all great comics, Dan favoured the under-dog. As the waiter he was big-eyed and hollow-cheeked and his husky voice had an endearing appeal.

"Yes, sir! No, sir! Yes, sir! When I first came here these trousers were knee-breeches. Legs worn down by waiting. Sir! What did you say? How long would your steak be? Oh, about four inches, I should say, about four inches."

At this point the pathetic little figure would fix his eye upon an imaginary plate, sensing the customer's complaint before it was uttered.

"Beg pardon, sir, I'm sure. My mistake, sir. You would have it so quickly that I got flurried and gave you the Spring Port and the '75 chicken."

There was somewhat more assurance in Mr. Meakins, the frock-coated shop-walker, but still it was essentially the little man, only too anxious to oblige.

"Yes, Ma'am. What, Ma'am? No, Ma'am. Red, Ma'am? Yes, Ma'am. I quite understand. I'm a married man myself." Then a little turn of the supple waist and Mr. Meakins was all attention to a new inquiry.

"Gloves, Ma'am? Yes, Ma'am. You want those in the window at three-three? Can't be done, Ma'am. Can't be done. Glued to the glass, glued to the glass!"

And, lastly, the japes attaching to the Grocer in "Our Stores."

"There is a sort of mystery in the word 'egg.' There are newly laid eggs, there are fresh eggs and there are eggs. That is the egg I am talking about. It is the egg which causes all the trouble. You dare not kick it. It's got no face."

But already Dan is off on another tack. "Those eggs exploded this morning." "My dear sir, you surprise me. Of course I'll change them. They were all so full of meat that they could not stand hot water."

And the riverside house, "where the river was at the bottom of the garden, or the garden was at the bottom of the river!"

The Eclipse of Variety

Lastly, 1s. 6d. was the cost of a pit seat and 5s. paid for a stall, with no entertainment tax. Those were the days for Variety.

Like the Palaces of Variety, the Syndicate Halls, as the Edwardian patrons of vaudeville knew them, barely survived the first World War. The salaries of the stars had risen too quickly. It was no longer possible to present twenty good turns a night, as had been the practice. Moreover, there was a tendency to rely too much upon established favourites, and songs and patter were repeated too frequently. Revue, which needed fewer stars and allowed the more easy invention of new songs, tended to take the place of Edwardian Variety, and a star like George Robey gratefully accepted the support of colourful backgrounds and well-trained choruses, the more because they permitted larger and even larger salaries. In the provinces, too, proprietary travelling revue companies came into being and managers found it more profitable to engage such a company, rather than search Europe for twenty attractive turns weekly.

At the end of the 'twenties, when the Talkie boom was beginning, there were fewer than a hundred music-halls throughout the British Isles, and it seemed that the talking film was killing Variety. However, the old-time interest in highly flavoured personalities and unbuttoned humour slowly reasserted itself and such firms as Moss Empires, B. and J. Theatres, and the Stoll Tour came back to Variety, though with big differences. Once more, instead of fewer than a hundred music-halls, Britain had well over a couple of hundred, not to mention the revue houses and the cabaret shows, and, all the time, music-hall entertainments were suffering slow but constant changes to fit them for mixed audiences, as opposed to the masculine audiences of Victorian times. One of the most effective factors bore no relation to the stage proper. It was the absence of the "No Smoking" rule, which governed theatres devoted to legitimate drama. A quarter of a century ago so many West End theatres banned smoking in their auditoriums that producers of drama found it difficult to attract paying audiences. Sir Arthur Pinero pointed out the cure. "Introduce the cigarette and the pipe, and you will fill your theatres once more," he said. Sir Arthur added that there had been a time when women objected to smoking in an auditorium. When they waived this objection to tobacco, a blow was struck at the popularity of the theatre. Be this as it may, by 1913 there were fully as many women in a West End music-hall as men. Man, a smoking animal, finding that his women-folk had no rooted objection to tobacco, took tickets for a music-hall, whereas five years earlier he would have chosen a musical comedy in a regular theatre.

The ever-rising rentals of London theatres between the two World Wars had abiding effects upon all forms of entertainment. By 1920, West End theatres were worth three times as much as they had been in 1914. A theatre might originally have been leased at £200 a week. By 1920, the renter could obtain £400 a week from a sub-lessee, and the latter was still able to make a profit upon the transaction. Moreover, at post-war costs, it was no longer profitable to build new theatres within "the charmed circle" which includes Shaftesbury Avenue, Leicester Square, the Haymarket, Charing Cross Road, the Strand, and Drury Lane. Something like £6,000 a year would have been asked as ground rent and another £40,000 would have been required for dispossessing existing tenants. These prime costs, together with £100,000 for actual building, meant that £400 a week was no more than a fair return to a speculative builder of a West End theatre, with a holding capacity of about 1,500 people, and a money capacity of, say, £250 a performance, that is, £2,000 a week. A big house, such as the Hippodrome, could not be built for anything like that price. Owners of a super-film could afford to pay £800 a week for such a house as the Palace and though the Co-Optimists were able to lease this theatre for a while, it was a hazardous venture, especially as, by May 1921, the post-war trading boom had collapsed and there were two and a half million unemployed in Britain. Thus it was that the larger London theatres were driven to stage expensive musical shows, while the smaller West End houses turned to intimate revue, a variant upon an art-form which had long attracted Parisians, but, thus far, had engaged no more than the passing attention of Londoners.

Chapter X

PIERROTS AND PIERETTES. FOLLIES AND CO-OPTIMISTS

APART FROM PATRONS OF MUSIC-HALLS, THEATRES, AND CABARET
shows, there has always been a considerable public desirous of what may be
described as non-theatre vaudeville. It may be that this public was originally
associated with a feeling which was very prevalent in the middle of the nineteenth
century, both in Britain and America, that is, that theatres and music-halls were
inventions of the devil, whereas concerts, even when the faces of the performers
were disguised with burnt cork, could be justified by the tenderest of consciences.

The earliest entertainments to cater for this demand in Victorian times were
the nigger minstrels, which had their origin, naturally enough, in the States,
though probably an equally enduring embodiment of the type flourished at St.
James's Hall, Piccadilly.

The American originator of the negro minstrels was one, Ned Christy, and
his first troupe numbered three, each disguised with plentiful applications of burnt
cork and, between them, manipulating five instruments: a banjo, a violin, a
tambourine, a triangle, and the all-important bones. Christy specialised in negro
melodies and most of them were traditional airs of the folk-song type. By 1847,
E. P. Christy's Minstrels were an established institution in America, and persuaded George Washington Moore to inaugurate his Nigger Minstrel show in
St. James's Hall (where Piccadilly Hotel now stands). The financial genius of
the partnership was Frederick Burgess. There were also the Mohawk Minstrels,
including Harry Hunter, who wrote the famous tongue-twister, "I saw Esau kissing
Kate," with its climax, "For I saw Esau and he saw me, and she saw that I saw
Esau." The well-known firm of Francis, Day and Hunter, music publishers,
was established upon the popularity of the songs of Harry Hunter in Victorian
times, the brothers Francis being members of the Moore and Burgess troupe and
David Day its business manager. So successful was Moore's venture that it gave
from nine to twelve performances weekly over a period of forty years, and in the
'eighties the Moore and Burgess Minstrels boasted seventy performers, eighteen of
whom were vocalists and ten comedians, while the company also had twelve
unrivalled clog and statuesque dancers, all magnificently costumed by Mrs. May.
The prices were suitable for family parties—Fauteuils, 5s.; Sofa Stalls, 3s.; Area,
2s.; Gallery, 1s. A national institution, this, if ever there was one in connection
with song and story.

The no less popular German Reed entertainments were staged at St. George's
Hall, which was opened in Langham Place in 1867, and leased to Thomas
German Reed. His first production was an operetta, *The Contrabandista*, by
Sullivan and Burnand, a show which was later transformed into *The Chieftain*.

Two operettas with music by Offenbach completed the bill. Later, W. S. Gilbert, the brothers a-Beckett, Robert Reece, Frederick Clay, Alfred Cellier, Edward Solomon, and Walter Slaughter contributed sketches, songs, and music; one of Gilbert's efforts being "Ages Ago," which was to be the basis of *Ruddigore*. Mrs. German Reed (Priscilla Horton) was a leading spirit in the enterprise, with her character sketches at the piano, Reed himself being her accompanist. The first entertainments were given at St. Martin's Hall in Long Acre, then at the Gallery of Illustration, Lower Regent Street, and, finally, between 1874 and 1895, at St. George's Hall, Langham Place.

In 1860, the German Reeds were joined by John Parry, who told stories and sang songs to his own accompaniment. When Richard Corney Grain, a young lawyer, took Parry's place at the piano, these medleys of song, character sketches, and recitations became the staple in German Reed entertainments. In twenty-five years Corney Grain did not exhaust his store of funny stories or his gift for kindly social satire. George Grossmith, senior, Yvette Guilbert, Albert Chevalier, Helen Mar, and Ruth Draper were among the vaudeville artists who have since exploited this highly specialised market. It is nearly allied to the market which supported the pierrot troupes during the summer holidays, institutions which eventually gave the Follies and the Co-Optimists to English vaudeville and assured Balieff's Chauve-Souris its welcome. The first London appearance of the Follies in the West End was at the Queen's Hall, in conjunction with Albert Chevalier and his Coster impersonations.

It was in the early years of the twentieth century that the vogue of nigger minstrels at English watering-places ended and pierrots took their places. Evidence, this, of a growing demand for a somewhat more sophisticated entertainment on pier or beach. An exceptionally gifted nigger troupe (say at Great Yarmouth or Llandudno) was able to meet the competition of the pierrots, but most dark-faced minstrels cleaned their faces and joined the new-comers. Here and there a clever manager engaged a small company and made quite big monies by working a successful "pitch" on shore or pier. Indeed, a really good "pitch" was so profitable that the Scarborough Corporation could charge £600 for a season, this amount guaranteeing a troupe from competition. Other seaside resorts erected pavilions and engaged troupes on a percentage basis, the members being largely recruited from the choruses of musical-comedy companies who chanced to be "resting" during the summer months and hoped, at least, to pay the expenses of a long holiday at the seaside. Perhaps an average wage was £4 a week.

The associations of the pierrots and pierrettes with the larger world of the theatre were innumerable. Wish Wynne, of happy memory, was a member of a troupe which sang and played on a stretch of waste ground in front of the West Riding police-station in Halifax. Thirty years ago Tom Walls was earning 45s. a week on Brighton front. Tom Walls, in turn, gave Bobbie Howes his first real opportunity, in a concert party working Welsh seaside resorts. Jack Hylton, the conductor, also graduated with seaside concert parties, of the pierrot type. His father at one time was a cotton spinner, who eked out an inadequate income by singing comic songs at smoking concerts; later, he passed into public-house proprietorship. Young Jack, at the age of ten, was appearing as "The Singing Mill Boy," with clogs, and by 1905 was starred as a boy vocalist with a pierrot company. In the winter Jack appeared in the singing-room of his dad's public-house, and in the summer was one of the Comedy Cameos at Rhyl. Later came an engagement at the old Embassy Club, in London, and, at last, the Queen's Hall Roof and fame.

Mention will be made later of "The March Hares," out of Cambridge University, and the Co-Optimists, which were an important consequence of the March Hares' Madness. A kindred show was "The Mad Hatters," featuring Bobby Comber, who later achieved Wireless fame. The "Tatlers" and "Scamps" gave Leslie Henson early opportunities, as Will Pepper's "White Coons" at Felixstowe nourished the budding talents of Harry S. Pepper. Catlin's Pierrots and resident troupes at such resorts as Llandudno and Lowestoft were other nurseries of vaudeville talent on the eve of the first World War.

The Follies

The first of the historic pierrot troupes was Pélissier's Follies, with their motto "Excelsior." The original company began its ascent to the heights of vaudeville from the London suburbs. At first there were ten members; then six, and at last, nine, the number of the children of Zeus and Mnemosyne, who constituted the Muses. Always at the head of the troupe was the burly Harry Gabriel Pélissier. Born in 1874, at the age of fifteen he was composer enough to persuade Jessie Bond of Savoy fame to sing his songs and singer enough to make the lady, in turn, play his accompaniments. To the eloquent and wise leader of the troupe was added in time Lewis Sydney, with the cleft palate, and his "Snoishtory of the Kishning Cup." Lewis Sydney was the Alfred Lester of the Follies and never enjoyed the mock life of pierrottery. He abandoned it for a business career.

As for the rest of the troupe, there were Muriel George and Ethel Allandale, singers of pretty songs; Effie Cook, the dancer of the party; Dan Everard and Morris Harvey, the heavier comedians (so far as any Folly was heavy); and the soubrettes, Gwennie Mars and Fay Compton. Of Fay Compton it need only be said that her fame eventually extended far beyond the Follies. Muriel George is remembered for her golden hair and her singing of "Moon, my Moon." Her mother was a well-known teacher of singing, and intended that her girl should become an operatic singer. But Muriel George met Ernest Butcher, the baritone, and together they discovered and sang folk-songs; the very talent which Pélissier wanted when he created the Follies.

To the Tuneful Nine were added sundry Loves and Doves, who appeared from time to time in the "beauty-full, grace-full and A-Muse-ing tableaux" of the Follies; among them Louis Laval and Maud Evans, in charge of the Double

Grand piano; Doris Brooke, Marjorie Napier, singing "I want somebody to love me"; Norman Blumé, Ronald Bagnall, Douglas Maclaren, and Evelyn Hughes.

Beginning as amateurs, run by the tennis-playing Baddeley Brothers, in the interests of charities in the London suburbs, Sherringham Chinn gave the Follies a professional twist, and the troupe accepted engagements at seaside piers, among them Southsea and Worthing. Eventually Pélissier purchased the goodwill of the concern from Sherringham Chinn and reduced the number of the company to six. Among them were Lewis Sydney, Ethel Allandale and himself, with Arthur Wimperis in the background as supplier of lyrics. Wimperis was also primarily responsible for the comic programmes of the Follies, with their illustrations, for he was an artist before he turned playwright. One of them lies before me as I write, with extracts from the Rules of the Lord Chamberlain.

"An egg-proof curtain will be lowered at least once during the performance for the protection of artists."

The comic "ads" in a Follies programme alone made half an hour's wait on a pit seat at the Apollo amusing. "Dewar's Soap for the Gullet." Smellin's Cod Liver Oil. Again "Tea (perhaps), per pot per person," and the instruction, "In case of Fire, cut along the dotted line!" This programme was concerned with the music-hall burlesque, which was a Follies triumph. Here are some items:

(i) Mic and Mac, Amurrica's slickest, quickest, cross-talk Comedians.
(ii) Mr. Ernest Bathos, The Great Actor Vocalist, in his world-famous beery pathetic ballad, "Give my love to Mother."
(iii) Colonel Swanky D. Codder (assisted by Miss A. Lotta Bulls) in their sensational Wild West Kilburn Shooting Act.
(iv) Miss Mona Yellba, the Australian Sopralto.
(v) Margaret Whooper and a Piano.
(vi) George Robeyville, the Refined Humorist.
(vii) Mr. Grandsby Billious, in his Drawing Room entertainment, entitled "What the Dickens."

And so on!

Everybody's Benefit, a burlesque of a benefit matinée, written and composed by Pélissier, with lyrics by Arthur Davenport, was an extravaganza of the same type as the potted music-hall entertainment. The honoured lady was Sarah Judkins, who was pictured twice on the special programme, first as a juvenile in tights and, secondly, as she was fifty years later. The following artistes reluctantly consented to appear by kind suggestion of their respective managers:

1. Signor Caroozo (by kind permission of the Gramophone Company).
2. Mr. Arthur Bradsmith and Chorus, from the *Gay Gazeekas*, in his celebrated song, "I want to be a Hero" (by kind permission of the audience).
10. The Supper Scene from *The School for Scandal*. Played entirely by Leading Actor Managers (by kind permission of each other).

The Follies
The Company in Costume
H. G. Pellisier trying his own voice

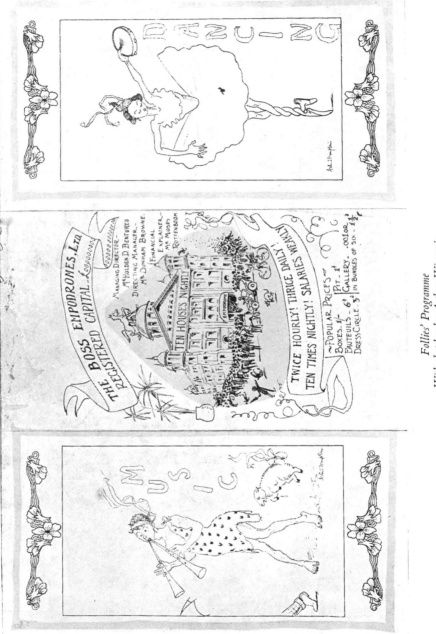

Follies' Programme

With sketches by Arthur Wimperis

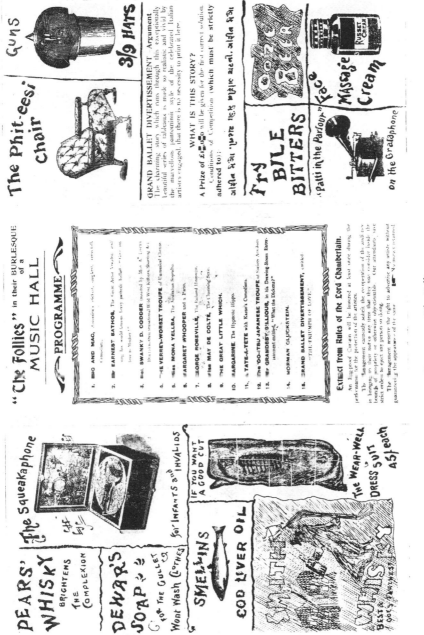

Programme: The Follies
In their Music Hall Burlesque

Laddie
Cliff

Gilbert
Childs

Betty Chester

Davy
Burnaby

Stanley
Holloway

The Co-Optimists

13. Act II of that screaming Farcical Comedy, *Where's My Wife?*
(Translated from the French and all the spice extracted by Comyns Brookfield.)
14. By general desire the Manager of "The Follies" Music Hall will recite *Kissing Cup's Race.*

And so on!

Again there was Pélissier's Potted Pageant.

EPISODE I

The Birth of Harmony

Being an authentic picture of prehistoric man in his habit, as he lived, introducing a promenade concert of the period. . . . It will be seen that these primitive creatures were the originators of a well-known entertainment now running in London.

EPISODE III

Lady Godiva's Ride

A beautifully and artistic picture showing this exquisitely lovely lady riding unclothed through the streets of Coventry. . . . An idea of the perfect dimensions of this lady can be gathered from the fact that she measures from the tip of the snout to the centre of the near fetlock exactly 4 feet $17\frac{1}{2}$ in., roughly speaking.

EPISODE IV

The Kings and Queens of England

This episode was invented by Mr. Arthur Wimperis in a moment of temporary mental aberration, while thinking of his ancestors.

EPISODE VI

The Hobby Horse

These mammals (*velocopaedia Brittanica*) were apparently still in existence at this period (whatever it is) and were ridden by most of the smart set at that time (whatever it was).

And so on!

Potted Pantomime and Pélissier's Potted Plays were other regular features in the Follies' bill. For the rest, here are a few extracts, selected at random from a number of surviving programmes:

Effie Cook will indulge in a fit of the dismals, *Never More* (Krenkel).
Beverage Quartettes: (1) Port, (2) Harrogate Wells, (3) Cyder, (4) Rum. (5) Blubber.
Gastronomic Quartettes (for six voices): (1) Missionary, (2) Baked Potatoes, (3) Haggis.
Ypsilanti: (Davenport and Pelissier) By Gwennie Mars.
Teddy Bear: (Words by Davenport, Music by Pelissier) By Ethel Allandale.
Morris Harvey: Will indulge in the Sincerest Form of Flattery.
Old English Glee: words by Davenport, music by Davenport and Pelissier—By The Follies.

H. G. Pélissier was the good genius of the troupe. His personal inspiration and the gusto which he put into the team-work lifted the entertainment into a diversion unique and entirely enjoyable. It was pierrot programme *in excelsis*. The Chief's infectious spirits did what a more brilliant composer, singer, and actor might have failed to achieve. He made his company a happy family, whose happiness communicated itself to the audience. It was a good day for Anglo-Saxon vaudeville when Pélissier refused to become a diamond merchant. For four years Pélissier built up the repertoire of the Follies and tuned up the individual turns, until the little company was up to the West End standard.

As has been said, the opportunity came when Albert Chevalier engaged the Follies to supplement his matinée recitals in the small Queen's Hall in 1898. The Chevalier recitals precisely met the demand created by those who enjoyed the thrill of theatrical production but feared the traditional associations of stage life. Here was a man who could act, and yet offered a blend of sentiment and actuality in which damsels in their 'teens, maiden aunts, and middle-aged parents could safely indulge. Admittedly, there was greater realism in the Cockney embodiments of Gus Elen and Alec Hurley at the Palaces of Variety or the Syndicate Halls, but Albert Chevalier's recitals justified a claim that here was the Laureate of Costerdom. Like Harry Lauder, with his Scottish songs, Chevalier devised a compromise with actuality, which allowed the humour and sentiment of the coster world full freedom, without a trace of vulgarity.

Chevalier had considerable experience as an actor before he touched fame as a singer of coster songs. His early stage appearances were made as a lad under the Bancrofts at the Prince of Wales's Theatre; thence he passed to John Hare's management at the Court, where he played in Pinero farces. Full fortune, however, only came when he persuaded the London Pavilion to allow him to sing coster songs; his claim being enforced by his success as an entertainer at Savage Club "Saturday Nights." When "Knocked 'em in the Old Kent Road," "Wot's the good of anyfink?" "Oh, Liza," "My Old Dutch," and "Our Little Nipper" followed hard upon "The Coster's Serenade," it was plain that a new star had arisen. Always, a Chevalier make-up was perfect, and the details of the character sketches were worked up with the utmost care. At his best the sentiment was unforced, but, in Chevalier's latter days, the singer tended to over-emphasise pauses. How good he was in the "Coster's Serenade"! The memory still brings to life half of London Town, as it was half a century ago:

> You ain't forgotten yet that night in May,
> Dahn at the Welsh 'Arp, which is 'Endon way.
> You fancied winkles and a pot of tea.
> "Four ale," I murmured, "'s good enough for me.
> Give me a word of 'ope that I may win"—
> You prods me gently with the winkle pin;
> We was as 'appy as could be that day,
> Dahn at the Welsh 'Arp, which is 'Endon way.

The association of the Follies with Chevalier at the small Queen's Hall was followed by music-hall appearances at the Tivoli, the Alhambra, and the Palace; and, at last, a Royal Command to Sandringham. The invitation was given by King Edward in connection with a Queen Alexandra birthday party. Such successes persuaded Pélissier to hire a theatre and offer the public a full evening's programme. The troupe was at the Royalty in 1907. Later, came appearances at the Apollo. Something on the Double Grand, perhaps Tchaikovsky's "Valse des Fleurs," then the Opening Chorus, followed by Kipling's "Just So" songs, with music by Edward German, maybe, or Lewis Sydney and Pélissier singing to one another, and a Potted Play. Pélissier, as actor, composer, manager, and producer attempted more than any one man could do. His early death was a result. This was in 1913 at the age of thirty-nine. Among Pélissier's songs were "Awake," "I want Somebody to Love Me," "In My Garden of Roses," and "Oh, what a Happy Land is England."

The first World War wrought great changes in social habits and corresponding changes in public entertainment. The Y.M.C.A. had done something to meet the need for organised amusement for troops in training, but real progress began when Oswestry Camp, under the guidance of Basil Dean, built a garrison theatre in 1916, canteen funds providing the original capital. Every evening at Oswestry two performances were given to crowded audiences, spectators in the pit frequently sitting upon each other's knees, rather than miss a selection from *Faust*, or what not. The success at Oswestry was so plain that the Canteen Board instructed Basil Dean to extend the experiment. A circuit of garrison theatres and cinemas was created, prices of admission ranging from 3*d.* to 2*s.* 6*d.* By November 1918 there were fifteen army theatres and seven cinemas, served by ten official companies. Three of them were playing musical comedies such as *The Merry Widow*, *Our Miss Gibbs*, and *The Maid of the Mountains*, while two vaudeville companies presented the best numbers in current London revue. Concert parties, working on Pélissier lines, staged entertainments at the smaller training centres or behind the lines in France, not only while fighting was in progress, but during the weary months of waiting which preceded demobilisation. Not a few well-known vaudeville players established their reputation by work of this kind; an outstanding example being Leslie Henson. Among the pierrot troupes, the Co-Optimists, working upon a nucleus of troop entertainers, achieved abiding fame.

The Co-Optimists

The Co-Optimists followed faithfully in the path cut by the Follies, and, like their predecessors, wore ruffles and skull-caps, the colours being purple and gold. The beginning came when four young Cambridge undergraduates, including Philip Braham and Davy Burnaby, founded an entertainment called *The March Hares* and toured the open-air pavilions, "Pa" Braham being the band of the combination. Solus, he manipulated piano, cymbals, drums, celeste, and triangle. Philip Braham is best known as the composer of "Limehouse Blues."

From The March Hares, Davy Burnaby went on to musical comedy, then to the Gaiety, where he was a portly foil to the slender Leslie Henson for some years. At the end of the first World War, Davy Burnaby was at the Casino Theatre, Wimereux, entertaining the troops, and with him were Phyllis Monkman, Melville Gideon, Gilbert Childs, Laddie Cliff, and Jack Buchanan. The party just sat in a semicircle round the stage and let the show run itself with the aid of two pianos. Melville Gideon expressly pleaded for a second piano, lest, when he had accompanied everyone else, he was left without the "pep" to get over his own songs. The extra pianist was Jack Hylton.

Now in June 1921 the genial Davy Burnaby was "resting." *A Night Out* had finished its run at the Winter Garden. Looking out for a new show, Burnaby bethought himself of *The March Hares* and the entertainers at Wimereux. Why not another pierrot troupe for London on the lines of the Follies? Over lunch at his Golf Club, Burnaby discussed the idea with Archibald de Bear, publicity manager at the Hippodrome. Doubtless to the surprise of Burnaby, Archie offered to put up £250 and, at once, the proposition took on a new glow. Then Laddie Cliff was interested and offered another £400. Amazing! The last £250 was put up by a young journalist, Clifford Whiteley. More Amazing! In a few years this initial £900 took £300,000 from the public. Most amazing!

The original production was by Hugh Willoughby, from settings and dresses he had designed while a prisoner of war in Holland and cost £300, a triumphant demonstration of the value of ingenuity and wit, as opposed to mere money. When the Co-Optimists opened at the Royalty, there remained just £200 in the bank for all emergencies. Questioned as to the financial prospects of the Co-Optimists in these early days, Laddie Cliff summed them up thus: "Three pioneers and two pianners—five in all."

Between them the plucky pioneers and pianners established the vogue of the Co-Optimists during eight years, and, in 1924, the members had the courage to rent the Palace Theatre at £750 a week, and stayed there a year. Only the ever-growing rentals charged for West End theatres ended their career of money making.

Throughout, Davy Burnaby was the leading spirit in the troupe, though he never had the commanding position of Pélissier in the Follies. A product of the "Manse" (English variety), he went to Haileybury, where one terminal report told an astonished parent: "Shows promise as an actor." At Cambridge, Burnaby sat for the Little-Go in 1900, though my informant, "Bucks," characteristically failed to state whether his friend passed the examination. Plainly, Davy did, as he became stage manager of the Footlights Club. Then came the call to the stage, and the gentle transition to the well-rounded *compère* of the Co-Optimists. As a writer of songs, Burnaby is remembered by "Reckless Reggie of the Regent Palace" and his ingenious *Initial Song* "I'll be your D.S.O. if you'll be my V.A.D." indicates the underlying idea.

Deep-voiced Betty Chester (Mrs. Billyard Leake) had been on the stage about seven years, playing in Shaw, Shakespeare, revue, cabaret, and musical comedy, but she appeared with the Co-Optimists so continuously that her name springs to mind when the feminine supporters of burly Burnaby and Laddie Cliff are recalled. There was nothing Betty Chester could not attempt. It might be an appearance as Carmencita, with Burnaby as Carmen and Gilbert Childs as Carmen-two-seater in the grand spectacular drama of the Bull-ring, entitled *Write to John Bull About It*, or it might be just singing the ever-popular Masefield lyric, "Sea Fever." When Betty Chester was playing elsewhere, Gwendoline Brogden sometimes wore the purple and gold in her stead.

It would be pleasant to recall many details of that eight years' pilgrimage through the pleasant dales of vaudeville, but a few glimpses must suffice to recall the pulsing whole, with its ever-growing intimacy between players and public which is the secret of abiding success. Elsa Macfarlane ("Take my hair as red") was the soprano of the party, Phyllis Monkman the dancer, while Babs Valerie was charged with the duty of filling the stage without attracting too much attention to her pretty self. As she said:

> I'm the baby of the party,
> And with chocolates I'm fed.
> And if I have too much to say
> Then I'll be put to bed.

Hermione Baddeley was not an original Co-Optimist, but came in when she was eighteen years old. She had leapt into theatrical fame a year earlier, as the coster girl in *The Likes of Her*. With Gilbert Childs, Hermione Baddeley played a tiny sketch, *Missing the Bus*, by Greatrex Newman. As a weary, bedraggled wife, returning with her husband from a musical evening laden with gramophone and records, she put in a great piece of miming.

Melville Gideon was, of course, *facile princeps* at Piano Number 1, but Herbert Hedley at times contributed the twiddley bits which the genius of Melville disdained. Wolseley Charles was another pianist, while Harry Pepper, son of White Coons' Pepper, was often called upon to open the show at the piano. Bow-wow! Apart from his skill as an accompanist, Melville Gideon wrote a round century of songs for the troupe and sang and acted with the best. His "Texas Love," supported by a full company of cowboys and cowgirls, will be remembered. It was written by Greatrex Newman, who wrote a number of successful sketches for the Co-Optimists. "Amapu," for which Edward Knoblock wrote the words for Gideon's music, was originally a skit upon the so-called Indian Love Lyrics, which failed to reach publication until it became part of the Co-Optimists' first programme.

How is this record to end? With Laddie Cliff, fresh from Margate singing "Coal Black Mammy"? When Laddie Cliff was lost to the troupe, Austin Melford took his place. You may remember his "I've fallen in love with twins," in this case Anita Elson and Doris Bentley. Stanley Holloway associates himself with pills and jail, but also with "The King who wanted jam for tea," and "Coaling." The music of the jam-loving King number was by Wolseley Charles, from County Clare. And there still remains the memories of little Doris Bentley, the soubrette, Cicily James, and Gilly Flower, who—

> don't take up much room,
> I've only just begun, you see,
> To burst forth into bloom.

No, there is only one conclusion to Co-Optimist memories—"And so to bed!" Nikita Balieff's La Chauve-Souris, from the Bat Theatre, Moscow, was not strictly English vaudeville, any more than it was characteristically Russian. It was a cosmopolitan effort, which made a niche for itself in London. Noel Coward has recorded his impression of a Balieff's speech:

> Ladies and gentlemen, Ass you see, I find him verrey deeficult to spik Eenglish. There iss an old Russian proberb wheech say that a dead rhinosceros iss nearer to the starrs than a leetle child who steecks a pean eento iss old grandmother, all of wheech have no bearing whatever upon the leetle scene wheech my company weel present.
>
> Eet iss a peecneeck een old Russia. (*The song of the Volga Boatmen is heard off and Balieff vanishes for a while.*)

The splendid team-work and the perfect rehearsal of the Chauve-Souris songs and sketches revealed the secret of success in such efforts, and made memorable the Dresden china trifle: "Sur le Pont D'Avignon," the Volga Boat song, with the men on the ropes, and Léon Jessel's "Parade of the Wooden Soldiers," to mention only three items in a typical programme. Much of the music was French or German, but the bright colours of the backgrounds and the costumes were derived from primitive Russian peasant art and they gave distinction to Balieff's productions.

Chapter XI

INTIMATE REVUE, FROM COCHRAN TO FARJEON
1914 TO 1944

SPECTACULAR REVUE, OWING SOMETHING TO THE GERMAN
Reinhardt but more to the American Florenz Ziegfeld, was introduced to London
by Albert de Courville, as the London popularity of a more witty and engaging
genre, Intimate Revue, stands to the credit of Charles Cochran. Whereas spectacular revue was usually staged at such houses as the Hippodrome and the
Coliseum, intimate revue established itself in smaller theatres, particularly the
Ambassadors and the Vaudeville. Later Charles Cochran was to rival de
Courville's most florid efforts, but it was as a populariser of the intimacies of
revue, rather than as a vendor of its colourful splendours, that Cochran proved his
worth, and it is his efforts in this direction which now claim attention.

Well before Cochran's tally of production was completed he had a round
score of revues to his credit, and they showed an average profit of £12,000 on
their London runs. Plainly, this is the record of a master-showman. As for the
players, Delysia, Evelyn Laye, Spinelly, Eve Lavallière, Betty Balfour, Jessie
Matthews, Maisie Gay, Tilly Losch, and Hermione Baddeley are some of the
women who figure in Cochran's revue programmes. Massine, Leon Morton,
Sonnie Hale, Ernest Thesiger, and Douglas Byng are among the men, while
Cochran authors include Harry Grattan, Noel Coward, Arthur Wimperis,
Beverley Nichols, and John Hastings Turner. Only a very shrewd judge of
potential talent and a man with wide-ranging sympathies could have collected
such teams, and only a man skilled in handling the personnel of the stage could
have persuaded such folk continually to give him of their best.

Charles Cochran was born in Sussex some seventy years ago. In early life he
chanced to see Arthur Roberts in pantomime at Brighton, and the experience
persuaded him to become a comedian. Oddly enough, Aubrey Beardsley and
Mabel Beardsley, his sister, were early friends and influences, so that, even as a
schoolboy, the characteristics of the master-showman were there, a vital interest
in the popular theatre and some association with the more bizarre forms of art.
Thanks to Arthur Roberts, the beginning of Cochran's stage experience was
singing comic songs at smoking concerts in South Coast resorts. With little
more professional experience, young Charles went to America in search of a
career. He reached Chicago with 25 cents in his pocket, and discovered his
mascot in Richard Mansfield, who has been described as the Henry Irving of
America. At any rate, Mansfield was a man of influence and standing, and made
the Englishman his personal secretary, having quickly reached the conclusion that
Cochran was never likely to be a comedian of worth. The career had commenced.

Cochran came back to London in search of plays for Richard Mansfield, and, after a spell as a music-hall agent, he tried his prentice skill as a theatrical producer. His first effort, *Sporting Simpson*, at the Royalty in 1904, was a failure. However, when wrestling enjoyed a music-hall boom, Cochran was in it, with Georges Hackenschmidt as his bright star. Roller-skating and boxing followed, and Cochran was in them. It will always be a mystery how "C. B." missed "going into the dogs." Lastly, the production of *The Miracle* at Olympia in 1911, with its cast of 1,500 performers, showed that a new force was at work in the theatrical world. In the early years after the first World War, he controlled seven theatres in the West End of London, and the productions included two revues, two straight comedies, a realistic drama, the Duse Season and the Guitry Season, not to mention a song and dance show, which was in rehearsal, when Cochran's record established itself.

There had been efforts at popularising intimate revue in London before those of Charles Cochran, including those of the ubiquitous Planché, Rouge Croix and burletta-scribe. Planché's first attempt was made in 1825, when the Adelphi Theatre was managed by Yates and Terry, Yates being the father of Edmund Yates of *The World*, and Terry the friend of Sir Walter Scott, whom he aided in dramatising some of the Waverley novels for Drury Lane. For Yates and Terry, Planché wrote *Success, or A Hit if You Like It*. The Lady Success was a daughter of Fashion, Grand Autocrat of all the World, and the curtain went up to the strains of "Rule Britannia":

> When Fashion first at Whim's command,
> In lieu of Common-sense began to reign,
> This was the chorus, the chorus of the land,
> And mantua-makers swelled the strain.
>
> Rule great Fashion! Where'er your sceptre waves,
> Both old and young be ever, ever, Fashion's slaves.

Planché failed to establish Parisian revue in London, partly because he hampered himself by having a single female character, Lady Success herself. There were, however, occasional efforts to give the type an English dress. Thus H. J. Byron, in 1863, wrote *Sensations of the Past Season* for the St. James's company, but it had no great success.

Under the Clock, by Charles Brookfield and Seymour Hicks, with music by Edward Jones, was a venture at the Court about the time Victorian burlesque was giving place to Edwardian musical comedy. Seymour Hicks scored a small triumph and secured a long engagement from George Edwardes at the Gaiety in consequence, but *Under the Clock* lacked the vitalising rhythm and pace, which persuade audiences that they are sharing memories and experiences with the stage players. The idea behind the extravaganza was that Brookfield was Sherlock Holmes and Seymour Hicks, Dr. Watson, and they were showing Emile Zola the theatrical sights of London. Among the sights was the Third Mrs. Tanqueray, who zigzagged around the stage, murmuring, "I can't go straight; I can't go straight!" With Pinero's heroine was telescoped Lottie Collins, in her famous song, and the item ended thus:

I'm wiser now than to allow
  Myself to go astray;
For I'm the Second Mrs. Boom
  Tarara-Tanqueray.

Lottie Venne, assuredly, was in her element when she essayed imitations of Mrs. Bancroft and Julia Neilson. So was the youthful Seymour Hicks as Irving and Wilson Barrett. Imitations alone, however, are meagre fare for a revue, even though it only occupies a single act and is part of a triple bill, as was *Under the Clock.*

Six years later, *Pot-Pourri, a Revue of 1899,* was produced at the Avenue, with a book by James Tanner and music by Napoleon Lambelet. A clever cast included Farren Soutar, a son of Nellie Farren, John le Hay, Marie Dainton the mimic, Claire Romaine, and Mlle Jane May, the latter disguising herself as Yvette Guilbert and also imitating La Grande Sarah, in the role of Hamlet. "A Thousand Leagues under the Sea" and "A Railway Station as it ought to be" were among the scenes. Again, there were too many imitations, and, in consequence, a marked absence of continuity.

Perhaps it was the memory of *Pot-Pourri* which persuaded Cochran to make his first timid effort to establish revue in London. With view to production at the Palace, Cochran commissioned Mostyn Piggott and Herman Finck to write a forty-minutes' revue, with Marie Dainton and Farren Soutar in leading roles. However, at the time London music-halls were forbidden to produce stage plays. Fearing litigation, the Palace management decided against the forty-minutes' revue and Charles Cochran momentarily turned his attention to other fields.

Another timorous effort in the direction of intimate revue was made when *Rogues and Vagabonds* was produced at the Empire in 1905. This was an invention of young George Grossmith, with aid from a Gaiety colleague, Harry Grattan, later Charles Cochran's first lieutenant in the establishment of intimate revue. One of the scenes in *Rogues and Vagabonds* was concerned with three chorus girls. Kitty Hanson (Mrs. "Bill" Berry) and Elsie Clare were two of them; the third was Grattan, who changed his disguise each night, now appearing as a char-woman, now, perhaps, as a giddy young flapper, and now as a principal boy, in the tights of the period. Grattan's lady companions in the scena never knew what to expect and were always in doubt how a new disguise might disturb their night's work.

What was wanting in English revue before Cochran's successes at the Ambassadors was tradition. None of the attempts at establishing the genre had been long-lived enough to collect and train a company able to establish community feeling between stage and auditorium, which is the life-blood of intimate revue.

12

A team is needed, not one or two lone comedians or comediennes. Thus, Robert Hale, father of Binnie Hale, fresh from a round of parts in Gaiety musical come, dies, had been playing in revue at the Empire and the Alhambra. In a single show Hale might burlesque a dozen topical personalities or institutions. Hunting, for example, with Hale as a Master of Fox Hounds, riding a restive hobby-horse and accompanied by a band of stuffed hounds. The delight of the audience was shown by the chorus of hunting cries which it evoked, cries which spurred the sharp-witted M.F.H. to renewed back-chat. Another Robert Hale triumph was his P. G. H. Fender, the Surrey and England cricketer and sporting journalist, with his long nose, his goggles, and his outsize sweater. Robert Hale's talent in revue was comparable with that of "Bunch" Keys, but he was a little in advance of the times (*Everybody's Doing It* dates from 1912), and he did not have the luck to come upon a Cochran, able to add the moral and material support required if intimate revue was to establish itself as a London institution and not merely as a passing craze.

When Charles Cochran gave London *Odds and Ends*, he was searching for an entertainment on the lines of that given at the Capucines, Paris, and the tiny Ambassadors Theatre in Seven Dials seemed a promising place. It was cheap, and cheapness was important, for it was the autumn of 1914, and the season was beset by the uncertainties of the early days of a World War. Moreover, Cochran contemplated an international flavour and realised that audiences able to appreciate international allusions would have to be built up by slow degrees. Happily, the ripe talent of Harry Grattan was to hand. He had first-hand experience of revue-writing and had known the feel of the "boards" from early childhood, having made his first appearance at the age of four, as one of "The Little Grattans." At twelve, Grattan was playing Captain Corcoran in a children's edition of *Pinafore*, this being a Christmas production at the Savoy and expressly devised by Gilbert, Sullivan, and D'Oyly Carte to encourage potential talent in the youth of the profession. Years of hard work in the provinces were followed by Grattan's appearances at the Gaiety in *The Toreador*, *The Orchid*, and *The Spring Chicken*. Thus Grattan was fully equipped when Cochran approached him in 1914 and called for the first rough scenario of *Odds and Ends*, with music by Edward Jones, who had written the music for *Under the Clock* and was now Cochran's musical director at the Ambassadors.

The scenery? There was no scenery. The revue opened upon a bare and empty stage. Later, there were black velvet curtains, a reminder that the influence of Reinhardt and Ernst Stern was already operating in Cochran-land.

Incidentally, intimate revue once more made the fourpenny or sixpenny programme worth the money asked, as it had been in the days of the Follies. It amused pit or gallery at the Ambassadors to receive the request: "Pray be seated punctually at 8.30, as the plot finishes at 8.25." The Bathing Revue, *Wash Me*, in which five million gallons of real water were *not* used, was equally typical of Mr. Grattan's facile invention.

"Pell Mell," An Ambassadors' Revue
Leon Morton and Alice Delysia, in 'The Arabian Nights'

The Crazy Gang at the Palladium
Flanagan and Allen; Nervo and Knox; Naughton and Gold

The Great Delysia

Apart from resurrecting Harry Grattan, Cochran's bit of luck was his discovery of Alice Delysia. She had been playing a small part at the Olympia, Paris, when Cochran offered her £6 a week to come to the Ambassadors. Delysia had personality, good looks, full assurance, and a splendid capacity for whole-hearted team-work. Moreover, in the French comedian, Leon Morton, Delysia found just the support she needed. No one ever sang Paul Rubens's recruiting song, "We don't want to lose you, but we think you ought to go," with more conviction that Delysia. Born in Paris in 1889, she began her career as a midinette, and first faced a large public when she entered for the Midinettes' Race through the French capital, and won it. Already there was vim and, slowly, stage experience was added, the beginning being in the chorus, when *The Belle of New York* was produced at the Old Moulin Rouge. From musical comedy Delysia passed to revue, and it was from revue at the Olympia, Paris, that Cochran enticed her to play "lead" in his war-time production at the little Ambassadors Theatre in West Street, Shaftesbury Avenue.

More *Odds and Ends* followed in 1915, and in it the inimitable Morton and Delysia, attended by eight pretty members of the Ambassadors chorus, four Cocodes and four Cocodettes, mimed and danced a wordless mid-Victorian scena, to music by Herman Darewski. In the absence of words, they had to guess what the scena was about. Effective, too, was Harry Grattan's happy fancy, whereby Leon Morton, in the role of Puck, invoked a band of fairies headed by Oberon and Titania and found them in rags and tatters. Apparently, in a materialist age, unemployment was rife in Fairyland.

For his third venture at the Ambassadors, Cochran commissioned Fred Thompson and Morris Harvey to write *Pell Mell*, the music this time being by the American Nat D. Ayer, who was later writing some telling tunes for *The Bing Boys*. *Pell Mell* ran for ten months. Just as Mr. Grattan had assured his hearers that *Odds and Ends* possessed no plot, so the authors of *Pell Mell* announced that their revue was fully as coherent played backwards as it was played forwards. In addition to Delysia and Leon Morton, Dorothy Minto was in the cast, not to mention Morris Harvey, with his provocative nose, singing "Dear Old Broadway," and dapper Nay Ayer, in a typewriting duet with Miss Minto. Miss Minto's other outstanding effort was the ragtime number, "What did Cleopatra do to make Mark Antony lo-ove?" Incidentally, in *Pell Mell*, Delysia demon-strated precisely how the long-limbed Leon should be shaved, but her daintiest piece of work was the Fragonard sketch, in which she permitted and even encouraged an elderly marquis to assist in putting on her stockings. Lastly, in the very spirit of Vaudeville were the seven scenes (or should it be eight) reviving memories of op'ra bouffe. The Two Gendarmes song from *Genevieve de Brabant*, the "Glou Glou" duet from *La Mascotte*, *La Legende de la Mère Angot*, Delysia singing the Letter Song from *Rip van Winkle*, were among the memories, the last one being a scena from *La Fille de Tambour Major*, and the whole concluding with a version of the same, "as treated by a modern revue composer."

There has never been more effective revue than Charles Cochran gave Ambassadors audiences in the years of the first World War. It steered clear of a certain bitterness which characterises a good deal of more recent intimate revue. But success brought disabilities in its train. Something bigger and more expensive was demanded, and bigger and more expensive meant a larger chorus, a bigger salary list, and a larger theatre. In 1918, Cochran took over the London Pavilion, intending to convert it from a music-hall into a house for revue, with rather more of spectacle than was possible at the Ambassadors.

As a variety house, the Pavilion had fallen upon evil days, the receipts being no more than a few hundred pounds a week, in spite of such stars as Marie Lloyd and the clown Grock heading the bill. There was no obstacle to the onrush of Charles Cochran by this time. Apart from the Ambassadors, he was in charge at the Empire, where Irving Berlin had composed the music for *Watch Your Step*, with a cast which included Ethel Levey, George Graves, pretty little June (then a dancer), Lupino Lane (a new-comer to London), and Joe Coyne.

As for the Pavilion venture, the production of *As You Were* in August 1918 converted the property from a heavy liability into a handsome profit-maker. Within a few months the proprietors found their annual income quadrupled. Delysia, who played the beauties of all time in *As You Were*, was the principal attraction and when she left the cast for six weeks the receipts fell by £1,000 a week, furnishing full justification for the generous salary she was now receiving in comparison with the £6 a week with which she began her career at the Ambassadors. Apart from her salary at the Pavilion, Delysia drew £50 a night for singing a couple of songs in cabaret at the Trocadero. Beyond a doubt revue had won a welcome in the West End of London. By this time Cochran had added the quicksilver wit of Arthur Wimperis to his assets on the authorship side and Herman Darewski was there with a store of tuneful musical numbers. He had learnt the tricks of his trade under Seymour Hicks. So far as actual stage production was concerned, the Cochran revues owed much of their slick competence to Frank Collins, C. B.'s second-in-command. There was also Elsie April, who supervised the musical arrangements in many Cochran productions, including Noel Coward's *Bitter Sweet*.

There is a wealth of theatrical wisdom in Israel Zangwill's gibe at the profession, "To the actor, the part is greater than the whole." The team-work which makes for final unification is important in every form of drama, but it is all-important in revue. Necessarily, the individual talents of singers and dancers, or those of show girls and chorus, in a speciality number, call for display, as a jewel of worth calls for a gold or platinum setting, but the truly successful revue is distinguished from the mediocre or the poor revue by the continuity of interest it arouses and the unity of effect it displays. This continuity and unification may be due to author or composer; more probably it is due to the producer. In Charles Cochran shows it was due, in the final analysis, to "C. B." We can see why this should be so if we visualise the conditions governing a revue in the making. When the principals have been engaged and scenery, wigs, and costumes are being designed and fashioned, sectional rehearsals are taking place in different parts of London, for a suitable theatre is seldom available. Usually, dialogue sketches are rehearsed in one place, dance-numbers in a second, and song-numbers in a third. A rehearsal-room may have a piano of sorts, a practice-bar for the dancers and a looking-glass for the show-girls, but the all-important glamour exists in imagina-tion only, in the imagination, let us say, of "C. B." The added glow of light and colour and the extra ounces of vim which will lift bleak professional craftsmanship into an irresistible temptation to spend 12s. 6d. or 15s. upon a stall are present only as an act of faith and in a Cochran venture it has always been C. B.'s task to see they were available by the opening night.

In practice, the intimacies of revue are seldom created by a book of the words or a musical score, valuable as these are, but by a popular actor or actress. Never-theless, a witty idea may help to give unity to a show. Such an idea was present in *As You Were*, when Arthur Wimperis had done playing about with a difficult French original by Rip. One after another the famous beauties of all time came to life on the stage, one of them being Ninon de l'Enclos, whose appearance allowed Herman Darewski to write a telling number for Delysia. He also wrote the tuneful "If you could care for me." In the role of Ninon, Delysia put across a question to John Humphries, which never failed to bring down a "house," largely made up of soldiers on leave.

"Are you single, married, or in Paris on leave?"

A typical Arthur Wimperis thrust this. Apart from revue, latter-day vaudeville has owed much to his ready wit. The son of the well-known water-colour painter, he was a schoolfellow of mine at Dulwich College. He it was who introduced me to *Ally Sloper*. When schooldays ended, he joined the *Daily Graphic* as a black-and-white artist. His pictorial contributions to the Follies' programmes have been recalled, as have his lyrics for such musical comedies as *The Gay Gordons* and *The Arcadians*. Like W. S. Gilbert, Wimperis has learnt the value of visual impressions in getting over vaudeville effects and the models he made for scenes in his plays were highly ingenious. Herman Darewski, who wrote numerous songs in collaboration with Wimperis, has told how lyricist and musician worked out an idea at a piano, writer and composer contributing suggestions in turn, until it was hard to say whether success meant that the melody precisely fitted the lyric or the lyric the melody.

It was Arthur Wimperis who was asked to sit through a vaudeville show, with a view to selecting the best items for a forthcoming revue. The verdict of Wimperis was devastating:

"My dear fellow a unique evening! I wouldn't have left a turn unstoned."

As You Were, being of French extraction, the English censor was suspicious, and the eagle eye of the Lord Chamberlain of the day caused changes in some of the dresses. In particular, there were complaints regarding a very effective skin-tight black silk net costume which Delysia wore as Lucifer in one scene, to which Delysia retorted, "The audience raises no objections." However, enough of Gallic sauce was left to justify a run of thirteen months and Cochran did not have to stage a successor at the Pavilion until *As You Were* had a record of 434 performances to its credit. As I have said, its final virtue was that, for once in a while, a revue had an intelligible and consistent plot. John Humphries, sick of the war and troubled by the levities of his wife, invested in a magic pill, which transported him into far-away times, where the clash of arms did not trouble society, but such fascinations as Cleopatra and Helen of Troy lived on. Leon Morton, singing "If you could care for me," was the eternal lover, who invariably turned up to deprive the elderly John Humphries of some beauty of the past whom his enterprise appeared to have earned.

In *London, Paris and New York* (1920), Wimperis was once more chief chef and Herman Darewski music provider at the Pavilion. This time Nelson Keys was the star and Wimperis gave "Bunch" excellent material. His first appearance was as an outsize German bandsman, and, a few minutes later, he was imitating Henry Ainley in a potted play. A Frenchman, ablaze with passion, followed and then, by a magical change of features, costume, and bodily bearing, a Spanish brigand emerged. Nelson Keys had to work hard to make the necessary changes in dress and make-up. And only half the evening's work was done, for "Bunch" still had to impersonate a street-ballad singer, a Beau Brummel character in Regency Brighton, and a Cockney tipster in the Five Shilling Ring. An evening of amazing transformations closed with Nelson Keys as the roué Admiral Sir Noazark, as a knut in evening attire (this being an approximation to "Bunch" as "Bunch" liked to know himself), and, at long last, as a Japanese juggler, with skull, eyes, and teeth all fully Oriental. The Oriental high cheek-bones had called for the drawing of two side molars, a sacrifice which Nelson Keys made upon the altar of vaudeville with admirable spirit. Less pleased was Mr. Cochran when he found that the set of false teeth had cost the Pavilion management £42. It was characteristic of "Bunch" Keys that he always wanted the best of everything.

An interesting feature in the production of *London, Paris and New York* was the return of Nellie Taylor to the West End stage, after a lengthy absence. She was obsessed by the fear that she might forget her lines, and this in spite of the fact that she had been on the stage for a decade or more and had played important principal parts. A Birmingham girl, she began as "The Pocket Vesta Tilley," singing at concerts, until Oswald Stoll offered her £4 10s. a week for a short music-hall engagement. Still no great success, but Nellie Taylor's high promise was justified when she secured an engagement as leading lady in *High Jinks* at the Adelphi, playing with W. H. Berry and Maisie Gay. As leading lady in *The Boy*, her salary was £100 a week. She was only 38 when she died.

Some Charlot Shows

With such a play as *London, Paris and New York*, Charles Cochran had travelled far from intimate revue, as it had been given at the Ambassadors and his later triumphs in the genre were more nearly akin to spectacular revue and, accordingly, will come up for discussion in a later chapter. But, first, a few words about revue at the smaller London theatres, where intimacy and continuity of ideas were easier to secure than they were at such a theatre as the Pavilion. For example, in Andre Charlot's production, *The Punch Bowl*, at the Duke of York's and the Vaudeville, the revue was planned upon the notion that each turn should be a spoonful from the exhilarating concoction which gave its name to the show. Similarly, *Bran Pie*, Andre Charlot's revue at the Prince of Wales's in 1919, was based upon ten dips in Act I and eleven dips in Act II, the last dip producing a series of dances, seen in reverie, beginning with a minuet and concluding with a jazz, headed by Beatie and Babs. Dip Nine in Act II was the typical Jack Hulbert number, "I did feel a dreadfully ass." All sorts of musicians, lyric writers, and speciality producers contributed to the bran-pie, and the dips justified more than 400 performances.

Apart from continuity, the other essential in revue is speed. Whereas a sketch in a variety entertainment gives body to a programme and occupies a substantial part of the evening, the snappier a revue sketch is the better. A long-drawn-out sketch somehow disturbs the all-important sense of quick-fire song and dance which is the primary aim in revue. Some idea of what a revue author should aim at is furnished by the following effort by Clarkson Rose in a Palladium revue. A married couple are having a meal in an hotel, when there is a sudden knock at the door and two gorgeously attired trumpeters march in. They bow ceremoniously, pose, and then blow a tremendous fanfare. Naturally astonished, the diners rise from their seats, the husband calls angrily for the hotel manager, who rushes in and attempts an explanation. The climax comes when the husband shouts:

"Fool, I ordered *crumpets!*"

Noel Coward, with his uncanny sense of what is effective on the stage, is a master in these catch-as-catch-can effects. A memorable one was in the competent hands of Maisie Gay in *This Year of Grace*. Ten minutes of dumb pantomime accompanied Maisie's effort to board a bus, the only word spoken in the sketch being the concluding exclamation, "Taxi!" The wordless sketch was a last-minute addition to the revue, following its trial trip in Manchester. Cochran came to the conclusion that another comedy scene for Maisie Gay was needed, and one Friday night he blandly told Noel that it had to be ready for use on the following Monday. Noel's far from bland reply was, "I'm dog-tired. I haven't an idea." However, by Sunday, the one-word sketch, with its climax, "Taxi!"

The elementary rule in sketch-writing, which Coward obeyed to the letter in this effort, was, "The biggest laugh must be on the last line before the black-out."

André Charlot has been mentioned. Born in 1882, Charlot gained his early theatrical experience as press manager at Parisian vaudeville houses, and was manager at the Alhambra in London during the first World War. Here he experimented with spectacular revue, but his most characteristic contribution was the series of intimate revues which he produced at the Vaudeville between 1916 and 1923. *Buzz-Buzz* at the Vaudeville in 1918 was typical. This was the revue in which "Bunch" Keys cemented his reputation as an actor in revue. A Jap, a Jew, José Collins in *The Maid of the Mountains*, and another version of Henry Ainley were some of them, a pleasant variant being the moments when Keys was allowed to be his amiable self and display top hat, tail coat, and nicely creased trousers as flawless as the shapely little man they encased and adorned. Nelson Keys singing "Coupons for Kisses" in company with Heather Thatcher is a *Buzz-Buzz* memory; so is Walter Williams in his stuttering song, "K . . . K . . . K . . . Katie." Theatre-lovers who chance to have preserved their programmes, like to remember that they recognised Gertrude Lawrence as a potentiality for the first time. She was Little Mr. Rain, who, in company with Miss Sunshine, popped in and out of the Swiss chalet barometer. Dance-lovers may also have noted one, June Tripp, among the "ponies," later to achieve fame as "June."

James Barrie once said of "Bunch" Keys, "Here comes the dramatic profession in a nutshell." No better definition of a first-class revue actor could be looked for. Nelson Keys was not a laughter-compeller of the "Bill" Berry type. He was a character actor, with a vast range and, when he took the trouble to build up an impersonation, the best mimic in the world. Once an author found an idea, Nelson Keys could make as much of it as any actor on the stage. By idea, I mean such a thing as "a gin-sodden Empire, telephoning home," which Ronald Jeans propounded to Nelson Keys in *After Dark*, at the Vaudeville in 1933. At once the Keys' mind was on the march. Costume, make-up, voice—all came to him, until much more was there than Nelson's author had imagined in his wildest dreams.

In a relatively short career, "Bunch" earned the better part of £250,000, though he hadn't a penny to bless himself with at the end. There were times when he earned £400 a week, and after he became a star he never took less than £150 a week, but he was temperamental. Moreover, his light, volatile methods called for a big, genial comedian as a foil, as Dan Leno wanted a Herbert Campbell, if he had to fill a stage for any length of time, and the all-important foil was not always available. In revue, Nelson Keys sometimes played a dozen or sixteen characters in an evening and each one as sharply differentiated as a character in a straight comedy. "Bunch" himself said, "I suppose I have a fly-paper mind. Things stick to it."

Nelson Keys was born in Lambeth in 1886, his father being an electrical engineer. His very first professional earnings followed an appearance at the Bull and Bush, where he recited a poem three times. At first, young Nelson was himself; then a Frenchman; and, finally, a baby, but each time repeating the same piece, with appropriate differences. The 10s. he received for this Bull and Bush effort persuaded the young man that there was a future for him on the stage. He joined a touring concert party, which had a stand on Herne Bay pier. Musical comedy engagements followed, and then a two years' engagement to play Jimmy Welch's part in *When Knights were Bold* on tour at £8 a week.

Young Keys was forging ahead, though, admittedly, his playing as Sir Guy de Vere was no more than clever mimicry. Realising this, Keys showed commend' able courage when he accepted an offer from Robert Courtneidge to play Bobby in *The Arcadians*. The pay was £3 less than he had been receiving in the provinces, but he was at a West End house, even if his part was confined to a single line— "They're off!" Robert Courtneidge made Nelson into an actor. He bullied the young man, calling him "Mumbler Keys" and insisting upon the necessity for amusing the boy at the back of the gallery, as well as the pretty young lady who clapped her gloved hands in a front'row stall. Gradually the role of Bobby expanded, and Nelson was allowed to add a song, "Back your Fancy." Lionel Monckton had written it as a quartet, but it failed and was rescued from oblivion when "Bunch" pleaded that he should be allowed to sing it solo.

In *The Mousmé*, playing a Japanese part, in *Princess Caprice*, in *Oh, Molly*, and *The Girl in the Taxi*, Nelson continued to enhance his reputation as actor, singer, and dancer, causing Arthur Wimperis to write a part for him in *Love and Laughter*, an early revue, which was given at the Empire in 1913. It was also Wimperis who persuaded Alfred Butt to add Nelson to the *The Passing Show*, the revue which was running at the Palace when the first war broke out, with the burly Arthur Playfair as foil to the diminutive "Bunch." Elsie Janis (and Mother), Gwendoline Brogden, singing Wimperis's recruiting song, "On Monday I walked out with a Soldier," and Basil Hallam were other stars. Hallam's six feet of lackadaisical manhood contrasted with the four feet odd of "Bunch" Keys as happily as did the square shoulders of Arthur Playfair. Basil Hallam knew how to dress and how to behave and, for some months in 1914, Gilbert the Filbert linked up with the long line of vaudeville dudes.

In 1936, when Nelson Keys was forty'nine, Herbert Farjeon wrote a book for the Saville, *Spread It Abroad*, and once more the little man scored. Ivy St. Helier, with her mingled comedy and pathos, was a perfect foil to "Bunch," as were the beauty and the dancing of Dorothy Dickson, the leading lady. "Keys, my boy, I'm proud of you," said old Robert Courtneidge, when he saw the show.

The economic factor can never be ignored in theatrical affairs, so I do not apologise for insisting upon it in connection with revues. Just as the talent of Harry Grattan became too expensive for the management at the Ambassadors, so the £100 a week which Delysia could command when the run of *Pell Mell* ended necessitated her transfer to a theatre larger than the Ambassadors. Indeed, for a time Cochran was doubtful if intimate revue itself was not being killed by the economic factor, and turned to other forms of vaudeville. At the end of the first World War the staging of an intimate revue in the West End of London cost perhaps £5,000, £3,000 being spent upon costumes, £1,500 upon scenery, and the rest upon rehearsals and other preliminaries. As for running expenses, they would be £1,100 or £1,200 a week and, given luck, the producer might look for a weekly return of £800 or £900 towards his production costs, and profits for the syndicate. The weekly bill of, say, £1,200 would include such items as the following:

Leading Comedian, £150; Leading Lady, £60 or £70; Other principals (total), £100; Chorus (16 girls at £4), £64; Orchestra (12 members), £100; Authors' fees, £100; Theatre rent, £400; Miscellaneous, £250.

However, thanks to Charles Cochran's example, several London managements had solved the various problems, theatrical and economic. Authors had been given confidence in the new genre; bodies of players, including such promising youngsters as Beatrice Lillie, Gertrude Lawrence, Jack Hulbert, and "Bunch" Keys, were there to put across songs and sketches. Tuneful music, appropriate scenery, and happy costume designs had been less difficult to find, as they belonged to the theatre world in general. Lastly, with the Garrick, the Pavilion, the Oxford, and the Aldwych all under Cochran's control, it was plain that successful revue production promised big financial rewards. In other words, C. B. had done the trick neatly, sweetly, and completely. The sequel to the successes of the momentous seven years between 1914 and 1921 belongs to a later chapter. But, first, the latest developments in intimate revue, those associated with Herbert Farjeon and the Gate Theatre, call for record.

Little Theatre Revue

Far and away the best thing in intimate revue since the early productions of Charles Cochran have been the "Little Theatre" revues from the pen of Herbert Farjeon, though by no means all were given at the Little Theatre itself. No writer has brought a fresher fancy and more satirical insight to the task of revue-making. Moreover, at the Little Theatre after 1938, he had the advantage of being his own manager and producer, though anything less like the typical controller of a vaudeville house can scarcely be imagined. Farjeon's approach to revue-creation was that of a student of social history with literary leanings, and he made it his job to force his company to think. His success was his triumph. A score of social problems reeled under the assaults which arose from Little Theatre revue. For example, Co-education:

> We don't have lessons, we don't have sports,
> We don't have rules of any sort,
> And the boys and the girls write their own reports,
> In Liberty Hall, the free school.

As for broadcasting, when Dorothy Dickson, Walter Crisham, and Bernard Miles appeared as Bebe Dickson, Walliver Crisham, and Ben Miles in the devastating "Lo Gang," the B.B.C. itself trembled. The only just criticism was that satire and the thing satirised were so nearly akin that one had to listen hard to be sure that one had not dropped in upon some Sunday evening at the B.B.C., and that Vic Oliver, Bebe Daniels, and their associates in *Hi Gang* had not materialised at Wyndhams to help in building up *Diversion No. 2*. For example, Bebe Dickson singing:

> I've got a date with a Dream,
> My Dream's got a date with me,
> If I never woke from that sweet Dream
> How sweet that Dream would be.

Farjeon loved to tilt at institutions and the B.B.C. wilted again and again under his thrusts. "Thank God for the B.B.C.," in *Nine Sharp* at the Little Theatre is such a memory. Father is discovered fiddling with the wireless and all sorts of strange turns materialise, including a potted version of *Hamlet* and an Empire Tour, the latter with up-lifting quotations from the poets. Thus Captain Snaggers, of the North Sea Bloater Fishing Fleet, brought forth, "Those that go down to the sea in ships!" "The Captains and the Kings depart!" and "Little drops of Water, little grains of Sand," a conjunction of apposites which would only occur to one born to a career in English letters. The B.B.C. com-mentator's farewell to Snaggers was, "Good-bye and good bloat-ing," which brought listeners-in once more to earth and ocean.

Born in 1887, Farjeon and his sister Eleanor, who collaborated with him in some of his stage work, came of literary and theatrical stock, with the em-phasis upon literature. Their father was a novelist, but one of their grandparents was Joseph Jefferson, the actor. Farjeon was also on the American stage for a number of years before he turned

Herbert Farjeon

to dramatic criticism. Thus he really did know what was wanted and wanting when he turned to revue-writing. *Picnic*, at the Arts Theatre Club in 1927, was an early effort in the revue form and it included a bright idea which Elsa Lanchester had been exploiting privately. "I've danced with a man, who's danced with a girl, who's danced with the Prince of Wales."

Farjeon has admitted that the song did not achieve the success he expected, but it is to the credit of vaudeville managers that *Picnic* and *Many Happy Returns*, which followed in 1928, persuaded them that a new talent was on the horizon. It reached full accomplishment in 1939, when war conditions put a premium upon simple and inexpensive productions, as war had done in 1914, when Cochran established intimate revue at the Ambassadors. This time it was in the Little Theatre, Adelphi, that intelligent satire triumphed. *Winter in Torquay*, with Hermione Baddeley as Mrs. Twiceover, the lady with the double mastoid, "like a gong; bong, bong, bong, gong!" and blood-pressure which constantly threatened "pouf, like a bicycle tyre!" was unforgettable, the climax being:

> It is always very pleasant
> To brighten up the present,
> By telling other people what you've had.

Equally caustic and of even wider application was Farjeon's tilt at certain cabaret singers, as rendered by Lyle Evans in *Spread It Abroad:*

> But when men who are really men go out
> With blondes who are really blondes,
> You give 'em smut,
> You give 'em dirt,
> In a nice white tie
> And a nice white shirt,
> And, they'll clap you loud,
> They'll clap you long,
> Till you give 'em a dirtier,
>   Dirty song.

In *Spread It Abroad* at the Saville, Farjeon had the assistance of a first-rate revue company, headed by Nelson Keys and Ivy St. Helier. "L'Absinthe" was a typical St. Helier number, with its Parisian background, but the actress was no less successful as the elderly Lilac Loveday, whose treacherous memory, recalling memories of the 'twenties and 'thirties, told of "the wild abandon of Gladys Cooper" and "the coy, piquant charm of Flora Robson." "The Charge of the Late Brigade" with Ivy as the lady who always arrives after the curtain had risen upon the show, was another number in *Spread It Abroad*, though it had not the perfect unity of Maisie Gay's eleven minutes of pantomime in *The 1930 Revue*, which also treated the late-comer to the stalls theme. If Noel Coward's uncanny intuition as to what will make effective "theatre" justifies a claim to the classic treatment of the late-comer theme, Farjeon was the happier when he essayed another well-tried theme, that of the father and the small boy instructing one another in the mysteries of life and sex. Noel Coward's effort in *Growing Pains* concluded:

The Boy: Why are you so nervous, Papa?
Papa: I am not in the least nervous, Herbert, but that which I have to tell you is rather delicate and—er—rather difficult.
The Boy: What is it you want to tell me, Papa?
Papa (with a gulp): My boy—there is no Santa Claus.

Personally, I prefer Herbert Farjeon's devastating:

Papa: And, by the way, I shouldn't tell your brother—not just yet.
The Boy: I see—does Mother know?

And this holds good, even if Farjeon may have been in some debt to Miles Malleson's line in *The Fanatics*, "Just one thing. Not a word of this business to your sister," a Victorianism which brought down the curtain with a roar, as brother and sister had been discussing that very matter at length before young Freeman's Dad arrived.

The war-time *Diversions* at Wyndhams in 1940, when the Battle of Britain was near its height, was in slightly different genre to the early Farjeon revues. There was more insistence upon artistry *qua* artistry, perhaps because Edith Evans, as actress, and Irene Eisinger, as singer, were at Farjeon's command. Irene sang Mozart and Rossini, while Edith Evans gave the Hop-picker monologue, which she dictated to Farjeon over the tea-cups at the Albany and brought to life by herself creating the East End coster woman who had been blitzed.

"Not a window; not a door; bombed right out; and there was my boots in the middle of the back-garden." ... But "Londoners can take it," 'e sez, "and I reckon that's right, Londoners can take it."

Or again, the hop-picker's, "What do you think I've got at the bottom of my basket? Jellied eels! I don't know what they'll be like when we get there, but they was grand when we started!"

In a very different mood, but indicative of Farjeon's range as a satirist, was his tilt at the ballet fans of the 'twenties and 'thirties:

How poetic! How lyrical! What a feat! What a miracle!
Oh, the sighing of the women and the swooning of the men!
When he twiddled and twirled for us, he created a world for us!
How we screamed and shrieked and hooted, how we whooped and how we howled!
We were ravished and uprooted! We were frequently disembowelled!
You will never know the throb, the glow, the bliss that we knew then,
When Bolonsky danced *Belushka* in September 1910.

Herbert Farjeon's quality as a creator of revue script is on permanent record in his *Omnibus*, and few of his rivals would submit their work to the acid test of reading in the quiet of a study, hours after the footlights were dimmed and only the memory of actors and actresses remained to vitalise what had once seemed so alive. One has to read Farjeon's commentary upon the Eric Maschwitz senti, mentality, "A Nightingale sang in Berkeley Square," to savour its full fruitiness, and this holds good while one admits that the wit and beauty of Dorothy Dickson put an unforgettable thing across the footlights when she sang the mock "Nightin, gale Song" in *Diversion No. 1*. However, it is in the nature of intimate revue that it invites sampling and re-sampling. No doubt, half a dozen hearings of Dorothy Dickson's "while nightingales sing in well-bred squares" would have revealed all the irony of Mr. Farjeon's satire and not a beggarly 20 per cent. Ivy St. Helier singing "L'Absinthe" furnishes another instance of a single hearing of a Farjeon lyric being insufficient, perhaps the highest compliment to be paid to a sketch or lyric-writer in revue. How seldom is anything left when the moment before the "black-out" has revealed the full invention of a revue author. The, death of Herbert Farjeon in May 1945, at the age of 58, was a real loss to Anglo, Saxon vaudeville.

The brilliant efforts of the Gate Theatre company in the late 'thirties have a special interest because they emphasise the value of the intensive training of principals in the ways of intimate and inexpensive revue if the best results are to arise. In particular, the Gate gave Londoners Hermione Gingold, whose gifts include authorship as well as presentation. In *Arsenic and Old Shows* she not only impersonated Lilian Braithwaite ("I've forgotten to put the gilt on the ginger-bread"), but also associated other members of the Ambassadors company with shows as various as *The Vagabond King* and *The Merry Widow*. A few months before Hermione Gingold had been working with Hermione Baddeley in *Rise Above It* at the Comedy. The memory drove a tearful Miss Gingold to the highly characteristic comment:

> I do miss Hermione badly,
> The show isn't really the same;
> I sit in my room just before we begin
> And imagine her back again, swiping my gin. . . .

A dozen delectable moments associate themselves with the sub-acidity of the typical Gingold attitude towards life. I will confine myself to three of them in *Sweet and Low*: Hermione, in *negligé*, and hugging her hot-water bottle, with the touching refrain, "Let me run to you"; Hermione as Brünhilde, with winged helmet and spear, singing of Valhalla; and Hermione as Carmen Miranda, making play with scarlet finger-nails, festoons of tropical fruit, and other para, phernalia which associated itself with the Brazilian diseuse, and at the same time maintaining contacts with such a topicality as A.R.P. work in war-time:

> Is your stirrup-pump still working,
> Colonel Hop-hop-hop-hop Hopkins?
> It's a long, long, long, long time since we had a blitz.

Nor must Miss Gingold's brilliant partner at the Gate and elsewhere be forgotten, Walter Crisham. He was a member of the Queeries Concert Party in *Rise Above It*, at the Comedy, a show within a show, which its compère described as "one of the horrors of modern warfare." An excellent dancer and deviser of dances, Walter Crisham.

If one had to select a typical number associated with the little Gate Theatre and the theatrical progeny to which it has given birth, I should choose the skit upon crooning which also happens to be concerned with successful motherhood:

> There's a Baby for Everybody somewhere,
> So don't be sad and blue;
> There's a Baby for Everybody somewhere,
> Don't weep the whole day through.
> Don't be lonesome, don't be sad,
> Dry your eyes and be downright glad;
> There's a Baby for Everybody somewhere,
> If you know just what to do!

Chapter XII

COCHRAN. THE LATER REVUES, WITH AN EXCURSUS
UPON NOEL COWARD

DURING THE FIRST WORLD WAR CHARLES COCHRAN'S ENERGIES
were by no means exhausted by his productions of intimate revue at the Ambassadors. In 1917, at the Prince of Wales's, he produced *Carminetta*, a skit upon
Bizet's *Carmen*, which Monckton Hoffe adapted for the English stage. Most of
the music was by Emile Lassaily, a disciple of Offenbach, though the highlight
in the operetta was Delysia's singing of Herman Darewski's "I love you, I hate
you," which brought down the curtain upon the heroine's unhappy loneliness.
Two years later, when the London Pavilion had passed into his control, Cochran
produced a daring but amusing operetta, *Afgar*, with music by Charles Cuvillier,
the composer of *The Lilac Domino*. The French version was shocking, as is
suggested by the fact that, even after the libretto had been purged for English
consumption, Harry Welchman, the Don Juan of the piece, owned a harem in
which Delysia was the prize item, along with five other wives. The plot included
a strike of the ladies of the harem, akin to that in the *Lysistrata* of Aristophanes.

On the border-line between musical comedy and revue was *Houp-la*, a Cochran
production at the St. Martin's Theatre in 1916. Fred Thompson and Hugh
Wright were responsible for the book and Nat Ayer and Howard Talbot for
the music, and as his cast was headed by Gertie Millar and George Graves,
Cochran considered that he was entitled to charge £1 1s. for stalls. St. Martin's
audiences disagreed and after a week Cochran reverted to the more popular
half-guinea. Paul Rubens was to have written and composed *Houp-la*, in company
with Nat Ayer, but was too ill to fulfil the contract.

Charles Cochran has always been proud that he brought that great comedienne,
Florence Mills, to London. Florence Mills was the daughter of a freed slave and
her talent as a vaudeville star was comparable with that of Paul Robeson, as a
factor in persuading the world to give justice to coloured folk. Like Robeson,
Florence Mills hoped by her acting, singing, and dancing to prove that the negro
race was fully worthy of a place in modern art. Her song, "I'm a little blackbird,
looking for a blue bird," had a mixture of pathos and charming impudence
which was irresistible. When she died all too soon, there was mass-singing of
"Bye-bye, Blackbird" at her graveside. The plantation folk knew that an influence
making for their welfare had passed away.

Florence Mills and a company of plantation singers had made a small sensation
at a Broadway restaurant when Cochran brought them to the Pavilion in 1923,
to make up the second act of *Dover Street to Dixie*. The first half of the show
had no great success, but when Will Vodery's coloured orchestra got to work at

the beginning of the second act, and the Plantation Chorus made its sensational rush towards the footlights, the Pavilion audience stirred in their seats. Something new. When Florence Mills passed on her dreams of the hills of Tennessee, the while displaying her gift of pathos, her flute-like trills, the sparkle of her eyes, and the grace of her fragile, chocolate-coloured limbs, Pavilion audiences were fully awake, not only to a novelty, but to something rich and rare, as is everything of real beauty.

There was a great deal of unemployment in 1923, and the Ministry of Labour put such pressure upon managers that coloured revues, not only at the Pavilion, but at the Empire, were withdrawn. For Florence Mills and the Plantation folk was substituted the film, *The Covered Wagon*. However, the triumph which was denied in 1923 was achieved in 1926, when Cochran brought Lew Leslie's *Black Birds* to the Pavilion.

Oddly enough, the success of *Black Birds* was a factor in the colossal failure of *White Birds*, which a wealthy Yorkshire business-man, Everard Gates, produced at His Majesty's Theatre in 1927, at a cost of £30,000. Mr. Gates's original idea was that Bernard Shaw and Sir James Barrie should write his record-breaking revue. This proved impossible, and Noel Coward and Beverley Nichols were interested in the scheme for a time, while William Nicholson and Nevinson were mentioned as scenic designers. Before *White Birds* actually reached its first night, Everard Gates's scheme resolved itself into spending £30,000, with the aid of Lew Leslie. Mr. Leslie carried out his task resolutely. The rent of His Majesty's Theatre was £600 a week, yet it was kept empty for six weeks for rehearsals of *White Birds*, though Maisie Gay, Maurice Chevalier of Paris, and other expensive stars were in the cast. "No wit in the words and no melody in the music," was the verdict of the critics when the play was finally produced.

Which brings up once more the problem of the economics of vaudeville, and a less happy phase of Cochran's career, that of his financial failures. As we have heard, a few hundred pounds had sufficed to launch the first *Odds and Ends*. By comparison, Cochran, in the post-war period, found himself spending £30,000 upon a highly spectacular revue, carrying, moreover, a salary list of £1,200 a week, in addition to the cost of his orchestra and his in-front-of-the-curtain staff. The time was now the spring of 1921 and the place was Oxford Music Hall, upon which £80,000 had been spent, in order that the New Oxford might be the best theatre in London for spectacular revue. Only crowded houses could justify such lavish expenditure, and Cochran searched three continents for talent.

The *League of Notions* at the New Oxford opened upon an impression of a London fog, in which a theatrical manager sought the aid of Pierrot, Columbine, and Harlequin in the composition of the revue. At once the old-timers offered their aid, and the curtain—a dazzling creation of silver tissue—rose to display a tailor's shop. The tailor was at work upon a crazy patchwork quilt, intended for the bed of the Dolly Sisters. The bed proved to be eight feet high and was

13

reached by means of a step-ladder. By the time the Dolly Sisters were safely in bed—and out of bed—the *League of Notions* was in being.

The *League of Notions* was produced by a young Anglo-American, John Murray Anderson, one of his inventions being "The Dance of the Silver Bubble," in which Rita Lee moved about the stage followed by a silver balloon, which seemed to obey her every whim. The lightest touch kept the balloon dancing. Another dancer, Grace Christie, achieved success in the turn in which she displayed grotesque masks designed by Benda, a Polish artist. Each mask was insured for £500 as a work of art. As final evidence of generous ingenuity, the Oxford management presented the audience with tambourines, which were used to accompany songs and dances. The Duke of York (King George VI) and his brother, Prince Henry, were in the stalls on the first night, and plied their tambourines with vigour.

Charles Cochran had intended to spend £25,000 upon converting the old Oxford Music Hall into a first-class musical-comedy and revue house. As has been said, the cost was £80,000. Moreover, when *The League of Notions* should have been produced, circumstances necessitated postponements and Cochran found himself saddled with an expenditure of £400 a day and nothing coming into the till. Lastly, Cochran was seriously ill and unable to give the production the personal attention needed. *The League of Notions* was in no sense a failure. It played to £4,000 a week and the production came back at the rate of £1,500 a week, but, in the end, the net profit was no more than £7,000, and this was much less than Cochran expected when he decided to convert the Old Oxford into the New Oxford.

And worse was to come. *Mayfair and Montmartre* followed, another expensive production, with a cast including Lady Tree, Nellie Taylor, Joyce Barbour, A. W. Baskcomb, and Delysia. A lovely Boccaccio scena and a superb Inca Ballet were obvious attractions and the production costs were coming back at the rate of £1,200 a week, when Delysia lost her voice. She had been working too continuously. Competent understudies did their best, but receipts fell away, and when the books covering *Mayfair and Montmartre* were finally balanced, a loss of £20,000 was revealed. In 1923, Mr. Cochran called his creditors together and got a year's grace, in the hope that the staging of the Rodeo might restore his fortunes. The hope did not materialise and bankruptcy could not be avoided.

Noel Coward, Revue Writer

No purpose will be served by recalling in detail all of Cochran's musical shows, the more because Mr. Cochran himself has told us so much in his own inimitable manner. But his association with Noel Coward helped to make vaudeville history in more than one direction. Born on December 16th, 1899, Noel's stage career began when he read an advertisement for a boy actor in a children's play at the Little Theatre, and an audition resulted in his first contract. Financially, it was to be eclipsed by many later contracts, but it had this virtue. The young player was to be a Prince in a production called *The Gold Fish*. A beginning had been made. Later, the boy was one of Italia Conti's children in *Where the Rainbow Ends*, and his first play came in 1920, when he was twenty-one. It had no great success, but a visit to America in the following year led to *The Vortex* of 1924, which, in turn, prepared the way for the intervention of Charles Cochran in Noel's fortunes and finally for the production of *This Year of Grace* and *Bitter Sweet* in 1928 and 1929. By this time Coward's contributions to British vaudeville were comparable to those he was to make to straight drama, as illustrated by the comedy, *Private Lives*, and the social pageantry of *Cavalcade*.

An early Noel Coward essay in revue-writing was Andre Charlot's production of *London Calling* at the Duke of York's. It included the impudent tilt at modern free-verse poetry, associated with an imaginary group which Noel entitled the Swiss Family Whittlebot. This consisted of Miss Hernia, a lady who appeared in undraped dyed sacking, together with Brother Gob (in cycling breeches) and Brother Sago. Mr. Coward has disclaimed any intention of directing his satire against any particular literary clique, and it was a pity that one such circle was unable to accept the witticisms as an "after-dinner digestive." However, all this happened in 1923, and we have Mr. Coward's assurance that any alimentary disturbance has long been forgiven. In any case, Noel was only twenty-four years old. More to the point is the fact that, though the relatively youthful author shared the book of the words with Ronald Jeans, Coward made himself responsible for *all* the lyrics and music and, moreover, played a leading part with Tubby Edlin, Gertrude Lawrence, and Maisie Gay in support.

If only because *London Calling* embodied the promise which was to be fully implemented in *This Year of Grace*, it will have a place in the story of British vaudeville. At last, a man of the theatre had arisen capable of doing for revue what Planché had done for Victorian extravaganza, that is, giving it the unity and driving force which can only arise from individual invention and direction. In *London Calling* the unifying device was twenty-five "calls," the twenty-fifth being Gertrude Lawrence and the Duke of York's company in the finale, *Follow a Star*. In response to Call Five, Maisie Gay, with aid from Ronald Jeans, showed herself "a ministering angel, Thou." Her bright bouncing bed manners as Nurse Doodah, in charge of a patient in a hospital for nerve trouble, reduced the sick-room to a state of chaos and stalls, circles, and gallery to hysterical laughter.

An American newspaper-man once described Maisie Gay as a comedienne with a Connie Ediss *chassis* and a 1922 top. The phrase happily described Maisie's contacts alike with the tested tradition of the theatre and the ever-changing world of men and women, contacts which must be maintained if intimate revue is to flourish. In a Charlot revue at the Prince of Wales's, for which no fewer than twenty writers were responsible, Maisie Gay did wonderful things as an elderly cocotte of the Parisian Moulin Rouge, beplumed for conquest, in the manner pictured by Felicien Rops. Maisie Gay was stricken with arthritis in 1932 and died in 1945, after thirteen years of suffering.

Maisie Gay was a character impersonator of genius and her range approximated to that of Nelson Keys. In one revue she gave no fewer than sixteen impersona-tions, and in *This Year of Grace* she made eleven changes of costume, giving just a minute and a half for each change. She has told us that, always in character impersonation, she began with the costume. Once that was decided upon, the voice and mannerisms arose naturally. An early effort was a Cockney charlady, and for this Maisie provided herself with the bonnet which Fred Emney had worn in "A Sister to Assist 'Er." Such is the value of tradition for those who have stage-lore in their blood, that Maisie always felt fully in character directly she had donned the historic bonnet.

In a different mood was Maisie Gay's Lady Kitty, a vaudeville star of uncertain age, though not so *passé* that she could no longer rely upon a chorus of admiring males. As she assured Duke of York's audiences:

> I am playful as a kitten,
> Love has seldom passed me by,
> I have more than once been bitten,
> But I'm hardly ever shy . . .

The conclusion of the song ran thus:

> Though at one time people always called me "Gladstone's Pet,"
> Still there's life in the old girl yet.

Another Maisie memory is Ivor Novello's mock patriotic song, "March with Me," which Miss Gay sang in apparent competition with Clara Butt's rendering of "Land of Hope and Glory." As the climax was reached, eight chorus girls marched in, bearing spears. They dropped to their knees in homage, with the result that the spearheads landed heavily upon poor Maisie's rump. Again, there was Maisie Gay in Noel Coward's *Bus Rush* scena. Lastly, Daisy Kipshaw, the Channel swimmer, singing "Britannia Rules the Waves," with the chorus. "Up girls and at 'em!" was unforgettable. A small girl dashed in.

Little Girl: Mother, mother, a great big whale.

The whale turned out to be a very large woman in a bathing-suit, who had just finished her weekly Channel swim. She proceeded to sing "Britannia Rules the Waves," with its refrain:

> We'll do our bit till our muscles crack,
> We'll put a frill on the Union Jack.
> Here's to the maid
> Who isn't afraid,
> Who shingles and shoots and shaves.
> Up, girls, and at 'em!
> Britannia rules the waves.

Noel Coward's stage association with Gertrude Lawrence in *London Calling* is one which all lovers of revue hope may be renewed. Its potentialities were revealed at the Phoenix Theatre in 1935 when the pair of them sang "Has anybody

seen our ship?" from the sketch *Red Peppers* in inimitable fashion. The way in
which the one passed the ball to the other could only have come from a long-
standing stage alliance. Londoners both, they had known one another profes-
sionally from childhood onwards, that is, from the days when Noel was a juvenile
Prince and Gertrude a fairy in a Brixton pantomime. By 1911, Miss Lawrence
was a child dancer in Cochran's production of *The Miracle*, at Olympia, earning
a pound a week or thereabouts, fame coming when Charlot sent her to the States,
as an understudy to Beatrice Lillie. But even fuller powers were revealed in
combination with Noel Coward, as author, producer, composer, and actor. In
particular, the presentation of the ruddy-wigged variety artists of *Red Peppers* who
found their turn ruined by a combination of temperamental temper and professional
jealousy; here was vaudeville stark naked, as it was to be found in a third-rate
sing-song music-hall thirty years or so ago.

This Year of Grace was not Coward's first Cochran revue. Three years earlier
he had written the book, the lyrics, and virtually all the music for *On With the
Dance*, though not quite all. His commission from Cochran was to do "the
book," but, characteristically, Noel so constructed the scenes that each led up to
a lyric and a lyric, moreover, which he alone could put to music. In the result
the long-suffering Philip Braham, who was to have done the music, found
himself with only three numbers to his credit. A "Cowardly" trick, but as Noel
was plainly a coming man, the management at the Pavilion did not raise any
undue objection to this assertive energy. *On With the Dance*, produced in 1925,
chanced to be one of the Coward vintage years. *Fallen Angels, The Vortex*, and
Hay Fever were running at other London theatres simultaneously with *On With
the Dance*.

Ernest Thesiger and Douglas Byng, in the cruel sketch of the *passé* ladies going
to bed, fixes itself in the memory and, of course, Alice Delysia, singing "Poor
Little Rich Girl." The ballet *Crescendo*, too, an invention of Leonide Massine,
who appeared as Bobo, the Spirit of Modernity, and made his puppets dance to
the rhythms of jazz, until, willy-nilly, they were swept up into a frenzied surge
of impressionistic movement. Massine was a Diaghileff discovery, a Sicilian,
but combining the melancholy of a Russian with the ardour of an Italian. He
was seventeen when Diaghileff saw him first and made his London debut in
The Legend of Joseph, characteristically bored by the advances of Potiphar's spouse.
A few years of intensive training and Massine showed himself, not only a youth
of remarkable beauty, but a dancer who was very apt to express the weary energies
of a war-worn age.

Cochran's 1926 Revue at the Pavilion was, nominally, by Ronald Jeans, but he
was assisted by a veritable committee of composers and writers, who provided
music and lyrics. A pity this, after the opportunities for individual invention
which Cochran had offered to Harry Grattan, Arthur Wimperis, and Noel
Coward. Perhaps this was why the best things in the 1926 Revue were the Leonide
Massine Boccaccio scena, "The Tub," with a Florentine background, and the

ballet *La Carmagnole*, with music by Adolf Stanislas, which featured Spinelly as the King's mistress. However, Mr. Cochran's error, if error it was, was rectified in 1928, when Noel Coward was given full responsibility for *This Year of Grace*, and the revue earned no less than £30,000 for the lucky author. Moreover, Noel Coward later appeared in Sonnie Hale's part in the New York version of the revue, earning £400 a week and having the satisfaction of partnering Beatrice Lillie, who took over the Maisie Gay sketches. Their joint success was such that ticket speculators ran the price of a 27s. stall up to the equivalent of £5.

In *This Year of Grace*, Noel Coward, exploiting the social philosophy already adumbrated in "Poor Little Rich Girl," wrote "Dance, Little Lady," the singer being Sonnie Hale, the dancer Lauri Devine, and the creator of the all-important masks, Oliver Messel. Once more Coward made himself the voice of the restless hirelings of Dame Pleasure, who came to womanhood during the post-war years:

> Though you're only seventeen,
> Far too much of life you've seen,
> Syncopated child; . . .
> But I know it's vain
> Trying to explain
> While there's this insane
> Music in your brain.

The negative side of the philosophy was embodied in an earlier number in the revue, given to Jessie Matthews and Mr. Cochran's Young Ladies, "Teach me to dance like Grandma," in which the younger generation resolutely refused to dance—Blues!

> Black Bottoms, Charlestons!
> What wind blew them in?
> Monkeys do them in Zoos.

Studying Noel Coward's social philosophy, far from the beat of the music and with only a dim memory of the orchestral colour, one does less than justice to these lyrics. To savour their real merit one must remember that the Coward method does not seek the singable rhymes which Gilbert provided for Sullivan, but more sophisticated lilts, which those familiar with the complexities of jazz and swing accept as authentic invention, just because they appear to be unfamiliar. "Mad dogs and Englishmen," from *Words and Music*, first given at the Adelphi in 1932, furnishes an example. One has to recall Coward himself speeding along the lines and finding the one and only concatenation of rhymes and pauses if the real thing is to be recovered. Here is the underlying idea:

> Mad dogs and Englishmen
> Go out in the midday sun.
> The Japanese don't care to,
> The Chinese wouldn't dare to.
> Hindoos and Argentines sleep firmly from
>   ten to one,
> But Englishmen detest a siesta!

And so on through the world atlas, leading up to the memorable climax:

> At twelve the natives swoon
> And no more work is done,
> But mad dogs and Englishmen
> Go out in the midday sun!

Similarly, Coward's *Operette*, dating from 1938, gave us "The Stately Homes of England." The composer was too young to be aware that Sydney Grundy's *Haddon Hall* opened with another "Stately Homes of England," which was sung by a hidden chorus of Simples and was furnished with a charming setting which Arthur Sullivan plainly intended should emphasise the pride of nationality associated with such a place as Haddon Hall. Mr. Coward's purpose was very different; he debunked "the stately homes" ideal with savage glee. The author-composer will forgive the quotation of a typical verse sung by a chorus of down-and-out aristocrats:

> The stately Homes of England,
> How beautiful they stand
> To prove the Upper Classés
> Have still the upper hand.
> Though the fact that they have to be rebuilt,
> And frequently mortgaged to the hilt,
> Is inclined to take the gilt
>   Off the gingerbread;
> And certainly damps the fun
>   Of the eldest son.
>
> But still we won't be beaten,
> We'll scrimp and screw and save,
> The playing-fields of Eton
> Have made us frightfully brave.
> And so, if the Van Dycks have to go
> And we pawn the Bechstein Grand,
> We'll stand by the stately Homes of England!

The virtue in a Noel Coward song or sketch is its actability. Here is an author who knows to a nicety what can be put across the footlights, though I think Mr. Coward has been misled by a law which he maintains is fundamental in modern revue-writing, that is, "the audience must never be kept waiting." The temptation to be slick becomes too great. Half-baked thought and meaningless motion are too apt to escape the diligent criticism which gave Gilbert's best work a life well beyond a single generation.

A characteristic piece of impudence in *This Year of Grace* was the inclusion of "Any Noel Coward Play" in a series of theatrical parodies. This reproduced the historic moment after the curtain fell for the last time upon *Sirocco*, Noel's dismal failure. Frances Doble had been summoned to the footlights and, amid cat-calls and booing, told an astonished audience:

"Ladies and gentlemen, this is the happiest moment of my life."

In the parody, a row of players, including Noel himself, was shown bowing, while an unseen audience booed and raspberried with fervour. When the leading lady stepped forward and, with tears in her voice, announced full contentment with her reception, the first-night audience gasped, then smiled and, finally, burst into a roar of full-throated laughter. Needless to say, Coward has always been very grateful to Charles Cochran for his ungrudging support in the difficult days following the disaster of *Sirocco*, and it is no less gratifying to record that passing failure was speedily eclipsed by the triumphs of *This Year of Grace*, *Bitter Sweet*, and *Cavalcade*.

Bitter Sweet (the title was suggested by Alfred Lunt) was produced at His Majesty's in July 1929. It was not only written and composed by Mr. Coward, but produced by him. The only thing Coward did not do was to orchestrate his own tunes, this being the work of Orellana, who had done a similar service for Lionel Monckton, Paul Rubens, and other makers of melodies fit for whistling. *Bitter Sweet* combined the virtues of a costume play with those of contemporary story and satire, as the period of the plot ranged from 1895 to 1929. Evelyn Laye and Nellie Taylor were early choices for the soprano role, but the honour fell to the American, Peggy Wood, and she proved an ideal Sarah Millick. Later, Evelyn Laye was the first to sing the role in America and was only less successful. No one could have looked more lovely than Miss Laye or sung the famous valse with more charm, but the acting of Peggy Wood as the silver-haired Marchioness made the part of Sarah Millick her very own. Memorable, too, were the Rou-manian Georges Metaxa as Carl Linden, Ivy St. Helier as La Crevette, and the faded, jaded boys who broke into:

> Ta-ra-ra-boom-de-ay,
> It's mental washing-day.

Ivy St. Helier, as her manner suggests, was a Jersey girl, and Seymour Hicks, a Jersey man, gave Ivy her first London chance. Noel Coward wrote the part of Manon La Crevette for her and she did it every justice, from the swing of the memorable bustle to the singing of "If love were all."

Coward wrote the second act of *Bitter Sweet* in hospital, while awaiting a painful but not dangerous operation, and the waltz "I'll see you again" came to him in a taxi during a twenty-minutes' traffic block. The play went into rehearsal in May 1929, and after a three weeks' trial run in Manchester, reached London, where the Lancashire triumph was repeated. Produced on July 18th, it ran for 673 performances and 800,000 people saw it at His Majesty's alone. The casino scene in the second act was designed by Ernst Stern and could not have been bettered. *Bitter Sweet* was easily the best comic opera in forty years. For a com-parable joy one had to go back to *The Gondoliers* of Gilbert and Sullivan.

The first time I saw *Bitter Sweet* was a matinée, and as I came into Pall Mall from His Majesty's, I found myself composing a letter of thanks to the author, composer, and producer, a thing I had not thought of doing after any vaudeville show before. I did not post the letter. One never does.

Cochran in the 'Thirties

By 1930, Beverley Nichols was established as librettist at the Pavilion, though the twenty-nine items in Mr. Cochran's revue of that year included many things for which the nominal author of the piece was in no way responsible. There was a ballet to the music of Lord Berners, entitled *The Freaks*, in which Alice Nikitina gave a one-legged dance, the assumption being that she was a freak, who had escaped from a circus. Another original item, *In a Venetian Theatre*, was a ballet for the arms only, performed by twelve masked girls in long white gloves, who appeared to be watching a performance from a stage box. Most daring of all was a *Heaven Scena*, dressed by Oliver Messel, in which the entire company was garbed in white, and by some strange fortune found itself translated to another world, where snow-white hansom-cabs, celestial constables, and other slightly disguised personalities and institutions assured Pavilion audiences that the New Heaven was very like the Old Earth.

For this revue, Mr. Cochran discovered a delightful romp in Ada May, an American girl, who appeared as a railway porter, a dairymaid, and a flag-seller, and, incidentally, did a dance with the aid of a large red balloon and a familiar Chopin air, which Pavilion audiences regarded as justifying Beverley Nichols's dictum that Ada May could caricature a complete cast with one of her high kicks. Unfortunately, Ada May was absent for thirty-two performances in the early days of the run of *The 1930 Revue* and the effect upon advance bookings was immediate. "House Full" signs were displayed, but crowded audiences dispersed, just a little disappointed that they had missed such a highlight of the show as the elfin Ada May.

The low comedy in Beverley Nichols's revue was in the capable hands of Maisie Gay, whose best opportunity came in *Cup and Lip*, a sketch in which the actress made an omelet, obeying instructions from "The Wireless." Maisie, entering the stalls of a theatre, long after the performance had begun, was an excellent bit of dumb-show. Stout in build and hampered by an abundance of wraps and belongings, she made her way to her seat, incidentally giving a display of bad manners, only too familiar to patrons of West End vaudeville houses. This well-loved player suffered from arthritis and had a room just inside the stage door, where she dressed with the Pavilion chorus. Her early withdrawal from Theatreland was a sad loss to vaudeville.

At the Palace, Cochran produced *Streamline* in 1934, this being his twenty-first revue. The opening scene revealed Shakespeare's Globe Theatre in the year 1593, but, quickly, the audience was transported to the Theatre Royal, 1934. By the end of the prologue Mr. Cochran's young ladies were wearing pink knickers and blue brassieres and topicalities were to the fore, so the new revue was launched. The pink knickers and blue brassieres scena proved to be a skit upon the masculine Black, Brown, and Red Shirts of contemporary European politics. The slogan, "Join the Blue Brassieres" was displayed on the one side of the stage, and supported by a party of suitably attired ladies of the chorus, threatening Meg Lemonnier's pink knickers brigade.

If full marks had to be awarded to an individual number in *Streamline* it would be to Florence Desmond, as the Arctic explorer, who was not only the first married woman to fly to the Pole, but the first woman to take her baby with her! "Dessie," as her friends call her, began stage work at the age of ten and already displayed considerable talent as a mimic. She reached the West End when Cochran engaged her for the chorus of *On With the Dance*, and her earliest singing number in Cochran revue dates from 1926. A year or two later her imitations, particularly those of Tallulah Bankhead and Mae West, engaged the attention of playgoers. The rolling walk, the flirtatious smile, and the veneer of naughtiness which constitute Mae West's contribution to vaudeville were there to the life. In *Streamline*, Florence Desmond took part in a Gilbert and Sullivan operetta, entitled *Perseverance*, with "Dessie" as a strictly Victorian-minded Patience. In general, however, *Streamline* owed its success to the dancers, headed by the delightful Tilly Losch, the dancers including the Young Ladies of Mr. Cochran's chorus, "alive and kicking."

Follow the Sun, the Cochran revue of 1936, was an Adelphi production, and Arthur Schwartz, of *Band Wagon* fame, provided the music. He was a New York barrister, and piano-playing was no more than a pleasant hobby before a song from his pen was accepted for Grand Street Follies in 1927. The price paid was eight dollars forty-two cents, but persuaded Arthur Schwartz to abandon Law. Coming to London, he wrote "High and Low" and "I'm like a Sailor" for the late Julian Wylie, who put them into his *Here Comes the Bride*. Then Fred and Adele Astaire won popularity for *The Band Wagon* in New York, and Arthur Schwartz, its musician, was a made man. He was a quick worker. Two hours after Schwartz was told the title of Cochran's 1936 revue, the music of the opening number, "Follow the Sun," was on Cochran's desk.

In this show Claire Luce was Cochran's leading lady. An American by birth, she came to London after a term with the Ziegfeld Follies and at once made her mark as Bonnie, the unhappy little wife of the vaudeville star in *Burlesque*, in which she appeared with Nelson Keys, who played the little comedian, Skid. *Burlesque* deserved more success than it achieved and Miss Luce's Bonnie was an astonishing emotional effort for a girl whose stage training had been confined to revue and there, principally, to dancing. Later, Claire Luce was to show a similar command of emotion as the unhappy heroine in *Of Mice and Men*. The gifts she displayed as a dancer when she partnered Fred Astaire in the "Night and Day" number in *Gay Divorce* offered Cochran an opportunity when he staged "The Lady with the Tap" scena in *Follow the Sun*. Here Claire impersonated a lovely

[Photo : Angus McBean

Bobby Howes and Bea Lillie singing 'Sic Transit Gloria,' in the Revue "All Clear"

[Photo : Sasha

Maisie Gay in "Cochran's 1930 Revue," in the sketch 'The Late Comer'

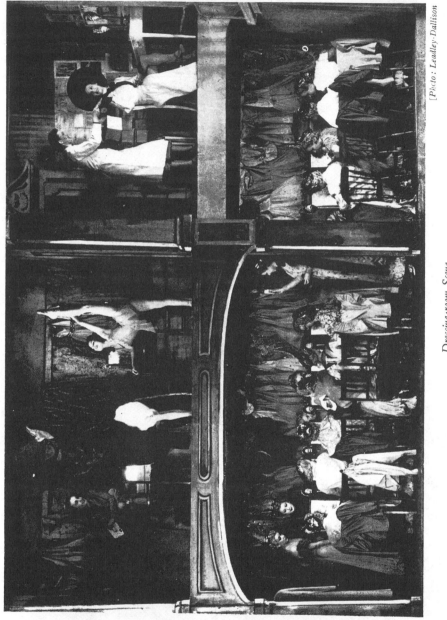

[*Photo: Leadley-Dallison*]

Dressing-room Scena

Cochran's Revue, "Follow the Sun," Adelphi Theatre, 1936

spy, charged with the duty of tap-dancing her way into a fortress manned by ladies of Mr. Cochran's chorus, in military attire which happily contrasted with the black and white displayed by the spy.

Miss Luce's other opportunity was in *The First Shoot*, a ballet devised by Osbert Sitwell, with music by William Walton. She played Connie Winsome, a Gaiety girl, who had married into the peerage and was entertaining her first shooting party as the wife of Lord de Fontenoy. The ballet included a dance of pheasants and ended when Lady de Fontenoy was unluckily shot by her admirer, Lord Charles Canterbury. Cecil Beaton, who designed the Edwardian suits and dresses, had a full share in the success of William Walton's ballet.

For the *décor* and stage settings in *Follow the Sun*, Cochran enlisted Ernst Stern, from the Reinhardt theatrical laboratory in Berlin. Stern was originally a cabaret artist, who began his career in Vienna, but went to Berlin, where, for a time, he made illustrations for the pre-1914 *Simplicissimus*. Max Reinhardt discovered that Stern's artistic talents could be diverted into theatrical channels and Stern's work for Cochran during the first production of *The Miracle* at Olympia revealed not only a high talent but amazing industry.

Follow the Sun cost Mr. Cochran £17,500, and *Home and Beauty*, the Coronation revue, considerably more; so, properly, it should have been as much better as it was more expensive. It was not. This time Nikolaus Brodszky provided the melodies, A. P. Herbert the wit, and Nelson Keys, Binnie Hale, and Gitta Alpar the star cast, but their joint efforts were obscured by the very generosity of Mr. Cochran's production. Nevertheless, Binnie Hale, as Rose Mellow in her bath at Mulberry Moat, challenging Miss Alpar to an operatic bout, was excellent burlesque, while, as a variant, there was "A Nice Cup of Tea," sung in the servants' hall, a lyric in A. P. Herbert's best manner, to the music of Henry Sullivan.

> They say it's not nutritious,
> But darn it, it's delicious,
> And that's all that matters to me.
> It turns your meat to leather,
> Well, let's all die together,
> The one drink in Paradise is tea!

Apart from his contribution to "A Nice Cup of Tea," as the Plumber to the 'tweenie of Binnie Hale, Nelson Keys's character sketches included three studies in senility, an elderly Harrovian in *Pass the Port*, an aged farmer who deplored the English weather, and an aristocratic old lady. All were good, but they failed to make their full effect in a theatre as large as the Adelphi. What was happening was that the stage pictures were "stealing" the show. What theatre-goers took away was the memory of Mr. Cochran's Young Ladies, in undress, standing before their lighted mirrors, or some other spectacle which owed more to John Murray Anderson, the producer, than it did to the high-salaried trio who consti- tuted the stars in *Home and Beauty*. As for the plot provided by A. P. Herbert, it was lost amid the myriad graces of its setting. Gitta Alpar suffered most, as she was a soprano of the grand-opera type and needed time to display her gifts, time which was occupied by the disclosure of the multitudinous backgrounds of *Home and Beauty*. On the Continent, Gitta Alpar created the title role of *The Dubarry*, which poor Anny Ahlers played with such success in London. Gitta Alpar should have had opportunities comparable with those in Millocker's operetta, instead of the bits and pieces vouchsafed in *Home and Beauty*.

Mr. Cochran celebrated the opening of the second World War by producing a Ronald Jeans revue at the Savoy, with music by Noel Gay. It opened with a black-out scene, which is sufficiently characterised by this exchange of experiences:

> *The Lady:* Gawd, what muscles that man has!
> *The Man:* That was a lamp-post, dearie.

Of course, the revue was named *Lights Up*. A pleasant turn was an adenoidal voice from the broadcasting station at Zeezen, reminding British listeners-in of the atrocities committed during the Battle of Hastings. Again, Doris Hare, disguised as a Cockney urchin, discussed evacuation problems and reached the conclusion, "I didn't really never ought to have went." With Evelyn Laye and Phyllis Stanley in the cast, theatre-goers were assured of songs well sung, Miss Laye being specially good as Cora Pearl singing "Only a Glass of Champagne," in what was described as a recension of a song and dance hall of the 1860's, from the pen of Arthur Wimperis. Miss Laye displayed an unexpected sense of characterisation in a number of roles; for example, as the uniformed assistant of Carlo the Illusionist, whose best tricks she botched with obstinate persistence. The turn was in quaint contrast to her earlier appearances in Ronald Jeans's "Four Stages of Marriage," in which the sentiment ranged from the ecstasy of the honeymoon era to the exasperated boredom of marital maturity. As her pretty self, Evelyn sang a charming Noel Gay number, "You've done something to my heart."

With Doris Zinkeisen responsible for the stage settings and costumes, Buddy Bradley in charge of the dancers and the dancing, and Mr. Cochran's Young Ladies displaying their graces in a typical day from their own lives, *Lights Up* was a worthy war-time effort, even if it does not stand out among its producer's contributions to the vaudeville of his era. Personally, I liked it better than Cochran's second war-time revue, *Big Top*, a production at His Majesty's, with a book by Herbert Farjeon. Cyril Ritchard and Fred Emney supported Beatrice Lillie, but Farjeon's canvas seemed over-large and, continually, one wanted to be nearer to the inimitable Bea, so that her talent might be fully sensed.

Chapter XIII

QUICK-FIRE MUSICAL COMEDY, MAINLY FROM AMERICA
1919 TO 1945

THE PASSING OF GEORGE EDWARDES WROUGHT MANY CHANGES
in the world of light music, but the goodwill he had built up was too valuable
to be sacrificed without an effort to carry it into the new generation of playgoers
which arose out of the first World War. In fact, what may be called the Gaiety
and Daly's tradition established more than one management and thus contributed
substantially to later vaudeville history. Indeed, the numerous revivals of George
Edwardes shows during the second World War show that the Edwardean outlook
was far from being ephemeral. This generation cannot fully recover the old-time
thrills, but the music, at any rate, lives on.

Reference has been made to Robert Evett's courageous venture at Daly's, after
Edwardes's death. At the Gaiety, the mantle of one amiable George passed to
another, George Grossmith, junior, who was partnered by an experienced man
of the theatre in Edward Laurillard. In the joint venture Grossmith provided
what artistry was called for and Laurillard the business capacity. Laurillard had
learnt his trade managing such productions as *The Gay Parisienne* and *The Lady
Slavey*, and then became interested in cinemas. No fewer than twenty-five cinema-
houses were under his control when he was persuaded to return to the musical-
comedy world in partnership with young Grossmith, with whom he had already
engaged in one very profitable gamble, the production of *Potash and Perlmutter*.

When Laurillard retired from the joint directorship after five years, Grossmith
joined forces with J. A. E. Malone, who had been responsible for the stage
management of almost every important Edwardes musical comedy between 1895
and 1915. The son of an Irish V.C., Malone was intended for medicine, but
joined Edwardes when a manager was wanted for a world tour of *A Gaiety Girl,
The Geisha, The Circus Girl, A Greek Slave, Kitty Grey, Lady Madcap*, and *The
Quaker Girl*, witness to Malone's versatility as a producer. A remarkable record
and, incidentally, a reminder of the debt which playgoers so often owe to a man
who has no more than a grudging line in a programme. "Stage Manager, J. A. E.
Malone," was the customary acknowledgment, and quite often there was only
a polite silence.

Of George Grossmith, junior, there is more to be said. Indeed, if anyone sported
the white waistcoat and black "tails" of the amiable George it was the amiable
"Gee-Gee." After his highly successful appearance as beautiful bountiful Bertie
in *The Shop Girl*, he left the Gaiety for several years and did not return until
The Toreador was produced in 1901. Thenceforward, he was not only a leading
player in the Gaiety company, but Edwardes's chief-of-staff and a generous

provider of books of the words, being author or part-author of *The Spring Chicken* (1905), *The Girls of Gottenburg* (1907), *Havana* (1908), *The Dollar Princess* (1908), *Peggy* (1911), and *Theodore and Company* (1916). And this record takes no account of the revues devised for the Empire from 1905 onwards. I do not pretend to any admiration for these literary efforts, but they witness to a very real affection for musical comedy. In later years "Gee-Gee" wrote a musical version of *A Night Out* for his management at the Winter Garden Theatre, *The Cabaret Girl* (1922), *The Beauty Prize* (1923), and *Primrose* (1924), and these at a time when he was also controlling the Shaftesbury and His Majesty's theatres, where one of his ventures was the brilliant production of Flecker's *Hassan*.

Beyond a doubt young Grossmith was a worker. Moreover, he could claim a long apprenticeship to the particular brand of entertainment in which the Gaiety specialised, when the Gaiety Company, Limited, decided to lease their theatre, the understanding being that Grossmith would produce and act, while Laurillard would be the responsible manager.

As the son of his father, young Grossmith drifted into vaudeville naturally enough and commenced by earning £1 a week, at the Criterion, where W. S. Gilbert's *Haste to the Wedding* was played to music composed by George Grossmith, senior. With "Gee-Gee" played Marie Studholme, also making her debut. A little later, an engagement to play Lord Percy Pimpleton in *Morocco Bound*, at the Shaftesbury in 1893, established young Grossmith as a player of dude parts in musical comedy. An original allowance of three lines of dialogue and an idiotic giggle were expanded by impromptu anecdotes, riddles, and the like, until the role had real importance and persuaded George Edwardes to transfer "Gee-Gee" to the Gaiety. Here he played in ten musical comedies, and almost always as Algie, Archie, or some other dude. Very characteristic was Sir Archibald's song in *The Toreador*, an early effort by Paul Rubens:

> Everybody's awfully good to me, don't you know!
> I'm just about as spoilt as I can be, don't you know!
> One day I introduced my wife to a friend of mine, named Brown,
> And he actually looked after her, while I was out of Town.
> It was so unselfish of him, for he's married, too, is Brown.
> Oh! everybody's awfully good to me.

The chappie, the masher, the Johnnie, the dude—call him what you will—has been a figure of fun in London vaudeville for close upon a century. The songs of Leybourne, Vance, and Macdermott gave rise to "Merry" Nellie Power's Crutch and Toothpick ditty, and thus became the forebear of George Grossmith's "Beautiful, Bountiful Bertie," Vesta Tilley's "Algy, with the little glass eye," and several roles played by G. P. Huntley.

The Johnnie was a figure of the 1890's and, by night, was distinguished by a gardenia or a few tuberoses, possibly connected with a water-holder, worn under the buttonhole of his dress-coat. After the Johnnie came the Knut, to be associated with the recollection of Basil Hallam, singing the Finck-Wimperis number in *The Passing Show* in 1914 at the Palace, "Gilbert the Filbert," the description being, of course, a tiny pun. When the first World War broke upon London in the late summer of 1914, Basil Hallam was a flapper's darling, until his women friends began to ask why their hero did not enlist. They did not know that a metal plate supported the ligaments of one of his feet. However, Hallam was finally accepted for the Army and the last song he sang at the Palace was the

Mr. Crutchpick Tooth

prophetic "Good-bye, girls, I'm through." He was in an observation balloon which broke loose, drifted over the German lines, was shot down, and the parachute failed to open. Elsie Janis took over the reversion of "Gilbert the Filbert."

To-day, the Johnnies, the Mashers, and the Knuts are represented by the Cads of the Western Brothers. In a swell restaurant (if "swell" is the appropriate adjective) at cabaret-time, two bored youths, wearing monocles, stroll on to the dancing floor and, without a smile, hail their audience, "Good evening, Cads!" The effrontery of the gesture in some curious way justifies the impudence, and George and Kenneth are hailed as conquerors, carrying on a tradition which connects them with a long series of vaudeville characters.

It is also to the credit of "Gee-Gee" that he popularised that intoxicating bit of nonsense, "Yip-i-addy-i-ay," in *Our Miss Gibbs*. Edwardes refused to see any fun in the song and signified his sense of its unimportance by paying a beggarly £5 for the English version of the lyric, which Grossmith himself provided. In the event, the encores seemed as if they would never end. Timed as young Grossmith timed it, and with a chorus which let the rhythm rip, the idiotic romance of "Herman von Bellow, a musical fellow, who played a big 'cello each night" still has power to excite:

> Yip-i-addy-i-ay, i-ay! Yip-i-addy-i-ay!
> I don't care what becomes of me,
> When he plays me that sweet mel-o-dy.
> Yip-i-addy-i-ay, i-ay! My heart wants to shout out "Hooray,"
> Sing of joy, sing of bliss, Home was never like this,
>   Yip-i-addy-i-ay.

The first Grossmith-Laurillard musical comedy at the Gaiety was *To-night's the Night*, a version of the famous Parisian farce, *Pink Dominoes*. It was followed by *Theodore and Company*, another Parisian importation, in which Leslie Henson began to make Gaiety history. The music was by youthful Ivor Novello and Jerome Kern, the first-named receiving the commission on the strength of the success of his war-time song, "Keep the Home Fires Burning." Teddy Payne was dead, so Leslie Henson was a welcome discovery. He owed his first engage-ment in West End musical comedy to Ernest Mayer, the play-broker, who saw Leslie in a pierrot show and registered him in his mind as "a stout, middle-aged" comedian. Indeed, Mayer remembered the tubbiness of Leslie Henson so vividly that he was inclined to refuse the youthful and slim Leslie an all-important introduction to Laurillard and George Grossmith, who were about to produce *To-night's the Night*. After an audition, Leslie was given a one-line part and £4 a week. A year later, in *Theodore and Company*, Leslie Henson as Pony Twitchin of *Crimson Comics*, ran away with the play, and the opening £4 bounded up to £100 a week.

Apart from the duet with Dave Burnaby, "Three hundred and sixty-five days" (Jerome Kern's first big song success), *Theodore and Company* is memorable for an exchange of personalities between Irene Richards and Adrah Fair. Irene, as Alma, was built on more substantial lines than the sylph-like Adrah, and the exchange took this form:

> *Alma* (Irene Richards): I've got the legs!
> *Cleo* (Adrah Fair): Yes, calves all the way down!
> *Alma*: That's better than ankles all the way up.

The Laurillard and Grossmith alliance lasted until 1921, but not at the Gaiety. It will be remembered that Grossmith's contract with the Gaiety Company, Limited, had called for personal appearances on the stage. These were no longer possible when Grossmith became a Lieutenant in the Royal Naval Volunteer Reserve, a war-service which called forth a cruel gibe from Nelson Keys, "He's one of the Epsom Salts." The Board of the Gaiety Company, accordingly, tore up their contract with Laurillard and Grossmith and tried to run the theatre themselves. With little success, be it said; musical-comedy production is not a venture which hard-headed business-men can indulge in as a part-time job. In such matters the Board of a limited liability company is a noun of multitude, signifying many but not much!

"Gee-Gee" Returns

As for Grossmith, he returned to musical comedy when the war ended, with enhanced vim, the more because he had made a lot of money as inventor and part-author of the famous *Bing Boy* productions at the Alhambra. Very soon the Laurillard and Grossmith syndicate was once more in command at the Gaiety, and this time with a long lease. They were also producing musical shows at the Adelphi.

The most spectacular enterprise of the partnership, however, was the building of the Winter Garden Theatre. Passing down Drury Lane after he had been demobilised, Grossmith stopped before what had once been the Old Mogul music-hall. It was entitled the New Middlesex and in the possession of Sir Oswald Stoll. Its potentialities as a West End theatre may be judged from the fact that the most expensive seats were 1*s*. 3*d*. apiece, but "Gee-Gee" had visions. The time was 11 a.m. Within an hour Grossmith was in conference with Sir Oswald and well on the way to buying the freehold of the premises which, with aid from the architect, Sir Charles Allom, were to become the Winter Garden Theatre.

During ten anxious weeks the Old Mogul suffered conversion, and a couple of days before the opening the wooden scaffolding was still so prominent that a Drury Lane wit described the place as "The Splinter Garden." The workmen were only just cleared out of the theatre as the first-night audience was ushered in. However, directly Ivan Caryll climbed into the conductor's chair, displaying the familiar fierce moustache and trimmed beard, it was plain that the old Gaiety atmosphere was being re-created and that the first-night audience at the Winter Garden was at one with the players on the big stage, as audiences had been when Hollingshead and George Edwardes controlled the Gaiety. Perhaps the intimacy was established the more quickly, because a party of chorus girls had been collected which vied with the Ziegfeld Beauties of New York.

The new Drury Lane house opened with *Kissing Time*, a New York production, originally named *The Girl behind the Gun*. Phyllis Dare and Yvonne Arnaud supported Grossmith, and Leslie Henson, with war honours thick upon him, assisted. He had been "Leslie of Lille" and had a big reputation as an entertainer of troops, so ex-soldiers spent their deferred pay generously upon stalls, pit seats, and gallery seats while *Kissing Time* was enjoying its long run. By this time Leslie Henson had revealed his full powers and had a position comparable with that of Teddy Payne. Henson's amazing powers of improvisation can be illustrated

14

from an episode associated with *Yes, Uncle,* which was produced at the Prince of Wales's and included a silent gagging scena, in company with the youthful Margaret Bannerman. The young lady had been entrusted with the line:

"Well, good-bye! I'm going out to buy some stuff for a petticoat."

There was a sofa as well as two big bolster cushions on the stage, and one night it struck Henson that a bolster cushion dimly resembled a roll of silk. Without a word to his stage-partner, he picked up the bolster, started to unroll the imagined silk, stroked it, and measured off a few yards. Finally, he snipped at the corner with imaginary scissors, before he tore off a length, folded it up and presented the imaginary packet to the amazed "Bunny." The "House" by this time was indulging in a continuous chuckle and Henson whispered:

"Quick, give me some money out of your handbag."

Miss Bannerman duly obliged, whereupon Leslie proceeded to pencil an elaborate bill, and sent it hurtling to an imaginary cashier, by means of an imaginary "ball," in which the bill and the cash were supposed to be enclosed. As the ball (in imagination) sped round an area about the line of the dress-circle, Leslie's comic eyes followed it, and when it returned with the precise change, he opened the ball, gave the money to "Bunny," and bowed her out of the imaginary shop.

"Bunny's" inexperience at the time was revealed at the next performance, when she said, "Well, I'm going out to buy some stuff for a petticoat," and then tripped off the stage, so that the best silent gag in musical comedy was lost to the audience. Her justification was that she thought "It was just Leslie's fun!"

Sally, one of many variants upon the Cinderella theme, dates from 1921, and was even more successful than *Kissing Time.* It made a profit of £40,000 and had a run of 387 performances. Grossmith called upon Jerome Kern, from New York, for the music, remembering his tuneful contributions to *Theodore and Company.* Guy Bolton and Clifford Grey did the book and lyrics and the experienced Edward Royce (son of the famous burlesque actor) produced. In New York, the title role had been played by the gifted Marilyn Miller and Kern was very suspicious when the role of Sally was given to the beautiful Dorothy Dickson. Kern and Ziegfeld, who had an interest in the English production, raised other objections, pointing out that Dorothy's only experience consisted of dance-turns in a Cochran revue, in company with her husband, Carl Hyson. However, they were wrong. Dorothy Dickson shared all the glory that was going and held her own with Leslie Henson and "Gee-Gee" themselves. Dorothy's reminiscences of Joan of Arc, prompting the reflection, "You can't keep a good girl down," the happy uplift of "Look for the silver lining," and her singing of "I'm but a wild, wild rose" (with male chorus) are outstanding memories, as is the Grand Duke's song, "Where the Schnitzer goes Down to the Sea."

Some years later *Sally* was revived at the Saville Theatre with Jessie Matthews in the role of the kitchen-maid turned Russian dancer and Richard Hearne as the Archdule turned waiter, but this time the piece was entitled *Wild Rose.* The wedding scene in the last act, which led up to the topical duet, "There's a church round the corner that's waiting for me, the corner of Madison Square," and the Flor Fina ballet, with music by Victor Herbert, are other *Sally* or *Wild Rose* memories.

It has been said that the management of a single theatre by no means exhausted the energies of George Grossmith. In 1920, he and Laurillard were producing *The Naughty Princess* at the Adelphi, this being a version of a French opéra bouffe, *La Reine S'Amuse*, with music by Cuvillier, who had written *The Lilac Domino*. Yvonne Arnaud assisted the French comedian Leon Morton to provide the Gallic atmosphere, the other stars being W. H. Berry, Heather Thatcher, then a budding actress fresh from one of Charlot's revues, and George Grossmith, as the Young Prince. Wearing a golden wig and taking a long pull and a strong pull at his waist-band, Grossmith managed to fake the youth of the Prince, as, by his own admission, he faked Cuvillier's music.

It was during the run of *The Naughty Princess* that Laurillard retired from his partnership with Grossmith to devote himself to films. In this capacity he built "the Marble Arch," the first real cinema-house in the West End of London. In his place J. A. E. Malone joined Grossmith, and soon Grossmith and Malone controlled six London theatres—His Majesty's, the Adelphi, the Gaiety, the Apollo, the Shaftesbury, and the Winter Garden. Their production of *The Beauty Prize* at the Winter Garden in 1923 included an ingenious chorus of Mah-Jongg beauties—winds, dragons, flowers, circles, and the rest—the Chinese game of Mah-Jongg being a craze at the time. P. G. Wodehouse collaborated with Grossmith in writing the "book" and Jerome Kern once more provided the music, the team being the same when *The Cabaret Girl* was produced at the Winter Garden Theatre a year earlier.

In curious contrast to the intensive efforts extending over years which W. S. Gilbert judged necessary when writing a Savoy opera, the book of *The Cabaret Girl* was written during a trip to America on the *Aquitania*. "Gee-Gee" strolled the decks gathering ideas, while Wodehouse, in his cabin, sought words to express them, adding typing talent sufficient to get the words upon paper, ready for Jerome Kern, who was already at work upon the music in New York. After talks with the composer, Grossmith and Wodehouse revised and re-typed their script, and it was ready for Leslie Henson, Dorothy Dickson, Heather Thatcher, and Enid Stamp-Taylor, who were eagerly awaiting it in London. In the event, Henson fell ill and his part was played by Norman Griffin at short notice. The personal triumph in *The Cabaret Girl* fell to Heather Thatcher as Little Ada.

After Jerome Kern came George Gershwin, who provided the music for *Primrose*, a book by Grossmith and Guy Bolton. It was given at the Winter Garden in 1924.

"No, No, Nanette" Comes to Town

Musical comedy at the Winter Garden, in general, followed Gaiety tradition, and it was left to another management and another theatre to discover a new thing, the quick-fire show which still passes for up-to-date musical comedy. The epoch-making play was *No, No, Nanette*. Curiously enough, this also had a Gaiety origin so far as London was concerned, as it was discovered by Herbert Clayton, the handsome Toreador in the play of that name, which had filled the Gaiety Theatre a quarter of a century earlier. During the years Clayton, like Grossmith, had drifted into management and, with Jack Waller, had made some money out of that excellent farce, *It Pays to Advertise*. The small fortune sufficed to rent the Palace Theatre, where *No, No, Nanette* was produced in 1925. The plot—for *No, No, Nanette* really had a plot—was derived from a novel by May Edginton, *His Lady Friends*, which Sir Charles Hawtrey had produced as a play at the St. James's in 1920. In the musical version, Joseph Coyne played Charles Hawtrey's part, "the good picker," with George Grossmith, Irene Browne, and pretty Binnie Hale, with her twinkling toes, assisting in the laughter-making and love-making departments.

Joseph Coyne is wedded to a wife who is absurdly over-scrupulous in money matters, thus forcing the unlucky Joseph to spend his extra money upon lady friends at Nice, Bath, and Harrogate. He visits them in turn, and none divine that Joseph is leading a double life, or rather a quadruple life. A strange fact, this. However, while the chorus—"I want to be Happy"—was being thundered at stalls, pit, circle, and gallery, few patrons of the Palace cared a couple of soft drink straws about the niceties of the story. Youth, professional efficiency, and high spirits made *No. No. Nanette*, the musical-comedy success of its generation, and every restaurant band was playing "Tea for Two" and "I want to be Happy," not daily, but hourly. The theme, "I want to be happy," indeed, characterised the years immediately following upon the World War, and in 1925, in spite of dull trade, there was still hope that the wish might become a reality. The General Strike came in 1926 to dissipate it. At any rate, while Binnie Hale, in the salmon and white bathing-suit, together with Coyne and Grossmith and a big chorus were at work, a couple of thousand Londoners forgot potential worries. For months *No, No, Nanette* returned £500 a week to its American adapters and Vincent Youmans, the composer. Indeed, in 1926, when *No, No, Nanette* was at the height of its earning capacity, £250,000 a year was being paid to writers and composers in the United States as a consequence of the vogue of American plays in London and, incidentally, not a penny of British income-tax was paid on these earnings.

No, No, Nanette initiated the vogue of quick-fire musical comedies which is with us to-day. Silk stockings disappeared as they had done from Russian ballet-dancing, bare legs being the rule. As for the speed of production, it is on record that Joseph Coyne and George Grossmith required the attention of masseurs during the interval between the acts. Otherwise, there would have been a danger of physical collapse, as neither were in their first youth. Indeed, a minor triumph won by Clayton and Waller lay in their choice of heroes. It was an act of real courage to hand over the lover-roles to two elderly comedians. It was a major triumph of the elderly comedians that they proved themselves more than the equals of the best among their youthful rivals. *No, No, Nanette*, indeed, was a triumph of casting. Irene Browne and Marie Hemingway as the wives, and Vera Pearce as Flora, the strong woman, ably supported their principals, and because there was a story to unfold their efferts proved fully worth while.

When the career of *No, No, Nanette* at the Palace ended, the play was replaced by *Princess Charming*. The story goes that Herbert Clayton went to New York in search of a musical play and found nothing until, in his last hours on shore, he came upon a poverty-stricken Hungarian composer, Albert Szirmai by name. The Hungarian played to his visitor for a couple of hours, during which time the occupants of the flat below were knocking hard, and protesting, "Music isn't allowed." Szirmai secured his contract, when Clayton was sailing. The next step was to find a plot and lyrics fitted for the music and the task was given to the highly experienced and ingenious Arthur Wimperis, who produced a Ruritanian comic opera, based upon an Austrian story. This element of improvisation runs through almost all modern vaudeville, and, in many cases, it can bring forward the excuse, "it works." Thanks to a gifted cast, the improvisation worked in the case of *Princess Charming*, for Delysia had the title role, with Grossmith as her Prince. The comedian, W. H. Berry, was an insurance agent. Two typical Wimperis lines were in Berry's charge. "Have you heard the good news?" asked someone. "You never do in my business," retorted the lugubrious Berry. At another stage the comedian remarked, "Smile at him in Yiddish. You've got your hands free." This to Delysia.

By this time the Clayton-Waller management was so well established that the Palace no longer sufficed. Such musicians as Jerome Kern and Vincent Youmans had pieces which called for production and naturally desired to be associated with the lucky pair who had given *No, No, Nanette* to the world. *Mercenary Mary*, with music by Friedlander and Con Conrad, was given at the Hippodrome, and it included the popular "Tie a string around your finger." Kern's *Sunny* followed, a musical comedy which was produced on a lavish scale, costing the Clayton-Waller management £17,000 before a penny was taken. However, the size of the Hippodrome fully justified the outlay, as well as the expense of a long cast. The principal episode was a realistic presentation of a wedding on board an ocean-going liner, and very beautiful it was.

The triumph of *No, No, Nanette* did more than establish Youmans in the front rank of song and dance composers. It raised Binnie Hale to stardom, and from the Palace she passed to the Adelphi, where *Mr. Cinders* was produced in 1929. This time the music came from two Englishmen, Vivian Ellis and Richard Myers, and the programme reveals that an astonishing team was necessary before a somewhat trite recension of the foolproof Cinderella theme could reach production. J. C. Williamson "presented," Julian Wylie "produced," Clifford Grey and Greatorex Newman wrote the book, with aid from the lyric writer, Leo Robin, while the dances were devised by Max Rivers, Fred Leslie, and Charles Brooks, a team of ten, including the music-makers.

And all this talent in order that Bobby Howes, as Jim, a neglected orphan, might fall in love with Jill, a millionaire's daughter. Of course, the millionaire gives a ball and Jim is not invited, though he comes in time to help in the pursuit of the thieves, who have abstracted Jill's pearl necklace. The gyrations of the plot allowed Jill to become a housemaid for a time and thus indulge in a flirtation with Jim, in the course of which the millionaire's daughter donned spectacles as well as a housemaid's cap and apron, and thus disguised, sang "Spread a little happiness," the theme-song of *Mr. Cinders*. Playgoers will also recall the lines, "Every moment I'm with you, I'm happy; every little moment without you I'm blue," this being a Rita Nugent and Jack Melford effort. They may seem small things, but they went round the world in association with their music. For the rest there is the picture of the unhappy Bobby Howes, clad in a beer-barrel and retorting upon the tyrannous Lady Lancaster, "It's women like you make men like me hate women like you," and the climax of the Cinderella story, when, the pearl necklace being recovered, a burly policeman fits little Jim's bowler hat upon little Jim's head, and thus completes the musical-comedy equivalent of the pantomime glass slipper scene:

> Even when the darkest clouds are in the sky,
>   When things go wrong,
>   You must smile and try
> To spread a little happiness as you go by.
> What's the use of worrying and feeling blue,
> When days seem long, keep smiling through
> And spread a little happiness till dreams come true.

Bobby Howes is a prime favourite at the Hippodrome, and during the years of the second World War, made his tenth appearance there in *Let's Face It*, an American musical, with Cole Porter lyrics and music and a production by George Black. The plot concerned itself with three middle-aged ladies who set out to entertain three young soldiers, to the distress of three younger girls, a promising beginning to a show which aimed, above all, at speed and colour. The highlight of the piece was Bobby Howes, portraying in dumb-show the whole career of a soldier, from medical examination on enlistment day to the big moment of decoration for duty well and fully done. Here was miming worthy of miming's long tradition in musical shows. Bobby Howes knew he was in competition with memories of Arthur Roberts, Leslie Henson, and Maisie Gay, to name only three, and he did not disappoint.

Yes, Madam?, in 1934, had brought Binnie Hale and Bobby Howes once more into partnership, this time at the Hippodrome, but more memorable is the fact that in *Yes, Madam?* Vera Pearce established herself as the accepted successor of Connie Ediss. At the night-club, "The Knuckle-Bone," she sang "Czecho-slovak Love," in company with the diminutive, but ever-smiling, Bobby Howes. As a ferociously amorous dame of ample proportions and immense physical strength, Vera flung Bobby about the stage, thus illustrating the probability of her house-rocking claim, "Two more women like me, and you'd fill the theatre." In *Please Teacher*, the Hippodrome success of 1935, Vera Pearce was a gymnasium mistress in a girls' school, and again she played opposite little Bobby Howes. The substantial Vera Pearce, in roomy "whites," exercising over a pair of parallel bars, with Bobby Howes enjoying the spectacle, made Glasgow audiences rock with joy during the preliminary run, and the Hippodrome folk in London were no less appreciative. The only fear was that too much gymnastic exercise might bring Miss Pearce back once more to her sylph-like proportions. Then the best of her jesting would vanish, as it would have vanished from a tenuous Connie Ediss. "Can I see you?" asked Bobby Howes diffidently, when he entered the gymnasium. The guffaw which arose was due entirely to the fact that Vera Pearce was far from invisible. When a song wanted singing in the old-time Gaiety-cum-music-hall manner, Miss Pearce could do the thing as well as any comedienne on the stage, as she showed in "The Girl the Soldiers always leave behind them," of *Yes, Madam?*

In *Big Business*, which was given at the Hippodrome in Coronation year, Miss Pearce was once more yoked to Mr. Howes, this time playing Robin Hood to his Little John, in a mock pageant. As Miss Belmore played Will Scarlett, Mr. Howes seemed in danger of losing life itself, seeing that two outsized come-diennes were joining issue with Little John. And, lastly, Vera Pearce, in *Wild Oats*, at the Prince's Theatre. This time she was in company with Sydney Howard, but once more in "whites," though, on this occasion, as a cricketer. Out by a catch made by her unhappy husband, it was only too plain that Sydney would hear about it all later. Musical-comedy fans look forward to a sequel to *Wild Oats*, in which Mrs. Cloppitt will deliver a Caudle lecture to the erring Sydney.

Spectacle and Dance

The mechanics of quick-fire musical comedy and revue are those of American mass-production. A lot for the money, with little or no regard to lasting quality; that is the outstanding characteristic. There is also continual insistence upon speed, due to anxiety lest the audience should find a moment in which to be bored. In comparison with their Edwardian equivalents, the musical comedy and revue of the 'thirties and the 'forties moved in high gear. One other factor must be added arising from the fact that the present generation has divined the miming and satirical potentialities of the dance. Dancing is now much more than an adornment to a taking tune. It may well be the end-all and be-all of a show, outstanding examples being the productions associated with the American, Fred Astaire.

Fred Astaire made his first London appearance when he was only twenty-three, when he appeared in *Stop Flirting*, in company with his sister, Adele, another genius who is largely responsible for giving dance the place it has in up-to-date musical shows. From her voice downwards to her twinkling feet, Adele Astaire was fashioned in the proportions of a sylph, such an one as danced attendance upon Belinda in Pope's *Rape of the Lock*. To a sense of rhythm as potent as that of her brother, Adele added a sense of impish character which momentarily recalled such a low comedienne as Louie Freear. The Astaires played in straight vaudeville long before they discovered that their specialised approach to an audience was through the limbs rather than voice. The phenomenal success of *Stop Flirting* (it was called *For Goodness' Sake* in America) revealed that a new type of vaudeville was in process of invention and a type, moreover, which had promise of a long life because it was to be much more than a show which included a lot of dancing. Fred and Adele had discovered that a great many things could be fully expressed "through the feet." Recall the Oompah Trot and the delightful "Night and Day" number in *Gay Divorce*, to the music of Cole Porter, as it was given at the Palace in the early 'thirties, years when London and New York badly needed cheerful entertainment. I have forgotten if *Top Hat* had a stage as well as a film presentation. If so, the "Cheek to Cheek" dance is another instance of the rhythm of limb and body giving sentiment a new meaning; a meaning, moreover, which helped to hide the absurdities of latter-day lyric-writing:

> My heart beats so that I can hardly speak,
> When we're out together, dancing cheek to cheek.

The gay (I had almost written careless) proficiency of such dancers as the Astaires can be infinitely attractive and even persuades the elderly that there is something, apart from increased tempo, in super-heated Fox-trot. At any rate, Fred Astaire finds no difficulty in expressing his stage personality to the full in his "mainly dancing" shows. A decade of exploration and invention has enabled American dancers of his type to give, let us say, tap-dancing, some of the virtues of expressive language, and it will be understood that this implies instructing audiences to see, as well as actors and actresses to dance. The gestures and momen-tary poses which tap-dancing encourages have developed significance, so that this generation of playgoers not only derives amusement from the movement, but divines that the whole gamut of stage potentialities is being illuminated. The dancing supplements the rhythmic pattern not only of music, but of the particular show, as the stage effects mirror the moods of the dancer or the dancing chorus.

It may well be that the full flavour of these high-speed song and dance shows cannot be savoured out of Broadway. We saw Cole Porter's *Dubarry was a Lady* in London during the early months of the second World War. But did Arthur Riscoe, even with the aid of that amazing chequered suit, put over the mingled impudence and vanity of the cloakroom attendant about to turn King of France, as did Bert Lahr in the New York production? Similarly, there was Frances Day putting over that super-heated ditty anent "Katie who went to Haiti," with the consequence that, richly as Katie loved Haiti, it was nothing to the loves which Haiti bestowed upon the generous-hearted Katie. Ethel Merman, in New York, was singing a song which was made to fit, whereas for Frances Day the song was

Dormitory Scene in "Please Teacher"
In centre: Winifred Izard, Sepha Treble and Pearl Greene

A. P. Herbert's "Derby Day"

[*Stage Photo Co.*

"The Du Barry," at His Majesty's Theatre, 1932

a reach-me-down; not a misfit, of course, but not quite what Cole Porter had in mind when he wrote the song for the Merman and Broadway audiences. However, the spectacle of the would-be King lying upon the Louis Seize table and nursing the arrow in his posterior, an accident which sadly cramped his love-making, showed a welcome vitality. Frances Day, as Madame Du Barry, in the gardens of the Petit Trianon, too, was a picture. It is not uncommon to leave a quick-fire musical which reaches London with a big American reputation, just a little disappointed; indeed, assured that something has been lost in the Atlantic passage. After all, quick-fire musical shows are probably America's top-ranking contribution to the stage and the reason for the disappointment may be that it is an art-form calling for teamwork of the highest order, a condition which American circumstances fulfil so well. The outstanding American vaudeville stars are usually those who profit most greatly by the teamwork of their colleagues, and whose clowning is best displayed against an energetic chorus and elaborate settings.

During the past quarter of a century one of the requisites in a really good modern musical has been a plot which offers opportunities for spectacle, as well as chances for displaying a well-trained chorus of singers and dancers. The reason is that, in the 'twenties, spectacular films such as *The Birth of a Nation* and Douglas Fairbanks's *The Thief of Bagdad* threatened serious danger to the theatre. The first of these films drew big audiences to Drury Lane and the running expenses were so low that, for a time, it seemed that no theatrical production could possibly compete. However, *Rose Marie*, produced early in 1925, ran for two years and a week at the Lane, following upon a big success in New York, where the part-author and producer, Oscar Hammerstein, junior, made a personal profit of £200,000 in seven months. When *Rose Marie* came to Drury Lane the American companies were still attracting audiences worth £35,000 a week. In a single week the box-office at Drury Lane took £5,900; in a year, £657,000. The actual profit was £185,000, while the theatre paid £87,000 in entertainment tax.

There was a big margin for spectacular production and an expensive body of players with such profits. The Totem scene, in which a chorus of seventy women and thirty men did some astonishing stage "falls," was the most memorable thing in *Rose Marie*, and, indeed, the most memorable thing of its kind in all vaudeville. For the rest, *Rose Marie* included a murder scene and could boast that it had no jazz music, so it had claims to originality apart from the size and energy of its outsize chorus. With Edith Day and Billy Merson as its stars, the Drury Lane production fully deserved its success.

The Desert Song, which followed *Rose Marie* at Drury Lane, was another production which owed much to spectacle. It was a sheikh story, with a Moroccan background and, once more, Edith Day was the heroine, the low comedy being in the capable hands of Gene Gerrard, as a society reporter. Gene Gerrard had made good at the Gaiety a couple of years or so earlier, playing an evening-dress comedian role in *Katja the Dancer*. A long struggle for recognition commenced before the first World War, when Gene was earning £3 a week as a comic bandsman in a George Mozart sketch. In those days Gene was known as Eugene O'Sullivan, and as the son of a tailor, whose shop was opposite the Holborn Empire. During an Australian tour Eugene O'Sullivan became Gene Gerrard and, when he was demobilised, he found his earning capacity had risen to £30 a week. After *Katja the Dancer* Gene Gerrard stepped into the £100 a week class, fully justifying the engagement as leading comedian at Drury Lane.

The Desert Song told of a young French officer who became the sheikh of an Arab tribe and abducted Edith Day to the Riff hills, and the plot sufficed, the more as it allowed of a chorus made up of the wives of French légionaires, wearing up-to-date Parisian gowns. Like *Show Boat, The Desert Song* was of United States origin, the principal author being Oscar Hammerstein, and the composer Sigmund Romberg. *The Desert Song* was revived at the Alhambra in 1931 and has since seen the footlights in 1936 and 1939. It is admirably fitted for less than critical audiences in outsize metropolitan theatres.

Show Boat, with Edna Ferber as romance-maker, Jerome Kern as musician, Florenz Ziegfeld as producer, and Oscar Hammerstein, junior, as author, was a Drury Lane triumph in 1928. I rank it with Noel Coward's *Bitter Sweet* among the fully successful musical plays of the century, satisfying as the *Yeomen of the Guard* and *The Gondoliers* were satisfying in their day and generation.

The making of *Show Boat* involved hard work in plenty. The beginning was a chance remark by Winthrop Ames, the American manager, during a trying rehearsal. Said Ames:

"Next time we won't bother with try-outs. We'll all charter a show-boat and drift down the river, playing to the towns as we come to them."

"What is a show-boat?" asked Edna Ferber.

"A show-boat is a floating theatre. The boats used to play up and down the rivers, in the Southern States, in particular along the Mississippi and the Missouri. The actors lived and slept right there on the boat."

Miss Ferber has told us that, at once, she sat up, and up and up, like a cobra uncoiling! Within a few days she was hot upon the trail of the old-time show-boats. At Winthrop's words a host of pictures, people, and happenings had welled up in her imagination, as the basis of *Cavalcade* fashioned itself for Noel Coward when he was idly turning over the Boer War issues of *Black and White*. A year was spent searching for material, including some weeks as a member of a show-boat company, during which Edna sold tickets, "walked on," and, in the intervals, talked with the riverside audiences. The writing of the novel took another year, and when it appeared 320,000 copies were quickly sold and no fewer than four separate film versions were made.

But the story called for the addition of music, and the music came when young Oscar Hammerstein offered to turn the novel into a musical play and proposed that Jerome Kern, then in the early forties and at the top of his form, should do the music. Hammerstein had no intention of wasting such a story upon the two acts and two set scenes of Edwardian musical comedy. He raised the curtain upon a river-bank along the Mississippi in 1890, with Captain Andy's floating theatre, *The Cotton Blossom*, moored to the jetty. Quickly the colourful South came to life in Julie, the half-blooded actress, with the negro melody, "Man o' Mine," which Marie Burke sang so delightfully in the original London production in 1928. Marie Burke's Julie lingers in the memory with Paul Robeson's Joe, singing "Ole Man River," and that is saying very much. The song established a great artist in the affections of London audiences.

> That old Man River,
> He don't say nuffin,
> He jest goes rollin' along.

Perhaps Robeson's song was the pick of the basket and, yet, Julie's:

> Fish gotta swim; birds gotta fly,
> I gotta love one man till I die;
> Can't help lovin' dat man o' mine.

was almost as effective.

The double love-story of *Show Boat*, the original rhythms of Jerome Kern's melodies, especially the numbers written under negro influences, and the varied and colourful backgrounds to the action, all helped to a triumph not only in America, but the world over. From the Mississippi waterside, the scenes passed to Chicago in 1893, the year of the World Fair, when Magnolia and her gambler husband are still enjoying prosperity enough to justify the haunting:

> *Gay:* Why do I love you?
> *Magnolia:* Why, do you love me?
> *Magnolia:* I'm a lucky girl.
> *Gay:* I'm a lucky boy, etc.

The duet is the counterpart of the earlier, "Let's imagine we've fallen in love," with its charming climax:

> Couldn't you? couldn't I?
> Couldn't we?—Make believe?

The two love-stories moved from the end of the 'eighties to the year 1927 before Edna Ferber had told us all there is to tell about Julie and Steve, Gaylor and Magnolia, and the fact indicates the essential difference between old-time comic opera or musical comedy and their latter-day equivalents. Less clear-cut and closely knit stories are called for to-day, together with quick changes of background and sentiment which would have been impossible with the two acts and two scenes of earlier custom. For her story Edna Ferber needed no fewer than fourteen scenes and a cast numbering 144.

It is not easy to find attractions capable of drawing paying audiences to Drury Lane, but, among Englishmen, Ivor Novello is admittedly of the number.

Undiluted sentiment, volatilised by full-throated orchestrations, characterises a typical Novello production, and again and again it has proved an assured draw at London's largest theatre, and this when other methods had manifestly failed to keep the great house open. Ivor Novello's career is analogous to that of Noel Coward. Both made contacts with the profession in boyhood and both scored sensational successes at a relatively early age. Both, therefore, have a keen sense of what is effective in a theatre, indeed, a sense which is so keen that, continually, it tempts them to the second-best which appeals to the undiscerning many rather than the best which can only reveal its full merits to critics with real discernment. Intellectually, however, Coward and Novello are the poles apart. Noel is the icy intellectual, fully sophisticated and readily bored, while Ivor is the warm of heart, emotional and uncritical as a British Celt should be. On the contrary, Ivor has never perpetrated anything so low-brow as some of the material Noel embodied in his early revues. The sketch *Oranges and Lemons*, of 1923, for example; or *The Order of the Day*, a trifle which dates from the relative maturity of 1928, but is frankly unworthy of talent and still more of genius.

Both Novello's parents were Welsh and both were musical, but Madam Novello Davies, the mother, was without doubt the formative agent. She was a gifted music teacher, and her Welsh choir won an international reputation, so her boy grew up in an atmosphere of music which was sound and, in the best sense, popular. Gifted with a soprano voice of exceptional charm, Ivor went to the Magdalen Choir School at Oxford and quickly became the leading soloist among the boys. When his voice broke it was natural enough that the young musician should turn to composition and, being greedy for applause, it was equally natural that he should turn to the musical-comedy stage, rather than to Church music, in which Arthur Sullivan had nursed his budding talent.

The choice was canny and enabled Ivor to avoid the painful years of struggle during which Noel Coward learnt stagecraft as a boy actor, under the eagle eye of Charles Hawtrey, and the even more painful years as a minor actor and author awaiting recognition. From 1910, when he made his first stage appearance, to 1924, when success came with a rush, thanks to the sensational production of *The Vortex*, Noel was learning in a hard school. Ivor, on the contrary, sat down at his mother's piano and tapped out "Keep the Home Fires Burning," and lo and behold, not only was a bank balance of 17s. miraculously increased by £16,000, but the Gaiety management commissioned the youth to partner Jerome Kern in composing the music for *Theodore and Company*. In the next twenty years, Ivor had eleven successful plays to his credit, ending with a memorable series at Drury Lane which fully solved the very difficult problem of filling that outsize stage and auditorium, as Noel Coward had done a few years earlier, when he handed the script of *Cavalcade* to Charles Cochran.

Seldom has so slender a vein of artistry produced financial rewards so generous. Putting aside the author and composer momentarily, and regarding Novello as an actor, it cannot be denied that what the public has asked for and received is

The 'Bridge of Lovers' from Ivor Novello's "Careless Rapture"

Top
Jessie Matthews (left)
Gertrude Lawrence (right)
in "Limehouse Blues"

Fred Astaire
in a Hot Dance

Ivor's second-best. After he put up a brilliant performance as Lord George Hell in Max Beerbolm's *The Happy Hypocrite*, an undiscerning public forced him into *Careless Rapture*. Its success was so persistent that "The Lane" abandoned its Christmas Pantomime, an unexpected tribute to talent, for pantomime at the Lane was generally regarded as a source of income which, if need be, would cover the financial year. Moreover, along with Dorothy Dickson, Ivor registered a personal triumph as leading man. Without a doubt here was Drury Lane entertainment *in excelsis*. The opening scene was on Hampstead Heath on a bank holiday afternoon, and the plot took the characters to China and allowed the curtain to fall upon a representation of an earthquake in the best Drury Lane manner. The West End "libraries" signified their appreciation of Ivor's success by subscribing close upon £100,000 worth of tickets for the Drury Lane season.

Later came Ivor's war-time success with *The Dancing Years*. On tour in 1939, the musical play attracted audiences numbering 15,000 weekly and, at a difficult time, gave work to more than a hundred people, eighty being players and twenty-four the theatre staff. And the success was Ivor Novello's and could be claimed by no one else. He was author, composer, and outstanding star, though Mary Ellis as the heroine was very delightful, while mention must be made of Roma Beaumont, the little Grete in the original Drury Lane production, whose simple charms disturbed Mary Ellis's romance so rudely. Nevertheless, what the public paid to see, first at Drury Lane and then in the provinces, and, finally, at the Adelphi was Ivor Novello as Rudi Klober, a penniless Viennese composer, to whom came Maria Ziegler, the comic-opera star, in love at once with the man and his music. Unwittingly, little Grete, by her adoration of Rudi, arouses the jealously of Maria and the singer leaves Rudi, to resume the romance thirteen years later, when the one-time lovers are in middle age. Indeed, Ivor brought his story down to the fateful year of 1938, not altogether to the advantage of the play, which scarcely had the strength to sustain the harsh realisms of Nazi-ridden Vienna.

There is no need to use a flail to separate the ripe grain from the straw and chaff in Novello vaudeville. Pleasant melody is there; so are sentimental action and a stage full of colourful people doing pleasant things. Judged by the standards properly applied to latter-day musical shows, the success is deserved, even if a lingering doubt obtrudes itself whether talents so easily come by should not properly give things of more abiding worth. To the present Ivor Novello has not given us his *Bitter Sweet*.

Chapter XIV

THIS'LL MAKE YOU WHISTLE, WITH AN EXCURSUS
UPON JAZZ

IT MAY BE DEBATABLE WHETHER THE SONGS OF HALF A CENTURY, and some account of their origin and popularity, properly belong to the story of vaudeville. Nevertheless, it is difficult to omit an aspect of a larger theme without sacrificing memories which seem to call for record.

What is it in a song which encourages the whistling habit? Plainly, not the worth of the music *qua* music. Few of us whistle the arias from *Don Giovanni*, though Figaro's "Here's an end to your games with the girls" shows that Mozart had the root of the matter within his grasp. Indeed, is the music necessarily all-important? May not it be some verbal factor?

1923 was the year in which "Bananas" flourished.

> Yes, we have no bananas,
> We have no bananas to-day!

A London publisher, the very knowledgeable Lawrence Wright, himself a song composer, was sure that a song with such silly words and such silly music could not possibly succeed, though he was persuaded to give the public an opportunity to approve. The composer, who admitted that he wrote the song before breakfast, also "thought nothing of it," causing "Mr. Punch" to comment, "And neither do we." Nevertheless, half a million copies were sold within a few weeks, and its vogue justified a sequal, "I've never seen a straight banana."

Of course, there was the quaint staccato rhythm associated with the song, but does it explain the sudden public interest in bananas? May it not be that the vogue of "bananas" had an origin similar to "Hello, who's your lady friend?" "Come up and see me some time," or "Hold your hand out, naughty boy"— catch phrases which owed their popularity largely to the ease with which they could be adapted to all sorts of social circumstances. Aldous Huxley, in *Texts and Pretexts*, considered a phase of the general problem, and, told of an eminent American divine who in a sermon pronounced a panegyric upon popular songs. "They are the repositories of wisdom and sound moral doctrine." It may be so, though I fancy the American clergyman founded his claim upon specially selected examples. The original versions of not a few popular songs trouble any conscience which is not easy.

The vogue of patriotic songs is easier to understand. Music-halls, revues, and musical comedies are natural forcing-grounds for the symbols, which are so potent in mass-suggestion. Rudyard Kipling, apropos of his own, "When I left Rome for Lalage's sake," in *Puck of Pook's Hill*, said of one great class of musical symbols, those which become marching songs for troops, "They run like a pestilence for six months or a year, till another one pleases the Legions and then they march on that."

"Lillibulero," with its nonsense title, is one of the oldest of the marching songs of the vaudeville type, a very different type, by the way, from the battle hymns which have a much longer history. With words by the Marquis of Wharton, "Lillibulero" summed up the hate Protestant Britain had for James II, and it was sung by the victors at the Boyne under the title, "The Protestant Boys." The song was not forgotten when Sterne created the immortal Uncle Toby in *Tristram Shandy*, and Gay rediscovered it when he and his musical advisers searched Britain's song-book for airs fitted for *The Beggar's Opera*. So did George Robey when he wanted music for:

> The little pigs lie on the best of straw,
> And what they can't eat they can jolly well gnaw.
> The little pigs run with their bumkins bare
> Because they have no breeches to wear.

Coming down to our own half-century, "Good-bye, Dolly Gray," "Soldiers of the Queen," and "The Absent-minded Beggar" were either marching songs of the Boer War period, or symbolic sources of patriotic energy. So was Lionel Monckton's "When the boys come home once more," when Marie Studholme sang it at the Gaiety.

Upon the Boer War of 1899 to 1902 there followed ten years of unpugnacious song, but international politics fostered a revival of the Jingo spirit about Christmastide in 1911, when *Hop o' My Thumb* at Drury Lane included the highly popular Bulldog's Bark, with its refrain:

> We mean to be the top-dog yet, bow-wow!

The sentiment was accentuated by the unfurling of a gigantic Union Jack, and a mighty "bow-wow" from the chorus. As a critic said: "One sees in a flash the whole complicated fabric of international relationships reduced to the level of a dog-fight":

> There are enemies around us who are jealous of our fame,
> We have made a mighty Empire, and they'd like to do the same.
> And they think the way to do it is to catch us as we nap,
> While they push our friends and neighbours from their places on the map.
> But if upon our property they'd trespass in the dark,
> They'll find a good old watch-dog that can bite as well as bark.

The international dog-fight was not long delayed, and with it came "Keep the Home Fires Burning" and "Tipperary" as typical marching songs. Florrie Forde sang "Tipperary" in the Isle of Man two years before the World War and requests from men in the trenches persuaded her to revive it in 1914. Actually, the first singer was Jack Judge, a part-author, with whom was associated Henry James

Williams, who died at Coventry in 1924. His gravestone is inscribed: "Author of 'It's a Long Way to Tipperary.'"

Another outstanding song of the first World War was written and sung well before fighting commenced. "On Sunday I walk out with a Soldier," with words by Arthur Wimperis and music by Herman Finck, of the Palace Theatre, and sung by Gwennie Brogden in a Palace revue, but when war broke out, it proved a recruiting song of astonishing potency, as Noel Coward recognised when he introduced it into *Cavalcade*:

> On Sunday I walk out with a soldier,
> On Monday I'm taken by a tar,
> On Tuesday I'm out with a baby boy scout,
> On Wednesday an Hussar.
> On Thursday I gang out wi' a Scottie,
> On Friday the captain of the crew—
> And on Saturday I'm willing,
> If you'll only take the shilling,
> To make a man of every one of you.

If the Finck-Wimperis song had a rival it was Paul Rubens's "We won't want to lose you, but we think you ought to go." Paul is said to have written it at a sitting, in response to an official demand for something which would help recruiting. He handed over the entire proceeds from the song, and they were considerable, to the Red Cross. My recollection is that nobody took the propaganda seriously and soldiers frankly laughed. The tune was what mattered—that it should be singable.

Much more acceptable to the fighting man was Alfred Lester's "Conscientious Objector's Lament," which had a great reception when it was given in *Round the Map* at the Alhambra:

> Call out the Boys of the Old Brigade,
> Who made our country free—
> Call out my Mother, my Sister and my Brother,
> But, for Heaven's sake, don't call me!

A rather more generous selection of the marching songs and uplift ditties of the second World War will justify itself, though the time for a final selection of the outstanding favourites has not yet come. When "Vi" Loraine went to France in December 1914, with Leslie Henson's concert-party, *Gaieties*, she scored a big success with a 1914-18 favourite:

> Some girl's got to darn his socks,
> So I've darned got to be that girl.

Dorothy Ward found her hit-song to be "Mademoiselle from the Maginot Line," while her most popular turn was calling a burly Tommy on to the improvised stage and singing a love song at him. "*That* always brought down the house," said Miss Ward afterwards. Noel Coward's big success was his singing of "Mad dogs and Englishmen."

Other songs owed their vogue to Gracie Fields, among them, "Run, Rabbit, run," "Sally," and "Little Sir Echo," originally composed with a waltz rhythm, which was changed to marching-time when the first invasion of France began. "So I'm sending a letter to Santa Claus to bring Daddy safely home to me" is another memory of Christmas 1939, and also associates itself with Gracie Fields. Nevertheless, it may be that the draw of all draws in the early days of the second World War was not Gracie Fields, comedienne, but Gracie singing "Ave Maria," or the Christmas hymn, "Come all ye faithful," even if her biggest laugh came from

> We're going to string old Hitler
> From the very highest bough
> Of the biggest aspidistra in the world.

And, lastly, that ditty of ill-omen:

> We're gonna hang out the washing on the Siegfried Line.
> Have you any dirty washing, mother dear?
> We're gonna hang out the washing on the Siegfried Line,
> 'Cos the washing day is here.
> Whether the weather may be wet or fine
> We'll just rub along without a care.
> We're gonna hang out the washing on the Siegfried Line,
> If the Siegfried Line's still there.

A mixed bag, and it is not easy to formulate the law of their selection. Fifty years ago the law of selection and survival was relatively simple. Your truly characteristic vaudeville song identified itself with a music-hall or musical-comedy star. This is not the case with the song-hits of recent years. Billy Merson, Will Fyffe, and half a dozen other comedians were equally identified with the vogue enjoyed by the mock-sentimentalities of:

> Will you love me when I'm mutton,
> As you do now I am lamb?

Similarly, if many pantomime-lovers recall the Scotsman, Tommy Lorne, singing "Give yourself a pat on the back," fully as many others associate the song with quite another singer. It belonged to general pantomime and was not personal property. Wee Georgie Wood sang "I'm in the mood for love" in a Birmingham pantomime, but, in the same year (1935), the song served equally well for Tommy Prior as the funny man in *Goldilocks*, or *The Three Bears*, at the Blackburn Grand. Indeed, the song would equally well have been handed over to a principal girl and, in fact, entered upon its public career when it was sung by Alice Fayre in the film *Every Night at Eight*.

Very different were circumstances before the first World War, when vaudeville stars jealously guarded the right to this or that song and as often as not owned the copyright.

15

The song-hits of Charles Coborn, still the grand old man of the halls,[1] furnish an example of Victorian and Edwardian practice. He owed one of his outstanding successes to Fred Gilbert, who wrote the words and music of "The Man who Broke the Bank at Monte Carlo." It was based upon the gambling exploits of a certain Charles Wells. Coborn paid Gilbert £10 for singing rights, though, fortunately, Gilbert signed a royalties agreement with his publishers and thus made £600, in place of the £30 for which he would willingly have sold the song

As I walk along the Bois Boo-long
With an independent air,
You can hear the girls declare,
"He must be a millionaire."
You can hear them sigh and wish to die,
You can see them wink the other eye,
At the man who broke the Bank at Monte Carlo.

outright. Coborn sang the song, wearing evening dress, top hat, and a sprig of lily of the valley in his buttonhole, not to mention an eyeglass and a cigar—altogether a tough Man-about-Town of the 'nineties. Barnard, the caricaturist, was tempted to a very different creation.

An earlier Coborn success was "Two Lovely Black Eyes," first given at the Paragon Music Hall in 1885. In this case the music was not original and had been sung in Italy, where it was associated with the words "Vieni sui mar" (Come to the Seas). Charles Coborn came across a nigger-minstrel version associated with the words, "My Nellie's blue eyes." Desiring lines with somewhat more

[1] Charles Coborn died in November 1945, when this book was in proof.

punch, Coborn decided to substitute "Two lovely black eyes," and then had to compose a suitable introduction to the new chorus. Walking through Stepney Green, on the Tuesday before the Saturday night upon which he was due to appear at the Paragon, Coborn delivered himself of the following:

> Strolling so happy down Stepney Green,
> This gay youth you might have seen,
> Tompkins and I, with his girl between.

A general election was pending and Home Rule for Ireland was in general debate. Accordingly, Coborn decided that the I of his song should give Tompkins the "two lovely black eyes."

Coborn sang the song dressed in a faded frock-coat, an old crush hat, and carrying a coloured cotton handkerchief. It was successful at once, helped by the fact that Coborn substituted the more populous Bethnal Green for the original Stepney Green. Soon East End costers and their donahs were shouting the chorus, as they too strolled so happy down Bethnal Green. Song-plugging was in being.

"Bill Sloggins," better known as "He's all right when you know him," was another Coborn "hit." The chorus was introduced by a snatch of East End dialogue:

> "Say, Jack, 'ave you 'eard the noos? Bill's cut 'is wife's froat."
> "No! 'Ave 'ee?"
> "Yas!"
> "Well, 'e warn't a bad sort, arter all, warn't Bill, when you knew 'im."

> *Chorus:*
> 'E's all right when you know 'im,
>   But 'e's angry when 'e's vexed.
> 'E'll black your eye one minute,
>   But 'e'll stand a pint the next.
> 'E wouldn't 'urt a baiby,
>   'E's a pal as you can trust;
> 'E's all right when you know 'im,
>   But you've got to know 'im fust.

Coborn was an out-of-the-way character in several directions. He wrote an amusing autobiography and was one of the first to suggest the use of the periscope in connection with trench warfare. In October 1914 he sent a home-made periscope to Lord Roberts, who arranged that the idea should be fully tested. After the Army had adopted the device, the Coborn periscope was publicly exhibited as "the father of the trench periscope."

Another star of the Victorian music-halls, who lived on into the second World War period, was Harry Champion. He died in 1941, aged seventy-six. Indeed, Champion owed not a little of his latter-day fame to his survival value, as one of the accepted old-time music-hall singers. He began in the 'eighties as a black-faced comedian, Will Conroy by name, but reached a much wider popularity as Harry Champion, the quick-fire comedian, who, he as said, sang six songs in a couple of minutes and got paid for it! His delivery was of the express order. In baggy trousers, with his billy-cock hat on the side of his head, Harry Champion rattled off "Any Old Iron," shuffling hands feet and body the while. "I'm Henery the Heighth, I am" was another of the high-speed songs, and "Boiled Beef and Carrots" was associated with him so definitely that cheap restaurants used to advertise, "A Harry Champion, 1s."

The association between song composer and singer in Victorian and Edwardian times can also be illustrated from the experiences of Joe Tabrar, who wrote

Joe Tabrar

"Daddy wouldn't buy me a bow-wow" for Vesta Victoria, but was also responsible for "Oh, You little darling, I love you" and "It ain't all Lavender," and then passed on his talent to a second generation, as Tabrar's son, Fred Earle, was responsible for the equally popular "He's waiting there for me."

Joseph Tabrar was a Cockney, born in Saffron Hill, and, as a boy, sang in the madrigal choir at Evans's Supper Rooms. When his voice broke, Joseph became a plumber and bell-hanger, but a plumber and bell-hanger who continuously dreamed of possible fame as a song writer. Chance required him to attend the great Ley-bourne in a professional capacity. It may be that the singer's bell-chords were out of order, thanks to the attention of one Bruggle-smith. At any rate, Tabrar seized upon the opportunity and indicated that he had written a song which might suit the Lion Comique, "Ting, ting, that's how the Bell Goes."

"Sit down at the Joanna, me boy," said the lordly one, "and whack on the dominoes."

Tabrar did, and "Ting, ting" was accepted.

In hours of need Tabrar often sold a song for a few shillings, but he had no doubt about his genius. "Arthur Sullivan," Tabrar once cried, "I can do all that he could an' more, while you wait—on the bit of old paper the 'trotters' are wrapped in." Indeed, this was the mood in which not a few music-hall early hits originated.

Tabrar had Vesta Victoria in mind when he wrote his famous "Bow-wow." "Baby Victoria," as she was originally called, was rehearsing on the Pavilion stage one Saturday morning, in company with Eugene Stratton, when Tabrar produced the manuscript. It chanced that Vesta had been given a kitten. When she sang Tabrar's song at the South London Palace on the following Monday night she brought the kitten on to the stage, hidden in a basket of flowers. Result, a furore of applause.

No, there was no doubt as to the proprietary rights in song-hits a quarter of a century ago. "Joshua, Joshua," was Clarice Mayne and no one else. She it was who brought about a tightening of the throat of her admirers, just by her timing of the chorus. Yet the theme was silly enough and the lyric no better. Something like this:

> Joshua, Joshua! Why don't you call and see Mama.
> She'll be pleased, you know; you are my best beau!
> Joshua, Joshua! Nicer than lemon squash, you are,
> Yes, by gosh, you are, Josh-u-osh-u-ah!

The girl's pride in possession, the greater because of the obvious element of doubt. Clarice passed on every throb, so that one forgot the special case propounded by the lyric writers and allowed the beat of the chorus to carry an emotion all could understand. Different was Clarice Mayne's early ragtime ditty, "Jerry Jeremiah," addressed to a supposed sweetheart, who was operating a trombone in a ragtime band:

> Jerry Jeremiah, my heart's on fire,
> Play again that sweet refrain,
> 　Ump-ta-ra! Ump-ta-ra-ra!
> Jerry Jeremiah, it's the finest tune I've known,
> Rag it, drag it, zigzag it, on your ragtime trombone.

Or again, Clarice singing "It's lovely to coo, it's lovely to woo, it's lovely to be in love." Can you see her, in a suit of silver armour, at the Hippodrome, in the first pantomime George Robey ever played in in London, singing James Tate's songs? He was her husband, and, on the halls, played her accompaniments, gazing soulfully the while, as though the singer was in very truth the Queen of his Heart that night.

But the outstanding example of the association between songs and singer was Harry Lauder, who rose to fame by virtue of pseudo-folk-songs, which he rendered in a pseudo-English dialect derived from Glasgow, and thus made acceptable to audiences the world over, which would have been mystified by Gaelic.

Enter Harry Lauder

Born in 1870, Lauder was the eldest of seven children and, in his boyhood, the seven were never far from the poverty-line. He was only eleven when his father died and Harry was glad to earn 10s. a week as a half-timer in a Lanarkshire coal-mine. Before he was fourteen, the boy had made public appearances as a singer and was recognised as "a bit of a comic." Building upon the Highland folk-songs he had heard his mother sing, Lauder found himself winning comic-singing competitions, the music, in many cases, being a simple melody which he wrote himself. The entertainments were known locally as "Glesca Bursts," and the harmonic society was willing to pay £1 a night to a singer as promising as Lauder, the Lanarkshire miner.

The competitions were truly testing. At the Scotia, Glasgow, when a trial turn did not commend itself to the audience, the singer or reciter was hauled off the stage by the manager, with the aid of a long hooked stick, which he put round the neck of the unfortunate performer. When Lauder was permitted to sing a couple of songs without attention from the hooked stick, he began to have visions of a stage career. But it was only when he was engaged for a month's tour of the Moss and Thornton halls in the North of England and sang his Scottish songs in English, with a strong Scottish accent, that Lauder felt assured of success and decided to have done with coal-mining.

Then came Lauder's first London triumph at Gatti's in Westminster Bridge Road, singing the familiar "Tobermory" and "Killiecrankie." Moderate success was hoped for when Harry came south, but what happened was in the nature of a vaudeville miracle. On reaching London, Lauder came to George Foster's agency in the Strand, opposite the Old Tivoli. Foster tells that Lauder was wearing a dickey, a bright red tie, vivid brown boots, a long frock-coat, and a tweed cap. It was not easy to accept his assurance:

"I'm a great comic, mon, a real divert on the stage, honest."

Foster took the Scottie's name to be "Louder." "No, the name is Lauder, sir. L A U D E R, and its a name the world will hear about, if you'll only gie me my chance, sir."

While Lauder was speaking Foster saw Tom Tinsley, manager of Gatti's, crossing the Strand outside. He asked Lauder to wait while he spoke to Tinsley. The manager had some trouble with his feet and could not easily get up the stairs to Foster's office. "I want a comic to-night," said Tinsley.

"I've got the very man for you, Tom. His name is Harry Lauder."

Seven pounds was the agreed fee and Lauder was overjoyed. That night his future was assured and during the next seven days Foster was busy booking Lauder at £10 a week. Hundreds of contracts were secured and Lauder signed them all—300 weeks' work at £10 a week. "Gie me your pen, quick, mon, I'll sign before I wake up."

Long before the six years were completed managers all over the country were willing to cancel the original contracts and sign new ones at double the money. A time was to come when Lauder would make £1,000 a week, this being his contract at the Pavilion, Glasgow, and Lauder was only less successful in Australia and America.

Harry Lauder was not an outstanding pantomime star, as were Dan Leno, Vesta Tilley, or Harry Randall, but he earned very big fees, and two pantomime appearances were associated with his most familiar songs, "I Love a Lassie" and "Roamin' in the Gloamin'." The first was introduced into *Aladdin* at the Theatre Royal, Glasgow, where it had a thirteen weeks' run in 1905. Lauder played Roderick McSwankey, a Glasgow boy who was apprenticed to the wicked magician of the fairy story, but it was the song that audiences demanded again and again and was, plainly, destined to make vaudeville history.

Five years later, Harry was engaged for another Glasgow pantomime, and he had a new song to hand, which he hoped would equal "Tobermory" and "I Love a Lassie" in popularity. A year or two earlier he had seen a couple of lovers spooning in the twilight and the phrase "roamin' in the gloamin' " flashed upon him. The very theme for a song. The song and the chorus were completed by the morning, but the patter and the accompanying facial expressions took months to make perfect. He tried a dozen costumes before he was satisfied and sang the song thousands of times before he considered it ready for the public. When he did sing it in 1910-11, "Roamin' in the Gloamin' " stopped the show. Without those months of rehearsal and selection even a Harry Lauder would not have achieved that sense of personal mastery over the emotions of a vast audience, which the singer himself has claimed to be the final evidence of success in his art. "Playing on the heartstrings of men and women," was Lauder's description of his purpose when he put over "I Love a Lassie" and "Roamin' in the Gloamin'."

Prior to 1914 such songs meant big monies for author, composer, or publisher, apart from the stage presentations. By the middle 'thirties, if a song was not exploited for all it was worth within a few weeks of publication, its popularity was exhausted by gramophone records, cabaret-singing, and dance broadcasts. No longer could a singer identify himself with a song and sing it for months and even years. Wireless had taken the place of the super-comedian or comedienne as the populariser of the tunes that the errand-boy whistled. Under the same influences, the sales of sheet-music fell away sharply. Instead of a royalty upon every copy sold, owners of a copyright song received an appointed share of the £100,000 or so paid out by the B.B.C. on account of copyright fees. The Performing Rights Society, acting for about 40,000 composers, collected payments for broadcasting on the basis of 5½d. each for the first million licensed listeners, 4½d. for the second million, 3½d. for the third, and 3¼d. thereafter. With nearly 8,000,000 listeners this worked out at about £100,000 per year. This sum was divided up on a "point" basis. A dance tune got one point each time it was played, and so on up to seven points for a symphonic work. Each year the P.R.S. analysed nearly 500,000 programmes containing more than 8,000,000 performances on behalf of their clients. The distribution of fees may be fair, but the days when an Ivor Novello, as the author of "Keep the Home Fires Burning," could make £16,000 for a few hours' work had gone, so far as sheet-music was concerned. Here is the evidence in statistical form:

	Sales of Sheet Music	Gramophone Royalties	Authors' and Composers' Royalties
1925	£566,459	£134,220	£123,493

(This year marked the early days of broadcasting and the increasing use of mechanical records.)

1929	£453,564	£296,871	£202,151

(The perfecting of electrical recording is reflected in the total of gramophone royalties.)

1933	£284,691	£93,911	£72,132

However, when the fees paid by dance bands and the value of gramophone rights and other profits are added, the worth of a popular song may still top the £10,000 mark. It is said that "Alexander's Ragtime Band" earned ten times as much for its composer, Irving Berlin. After Gershwin wrote "Swanee" in 1919 and Jolson popularised it in the extravaganza, *Sinbad*, a fabulous number of gramophone records were sold.

Pantomime Songs

The influence of the pantomime market upon song production must never be forgotten. A quarter of a century ago not a few of the most famous songs were written expressly for the pantomime market—a big chorus number for the principal boy, with appropriate spectacle, a sentimental ballad for the principal girl, or a comedy number for the Dame. The songs were kept in store against Christmas-time, whereas, to-day, similar songs have probably enjoyed a preliminary popu-larity in connection with a film or on the wireless. The property was too valuable to be kept in store against Christmas. However, principal boys and principal girls, or the agents who represent them, tumble over one another in their efforts to secure such a winner as Eric Maschwitz's "Nightingale sang in Berkeley Square." It may well be an essential ingredient in a successful Christmas show.

After the first World War pantomimes, not only in London, but in the provinces, dwindled in number and richness of setting, chiefly owing to the competition of spectacular revues, though in the middle 'thirties, at least a hundred were still being produced in Britain each year, so the genre had not lost all its vitality. A census in the 'thirties showed that *Cinderella* was the favourite story, being played at twenty-two theatres, compared with twenty in which *Dick Whittington* was the theme. *Red Riding Hood* was third on the list, being played at nine theatres, *Robinson Crusoe* having eight to his credit. The one-time favourite, *The Forty Thieves*, oddly enough, only drew audiences to two theatres.

Nevertheless, changes in popular taste were to be detected. In the absence of comedians and comediennes, tried out in the hard school of late Victorian music-halls, Dame Twankeys and their kindred seemed less important, though the five Georges—Graves, Lacy, Jackley, Wood, and Robey—were exceptions to the rule that relatively few "comics" can now fill a Christmas stage. Nelson Keys was once persuaded to test his powers as Old Mother Hubbard in *Red Riding Hood* at Covent Garden. His fragile Mother had charm, but, somehow, charm was not quite what was called for and the run ended after eight weeks.

Lack of inches and the presence of charm are not necessarily handicaps to successful pantomime appearances, as the success of Georgie Wood shows. "Wee Georgie," with his disarming smile, coupled with the face and form of fifteen and the mature wisdom of forty-five, established himself as a pantomime favourite as Wishie Washee in *Aladdin* and later showed himself a precocious Buttons, singing "I'm in the mood for love."

A year earlier, George Jackley, at the London Lyceum, was singing:

> Two little Tom-tits were tweeting
>   On the tip-top of a tree.
> Tunefully they were tweet-tweeting
>   On the tip-top of a tree,
> While cats were meowing and dogs were bow-wowing
>   And bumble bees buzzed busily.
> Two little Tom-tits were tweeting
>   On the tip-top of a tree.

George Jackley began his career in vaudeville as a member of the Jackley Wonders, an acrobatic troupe, who set up piles of tables on the stage and somersaulted over them. George was the small boy who made funny noises as he did his tricks. He utilised the same funny noises to raise laughs in Lyceum pantomime.

Jackley is one of the exceptions to the latter-day rule, whereby Francis Laidler, with thirty years' experience of pantomime production behind him, was so impressed with the dearth of trusty comedians that he defied tradition and engaged actresses for his "dame" parts. "There are not enough funny men to go round; better find a funny woman!" said Mr. Laidler.

Francis Laidler was a pioneer in what the profession calls "panto babes." In the 'thirties he used to collect "Sunbeams," mostly from homes in the Midlands and the North of England. Eighty "Sunbeams" in a year, aged twelve to fourteen, and none more than four feet five inches high. They served the seven or eight pantomimes which Laidler staged each Christmas. He it was who discovered George Lacy, a famous Mother Goose. A typical Laidler pantomime was the Coliseum *Cinderella* of 1936–7, with Edna Best in the title role, Madge Elliott as principal boy, and Douglas Wakefield and Billy Nelson as the ugly sisters.

The Onion Market

By 1930 Fay Compton, like Phyllis Neilson Terry and other heroines of real drama, had been persuaded to essay pantomime roles, Miss Compton being a delightful Dick Whittington at the Theatre Royal, Glasgow, in 1931. A year later Fay was at the London Hippodrome, singing "Round the Bend of the Road," the Onion of its Year:

> There'll be no more pickin', no more choosin',
>   Round the Bend of the Road;
> No more winnin', no more losin',
> No more askin', and no more refusin',
>   Round the Bend of the Road;
> No more grumblin', no more row-in',
> No more scrapin', no more bow-in',
>   Round the Bend of the Road.

Akin is Vivian Ellis's "I'm so terribly in love with you," first sung by Evelyn

Laye in *Merely Molly*, but transferred to pantomime directly the musical comedy run ended.

> I'm so terribly in love with you,
> I'd be happy if I only knew
> How to make you care a little too,
> Tell me do, Could you? Would you?
> If you ever care to answer "Yes,"
> Paradise will be our home address,
> Just a heaven built for two
> With room enough for me and you.

Another sentimental number of the early 'thirties was "A Shanty in old Shanty Town." Picture Dorothy Ward, at the King's Theatre, Edinburgh, in the glory of her manly inches, suddenly realising the futility of the civilisation which was still making pantomime a paying proposition at Christmastide. As she did so, her fancy wandered back to the place of her upbringing, and she gave utterance to this:

> But my tumbled-down shack
> By an old rail-road track,
> Like a millionaire's mansion is calling me back.
> For a queen's waiting there, with a silvery crown,
> In a Shanty in old Shanty Town.

Reference has been made to the songs from the States, headed by those of Irving Berlin, who led the cavalcade of jazz composers. The leadership was not only due to the success of "Alexander's Ragtime Band," but to an apparently unending series of "hits" which followed from his fertile pen. He it was who provided Beatrice Lillie with "I was born in Michigan":

> I want to go back, I want to go back, I want to go
>   back to the farm,
> Far away from harm,
> With a milk-pail on my arm.
> I miss the rooster,
> The one that use-ter
> Wake me up at four a.m. . . . .

Other Irving Berlin songs were "Let's take the music and dance" (a Jack Buchanan effort), "I left my heart at the stage-door canteen, It is there with a girl called Eileen," and "Heaven, I'm in Heaven," in which the immediate reason for elation was dancing cheek to cheek. It is a virtue in Irving Berlin's musical make-up that he can compose waltzes worthy of comparison with the good ones of the old-time tradition.

Cole Porter made his bow towards the end of the first World War and Londoners recognised "Let's do it; let's fall in love" as something new, directly C. B. Cochran introduced the song into one of his revues. However, a decade was to go by before Cole Porter was given a chance to take full musical control of a show, this including the writing of the lyrics as well as the melodies. *Gay Divorce* dates from 1932, *Du Barry was a Lady* from 1939, and *Something for the Boys* from 1942/3. If one had to name a single Cole Porter lyric and melody as fully characteristic, it would be:

> You're the top,
> You're the Leaning Tower of Pisa;
> You're the smile on the Mona Lisa;
> I'm a worthless cheque, a total wreck, a flop,
> But if, Baby, I'm the bottom,
> You're the top!

To-day, Cole Porter's gift is his ability to write "hit numbers" which Broadway stars can put over. Plainly, it is useless to write an operatic number for Fred Astaire, seeing that his vocal range is limited to three notes over an octave. As for Ethel Merman, who put over "Katie was a Lady" in the American version of *Du Barry*, Cole Porter has said that he knows her capacity so perfectly that "he writes for her now as if she was an instrument." This represents a healthy reversion to the Victorian and Edwardian method, when the best of the songs were composed for accepted stars, whose personality was the principal factor in sending them down the ages. The outstanding difference between then and now lies in the relative importance of lavish display in dress, scenery, and chorus work in popularising a song number. Cole Porter's sense of the theatre is keen enough to work with certainty within the limitations imposed. This is his genius, and the genius of Irving Berlin and Jerome Kern, the other recognised composers of Broadway musical comedy, is akin. Like Noel Coward, Cole Porter does not orchestrate his own songs, preferring to leave this part of the work to experts. The deeper truth with both composers is that their rhythmic patterns largely orchestrate themselves.

The Origins of Jazz

No study of current song-hits would be complete without a definition of the term "jazz" and some indication of its sources. Authority in the realm of music does not recognise any such thing as a jazz melody. It is pointed out that some tunes lend themselves more readily to jazz treatment than others, but that is all. As we know, the jazzing of classical melodies is among the minor tragedies of modern entertainment.

Essentially, jazz is musical improvisation and is created by the performers rather than a composer. A conductor of European reputation, Ernest Ansermet, writing in 1919, pointed out that no written score could give any idea of jazz-playing. There are thirds which are neither major nor minor. Nevertheless, the jazz players hit upon the natural harmonies of a given note. The fact is that the illiterates who made jazz knew so little of what the educated called music that they happened upon the virtue that lies in intervals which owe nothing to the metronome.

Jazz may be described as the latest of a series of revolutions which have extended the range of music from time to time, ever since man first beat time upon a calabash or picked out the notes of an octave upon the Aurignacian equivalent of the penny whistle. European music entered upon a connected history when Gregory the Great organised the plain chant for the choral services of Christendom, but this was only the beginning. By slow degrees, extending over centuries, polyphony was evolved from plain song. There followed the changes in style and orchestration which led to the development of the sonata form. Then came opera as an art of dramatic declamation, virtuoso concert singing, and, finally, the establishment of the orchestra in the dominant position it holds in modern music.

I believe it is quite inaccurate to describe jazz as negroid. There is a tom-tom element in African music which in no way characterises the jazz of the modern stage or dancing-hall. Moreover, the element in modern jazz due to the negro spirituals of the cotton plantations is small. As for the large proportion of coloured players in the world of jazz, there are economic reasons which sufficiently account for it. Vaudeville is almost the only important sphere of public activity open to the American negro.

To discover the origins of jazz one must go back to New Orleans about the turn of the century. The first executants were New Orleans "spasm bands," manned by youthful performers armed with cow-bells, cigar-box fiddles, old kettles, lengths of gas-piping, and even sugar barrels. All sorts of airs were drawn upon; marching songs of the Civil War period, work songs by the railwaymen, hymn tunes, and the rest. Even chain-gang songs, sung by convicts shovelling earth into trucks, were utilised in the realm of jazz. Just because jazz was the music of an illiterate class which knew little or nothing of what sophisticated musicians recognised as music, its creators hit upon a distinctive tonality and explored the virtues of unorthodox intervals.

Largely through the Mississippi dancing saloons (such as *Show Boat*), new rhythms passed on to United States railway centres such as Memphis, St. Louis, and when the underworld of Al Capone in Chicago adopted it during the first World War, jazz achieved national fame. When big business, in the form of gramophone recorders, band leaders such as Paul Whiteman, makers of instruments, night-club hostesses, and the song publishers of Tin Pan Alley were added, jazz was internationalised and the musical revolution was completed.

In origin, jazz was "tough," and the element of toughness remains, though some of the crudities have been polished off in what is known as "Swing."

The form of jazz known as "blues" usually consists of twelve bars of music in common time, and they are in groups of four bars apiece, but always there was the element of improvisation. The words were not made by professional lyric writers but by the singers, to express a passing emotion:

Ballet
in Offenbach's "Tales of Hoffmann"
Strand Theatre

Viennese Waltz
in "La Revue Splendide"
Prince of Wales Theatre

SUNG NIGHTLY BY MISS LOTTIE COLLINS AT THE GAIETY THEATRE

This Song may be Sung in Public without fee or Licence Except at Theatres and Music Halls, for which the written Permission of the Publishers must be Obtained

TA-RA-RA-BOOM-DE-AY!

Written by
RICHARD MORTON,

Music Arranged By
ANGELO A. ASHER.

On Melody Composed by
ALFRED MOOR-KING.

TA-RA-RA-BOOM-DE-AY.
DANCE MUSIC.
Price 2/- each nett.
Polka, by Josef Meissler.
Waltz, by Josef Meissler.
Galop, by Josef Meissler.
Polka March for Pianoforte by Theo. Bonheur.
Ditto - Ditto - for Banjo and Piano
Lancers, by John Crook.

F.A. TOWNSEND DEL.

REPRODUCED BY PERMISSION FROM THE LADY'S PICTORIAL.

"THE TIMES" says
MISS LOTTIE COLLINS as ALICE FITZWARREN in the Pantomime DICK WHITTINGTON at the Grand Theatre, Islington, Sang and Danced with the Utmost Verve, in the Case of her Song "TA-RA-RA-BOOM-DE-AY" Receiving a Double Encore.

LOTTIE COLLINS'S GREATEST CREATION.

Copyright
LONDON.
CHARLES SHEARD & Cº Music Publishers & Printers, 192 High Holborn, W.C.
W.T. STANNARD. Imp.

> I love that man; tell the world!
> Yes, I love that man; tell the world I do,
> But when he mistreats me, it makes me feel so blue.

"Blues" are not necessarily unhappy lyrics. There are cheerful blues, though the tribulations and joys of "Daddy"—a slang word meaning "lover"—occur with great frequency. Here is a typical "blue" of the Daddy type:

> My daddy rocks me with one steady roll,
> There's no slippin' when he once takes hold.
> I looked at the clock and the clock struck one,
> I said, "Oh, Daddy, ain't we got fun?"
> An' he kept on rockin' me with that steady roll.

Coming of Cabaret

Jazz was just the sort of thing to appeal to cabaret performers and audiences, and with the growth of cabaret in London, New York, Paris, and elsewhere, the element of improvisation in lyric-writing, music, and dance flourished. In fact, the growth of the cabaret habit in the West End in the 'twenties was less of a novelty than many Londoners supposed. Comedians, among them Arthur Roberts, used to go round to Evans's Supper Rooms in Victorian times, after their music-hall appearances, and they entertained Evans's guests well into the small hours of the morning. The cabaret craze which established itself in the winter of 1921–2 was more than this. Its economic basis was that an expensive jazz band and super-dancing facilities no longer sufficed for certain London restaurants and supper clubs. Competition for famous singers and comedians reached fabulous limits. At one time, Sophie Tucker earned £500 in a week at the Kit-Cat for cabaret work. The mixture of variety and dance constituted English cabaret.

In its twentieth-century form cabaret derived from New York. After the Armistice of 1918 there were New York restaurants, with dancing-space and roomy platforms, which could be moved up or down, forward or backwards, upon which a comedian could sing or a party of pretty girls display their lack of costume. The shows were timed to begin about midnight, when the New York theatres had closed. "Gee-Gee" Grossmith visited one of these restaurants, and when he returned to London the American idea received a London setting at the Metropole (the Whitehall Rooms). After a special dancing-floor was laid and stepped supper-tables built, the Midnight Follies were inaugurated on a November night in 1922.

The then Prince of Wales (Edward the Eighth) and his brothers were early patrons of the Midnight Follies and soon all smart London flocked to the Whitehall Rooms. There was some trouble with the London County Council, which required the performers to be limited to six and put a ban upon scenery and stage costumes, after the pros and cons were argued in the Law Courts. The verdict went against cabaret, but the new entertainment managed to survive. In the world of the theatre, an early repercussion was George Grossmith's production of *The Cabaret Girl* at the Winter Garden.

I am aware that ten years earlier, in 1912, there had been efforts to establish cabarets of the Parisian sort in London, in the Clavier Hall, Hanover Square, for example, and at Earl's Court, but both enterprises were on a small scale. Cabaret only came to its own in London after the Midnight Follies established their popularity. By the end of 1924, there were a dozen cabarets in the West End, where one paid a guinea or 30s. a head for supper and a short variety entertainment.

Recall the Cabaret Follies at Queen's Hall, in 1922. A visit began with a taxi-drive to the head of Regent Street, followed by a climb to the hall, built in the roof of the better-known Queen's Hall. The reward was a brilliantly lighted supper-room, with tiny tables set against the walls, permitting young men and maidens dancing in the central space. From time to time, the hall would be plunged into darkness and a revue or musical-comedy actress would occupy the dancing area.

Even more characteristic of London's cabaret was the Embassy under the management of Luigi, when Mrs. Vernon Castle (Irene Castle), with her curly head, boyish figure, and arrow-like limbs, created the type of the girl of the 'twenties. Her husband had been killed in 1918. At the Embassy, throwing off a wonderful ermine wrap, Mrs. Castle might appear in an orange chiffon gown, trimmed with flower petals of a slightly different shade, but always grace incarnate, so that every woman who watched her wanted to be an Irene. Her first dance, maybe, was to the music of the Illusion Waltz, while her last wild revel recalled Pavlova's "Bacchanale." Mrs. Castle was unconventional in her methods. Instead of leaving the hall after a dance, she sat at a table with her partner, sipping iced water, until the time came for another appearance. Later she joined in the ordinary fox-trots on the Embassy floor, accepting as a partner any gifted amateur who presented himself.

There was an economic justification for membership of a smart club like the Embassy in 1923, when the post-war boom collapsed and even rich folk began to count their sixpences. With income-tax at 4s. 6d. in the pound and super-tax to follow, even the well-to-do found it desirable to engage a table at the Embassy and entertain their friends at £3 a head.

Following in the wake of Mr. and Mrs. Castle numerous dancing teams established themselves, though not without heavy capital expenditure, for the wages of skilled accompanists, monies due to composers, publicity, and clothes are all expensive. A man in a dancing couple requires a couple of dozen dress-suits and eighty pairs of dancing shoes, while his lady partner will keep between thirty and forty dresses going during a six weeks' engagement. There is also the cost of dancing lessons, for slaps, pick-ups, pull-backs, and triples have to be learnt in an expensive school, perhaps that of the celebrated Buddy Bradley in Soho, where Jessie Matthews was taught the steps which she displayed with such effect in *Evergreen*.

The revolution which encouraged cabaret shows and dancing-halls established itself because war-weary youth felt that a bit of a riot was only its due, and the rhythms associated with jazz stood for a free and easy form of dancing, which was likely to be popular with young men fresh from "the Front," and V.A.D.'s, W.A.A.C.'s and W.R.E.N.'s who had been awaiting the return of the said young men for four long years. At any rate, music arising from sliding trombones, clarinets, drums, saxophones, and banjos proved much nearer to the post-war mood than the "Blue Danube" or the "Merry Widow Waltz." The saxophone was "the heart, soul, mind, body, and spirit" of the new dance bands, and it is noteworthy that it is the only reed instrument made of brass. The clarinet, the oboe, and the bassoon are all wood instruments. The stridency of metal was in jazz from the beginning and a certain stridency characterises the songs and dances which associate themselves with jazz. All are expressions of a desire to get a kick out of life, which Victorians and Edwardians would neither have looked for nor approved.

The later blues—particularly "Saturday Blues"—with their mock pathos—showed how syncopated music and dance could answer to moods of sentiment which alternated with the romps of the jazz age. Between 1924 and 1930 the one-step tended to disappear and fox-trots (slow, quick-step, and "blues") took their place, among the quick-steps being "All the King's Horses," by Noel Gay, which Cicely Courtneidge popularised in revue. Later, Noel Gay added "The Lambeth Walk" to contemporary dance.

Other dances of the 1920's were more exotic. Thus the Black Bottom derived its name from the silt on the banks of the Mississippi, upon which the dusky toilers in the cotton-fields danced with strange footshakes, due to the muddy nature of the dancing floor. Like the Charleston, it was a short-skirt dance. The numerous kicks, shuffles, and wriggles of the Charleston, however, proved to be beyond London's receptive powers. When the aid of a St. John's ambulance was required for dancers injured during a rowdy Charleston, the hotel authorities intervened. Politely, but firmly, they intimated: "You are requested *not* to dance the Charleston."

And behind this vast social revolution was the money-factor, directing and exploiting each passing craze. What happened was that Tin Pan Alley (the music-publishing centre in the States), with gramophone, broadcasting, and film music royalties in mind, decided to exploit the new music until a vast business organisation was associated with jazz and rhythms and its derivatives in dancing-halls, on the wireless, on gramophone records and in vaudeville. In Britain alone sixty million dance records for gramophones were sold annually in the years immediately preceding the second World War. Mabel Wayne, the composer of "Ramona" and "Little man, you've had a busy day," earned tens of thousands of pounds a year, so it is said.

And this was only the beginning. In the 1920's a popular negro band was a fortune-maker. The cost of the bands at the Piccadilly Hotel was no less than

£68,000 a year and the fees for speciality dancers, singers, and entertainers accounted for £32,000 more. Nor is there reason to believe the expenditure was unprofitable. In a single week in 1924 the Piccadilly Cabaret took £1,900, a figure which compared favourably with the box-office receipts of a successful revue or musical comedy. In 1927 the famous Ambrose, with his band, was tempted to leave the Embassy Club for the Mayfair Hotel. A personal salary of £10,000 a year made Ambrose, for the time being, the most highly paid band conductor in the world. In the same year, the reorganised Kit-Cat was paying Teddy Brown's band £1,000 a week.

Another resort of the 'twenties was the *Cave of Harmony*, which was established in Gower Street in the 'twenties, with Elsa Lanchester as the presiding genius. Her idea was to devise an English equivalent of the famous entertainment given at the Moscow Bat.

Elsa Lanchester was an interesting woman. Born in Clapham, at the age of seven she was sent to Isadora Duncan's School of Dancing in Paris. Coming to womanhood, she became a pupil-teacher at the Margaret Morris School of Dancing and later established a Children's Theatre in Soho, which she was to convert into the *Cave of Harmony*, though the place could not even boast a drink licence, which most producers of cabaret judged the primary essential. All sorts of amusing things were attempted and, as the *Cave* only opened when the theatres had closed, competent actors and actresses could be engaged. Novelties by Chekhov and Pirandello were produced, usually with a plain curtain back-ground. One of Elsa Lanchester's own songs, "I've danced with a man, who's danced with a girl, who's danced with the Prince of Wales," has been mentioned. Yet another novelty was entitled *The Old Mahogany Bar*, concerned with an imaginary public-house which had suffered conversion into a mission-hall. The jest was to sing the Band of Hope ditties of Victorian times in these surroundings. For example:

> Please sell no more drink to my father,
> It makes him so strange and so wild.
> Heed the prayer of my heart-broken mother
> And pity the poor drunkard's child.

The *Cave of Harmony* later found a home in Gower Street, where entrance was obtained through a mews and stables. Miss Lanchester herself lived in a balcony loft nearby, and reached her room by a ladder. Proprietor and assistants at the *Cave of Harmony* were well content to work for pocket-money and fame, and this eventually came to Elsa Lanchester herself. Nigel Playfair gave her a part in Karel Kapek's *Insect Play*, and thus Elsa met her husband and became Mrs. Charles Laughton.

The economic crisis of the 'thirties brought disaster upon these small ventures. When trade was normal they could struggle along, but their functions finally passed to well-endowed restaurants such as the Dorchester and Grosvenor House.

In 1933, the Dorchester Cabaret employed thirty performers, of whom eighteen had appeared with the Ziegfeld Follies of New York. About the same time, the Grosvenor was staging miniature musical comedy, with scenery and a company of twenty-seven.

And, lastly, that interesting venture, *Revudeville*, at the Windmill Theatre off Piccadilly Circus, which is not quite a theatrical production, nor yet a cabaret show, but a betwixt and between, being non-stop revue. As *Revudeville* at the Windmill has now achieved a run of some thirteen years, and its editions run into hundreds rather than scores, it may be regarded as a London institution. I do not pretend to like the entertainment, and what Mr. Van Damm, the Windmill's manager, calls "the artistry of its nudity" seems to me specially objectionable, whether regarded as art or nudity.

The Windmill employs two companies, the technique of *Revudeville* requiring a fresh show every three weeks. When one three weeks ends another company takes the stage, while the other has a short holiday and invents, rehearses, and produces the succeeding show. Regarded from the professional standpoint, there is much to be said for *Revudeville*, as practised at the Windmill. The players are always in employment and receive full pay during the rehearsals. No chorus girl gets less than £4 a week, and the show girls can earn up to £10 or £12, apart from the chance of selection for soubrette work. The Windmill was built in 1931 as an intimate theatre for straight plays, and as it only had seating accommodation for 300 people, it failed. Indeed, the plucky builder, Mrs. Laura Henderson, began by losing £25,000, but persevered until the venture was making £11,000 a year. Even the Nazi blitz of 1940–41 did not close the Windmill, and Lesley Storm's play, *The Heart of a City*, witnesses to the fact.

Chapter XV

THE LADIES OF VAUDEVILLE, FROM VESTA TILLEY TO
BEA LILLIE

IN VAUDEVILLE, WHAT HAS HAPPENED WITHIN THE PAST FIFTY
years has been the introduction of women into what was primarily a masculine
institution. It would be strange if the disappearance of the markedly masculine
atmosphere of the old-time "free and easy" had not been followed by changes in
the ladies on the stage side of the safety-curtain and the songs and dances they
offered to their patrons in front. It is the purpose of this chapter in the story of
Vaudeville to specify the feminine changes due to the passing years.

The Victorian music-halls and vaudeville houses tended to put a premium
upon comedians, as opposed to comediennes. Nevertheless, if Gus Elen and
Albert Chevalier put over coster songs, so did Bessie Bellwood, while Vesta
Victoria's character sketches were not unworthy to rank with those of T. E.
Dunville. As for Marie Lloyd and Vesta Tilley, they were attractions as well
assured of their welcome as the great Dan Leno himself.

One of Bessie Bellwood's classic efforts carries us right back to the free and
easies. It told of one, Maria, who, dressed in her best, joined the "toffs" at the
high-table in the old-time sing-song. Wearing a wine-coloured frock, a befrilled
skirt, and a rorty hat topped with a red and white feather, Miss Bellwood was
manifestly assured that Maria was making a big jump towards Society with a
capital S. She had worked as a rabbit-skinner in the New Cut, before her talent
as a singer revealed itself. "Wot cheer, Ria" is self-explanatory:

> I am a girl what's a-doing werry well in the wegetable line,
> And as I'd saved a bob or two I thought I'd cut a shine;
> So I goes and buys some toggery, these 'ere werry clothes you see,
> And with the money I had left, I thought I'd have a spree.
> So I goes inside a music-hall, where I'd often been afore,
> I don't go in the gallery, but on the bottom floor.
> I sits down by the Chairman, and calls for a pot of stout,
> My pals in the gallery spotted me, and they all commenced to shout.
>
> *Chorus:*
> Wot cheer, 'Ria! 'Ria's on the job!
> Wot cheer, 'Ria! Did you speculate a bob?
> Oh, 'Ria, she's a toff and she looks immensikoff,
> So it's wot cheer, 'Ria! 'Ria! Hi, hi, hi!

Bessie, from the New Cut, had Irish-Cockney impudence in plenty, and was
a past-mistress of back-chat, but her rival, Jenny Hill, had greater variety and a

better-endowed talent as a character actress. Victorian audiences nicknamed her "the Vital Spark." She was the daughter of a cab-driver attached to a Marylebone rank, and he apprenticed his little girl to a North Country publican. Rising from her slumbers at 5 a.m. to polish the "pub's" pewter, Jenny sang songs and danced to the farmers of the district at night until 2 a.m. Deciding that no gamble could be more unfortunate, she wedded an acrobat, who left her with a baby

'ARRY'

SUNG WITH GREAT SUCCESS BY

MISS JENNY HILL.

WRITTEN & COMPOSED BY

E. V. PAGE.

when she was barely out of her 'teens. Thus, dire necessity brought Jenny back to London, where a music-hall agent sent her to the Pavilion with a note, "Don't trouble to see this girl, she's troublesome!" Fortunately, the Pavilion manager judged for himself, and, that night, Jenny "stopped the show." The great Leybourne, who was to follow her, was kept waiting. With commendable generosity, he carried the little woman on to the stage for a final encore and held her up to view to an applauding audience.

That arch-sentimentality, "I've been a good woman to you," was a Jenny Hill success, but the gift for putting over a song was only the beginning of her talents. She could impersonate a London street Arab or, if need be, a pathetic old lady. In "'Arry," wearing bell-bottomed trousers, a shapely coatee over an expanse of white shirt, and a saucy little bowler hat, she twitted an uncomfortable coster, dressed in his Sunday best, who was on the stage with her:

> Oh, 'Arry, what 'Arry!
> There you are then, 'Arry!
> I say, 'Arry!
>   By Jove! you are a don!
> Oh! 'Arry! 'Arry!
> There you are then, 'Arry!
> Where are you going on Sunday, 'Arry?
> Now you've got 'em on.

Jenny Hill died in 1896, aged forty-six, and her daughter was Peggy Pryde, of whom George Belmont, of the Sebright, wrote: "The Wittiest Chin-wagging Woman in the World, the Tricky-tongued, Tale-pitching Pet of the Populace."

And Lottie Collins of "Ta-ra-ra-boom-de-ay" fame? The song not only made her, but killed her. At forty-four she died of heart disease and the doctors were assured that the seeds of the trouble were sown when the meek little widow of the song burst, on a sudden, into frenzied dance. Lottie Collins began her music-hall career as a skipping-rope expert, but, on a certain Saturday afternoon in October 1891, at the age of twenty-three, she electrified a Tivoli audience by the amazing abandon of the dance, assisted by the beat of a big drum and an excited foam of lace petticoat, which was in such curious contrast to the quiet opening:

> A smart and stylish girl you see,
> The belle of high society;
> Fond of fun as fond could be
> When it's on the strict Q.T.
> Not too young, and not too old,
> Not too timid, not too bold,
> But just the very thing, I'm told.
> That in your arms, you'd like to hold!
>   Ta-ra-ra Boom-de-ay! . . .

Lottie wore a big Gainsborough hat and a short frock of red silk, which readily displayed the wealth of white petticoat and the excitement began with a clash of cymbals which accompanied the opening "Boom." At first there was apparent diffidence, the tremble in the voice being emphasised by nervous little gestures with a handkerchief. Then, as Lottie reached the chorus, she put her hands to her hips, below the corsetted waist of the period, and broke into the intoxicating dance, the music of the orchestra mingling with every swirl of those maddened and maddening petticoats. No one else ever sang the song with similar effect, and Lottie Collins never did anything else comparable, but Lottie, plus that crazy chorus, were irresistible in the early 'nineties.

At Christmas 1891, Lottie Collins went into pantomime and her song enjoyed a fresh fame at the Grand, Islington. By March 1892, it was at the Gaiety, where Lottie Collins took £150 a week from George Edwardes for what amounted to a fifteen-minutes' turn. The Gaiety burlesque was not very successful. Within a week the receipts for *Cinder Ellen Up Too Late* increased by £600, so Blue-eyed George's bargain was a good one.

By the way, a romance also associates itself with the tune. It was composed by a well-known London musician—Mr. Gilbert, father of the sculptor, Sir Alfred Gilbert, R.A. Old Mr. Gilbert had no interest whatever in music-halls, and wrote the air as a mock coon song. It was published and drifted over the Atlantic, where it was lost for over twenty years, until it was included in a musical play, *Tuxedo*, by Henry S. Sayers, with music by Paul Stanley. It was plain, however, that what mattered in "Ta-ra-ra-boom-de-ay!" was contained in the first eight bars of the Finale of Gilbert's *Abdallah, the Last Moorish King*, written for the Merchant Taylors' Choral Society.

Mr. Gilbert, senior, only came into the story of the song after it achieved world fame. One Sunday evening someone chanced to strum a few bars of the "new song" and Gilbert recognised the melody. As it had been published, he still controlled the copyright. A claim was made upon the publishers, and Mr. Gilbert received an utterly unexpected cheque for £250.

If the air was adaptable, the words proved scarcely less so. During the Hooley mania, Lottie Collins altered the last refrain to "Te-ra-rah-Hool-e-ay," to the delight of stalls and gallery. During the Greco-Turkish War the song momentarily attained the dignity of a national anthem. In 1897, a party of British volunteers were visiting a small restaurant in Athens, where the Greeks happened to sing their own national anthem, and the Englishmen joined in. Not to be eclipsed in courtesy, one of the Greeks suggested singing the British National Anthem. He thereupon burst into the chorus of "Ta-ra-ra-boom-de-ay." The Englishmen had to stand, with caps doffed and faces all solemnity, until the Greeks had picked up the air. Then one of the volunteers sang a verse of the song, and the Greeks repeated the chorus.

Nor was the furore confined to Europe.

Charles Frohman brought Miss Collins to America and engaged her to sing "Ta-ra-ra-boom-de-ay" between the acts of a musical comedy called *June*. Receiving £200 a week, Lottie Collins cleared £5,000 by her tour, a large sum in the 'nineties.

The Two Vestas

And Vesta Tilley. Is there any chance of doing justice to the career of this trim little packet of mingled charm, good-nature, and impudence? Perhaps she was at her glorious best at the time of the Boer War, when no male impersonator could approach her dapper soldiers and sailors. Here was a girl who really did wear the clothes of a man with grace. No corsets, no high-heeled shoes, for Vesta Tilley. Previously most girls had played boy parts in tights, and a feminine dinner-jacket. An eyeglass, an opera hat, and a walking-stick completed the disguise, but it deceived no one.

Vesta Tilley's father was one Harry Powles, manager of a popular "sing-song" in Nottingham and generally known as Harry Ball. His daughter was born in 1864 and was christened Matilda, her stage name coming from the well-known match. From the first, Tilly Ball was recognised as another "vital spark" and at four years of age she was making her first stage appearance as a mimic. Then Miss Ball blossomed into the Great Little Tilley, and was accepted as a budding tenor by variety patrons throughout the Midlands—the pocket Sims Reeves. The first London appearance came in 1878, when Vesta Tilley was thirteen. The Great Little Tilley was henceforward billed as "The London Idol," and the epithet accurately described the little lady for the rest of her fifty years of stage life. In her late 'teens Vesta Tilley was principal boy at Drury Lane in *Sinbad the Sailor*. To her lasting regret, this was her only appearance as principal boy at "The Lane." Afterwards, Miss Tilley reserved her pantomime triumphs for the provinces. Lucky provinces. Later, she won special popularity in the Isle of Man, where a new concert-hall was built for her. Ten thousand holiday-makers would stand night after night, listening to the little lady rolling her "r's" and singing "Jolly good luck to the girl that loves a sailor," or the inimitable:

> He's verry well-known is Algy, to the ladies on the stage;
> Such a jolly good chap is Algy, just now he's all the rage.
> And a jolly big favourite, Algy, with the barmaids at the "Cri."
> He's verry well-known is Algy,
> As the Piccadilly Johnny with the little glass eye.

Vesta Tilley married Walter de Frece, who had an interest in the de Frece circuit of music-halls and, when her husband was knighted as an M.P., London's idol became Lady de Frece. It was a characteristic of her fifty years of life on the stage that she was as popular with the women as with men and, moreover, as popular behind the drop-curtain as she was in front of the footlights.

The second Vesta of the Halls, Vesta Victoria, was a character actress, and she had a talent for finding songs which gave her full opportunities. Singing "It's all right in the summer-time," she was wedded to a sign-painter, who had ambitions as a painter of "the altogether," for which his wife was required to pose. As Vesta Victoria said:

> It's all right in the summer-time,
> In the summer-time it's lovely.
> While my old man's a' paintin' 'ard,
> Standin' 'ere a' posin' in the old back-yard.
> But, oh my, in the winter-time;
> It's a different thing, you know,
> With a red, red nose and very few clothes
> And the stormy winds do blow.

Dressed in a prim white frock, black stockings and black shoes, Miss Victoria also sang "Our Lodger's such a Nice Young Man." "He calls me his own Grace Darling" ran in this fashion:

> And he calls me 'is own Grace Darling,
> 'E says that I'm 'is pet.
> I've filled each "plaice" within 'is sole—
> That ain't no cod, you bet!
> When 'e arsked me if I lov'd 'im,
> I said, "Wot O, not 'arf!
> Why I likes you just for your whiskers,
> 'Cos they tickle me and make me larf!"

Florrie Forde associated herself with "Waltz me around again, Willie," "Down at the old Bull and Bush," "Oh, Oh, Antonio," "Hold your hand out, Naughty Boy," "Has anybody here seen Kelly?", "Pack up your troubles in your old kit bag," and "Who's your lady friend?"—a noble series, and all of them Florrie's own choice. Her invariable test was, "Will the audience pick up the chorus on the first night?" If not, Florrie had no use for the song. "Looping the loop with Lucy" cost her a guinea—"sole rights." She never paid more than £25 for a song.

Florrie Forde was a Melbourne girl, by name Flanagan, and ran away from home when she was fourteen. The theatre was calling. At Sydney, where an aunt received the runaway, she found a sympathetic theatre manager, who allowed her to appear in ballad and dance. The refrain began: "He kissed me when he left me, and told me to be brave." The manager sent her home to learn a more suitable song, and Florrie Forde appeared on the following Monday, priced 15s. a week. Years as principal boy in pantomime followed, and in their course Miss Forde made a reputation not only in Australia, but in England, whither she came in 1897 on the advice of Chirgwin, the White-eyed Kaffir, who had been touring "down South." Derby Castle, Douglas, Isle of Man, was *par excellence* the place to hear Florrie Forde.

Florrie Forde was one of the earliest and most successful singers of "Tipperary." The script reached the theatre in the Isle of Man at four o'clock one afternoon and the management wanted the song in the evening bill. In order to comply, Florrie arranged that the words of the chorus should be printed in letters an inch high and displayed on the stage near the footlights, and thousands sang it. Fortunate to the last, she spent an afternoon singing in a naval hospital during the second World War and died a few hours later, aged sixty-four.

The One and Only Marie

Marie Lloyd's first big success came with "Oh, Mr. Porter," and upon this foundation she was raised to the rank of a national institution. When music-hall patrons flocked to the Royal, Holborn, in 1893 to hear Marie sing:

> Oh, Mr. Porter,
> What shall I do?
> I want to go to Birmingham,
> And they've sent me on to Crewe,

her turn was valued at £20 a hall, and her earning capacity was already £100 a week. She earned upwards of £250,000 during the thirty-five or forty years of her working life, and was making £200 a week at the end. Yet she died apparently possessed of little more than her salary for the preceding week. Her weakness was a crazy generosity. On one occasion she bought the entire contents of an East End shop. Sitting behind the counter, in her big hat, she handed over her wares, refusing all payment. When the goods were exhausted Marie distributed silver to late-comers. Mr. Butler, one-time landlord of the King's Head, Peckham, has told us: "Swells used to go to the theatre to see Marie. She'd say, 'You go round to the Green Room and have some supper; I'll be round later.'" Mr. Butler added, "They'd come and order champagne and whatever they liked, and it would all go down to her. I've taken as much as £30 or £40 a week from Marie. There was a special kind of brandy she had that cost me £2 10s. a bottle."

Much of the scandal told of Marie was apocryphal. Her own comment was: "I seem to have had a busy life, eh? Wonderful constitution they must think I have!"

Born in 1870 and the daughter of one Brush Wood, a waiter at a Hoxton tavern, Marie's professional beginnings were songs at free and easies, held on Saturday and Monday nights at the Eagle Assembly Rooms, Shepherdess Walk, Finsbury. The very first effort was "In the Good Old Days of Long Ago," sung in the guise of an elderly lady, wearing a black shawl and spectacles. Matilda Wood was now fifteen years old, and she passed on to the Sebright, Hackney, the Grecian Assembly Rooms, and the Star, Bermondsey, at a salary which was now 15s. a week. By this time "Tilly" Wood had become Bella Delmere, though the label somehow seemed to lack a democratic ring, and another was sought. Everyone, in 1885, had heard of the popular weekly newspaper, *Lloyd's News*. Accordingly, Bella Delmere became Marie Lloyd. An early act of generosity as an accepted star was to buy eighty pairs of shoes, one pair for each of the children in the Hoxton School, where "Tilly" Wood had been educated.

Two years later (in 1887) Marie was at Collins Music Hall, Islington Green, wearing a short skirt and white socks, her ever-laughing mouth displaying some nice teeth, which protruded a thought too far from the lips. She sang:

> My Harry's a sailor
> On board of a whaler,

and ended with a hornpipe.

About this time Marie was engaged to George Foster, the music-hall agent. Foster chanced to introduce his fiancée to Percy Courtney, a young man-about-town, who was interested in racing. The Marie-cum-George engagement was called off and Miss Tilly Wood became Mrs. Percy Courtney for a time, while vaudeville profited directly as the coster song, "Never introduce your Donah to a Pal," enshrined the incident.

Possibly the welcome which the gallery boys at the Old Mo extended to "The boy that I love sits up in the gallery" was the turning-point in Marie Lloyd's career. The welcome made every music-hall manager in Town want plump little Marie from Hoxton, with her blue eyes, her golden hair, her husky voice, her wink, and her capacity for creating "publicity stunts." One after another, popular songs were discovered, characterised, and put over the footlights. Perhaps a coster-woman, whose bloke joined up. This was Marie's comment:

> I do feel so proud of you, I do, honour bright.
> I'm going to give you an extra cuddle to-night.

Or it might be:

> I hate the horrid School Board,
> So does Brother Jack—
> Nothing but a wacky, wacky, whack, whack, whack!

"Then you Wink the other Eye," "Twiggy Voo," and "You can't stop a Girl from Thinking" were other successes. Once Marie came into collision with the licensing authorities over a certain song, anent a young lady who had a garden. Objection was taken to a phrase, and Marie altered it. Still the authorities were doubtful. In the end Miss Lloyd was asked to go through her repertoire before a London County Council committee. Everyone was satisfied, for Marie cut out all the winks and nods which gave her songs dubious significance.

"Thank you," said Marie, when the verdict was announced. "And now may I sing you a real song, such as your wives and daughters sing at home?"

Very foolishly, the County Councillors allowed the pianist to get to work upon "Come into the Garden, Maud." The elderly councillors were electrified. They had not guessed that such depravity existed in accepted songland.

It must be admitted that the Cockney of Cockneys was sometimes a very naughty little woman. Always, she was quick to see temptation and quick to fall into it. She was once playing in pantomime for "Gus" Harris, the story being *Little Bo Peep*. Very unwisely, "Druriolanus" suggested that Marie should kneel for a few moments by Grandmama's bedside.

"Look under the bed, Marie," whispered Dan Leno.

Marie did, and Sir Augustus was very angry.

On one occasion, a voice from the gallery called, "Marie, give us a dirty look!" Marie looked up, facing the speaker, and "brought down the house" with her retort:

"No need, you've got one."

Nevertheless, when she put on the demure white frock of the small girl to sing "Johnny Jones," and shouldered the wooden hoop, Marie offered temptations to the gallery boys who understood her so well. There was a highly provocative wink when Marie came to the end of the refrain:

> What's that for, eh? Oh! tell me, Ma!
> If you won't tell me, I'll ask Pa!
> But Ma said, "Oh, it's nothing, shut your row!"
> Well, I've asked Johnny Jones, see,
> So I know now!

All audiences were not equally receptive. At the Palace, with its pseudo-aristocratic atmosphere, Marie had to work very hard for her welcome. Night after night she tried out a new song and was on the point of admitting defeat when this bit of nonsense, set to a telling melody by the American composer, Nevin, "got" stalls, circles, and galleries at the Palace:

> There they are,
> The two of them on their own;
> In the parlour
> Alone, alone, alone;
> They gave me half a crown
> To run away and play—
> Umpty iddle-y, umpty iddle-y,
> Umpty iddle-y-ay.

Insistence upon one phase of Marie Lloyd's talent as an entertainer does less than justice to her gifts as a character actress. There was, for example, the impersonation of a Cockney charwoman who was moving house. She had lost the furniture van, she had lost her husband, she had lost her way. All that remained was a pet linnet, sole survivor of a sad day:

> Away went the van with me old man in it.
> I stayed be'ind with me old cock linnet,
> But I dillied . . . and dallied . . .

A snatch of song opened and closed the sketch; but what mattered was Marie's monologue telling the life-story of a London "char," born and bred in Seven Dials and accepting a black eye from her husband, now as a corrective, now as a compliment. Such an impersonation was on a higher plane than "A Little Bit of What You Fancy Does You Good," in which every point was emphasised by a leer or a wink from Marie's blue eyes.

At the end, Marie Lloyd struggled bravely with a mortal illness, and there was a personal significance in her last song, "I'm one of the ruins Cromwell knocked about a bit." At her last London appearance, when the inevitable encore came, she stepped forward and said quietly:

"When I was first a star I stood here—it was the Royal, Holborn, then—and sang a song that everyone sang, and it wasn't rude. Sing it with me now."

The band broke into the familiar "Oh, Mr. Porter."

She died in 1922, aged fifty-two. Fifty thousand Londoners attended her funeral. One huge wreath came from the Costermongers' Union, Farringdon Road; to another, consisting of a horseshoe of white chrysanthemums, were attached spurs, a whip, a cap of blue flowers. It was from "Her Jockey Pals," among them being Frank Bullock, "Brownie" Carslake, "Steve" Donoghue, and Herbert Jones. Every Londoner loved Marie. Her frailties were blessedly human.

Gracie, Ee Ba-Goom!

No one fills the niche left vacant when Marie Lloyd passed from vaudeville, but she has a successor in Gracie Fields. The wink which Gracie added to "When the he-lamb gives the she-lamb the once-over" recalled Marie and Gracie's treatment of a curtain call, twice, thrice, ten times repeated is typical Marie Lloyd. Weary of the repeated "calls," Gracie would come before the curtain, jerk her head sideways in the direction of the thumb which was directed over her shoulder. Of course every music-hall *habitué* recognised the signal. It signified that this was the end of a happy day and that Gracie would be found partaking refreshment at a mythical bar, behind the footlights. But there were other methods of farewell. Gracie might equally well close on quite a different note, that is, with a fervent, "I really do want to thank you—honest to Gawd!"

Gracie's father was a working engineer in Rochdale, Stansfield by name, and, at ten years of age, Gracie, in clogs and shawl, sought out a job as a half-timer in a local cotton mill, as a Lancashire lass should. But already Gracie Stansfield had won some success as an entertainer. Her family had theatrical interests and, at eight, the girl won a competition at a Rochdale cinema. The first prize was a 30s. engagement to sing "What makes you love me, as I love you?" through a week. Sometimes, too, Gracie was asked to sing a song on benefit nights, the pay taking the form of twopenny pies. When the reward was a silver coin Gracie spent the money at local music-halls, thus picking up the tricks of the entertainment trade. Her general conclusion was, "Gracie, this is the job for you." As it was plain Gracie had a voice of considerable range, her mother was inclined to agree, but Gracie's father remained a sceptic. He said: "Don't be daft, Jinny. Shove her in t' factory!"

In the struggle between the arts and industry, the arts were victorious. Before her eleventh birthday Gracie, tall for her age and long of leg, was touring with Haley's Juveniles and receiving a shilling a week, plus board and lodgings, this stage-work being varied with spells as an errand girl to a Rochdale confectioner. In the early years, her most promising talent was as a mimic, Gertie Gitana, George Formby, and Victoria Monks being among her victims. "Rochdale's Juvenile Mimic" was one line on the theatre bills. But the wide range of Gracie's voice also brought considerable success as a singer of "sob stuff," the attraction being grown-up songs, rendered by a small girl. The decisive step towards stardom came when Gracie developed a talent for "foony noises" and simultaneously came to the conclusion that sentimental songs, sung to the accompaniment of the shuffling feet of late entrants, gave no promise of a worth-while career. Chance showed her that a way out was to add a touch of burlesque to the sob stuff. No sooner thought of than tested. On the very next night, instead of singing the second verse of her ballad as straightforward sentiment, she "clowned" it and included some falsetto passages. The audience chuckled and then laughed and soon applause showed that a new Lancashire "comic" had arrived.

Thus Gracie Stansfield became Gracie Fields, though financial success was still far away. That came after Gracie met Archie Pitt, and she accepted the post of leading lady in a revue he had written. It was to include an imitation of Charlie Chaplin by Gracie, in the best Rochdale manner.

"It's a bargain," said Gracie, and she held out her hand.

"It is," rejoined Pitt, "and, what's more, that's what we'll call the show—*It's a Bargain*."

Within three weeks *It's a Bargain* was in difficulties. It was saved by one of those curious bits of good fortune which usually associate themselves with theatrical ventures in novelettes. A young professional had enjoyed *It's a Bargain*, and he came round to Archie Pitt's dressing-room to say so.

"I bet you're making a packet out of it."

Archie Pitt would have liked to agree, but honesty forbade. He explained the real position, which was that he was broke. The stranger put his hand in his pocket and produced forty pounds in notes.

"Take this," he said.

"But I've no security," responded Pitt.

"Security be blowed! Pay me when the ship comes home."

Archie accepted the loan, and the forty pounds enabled *It's a Bargain* to continue its run for nearly three years. At the end it gave place to *Mr. Tower of London*, with Gracie playing Sally Perkins. It was played 5,824 times in seven years, including two London runs at the Alhambra and brought in £400,000 to the box-office. Already Gracie was a star, and still in her 'teens.

For the vaudeville singer who seeks artistic refinements, Gracie Fields has little sympathy. When she went to New York for the first time, her American fellow-comedians set their faces firmly against the Englishwoman's slap-stick comedy. Gracie's reaction was to relapse into broad Lancashire:

"Say, mister! You may think I'm Lady Tissue Paper, but I'm not. I don't know you, but I bet I'm commoner than you are and every bit as rough. If you won't come in on my act, I'm coming in on yours!"

And Gracie did, with such effect that Broadway acclaimed her efforts as Rochdale had done and a second continent was ready to welcome the girl from Lancashire.

Very characteristic of the artist and the woman, if the two are separable in Gracie Fields's case, was her appearance at the Gaiety, London, in 1928. The Duncan Sisters had invested their savings in a nondescript musical show entitled *Topsy and Eva*, in which Rosetta Duncan blacked her face and played a nigger part. When Rosetta fell ill, Vivien Duncan found she could not hold the show together alone, and it seemed as if the company and stage hands would be "out of a shop," as Lancashire has it. Gracie learnt of the threatened calamity and telegraphed to Vivien Duncan, "I'll take Rosetta's part." As a Lancashire woman, she knew what "being out of a shop" meant.

Two days later Gracie was on the Gaiety stage, her face as well blacked as Rosetta's had been. Against the background of the Mississippi cotton plantations, Gracie thrust in "Ramona," "Why does an Hyena laugh?", and other Rochdale triumphs, defying criticism. Gags about Wigan and the tripe of Lancashire made their familiar appeal, and the closing night at the Gaiety was a triumph. At the stage door a big crowd was calling "Gracie." When she came out under police escort, the crowd took the little woman up bodily and chaired her. Of course, it was a Lancashire demonstration and Lancashire did it because Gracie had "saved a shop."

Similar in kind and even more momentous in consequences were Gracie Fields's appearances in France during the winter of 1939. Though far from well, she was unsparing in her efforts to amuse the troops in the field. There were times when Gracie sang thirty songs in a day and on one occasion she held the stage in a field theatre alone for seventy-nine minutes. Only a physique built up in the hardy North would have attempted the feat.

> Every tinker, every tailor,
> Every soldier, every sailor,
> They adored her!

Nor must the high spirits of the woman, as they were displayed at the Palladium in the days of the Crazy Gang, escape recording. Twice nightly Gracie donned Knox's trousers, Eddie Gray's blazer, Bud Flanagan's hat, Allen's shirt, and Jimmy Nervo's shoes, and sang, "Little Man, you've had a busy day," until as a fitting climax the public was invited to gaze upon the Carsons picking out Gracie's trim figure with their juggling knives.

There remain the songs which Gracie made famous. The classics of the second World War have been mentioned. The familiar "Why does the Hyena laugh?" was a John P. Long effort, and had its origin in a small boy at the Zoo remarking, 'I don't know what he's got to laugh at with a face like that." "She fought like a Tiger for 'er 'onour" came from Will Haines and Jimmy Harper, who also provided Gracie with that curious ditty, "Shall I be an Old Man's Darling?" Needless to say, a characteristic opportunity for mingling pathos and comedy into a typical Gracie Fields amalgam was offered by "An Old Man's Darling," in which the emotional problem was thus expounded:

> Mother keeps on nagging, all day long her tongue is wagging,
> Says that love is just a lot of tommy-rot.
> Better wed for wealth and ease,
> Love develops housemaid's knees,

You'll slave just like a nigger and you'll lose your lovely figure
And the beautiful proportions that you've got.
Well, maybe, I could do much worse
Than be a Rip van Winkle's nurse.

The refrain went on to emphasise the dilemma, "Should Gracie be an old man's darling or a young man's slave," but it did not straighten out the tangle, though one hoped Gracie's David would earn money enough to save his little Venus, together with her Marcel Wave.

In another song Gracie Fields propounded yet another interesting song question:

What can you give a Nudist on his birthday?
What sort of birthday present can you buy?
I *have* heard they play hockey, so something I had got,
But I *don't* know for certain if they wear shin-guards or not.
What can you give a Nudist for a present?
A shopgirl told me spats would be all wrong—
She said, "Good gracious, Madam, just imagine spats on Adam!"
What can you give a Nudist when his birthday comes along?

It was a sad day when America annexed the lady whom Lancashire christened "Our Gracie," and a happy one when she returned.

The vast majority of vaudeville stars to-day reach fame by a much less exacting route than that taken by Gracie Fields. There are a dozen anxious managers searching for a Jessie Matthews, a Beatrice Lillie, a Gertrude Lawrence, or a Claire Luce and, once found, the way to the top can be very easy, in comparison with the struggle which the stars of times past had to face before they found fame. Moreover, when they face the footlights, the latter-day stars command aids to success which the stars of Victorian and Edwardian times would have scorned. Marie Lloyd did not need the glamour of half a hundred chorus girls and elaborate lighting effects which convert a back-curtain into animated fairyland. Similarly, Gracie Fields is one of the few who can put over a song without these extraneous aids. Nellie Wallace, with a talent akin to that of the ever-memorable Louie Freear, is another. Nellie Wallace, as a washerwoman ironing a basketful of unmention-ables, is among the outstanding memories of present-day vaudeville.

As for the circumstances under which talent is discovered, recall the story of Jessie Matthews. She was born in 1907, in the heart of London's theatre world (Soho). First an exacting but admiring sister and then a Soho dancing mistress detected the promise of a stage dancer in the tall, slim, and long-legged Jessie. Their efforts resulted in an opportunity in a juvenile pantomime, so that, when she heard that Cochran's *Music Box* revue was to be given at the Palace, Jessie was ready to present herself for an audition. At first sight, Jessie was little more than a child with big eyes, a funny little nose, and a decidedly curious taste in dress, but C. B. has an eye for potential talent and decided to let her play the part of a chicken, in a number composed by Irving Berlin.

Then London managements forgot about Miss Jessie and she went off to America as a chorus girl in a Charlot revue. During the tour she had the luck to replace Gertrude Lawrence, Charlot's leading lady, for a while, and her singing of "My heart stood still" and "Dancing on the ceiling" suggested that a star was in the making. Back in London, Mr. Cochran was glad to bring back his little chicken of the Palace Theatre to play a leading part at the Pavilion. She signed on for four shows: £60 a week for the first, £100 the second, £150 the third, and £200 the fourth. As Miss Matthews said, "Not bad for twenty," particularly as the shows proved to be *One Dam Thing after Another*, *This Year of Grace*, *Wake Up and Dream*, and *Evergreen*. In *Wake Up and Dream* Jessie sang "Let's do it" with Sonnie Hale. It was a Cole Porter lyric:

> The nightingales in the dark do it.
> Larks, crazy for a lark, do it.
> Let's do it, let's fall in love.
> Canaries, caged in the house, do it;
> When they're out of season grouse do it.
> Let's do it, let's fall in love.

It was that wonderful trouper, Maisie Gay, who impressed upon Jessie the all-important truth:

"Develop your own personality, and don't mimic. Think of your own face. Never forget your round face, straight hair, and fringe. Visualise it all the time, while you are working, and exploit it for all you are worth."

In Noel Coward's *This Year of Grace*, Jessie Matthews showed that she had added a full measure of personality to her considerable skill as a dancer. Still more substantial success attended *Evergreen*, a musical comedy at the Adelphi, with a story by Benn Levy, songs by Lorenz Hart and Richard Rodgers, and dances by Billy Pierce and Buddy Bradley. The story was expressly written to exploit the graces of Jessie Matthews and the energy and humour of Sonnie Hale. It told how a young woman substituted her mother's birth certificate for her own and thus was able to pose as an elderly beauty who had been miraculously rejuvenated by the daughter's beauty preparations. The Neuilly Fair scene devised by Ernst Stern, with aid from the Adelphi revolving stage, was a feature of the show, but *Evergreen* is memorable because it showed how good Jessie Matthews really was and how much better she was likely to be with hard work and full experience.

The spotlight fantasia, *Dancing on the Ceiling*, links itself in the memory with Gertie Millar's *Moonstruck*. Richard Rodgers, the principal composer, Lorenz Hart, the lyric writer, Benn Levy who wrote the book, and Charles Cochran, the producer, were all on toe-tips when *Evergreen* was in the making, and the result was something which vaudeville lovers will not forget.

Or pretty Pat Kirkwood, out of Manchester, who first thrust her talents upon London audiences in *Black Velvet*, and went on to prove her gifts as a principal boy in pantomime, this being a well-approved approach to stardom. "Well-earned success after a long and strenuous training in the provinces." "Difficult years in the chorus." Not a bit of it. Pat Kirkwood was not nineteen when she displayed the capacity to impress her personality upon Hippodrome audiences, that is to say, upon something like twenty thousand men and women in a single week. Such audiences make the quick rise to fame possible. With a wink, an outsize smile, and a display of her pretty teeth, Pat Kirkwood put over the cynicism of "My Heart belongs to Daddy," which made much the same appeal to sophisticated vaudeville-lovers of our day as did the pseudo-sentimentality of Vesta Victoria singing "Daddy wouldn't buy me a bow-wow" in Victorian times. Pat Kirk-wood's other favourite was "Oh, Johnny," in praise of a young man who was no great shakes in the beauty market, but knew all the tricks of love-making:

> Oh, Johnny, oh, Johnny, how you can love,
> Oh, Johnny, oh, Johnny, heavens above . . .
> What makes me love you so?
> You're not handsome, it's true,
> But when I look at you,
> I just "Oh, Johnny, oh, Johnny, oh."

It will be interesting to see if Pat Kirkwood goes as far as Cicely Courtneidge, who had a far more strenuous struggle for public recognition, though she started out with all the advantages arising from being her father's daughter.

A Past Mistress of Bathos

If a fully typical lady of latter-day vaudeville had to be selected it would be a somewhat more cosmopolitan figure than Jessie Matthews or Mistress Jack Hulbert. Picture the lady of my choice, with close-cropped hair, so that you would be forgiven if you mistook her for a boy, though, in fact, she has been the delight of Johnnydom since Andre Charlot, at the Alhambra, had the wit to discover the budding starlet in his own chorus, and thus made it possible for the young lady to shed her lambent beams upon two continents.

Sing, of course she can sing, after a fashion, *her* fashion. And dance, of course she can dance in a fashion all her own. Moreover, she can raise a chuckle with smaller facial or bodily gesture than any woman in the profession, though her sufferings in "Rough Stuff" were an exception to the general rule, as was shown by the agility with which she broke from an over-strenuous wooer on the stage and sought refuge in the stalls. The masculine twelve-and-sixpennyites of those days knew they had not wasted their money when the opportunity for assisting this distressed damsel presented itself night after night at a certain vaudeville house in mid-Strand.

Again, and once more in the Strand, when the lady of our choice sailed off upon a silvery moon, pausing occasionally to dangle a garter above her admirers in the stalls, until one of them was clever enough to catch the dainty pale pink and blue satin thing from the prettily turned ankle. Nor was this the complete turn, for the lady was seated upon a wibbly, wobbly crescent, and the wibbles and the wobbles fitted with comic certainty into the bits of this and the bits of that which constitute musical rhythm when our heroine is singing. There was also to be added the twitch of the eyebrows which indicated a fugitive nausea as the wibbly-wobbly moon swayed and dipped, to be followed by a suggestion of ineffable relief when the seat returned to the level after its momentary flutter above the stalls.

And this imp of amiable mischief is . . .? Of course, "Bea" Lillie. Born in 1898, a year before Noel Coward, Miss Lillie came from Canada in company with a gifted mother who played the organ, and a sister who had skill enough to persuade the good people of Toronto to pay the family's expenses to London, that a professional career as a pianist might be assured. Poor little Bea apparently had no qualification for the London trip other than a liking for amateur theatricals, though this sufficed to secure a stage appearance in Alhambra revue when "Bea" was only sixteen, and a speaking part in *Now is the Time.* another Charlot production at the Alhambra.

Then came the first American tour, a triumph, which was repeated when Miss Lillie returned to London. The demand for tickets at the Vaudeville was so great that Manager Charlot arranged *two* first nights. That the second audience might reach home in time for a sleep before the next day's work, a supply of omnibuses was chartered and retailed at one shilling a seat. It was close upon three o'clock when the second of the first nights ended, and it is on record that three thousand waffles and griddle-cakes were sold in the small hours of that memorable morning, doubtless to those who had been wishing the lady with the close-cropped head many such happy returns.

Bea's speciality is emphasising the minor futilities of social intercourse. She is a past-mistress of bathos. With a gesture which may easily escape notice she can throw an entire male chorus into troubled doubt by giving an instinctive hitch at a dropping suspender. Or she may essay a song and, as the critical high note is reached, break into a falsetto which guys the piece fully as effectively as Gracie Fields at her wickedest. And, always, utterly unperturbed, for "Bea" knows that her timing will be exact, whether she is aiming at the just right or the just wrong. When the small voice breaks at just the wrong moment, the lift of the eyelids is forthcoming at the split second which fits the incident.

Here is an art of burlesque in which purposeful vagueness is substituted for the full-blooded exaggerations of most comic acting. Assuredly, there is nothing of the knockabout comedienne in Beatrice Lillie. What she relies upon is a vacuous smile, which proves to be fully intelligent a second later, while the whole bag-of-tricks is unified by complete unconcern as to consequences. The songs "L'amour the merrier" and "Snoops the Lawyer" associate themselves with "Bea," so does her effort in *At Home and Abroad* to order "two-dozen double-damask dinner napkins" from a departmental store clerk.

17

And the versatility of the lady. Recall *All Clear*, the war-time revue which H. M. Tennent staged at the Queen's Theatre in 1940, in which she starred with Bobby Howes and revealed how perfect a boy she could be when she put her mind to it. There never was a more angelic chorister than Master Ernest in *Evacuees*, a sketch featuring a couple of ultra-sophisticated choirboys evacuated from some Mayfair church and singing "Sic Transit Gloria":

> Although it may seem a bit caddish to yearn,
> We just can't help regretting the fun
> Of the days when we two were a sort of star turn
> At a very posh church in W.1.

And this study in depraved youth was only one among half a dozen turns centring upon Lillie. There was the star in "Entertaining the Troops," dead keen to do her bit, if this meant no more than introducing a shy recruit to the glamour which had been but now was passing. Bea's whisper to the shy youth, "Keep your hand upon the material," displayed genius. In delightful contrast was Marion Day, the bored night-club singer, with her bejewelled gas-mask and other evidences of successful gold-digging, and yet only too aware that she was "Weary of It All." This was a Noel Coward contribution to *All Clear*, as was *Marvellous Party*, the song-sketch in which "Bea" appeared in big black goggles and a Riviera beach-suit. A third Noel Coward contribution was *Cat's Cradle*, with Bobby Howes as Lilian Mawdsley and "Bea" playing Eva Tassel, a spinster of uncertain age, who kept cats. Miss Mawdsley had suggested that the cats, one male and the other female, might be friends, to which suggestion Miss Tassel responded by raising her pince-nez and saying, "False modesty's one thing; loose thinking's another."

In 1925, Miss Lillie married Robert Peel, great-grandson of the Prime Minister and heir to a baronetcy. Someone suggested "Bea" might leave the stage. "Leave the stage?" repeated Miss Lillie, "I should be like a duck without a pond."

B.B.C. Discoveries

The size of the audience in a modern super-theatre, and the advertising which modern methods make so easy, largely account for the ease with which reputations are made to-day in comparison with twenty-five years ago, though a sudden jump to fame has always been a theatrical possibility. To-day, a single song on the wireless may do the trick; or a few funny stories, associated with a touch of originality, the originality, let us say, of Suzette Tarri or Elsie and Doris Waters. In the latter combination Doris is "Daisy" and Elsie "Gert," Elsie contributing the words and Doris the music. They had been content with straight music, ballads, violin-playing, and the like, when, one day, they chanced to be watching a fashionable wedding. Two Cockney girls were standing near them and their comments aroused the interest of the Misses Waters, who introduced them to the public in the form of a gramophone record, but soon Bert, Gert and Daisy, and their relatives and friends were alive for music-hall, cabaret, and revue audiences. Daisy's raincoat, Gert's yellow jumper, and the string bag passed into the story of vaudeville. So did the familiar commentary upon lumbago:

Gert: 'E's got lumbago.
Daisy: 'As 'e 'ad it before?
Gert: No, 'e always 'as it behind.

Here is another:

Gert: Where's your old man?
Daisy: At an identification parade.
Gert: That won't take 'im long.
Daisy: Last time it took 'im three months.

Two other stars whose fame owes much to broadcasting are Ethel Revnell and Gracie West. They began at the microphone on a Saturday afternoon series, which the B.B.C. entitled "First Time Here," and filled a gap due to a singer being ill. Ethel and Gracie had worked out what they called a "Kid Act," when engaged by a Margate concert-party, based upon impressions derived from watching Cockney children at a Sunday-school treat.

Suzette Tarri is another discovery of wireless who has achieved vaudeville fame. She is no singer and has no great skill as an actress, but the speed and certainty with which she puts her wise-cracks over the footlights is inimitable. Scarcely one of them fails to create character, as well as raise a laugh, this being the conjunction of results called for in wise-crackery. Recall her comment upon her birthday:

"Another ring on my bark! I had two presents, four birthday cards, and a notice to have my gutter cleared out."

One of the presents was a bottle of wine. "I like wine," mused Miss Tarri. "After a glass I feel ready to undo all the good I've done in a lifetime."

Poor Suzette! She has always been unlucky in her love-affairs. "In twenty-seven years I've never had a proposal of marriage that was not accompanied by hiccups."

Then there was Miss Tarri's gardener friend, "who got his aerial crossed with a lettuce and got Mr. Middleton." And Alf, who so unexpectedly spent £20 or so upon a site for a grave. "Alf always does-look after his own comfort." Or the barmaid at the Rose and Crown, who, for twenty-seven years, fought a losing battle against drought, and tried devilled kidneys upon a man whose kidneys hurt like the devil!

Yes, during three "degenerations" Suzette's waitress learnt many things, among them the fact that "one man's meat is another man's rissole." And, lastly, the note of wonderment which crept into Suzette's query:

"Is the customer always right? Is he right when he picks his teeth with a fork? No! If so, what's a tram ticket for?

Chapter XVI

THE FORTIES OF THE TWENTIETH CENTURY

THE CURTAIN FALLS

EDUCATED TO ENJOY RAVISHING SPECTACLES IN AN OUTSIZE
theatre, where elaborate scenery and lighting effects are essential, is it not folly to
bewail the shortage of outstanding stage personalities? If the mirthful song and
character-creating patter were there as of old, audiences could not give them full
attention. The funniest of funny men cannot hold his own against eighty or a
hundred "lovelies," descending a golden staircase in an Earl Carroll or Florenz
Ziegfeld revue. It must be accepted that stage pictures are meant to be theatre-
fillers, and constitute the show, rather than tuneful song and mirthful humour.

Recall Oliver Messel's all-white scene in Offenbach's *Helen*, when Charles
Cochran presented it at the Adelphi, with Evelyn Laye as Helen and George
Robey as the long-suffering Menelaus. Helen's great circular bed was set in an
alcove at the back of the stage and was decorated with two gigantic swans. Above
hung a great lamp, and, over the sleeper's head, a dancing Love, while four
lovely wisps of drapery fell from the overhanging canopy, or were looped up
to the ceiling. Doris Zinkeisen, herself a stage-designer of genius, described
Messel's scenery in *Helen* as itself "acting a part." Little imagination is required
to gauge the difficulty of being really funny in such surroundings. The bed with
the outsize swans subdued even George Robey.

What has happened is that the second World War demands and secures a
measure of the magnificent spectacle it has learnt to expect from Hollywood and
Elstree. The Old Gaiety, the old Pavilion, the old Adelphi, and the rest served
their day and generation, but the stage of a Hippodrome or a Coliseum must be
filled sufficiently to amuse two or three thousand spectators twice daily. So it is
upon one of these outsize houses that we will ring down our final curtain.

Let it be the Palladium, which arose on the site of Hengler's Circus in Argyll
Street in 1911. It is the second biggest theatre in London and owes its prosperity
to the late George Black. As Morton, Moss, and Stoll were the creators of the
earliest large vaudeville houses of the modern type, so George Black has demon-
strated how the big Palaces of Variety could be saved from the all-conquering
Movies. In general, George Black's method was that of Albert de Courville, rather
than the eclecticism of Charles Cochran or the jolly catch-as-catch-can methods
of Jack Hulbert. "You just run things in quickly" and the "things" include a
cast of seventy or eighty, in order that the stage may really seem full during a
spectacular finale. There are also twenty tons or more of scenery, four tons of
properties, and three tons of costumes, the figures covering a single Palladium
production in the 1930's, when Bud Flanagan led the Palladium Crazy Gang.

Though incessant change and express speed are judged all-important, important production problems remain. The episodes must be blended in such a manner that audiences sense a logical continuity, even if words fail to express the "story" or the development of ideas. Moreover, there is the ever-present fact of the fewness of the available stars. Beauty and charm in a woman, vigour and strength in a man, allied with personality and the technical skill required to fill a large theatre, constitute a combination which is necessarily rare. "Tops, we must have Tops."

Nevertheless, even when revue is professedly being played, a George Black production at the Palladium is more akin to old-time variety than the majority of modern revues. *O-Kay for Sound*, the 1936-7 production at the Palladium, had little more than the theme song to lend cohesion to a go-as-you-please entertainment. The show opened in a studio where a musical film was in production, and this allowed of a variation upon the theme of Don Juan, with music by Mozart, as well as a burlesque of the same story, in the trusty hands of Nervo and Knox. A couple of Navy scenes and an Apache dance followed, until, in the second half of the show, even the faintest semblance of a plot was abandoned, and the audience was shown the exterior of a West End theatre, with "pittites" in the queue being entertained by varied "turns."

Well, effectiveness may be the proper test, not verisimilitude. One recalls an amazing skit upon the Aldershot Tattoo, during which someone sang, "You push the damper in and you pull the damper out, but the smoke goes up the chimney just the same," to the tune of "John Brown's body lies a-mouldering in his grave." Again, in the revue *The Little Dog Laughed*, the song "You can't ration sunshine" was sung to an air which was first published in the *War Cry*, and was written by a Salvation Army song-leader, Mr. Oliver Cooke, for audiences very different from those at the Palladium. George Black promptly converted the air, holding the view that there was no reason why the Churches should have a monopoly of the good tunes, in which for once his views coincided with the sentiments of the late General Booth.

Who among latter-day stars can dominate a large stage as did George Robey or George Graves in their prime? Billy Bennett, "almost a gentleman," could do so for a few minutes, and Billy Bennett is dead. Moreover, Billy was brought up in a harder school than latter-day stars look for. He began in pantomime as the hind-legs of an elephant, Mr. Bennett, senior, being a partner in a knockabout turn, Bennett and Martell. Later, young Billy was an acrobat. Then came the first World War and experience as a canteen comedian enabled him to return to the stage as a Soldier Comic, his speciality being travesties of familiar recitations, such as:

> There's a cock-eyed yellow poodle to the north of Waterloo,
> There's a little hot cross bun that's turning green,
> There's a double-jointed woman doing tricks in *Chu-Chin-Chow*,
> And you're a better man than I am, Gunga Din.

Max Miller, with high-speed "cheeky chappie" dialogue as his speciality, is another comedian of the day with an assured welcome. Max is fond of informing audiences that he views the blue pencil of the stage censor with no favour. The ginger-wigged Billy Merson, too, whose strength lies in his capacity to write songs which fit his personality, which is an old-fashioned approach to stardom. "She'll think of her soldier-boy" was an early best effort. Billy Merson's biggest hit was "The Spaniard who blighted my life," with a serio-recitative verse, and an idiotic chorus:

> He shall die!
> He shall die . . . ie!
> He shall die . . . tiddley-i-ti-i-i-i-i.
> He shall die . . . He shall die,
> And I'll raise such a bunion on his Spanish onion
> If I catch him bending to-night.

As the Holborn Empire was the happy hunting-ground of Max Miller, so Billy Merson was dear to audiences at the Palladium.

Tommy Trinder is less easy to characterise. He reached stardom through a talent for publicising himself. The poster, "You Lucky People," will be remembered. He has been known to go on the stage with a pocketful of photographs of himself, which he handed out to lucky ones in the audience. The Duke of Kent once collected a dozen in an evening, one for every laugh. However, there can be no doubt about the welcome managers and audiences alike give to Tommy Trinder. A typical Trinder week may involve a dozen performances at the London Palladium, followed by a dozen appearances in cabaret at Grosvenor House, beginning at midnight. Born in Streatham, Tommy Trinder began his career as a boy vocalist and when his voice broke, he entertained working-men's clubs at 7s. 6d. a night. Then he joined Archie Pitt as a comedian, doing concert-party work at southern watering-places in the holiday seasons. Slowly but surely, Tommy Trinder gathered the assurance which allows him to greet a late-comer to the stalls of the Palladium with "Get yourself mechanised, sir."

A London discovery of 1943 was Sid Field, who came to the Prince of Wales's in a George Black revue, *Strike a New Note*, and established his welcome at once. A characteristic Sid Field effort was the song, "Little Ball's going Ta-ta!", in a golfing scena with Jerry Desmonde.

> *Jerry:* Get behind the ball!
> *Sid.:* But it's behind the ball all round.

London audiences took a long time to discover Sid Field, the underlying reason being that the said Sid was fully content with the welcome which provincial audiences had extended to his funniments for years. However, when the successor to *Strike a New Note* was required, Sid Field was at the top of the bill and *Strike It Again* played to capacity houses for months. Mr. Agate, in a brilliant historical analysis which went back to the comics of Shakespeare, failed to isolate Sid Field's specific "mask," but reached the conclusion that "in the whole range of leer and innuendo from Hogarth to Ally Sloper, Field is all the corner boys of Cockaigne." Then, characteristically, he escaped with an apt quotation from A. B. Walkley, content that he had established Sid Field among the great comedians.

A South African girl, the red-haired Zoe Gail, furnished another bull-point for *Strike a New Note*, particularly in her energetic dances with Jack Billings. Zoe Gail's song displayed a measure of the full-blooded vulgarity which has characterised very much of vaudeville, since the art-form first took root in the Vire Valley. One verse of the song ran thus:

> When someone shouts "The Fight's up,"
> And "It's time to put the lights up,"
> Then the first thing to be lit up will be me!
> You will find me on the tiles,
> You will find me wreathed in smiles,
> I'm going to get so lit up I'll be visible for miles,
> Through the day and through the night,
> Signal beacons they will light,
> "England this day expects the nation to be tight!"
> What a shindy we will kick up,
> Old Big Ben will chime a hiccough
> To epitomise the sentiments we feel.

It is not surprising that Zoe Gail's effort achieved the distinction of a spirited protest from Mr. J. B. Priestley. *Strike a New Note* and *Strike It Again* represented an effort to find new talent and a number of hot numbers were thrust upon London, if not by stars, then by comets, which, in this connection, may be described as starlets in the making.

Vic Oliver and Ronald Frankau specialise in wise-crackery, and, like Max Miller, are less than fond of stage-censoring. Highly competent folk, but altogether too-knowing. Their social contacts seem to cramp their style. Looking back to the days of the one and only Dan, one recalls that he immortalised the failures, not the successes, of his generation. What interested Dan were the heirs to the kicks, not the heirs to the halfpence, as they interested Bud Flanagan and his associates when they put over "Underneath the Arches."

There are lovers of vaudeville who rank Flanagan and Chesney Allen close to the top of their profession. If they have a fault, it is that their methods tend to be so casual that one can never be certain that success is not a happy chance rather than the product of craft skill, but then this comment applies to so much of current art. Remember Bud Flanagan's commentary upon Somerset Maugham's "Rain," when he played the beachcomber in *Black Vanities*, and Flanagan's best seems very good.

We last heard of Jack Buchanan at Wimereux, with the March Hares, contemplating a future with pierrot troupes. In fact, in intervals between film production, Jack Buchanan made good as a vaudeville hero, broad enough in

method and masculine enough in mood, to star in quick-fire musical shows at
the larger theatres. Buchanan was the son of an auctioneer, and made his stage
debut at the Grand, Glasgow, in 1912. Touring in *To-night's the Night*, he
attracted attention as a light comedian of the Louis Bradfield-Seymour Hicks
type, and a series of London appearances followed. By 1928, his popularity was
so plain that when he dropped out of the cast of *That's a Good Girl* for a short
time, the receipts fell by £1,300 a week, evidence enough of stardom.

Jack Buchanan has played more than once with June, the pocket Venus of
the London stage. The two were specially good in *Toni*, a comedy, with music
by Hugo Hirsch. When the curtain rises Toni is in charge of a milliner's shop
with a bevy of pretty modistes in attendance, so it is not quite plain why Princess
Stephanie of Mettopolachia should choose this particular man to command her
personal bodyguard. However, after several scenes of abnegation in the accepted
Ruritanian manner, Toni is installed by curtain-fall as Stephanie's lover, and
presumably the future ruler of Mettopolachia.

Up and Doing, which Firth Shephard produced at the Saville, was characteristic
war-time variety, the 1941 equivalent of shows at the Empire or the Alhambra
in the first ten years of the century. In place of individual turns, each designated
by a number, a clever troupe, led by Leslie Henson, did their several bits, alone
or in company, and then went to their dressing-rooms to prepare for a reappearance
in another costume. Cyril Ritchard, for instance, began with his "Whitehall
Warrior," in which he guyed brasshats, to the delight of all who were serving in
the field. The ferocity with which Cyril, displaying his red tabs, put over the
verses had to be seen to be believed. They included an admission reminiscent
of *Pinafore*:   When the sirens start to blow,
                    I'm the first to go below.

In the second part of *Up and Doing* Cyril Ritchard was again in uniform, this
time in a stage-box and dressed as a cork-helmeted Pukka Sahib, in company
with Leslie Henson, the two being bent upon spoiling Stanley Holloway's efforts
to recite "The Green Eye of the Little Yellow God." But equally characteristic
of the entertainment were Patricia Burke and Graham Payn singing "I've got you
where I want you," or Binnie Hale in the Noel Coward number, "London Pride."
Scraps of entertaining sentiment or nonsense had been collected and put into
some sort of shape, with a little guidance from a prince among entertainers, Leslie
Henson. Apart from Leslie, Firth Shephard, Carroll Gibbons and his band,
and the Ladies of the Saville Chorus, at least fifteen authors and composers
contributed items to *Up and Doing*. Such an entertainment defies any classification
other than Variety.

Jack Hulbert and Cicely Courtneidge

The Hulberts, Jack and Cicely, are usually responsible for shows which have
a little more coherence than a Crazy Gang effort at the Palladium, or such a

Hermione Gingold as Lucrezia Borgia, in "Sweeter and Lower,"
at the Ambassadors

Bobby Howes and Cicely Courtneidge in "Hide and Seek,"
the Hippodrome

"Wiz Generaux and G.I. Joes I'm busing making dates.
I charge zem on a sliding scale as circumstance dictates
My French is getting quite as good as Mr. James Agate's,
Mais oui, mais oui, Fifi."

Hermione Gingold as Fifi in "Sweeter and Lower," at the Ambassadors

variety entertainment as *Up and Doing*. The fund of humour upon which they draw is also well enough endowed to enable them to dispense with the elaborate spectacle which other entertainers of the day seem to need. Given a well-written song, Cicely can put it over the footlights with as much assurance and sustained success as anyone in the profession.

Jack Hulbert and his brother Claude were the sons of a doctor, who specialised in defective speech, and, as a consequence, was one of the most effective teachers of elocution in his generation. This is no doubt why his boys passed to the stage by way of Westminster School and Caius College, Cambridge. Both were members of the Footlights Dramatic Club, and Jack's stage career began in earnest when Robert Courtneidge chanced to see him in a Footlights' production in 1913, entitled *Cheer Oh! Cambridge*. Jack was playing an "Algy" part which the Co-Optimists later characterised in this ditty:

> How d'you awfully do, old things?
> I'm Hulbert—frightfully Jack.
> I'm just popping off for a short vacash—
> But I'll soon be terribly back.
>
> They've offered me "Chin" in *Chu-Chin-Chow*,
> But I think I'll let it pass;
> If my chin gets as long as "Chu-Chin-Chow's"
> I shall feel a fearfully ass!

Mr. Courtneidge thought he had happened upon a pleasant variant upon the familiar dude of musical comedy when he added Hulbert to the Shaftesbury Theatre company. In fact, he happened upon a son-in-law, for Jack married Cicely Courtneidge.

Jack Hulbert's cheerful grin has saved many an evening from a threat of boredom, but it may well be that his place in vaudeville is best assured by his talent as a trainer of chorus girls. Sixteen pretty and sprightly "ponies," singing and dancing in perfect time, may be a sure cement for the necessarily varied items which constitute intimate revue and Hulbert is equally capable of training twice or three times as many if spectacle is called for. He has a genius for maintaining vim in a chorus of singers and dancers and because a lovely chorus is so important in the larger theatres, with their aid, he is one of the few stars who can hope to attract paying houses to such a theatre as the Palace.

Under Your Hat, in which Jack Hulbert and Cicely Courtneidge appeared in 1939, was seen by 300,000 playgoers before its run was interrupted by the declaration of war and the weekly takings at the Palace averaged £4,200. In fact, the Hulberts did for the Palace Theatre Company what Noel Coward and Ivor Novello had done for Drury Lane, Limited. They solved the problem of half-filled stalls which spell financial disaster. Early in 1938 the Company had a debit bank balance of £25,000. The rental paid by Hulbert and his associates brought all the lost money back and even promised a dividend to the Palace shareholders. It has been said that Jack Hulbert had the wit and good fortune to marry Cicely

Courtneidge, the best-equipped low comedienne of her decade in the British Isles. Her contacts with the musical shows of her time would have been even more numerous if she and her husband had not been forced to spend several valuable years making films, this being their method of restoring their personal fortunes after some unlucky theatrical speculations.

Fathered by Robert Courtneidge, Cicely made acquaintance with the footlights very early. At eight she was playing Peaseblossom. In 1907, when she was fourteen, she was playing Rosie Lucas, in *Tom Jones*. As Chrysea singing "I like London," and as Eileen Cavanagh, she appeared in *The Arcadians*, these musical-comedy parts leading up to Cicely's discovery of herself as a variety star.

Cicely has told us how it came about. It was during the first World War, when Jack was in the Army and Cicely had chosen a selection of songs mingling pathos and comedy, following one of her father's injunctions, "Make 'em cry, and then make 'em laugh." There was just a chance that one of Jack's leaves would coincide with her first appearance in variety at Colchester, but the curtain went up and no sign of the husband. More than once Cicely peeped through a hole in the curtain only to be disappointed, but, after the interval, there was the familiar grin, above a Tommy's uniform, lighting up the second row of stalls. Cicely said she wanted to shout. Well, the house lights went down and Cicely's number went up and she came on singing a sentimental number of the roses, roses all the way type. An Army nurse song followed, this being the "make 'em cry" item, and then the surprise, Cicely in her first male impersonation and wearing the "bags" of the Royal Flying Corps. This really did awaken Colchester to the sense that a real comedienne was making good. When the sketch ended, Jack came crashing into his wife's dressing-room. "They ate you up, Bob. You paralysed 'em. They are all chloroformed," which is just what Jack Hulbert would have said, if he had been following a "book." Next week, Cicely opened at the Victoria Palace in London, and she has never looked back since. The R.F.C. "bags" had done it. They had given Cicely the essential confidence.

For the rest, Cicely was in debt to Ivor Novello, who wrote the R.F.C. song for her. Her best efforts in revue were in company with Nelson Keys. "Cis can act. She's with you all the time," said "Bunch." And, incidentally, Jack Hulbert's strict attention to the business of the stage was good for Keys. In *Folly to be Wise*, at the Piccadilly in 1931, with a clever book by Dion Titheradge and tuneful music by Vivian Ellis, Cicely and "Bunch" played a straight comedy scena in which a charming spinster lady was asked to sell her home to a typical North Country business-man, bent upon putting up a super-cinema. The tragi-comedy could not have been acted more realistically if it had been written by Stanley Houghton, in the Manchester manner. Yet a few minutes later Cicely was in the attire of a smart young Guardsmen, side by side with the immaculate Nelson, singing Noel Gay's "The King's Horses." In the second edition of *Folly to be Wise*, the young Guardsmen became two youthful naval commanders, and they sang "The King's Navy," another Gay melody.

PALACE THEATRE

SHAFTESBURY AVENUE   **LONDON, W.I**

LEE EPHRAIM

PRESENTS

IN

"UNDER YOUR HAT"

Unlike Nelson Keys, who was never at his best in a large theatre, Cicely Courtneidge's methods are on a big enough scale to fill the largest house. Thus, Cicely starred with Bobby Howes in *Hide and Seek* at the Hippodrome in 1937. Nominally a musical comedy, there was a substratum of revue in *Hide and Seek*, the hero and heroine being members of a seaside concert-party, and the plot including a "flash-back", in the course of which Cicely impersonated a peroxided barmaid of the 1890's. "Desist!" said Cicely's eyebrows, after the Robey fashion, and the patrons of that Epsom bar desisted.

More characteristic of the Hulberts, indeed absolutely characteristic, was *The House that Jack Built*, which Jack "devised, arranged, and produced," with aid from two authors, a lyric-writer, and three musicians. Jack and Cicely played a Ronald Jeans sketch, with the scene laid in a lower middle-class villa in suburban Harringay, and they were at their best as Henry and his sub-acid spouse, reproving Carroway, an errant daughter for doings during a holiday at Clacton. "What I says at Christmas, Hi adheres to in Haugust."

Jack is acceptable in dude parts, but he is more effective in sharply characterised social types, the heavily moustached plumber, for example, in *Under Your Hat*. But a score of memories arise. Cicely, for example, in gymnastic shorts, lying over a chair and vainly endeavouring to keep pace with the B.B.C. announcer's instruction during the Daily Dozen. Or leading Vivian Ellis's mock-patriotic ballad, "The Empire Depends on You." The song was a highlight in *Under Your Hat*, and Cicely and Hulbert had been impersonating Colonel and Mrs. Sheepshanks, out of Poona. When the gyrations of the plot offered an opportunity, Mrs. Sheepshanks, a bespectacled mem-sahib, instructed a girls' school in their duties as Empire-builders, shouldering her umbrella as though it was a rifle and leading a triumphal march which made Palace audiences feel that here was the real thing, a first-rate vaudeville artist making good.

As musical plays go nowadays, *Under Your Hat* could claim a recognisable plot, though it took fifteen scenes to unravel. However, the fifteen scenes afforded ample opportunities for the stage disguises which theatre-goers expect from the Hulberts, so the happy financial results were not to be wondered at.

Doing the Lambeth Walk

One comedian, however, maintains contact with the tradition that your truly funny man mingles tears with laughter—Lupino Lane. Tears is not quite the word in this case, but rather a sentimental attachment for the Little Man from the Suburbs. Here is the air which recalls Lupino's most famous effort:

> Any time you're Lambeth way,
> Any evening, any day,
> You'll find us all doin' the Lambeth Walk.
> Ev'ry little Lambeth gal,
> With her little Lambeth pal,
> You'll find 'em all doin' the Lambeth Walk.

This snatch of verse by Douglas Furber associates itself with the last tune of Anglo-Saxon origin, which established itself not only as a whistleable song, but as a dance, and, moreover, all over the world. It is on record that Parisians at the time of the Munich crisis stood to attention when Noel Gay's tune was played, regarding it, apparently, as a sort of national anthem of those curious creatures, the English, associated in some vague way with Neville Chamberlain, who was the toast of the month in Parisian cafés. The music was written for a coster comic opera, *Me and My Girl*, and was by Noel Gay, who had already given his countrymen "The King's Horses" and "Something About a Soldier."

Me and My Girl was produced at the Victoria Palace about Christmas-time in 1937, with little Lupino Lane in the role of Bill Snibson, a Cockney from Lambeth. Snibson had inherited an earldom, but could not shed his Cockney habits. Consequently, during a week-end party at Hereford Hall, Dukes and Duchesses, Earls and Countesses, Lords and Ladies and the rest of them, were persuaded to slap their knees, cock their thumbs, and cry "Oi" in the approved Lambeth manner—surely a triumph of Dame Nature over social artifice. When the curtain fell upon the aristocrats rolling their shoulders and hips in time with Snibson's friends from Lambeth, the triumph of the Little Man seemed theatrically complete.

A good many years had passed since a show so brimful of laughter had appeared on the West End stage. For more than a thousand performances crowded houses rocked as they watched Lupino struggling with the robes and coronet of a peer, and there was not one who did not approve his sentiment, "You'll never alter my ball of chalk." As George Graves, in the role of a bibulous aristocrat, told Lupino, "You're one of Nature's gentlemen."

Maybe. Certainly, the Lambeth Walk, as song and dance, had very natural beginnings. Its origin had been the harmonic meetings in South London pubs, during which "Chase me, Charlie" and "Knees up, knees up, don't get the breezup; knees up, Mother Brown!" were sung with appropriate jig movements, men dancing with men, women with women, if that particular partnership was suggested by the set to partners. If and when the pubs were closed, "Chase me, Charlie" and "Knees up, Mother Brown" were equally popular on an open Lambeth pavement.

As a dance number, the Lambeth Walk established itself when Miss Adele England took over the air, with the intention of devising movements which everyone could dance without instruction. Her special contributions were knee-slapping in place of the original skirt-raising, and the very important addition of the characteristic Cockney "Oi," at the end of each verse, an invocation which became "Och aye" in Glasgow and "Ee, by gum; it's champion!" in Blackpool and other Lancashire dancing centres. When Miss England had done her best, the Lambeth Walk was truly "free and easy; do as you darn-well pleasey," and, therefore, fitted for public consumption on a grand scale. The Locarno Dance Circuit, with which Miss England was associated, alone controlled 300 dance bands. All were instructed to plug the measure, which, historically, will be recalled as the signature tune of the second World War.

War conditions encouraged "mateyness" and discouraged the dancing habit of the 'twenties, whereby one partner might suffice for a whole evening. When lads and lassies alike were in khaki or blue and tailed coats and starched shirts were discarded for the war period, there was a place for a dance measure which actually encouraged change in partners and even boisterous tomfoolery. Indeed, at more than one famous restaurant, dancing-floors which had been built for the gliding waltz or fox-trot, had to be relaid with special shock-absorbing devices, in order to withstand the sudden stamping of feet which accompanied the "Oi" of the Lambeth Walk. The song and dance took about six months fully to establish themselves, but by the middle of 1938 the Lambeth Walk was an institution. A B.B.C. broadcast was the primary agent. Until it was given, *Me and My Girl* was a doubtful winner. The broadcast set the box-office telephone at the Victoria Palace really ringing; receipts were quadrupled in a day. After 500 performances Lupino Lane and his associates had made a profit of £40,000 upon the London run alone, and thus assured the little comedian a handsome profit upon the £4,000 which he put into the venture.

Lupino Lane's Bill Fish, the Cockney porter in *Meet Me, Victoria* (1944) was another variant upon the small-man theme. This time Lupino was a railway porter and the fun arose from a conflict with Dorothy Ward, a stalwart emigrant from the Continent, bent upon securing a husband who could, at any rate, ensure her British citizenship. For a time Phyllis Robins, the Pimlico buffet attendant, Lupino's real love, fared badly in the contest with Dorothy Ward, but the proposed marriages proved to have been faked and the story ended happily in the Bridal Suite of the Brighton hotel. Moreover, the little railway porter by now had exchanged the old-time bowler for a top hat, preparatory to being now installed as stationmaster at Victoria.

Noel Gay again provided the music, the best song being the Phyllis Robins and Lupino Lane duet, "You're a Nice Little Baggage." Lupino's gyrations upon a mysterious stool, which consistently refused to maintain an upright posture, were laughter-provoking in a high degree. Indeed, the virtue of *Me and My Girl* and *Meet Me, Victoria* lay in the fact that they made big audiences laugh, and not just giggle.

Apart from the two Bills, Lupino Lane is, perhaps, best remembered for his appearance in *Silver Wings* at the Dominion Theatre, singing:

> When I am with you, I'm happy,
> And when I'm without you, I'm blue.
> I'm all at sea without,
> I couldn't be without
> Sweet, indispensable you!
> You are the why and the wherefore,
> Of any old thing I do.

"Hamlet" Burlesque in Charlot's "Char-a-Banc," at the Vaudeville

Lupino Lane, in "Me and My Girl," at the Victoria Palace

Frances Day, Stanley Lupino, Adele Dixon and Ralph Reader
in "The Fleet's Lit Up"

John Tilley and Douglas Byng
in 'Sweet Nell of Old Drury,' from a Charlot Revue

I'm all at sea without,
I couldn't be without
Sweet, indispensable you!

A very readable history of English Variety entertainment could be written around the adventures of the Lupino family, past and present. The first advertised appearance of the clan was associated with the famous St. Bartholomew's Fair in Smithfield in the year 1642, but for more than a century the Lupinos had been starring in a novel form of *Punch and Judy*. By 1784, Georgius (great-grandfather of Lupino Lane) was near enough to stardom to announce his "inimitable dexterity of hand in the Display of the Original and Universally admired Italian Puppets." From the open-air performances in Smithfield, Georgius went on to Drury Lane and Covent Garden, where he became ballet-master, marrying the wardrobe mistress at the Haymarket, another patent theatre of fame, who presented Georgius with a large family. Almost all of them achieved some sort of fame in the Victorian theatre world, George Lupino, father of the present generation, becoming "England's oldest clown." Lupino's mother was a niece of the well-known Sara Lane, who presided over the fortunes of the Britannia, Hoxton, for so many years. Lupino Lane takes his present surname from his aunt. It was bestowed at a time when Sara Lane seemed in need of an heir with "theatre" in his bloodstream, but, in the event, the sacrifice of the birth-name proved valueless, as Sara Lane left her considerable fortune elsewhere.

Stanley Lupino, a relative of Lupino Lane, also helped to make vaudeville history between the two wars, in particular when he was in partnership with Laddie Cliff at the Gaiety. *Love Lies*, *The Love Race*, and *Sporting Love* were among their ventures. Laddie Cliff, who died in 1937 when he was only forty-six, made his first appearance as a child-actor but sprung into fame when he sang "Swanee" in *Jig Saw*. In partnership with Archie de Bear and Clifford Whiteley he founded the Co-Optimists, incidentally this being the reason why he married Phyllis Monkman, a fellow Co-Optimist. He left pierrot trouping and after a series of appearances in revue and comic opera, actor-management, this inaugurating the partnership with Stanley Lupino.

Stanley's own career was even more varied and far more stormy than that of Laddie Cliff. He once told the Gallery First Nighters that on the day his mother was carried to her grave, the brokers were in the home, and the furniture was taken away. For a time the small boy sold newspapers in Camberwell, his first theatrical job being at the Rotunda, Liverpool, at 15s. a week. "Good old days," said Stanley, with a significant shrug of the shoulders, which the Gallery First Nighters fully appreciated. An appearance as the Cat in a Lyceum pantomime was another early experience, leading up to a memorable Buttons in a *Cinderella*, in which Madge Elliott was a lissom and attractive Prince Charming. A highlight in the pantomime was a song with chorus, in which Stanley enlisted the aid of the children in the audience, so that he could gather up all the kisses they desired to bestow upon the heroine (played by Greta Fayne) and bring them together into one huge presentation kiss for Cinderella.

Stanley Lupino had a genius for getting on familiar terms with audiences, as he showed when he put over Leslie Sarony's comedy fox-trot in *Love Lies*. The beginning was a catch phrase, "Now, Now! Come, Come!" which Leslie Sarony elaborated into:

> I lift up my finger,
> And I say, "Tweet, tweet";
> Shush, shush; now, now; come, come!

When Stanley introduced the number into *Love Lies*, Gaiety audiences were induced to join in, the joke being that all lifted up their fingers as they said, "Tweet, tweet." In the result, the number furnished the catch phrase of its season and was the hit number in *Love Lies*. In one of his last appearances Stanley Lupino was a would-be naval officer in *The Fleet's Lit Up*, in which he gaily sailed a model yacht on the Round Pond, Kensington Gardens, in preparation for his appointment as Admiral of the Fleet to the Ranee of Zabalon, an imaginary island in a tropical Ruritania.

And as a final memory, what more appropriate than Frances Day, in this same bit of colourful nonsense, singing, "It's delightful, it's delicious, it's electrical, it's delirious, it's the limit." The record of any half-century of popular entertainment, largely concerned as it has been with go-as-you-please invention, must long have exhausted the recorder's store of suitable adjectives. One or other of those at Frances Day's command will serve as a belated tribute to those whom this story of Anglo-Saxon vaudeville has omitted. To *all* who have filled our idle hours, Thank you!

INDEX

Names of Plays and Sketches in italics.

18   255

Index